Hardy, Conrad and the Senses

Man perceives in the world only what already lies within him; but to perceive what lies within him man needs the world; for this, however, activity and suffering are indispensable.

Hugo von Hofmannsthal, *The Book of Friends* (1921)

Every objectively real thing is thus a term in numberless series of mutual implications . . .

J. B. Stallo, *The Concepts and Theories of Modern Physics* (1882)

Hardy, Conrad and the Senses

Hugh Epstein

EDINBURGH
University Press

Edinburgh University Press is one of the leading university presses in the UK. We publish academic books and journals in our selected subject areas across the humanities and social sciences, combining cutting-edge scholarship with high editorial and production values to produce academic works of lasting importance. For more information visit our website: edinburghuniversitypress.com

© Hugh Epstein, 2020, 2021

Edinburgh University Press Ltd
The Tun – Holyrood Road
12(2f) Jackson's Entry
Edinburgh EH8 8PJ

First published in hardback by Edinburgh University Press 2020

Typeset in 11/13 Adobe Sabon by
IDSUK (DataConnection) Ltd, and
printed and bound by CPI Group (UK) Ltd,
Croydon, CR0 4YY

A CIP record for this book is available from the British Library

ISBN 978 1 4744 4986 1 (hardback)
ISBN 978 1 4744 4987 8 (paperback)
ISBN 978 1 4744 4988 5 (webready PDF)
ISBN 978 1 4744 4989 2 (epub)

The right of Hugh Epstein to be identified as the author of this work has been asserted in accordance with the Copyright, Designs and Patents Act 1988, and the Copyright and Related Rights Regulations 2003 (SI No. 2498).

Contents

Acknowledgements		vii
Abbreviations		viii
Introduction		1
Chapter One	The Physiology of Sensation and Literary Style *Desperate Remedies* and *The Rescue*	21
Chapter Two	Facing Nature	59
Chapter Three	The Visible World	79
	1 Fiction and Physics: Appearances in the Light *Far From the Madding Crowd* and *Lord Jim*	79
	2 Searching Space *A Laodicean* and 'The End of the Tether'	119
Chapter Four	An Audible World	139
	1 Sonic Imaging *The Return of the Native* and 'Heart of Darkness'	148
	2 The Sound of History *Nostromo*	177
Chapter Five	Identity and Margin	193
	1 Inspection, Immersion *The Mayor of Casterbridge*	194
	2 Widening Margins *Tess of the d'Urbervilles* and *Nostromo*	209

Chapter Six	**Minding the Senses** *Jude the Obscure* and *Under Western Eyes*	**243**
	Postscript	270
Bibliography		273
Index		293

Acknowledgements

I wish to thank Phillip Mallett and Allan Simmons for their patience and encouragement when reading very early drafts of what has become this book, and to record the friendship of very many members of the Thomas Hardy and Joseph Conrad Societies over the years. Sections of Chapter 1 and Chapter 3 have appeared in other versions in *The Thomas Hardy Society Journal*, *Conradiana*, *Thomas Hardy: Far From the Madding Crowd* (Cycnos), and *The Hardy Review*. Small sections of Chapter 3 and Chapter 5 have appeared in a different version in *Conrad and Nature* (Routledge, 2019). I am grateful for the permission to reproduce some of this material. I wish to thank Michelle Houston of Edinburgh University Press for her invaluable support in getting this book into print, and Tim Clark for his expert copy editing.

Abbreviations

CL *The Collected Letters of Thomas Hardy* (7 vols), ed. Richard Little Purdy and Michael Millgate. Oxford: The Clarendon Press, 1978–1988.
CL *The Collected Letters of Joseph Conrad* (9 vols), ed. Frederick R. Karl, Laurence Davies, et al. Cambridge: Cambridge University Press, 1983–2007.
LN *The Literary Notebooks of Thomas Hardy* (2 vols), ed. Lennart A. Bjork. Basingstoke: Macmillan, 1985.
LW *The Life and Work of Thomas Hardy* by Thomas Hardy, ed. Michael Millgate. Basingstoke: Macmillan, 1989.

Editions of Hardy's novels used are given in the footnotes and the Bibliography. Where available, I have used the Cambridge Edition of the Works of Joseph Conrad. Otherwise I have used the Dent Collected Edition (1947–54).

Introduction

On 3 September 1922, the Japanese professor Tadaichi Hidaka visited Conrad at Oswalds, the novelist's home in Kent. He later gathered his impressions under the title 'A Visit to Conrad', including this conversation, with Hidaka speaking first and Conrad responding:

> 'I visited Mr Thomas Hardy last month. He's quite advanced in years, isn't he?'
> 'Did you? That's nice. I used to see him quite often before, but I haven't had a chance to see him recently. He's more than twenty years older than I.'
> 'The impression left by Mr Hardy is very different from the impression left by you.'
> 'I'm sure it is. I've spent most of my days at sea.'
> 'His works differ a lot from yours.'
> 'They must do. In facing nature, Mr Hardy faces static nature, whereas I face dynamic, active nature, so we are naturally different. It's possible to find movement in stillness, and stillness in movement. Naturally the way they are expressed are [sic] different also.'[1]

Hardy and Conrad did not talk or write much about each other. Yet Conrad's phrase, 'In facing nature', recognises a shared enterprise in their writing, for all that he insists on the differences, which rings true in a way that could not be extended to George Eliot, or to James, Gissing, Kipling, Bennett, even Meredith.[2] Maupassant and Zola can more readily be seen to be 'facing nature' than their English counterparts of the period, but with something of the scientific detachment of

---

[1] Translation by Yoko Okuda, from her article 'East Meets West', *The Conradian* 23:2 (Autumn 1998), 73–87. Martin Ray's 'Hardy and Conrad' in the *Thomas Hardy Journal* 12:2 (May 1996) reviews the meetings between the two novelists.
[2] In conversation with H.-R. Lenormand, Conrad 'praised Kipling, Hardy and Bennett, but detested Meredith' (reported in Martin Ray, 'Interviews and Recollections', *The Conradian* 13:1, 1988, 57, entry no. 136).

the laboratory. Both Hardy and Conrad allow a more vital place for the determinations of consciousness, and not only the determinism of physical and social forces.

What I wish to show in this book is that an art made from impressions upon the senses – as an aspect of consciousness – appears more vividly when Hardy and Conrad are read alongside each other in their portrayals of humanity facing nature, rather than received in containers labelled 'Victorian' and 'Modernist' for separate consumption. For all the evident differences and incompatibilities between their works, this shared primary way of knowing the world makes them distinctive congeners in the novelist's business of rendering, in the direct, clear-eyed but feeling phrase from *Tess*, 'the plight of being alive' (134). They are the novelists, in late-Victorian England, who most fulfil the desire for 'cosmic emotion' proposed by the mathematician W. K. Clifford, 'an emotion which is felt in regard to the universe or sum of things'. Equally, their novels answer, with conspicuous directness, to Clifford's Positivist credo: 'For the interrogation of nature, without and within him, is the most momentous part of the work of man on this earth, seeing how all his progress has depended upon conscious or unconscious labour at this task.'[3]

Hardy and Conrad are alike in most readers' minds only to the extent of having an equivalently pessimistic vision of human existence lived under circumstances in which Providence is notably absent.[4] Although Faulkner said, 'I can find similarities between Conrad and Hardy,'[5] there is no attempt here to make particular works with so many and such obvious differences similar to one another. The intention, rather, is to explore the shared basis of

---

[3] 'Cosmic Emotion' (*Nineteenth Century*, October 1877), in *Lectures and Essays*, edited by Leslie Stephen and Frederick Pollock (1901), vol. 2, 257, 280. We have to except Conrad from the Positivist emphasis on progress. Hardy described himself as a 'meliorist', but Conrad writes to Bertrand Russell: 'I have never been able to find in any man's book or any man's talk anything convincing enough to stand up for a moment against my deep-seated sense of fatality governing this man-inhabited world' (*CL* 7:543).

[4] I am not concerned in this study with either writer's 'philosophy' and, of course, they both denied that they had one. See Phillip Mallett, 'Hardy and Philosophy', in Wilson ed., *A Companion to Thomas Hardy* (2009), 21–35; and Ludwig Schnauder's 'The Conradian World Picture' (79–99), in his *Free Will and Determinism in Joseph Conrad's Major Novels* (2009).

[5] Gwynn and Blotner eds, *Faulkner in the University* (1995), 142.

what has always been appreciated as characteristic of each novelist individually: a great power to evoke atmosphere and mood. In its external form, Lionel Johnson, in the earliest critical account of Hardy, read it thus: 'Not the looks of definite objects only, but their surrounding and intervening atmospheres, become plain to us; the blue mists or dusty gold lights, or thin gray breaths of air . . .'; and D. H. Lawrence wrote to Edward Garnett, 'Of course Conrad should always do the beautiful, magic atmospheres.' In its more inward form, Lascelles Abercrombie suggested of Hardy's tragic novels, 'the background of nature seems to exist chiefly as a spectacular variation of human moods'; while Hunter S. Stagg, reviewing *The Rover*, praised Conrad's 'gift of subjecting himself to the mood' of his scenes and characters, and thereby achieving 'mastery over the mood of the reader'.[6] This dual aspect of 'atmosphere' in writing has frequently led to Conrad being deemed an 'Impressionist', though Hardy only rarely so;[7] but it is Hardy's comment in his Preface to 'Poems of the Past and Present' (1901) which provides more precisely the focus on impressions taken here: 'Unadjusted impressions have their value, and the road to a true philosophy of life seems to lie in humbly recording diverse readings of its phenomena as they are forced upon us by chance and change.'[8] Recording readings of phenomena is both the province and the language of the physical sciences; and recovering the intense interest in sense impressions, their status in mediating between the external world and the internal, which manifested itself in so much empiricist writing of the second half of the nineteenth century, provides the context that I use for reading Hardy and Conrad *together*.

'Phenomena' is a key word in the empirical science of this period, as it is in the vocabulary and thinking of both Hardy and Conrad. Edward S. Reed, in his fine study of the development of psychology, marks out the conceptual moment within which

---

[6] Lionel Johnson, *The Art of Thomas Hardy* (1894), 69; Lawrence to Garnett, October 1912, *The Letters of D. H. Lawrence* (Aldous Huxley ed., 1937), 70; Lascelles Abercrombie, *Thomas Hardy: A Critical Study* (1912), 44; Hunter S. Stagg, 'A Novelist of Mood', *Reviewer* 4:2 (January 1924), quoted in Peter Mallios, *Our Conrad: Constituting American Modernity* (2010), 273.
[7] Jesse Matz, however, is forthright: 'Hardy was an Impressionist' (*Literary Impressionism and Modernist Aesthetics*, 2001, 121). Conrad says of himself, in a letter to E. L. Sanderson in 1897, 'I am impressionist from instinct' (*CL* 1:398).
[8] Thomas Hardy, *The Complete Poems* (1988), 84.

Hardy is writing, and from which Conrad has not escaped into twentieth-century relativities:[9]

> Before 1850 or so, perceptual evidence was always taken by scientists at face value: the rock is here, this meter reads thus and so. Now even such ordinary observations were subjected to a kind of sceptical reduction into sensationalist 'phenomena': I have sensations from which I infer that the rock is here, or that the meter reads thus and so.[10]

Hardy and Conrad, in my account, are alike primarily insofar as they work within this dimension of *encounter* as a staple position in their fiction, drawn to sensation, to surfaces, to the meeting point of self and surrounding world. Their novels are novels of inference. Acknowledging an adherence to physical manifestations in Conrad's writing, Arthur Symons (who dedicated his *Spiritual Adventures* of 1905 to Hardy) says of him what can equally be said of Hardy: 'The rarest subtlety in prose is its physiological quality; for prose listens at the doors of all the senses, and repeats their speech almost in their own tones.'[11] How prose fiction 'listens' to the senses, a subject also of great scrutiny by the physical sciences of the later Victorian period, is the subject of this book. This study thus gives an undeniably Victorian cast to writers who both have a claim to a twentieth-century modernity; but then Hardy lived sixty of his eighty-eight years in the nineteenth century, and Conrad forty-three of his sixty-six years, a scarcely smaller proportion. 'The most Victorian thing about his novels', writes John Bayley of Hardy, 'is their plot: the least, their sense of time, place, and event'.[12] The chronological disruptions involved in Conrad's plotting are often thought, in contrast, to be very modern; but what I hope to show is that in their sense of

---

[9] Indeed, Redmond O'Hanlon attributes Conrad's breakdown in 1910 to the way in which the new science of relativity loosened the certainties of Newtonian physics (*Changing Scientific Concepts of Nature in the English Novel 1850–1920*, PhD thesis, 1977, 5). He cuts this specific claim from his book, *Joseph Conrad and Charles Darwin* (1984).

[10] Edward S. Reed, *From Soul to Mind: The Emergence of Psychology from Erasmus Darwin to William James* (1997), 161. Vernon Lee's 1897 *Contemporary Review* article 'Beauty and Ugliness' suggests the erosion of this perceptual attentiveness fifty years later: 'the formula of perception has become not "I *feel* roundness, or height, or symmetry," but "this or that object *is* round or high or symmetrical"' (*Beauty and Ugliness and Other Studies in Psychological Aesthetics*, 1912, 159).

[11] Arthur Symons, *Notes on Joseph Conrad* (1925), 37.

[12] John Bayley, *An Essay on Hardy* (1978), 13.

space and event, if not exactly of place and time, the two novelists share some significant practices, and that the 'modernity' of these is more Victorian than is often assumed.

In the account to follow, then, Hardy and Conrad take their place not as figures 'in transition' in a literary teleology whose goal is Modernist interiority,[13] but as novelists whose work contributes distinctively to a condition in the novel in which, as Sara Danius notes, 'the emergence of realist discourse meant that description began to pervade the art of narration'.[14] Alan Spiegel asks, 'Why is there so much to look at, so much purely visual information, in the nineteenth century novel – particularly in the latter half of the period – and so much less to look at in earlier novels?'[15] *Hardy, Conrad and the Senses* is a discussion of descriptive writing, in which the world is brought to the senses both of the characters in the novels and of the reader. What, for instance, is the 'visual information' contained in the prolonged gaze 'through the opening afforded by a field-gate at the undulating stretch of country beyond' which opens Hardy's *Two on a Tower* (1882), when read in proximity to the opening of Conrad's first published short story, 'The Idiots' (*The Savoy*, 1896), with its declaration, 'The sun was shining violently upon the undulating surface of the land'? Both scenes present a carriage and a road, a getting down, a remark, and an injunction to look at a landscape to discern something unusual there, though 'the undulating country beyond' suggests something more culturally assimilated, more of a habitation, than Conrad's barer, resistant, 'undulating surface of the land'. Hardy's opening three paragraphs proceed by gradual geometric extensions until they envision the tower of the novel's title, but they begin, 'On an early winter afternoon, clear but not cold, when the vegetable world was a weird multitude of skeletons through whose ribs the sun shone freely' – a startlingly illuminated ocular performance which instantly seizes hold of a reader's perspective and thrusts it

---

[13] The most recent discussion of Hardy's supposedly 'transitional' status is that by Ken Ireland in *Thomas Hardy, Time and Narrative* (2014), 209/10. He concludes his study by comparing Hardy, 'as a bridge between nineteenth and twentieth centuries', with Conrad, who 'invents storyworlds which by their radicalism might have dwarfed the rural stage of Hardy's Wessex' (216). See also Linda Dryden, Stephen Arata, Eric Massey eds, *Robert Louis Stevenson and Joseph Conrad: Writers of Transition* (2009).

[14] Sara Danius, *The Prose of the World: Flaubert and the Art of Making Things Visible* (2006), 26.

[15] Alan Spiegel, *Fiction and the Camera Eye: Visual Consciousness in Film and the Modern Novel* (1976), x.

into an elemental intimacy with the material substance of the scene. Conrad, even more abrupt and with a more angular syntax, demands attention to 'clumps of meagre trees, with their branches showing high on the sky as if they had been perched upon stilts', a graceless and dour immobility that will go on to be coloured more in Fauvist than in Impressionist style.[16] Then, at carriage-wheel level, the narrator will be confronted by his first sight of one of the idiots of the story's title, whom the reader might feel to be the object of a brutal visual joke: 'The imbecile face was red, and the bullet head with close cropped hair seemed to lay alone, its chin in the dust.'[17]

Both passages track a series of perceptual events in the few moments of a beholding. Hardy provides a powerful statement of how this is achieved as a literary effect in his reflection of 5 August 1890: 'Art is a changing of the actual proportion and order of things, so as to bring out more forcibly than might otherwise be done that feature in them which appeals most strongly to the idiosyncrasy of the artist. . . . Art is a disproportioning' (*LW* 239). And with 'forcibly' in mind, the feeling of a slightly disconcerting assault upon the senses that reading so much of Conrad produces has been nowhere more brilliantly characterised than by Ford Madox Ford in his Introduction to *The Sisters* (published in 1925, after Conrad's death), in which he writes, 'if you read Conrad sentence by sentence with minute care you will see that each sentence is a mosaic of little crepitations of surprise and that practically every paragraph contains its little jolt'.[18] However different the idiosyncratic temperament displayed by each writer, the epistemological predicate is the same. As Merleau-Ponty wrote of Cézanne, he wished 'to make *visible* how the world *touches* us'.[19] What I show in detail in this book is that Hardy's and Conrad's novels create a distinct medium of sensational relations in which the facts of the external world are paramount, but truth to the mood in which those facts are apprehended is the route

---

[16] A late entry copied into Hardy's *Literary Notebooks* reads, '"Monet was concerned with what one saw; Cezanne with what one remembered. The impr.st landscape is the presentation of a momentary glance . . . Fauvism is concerned with the essentials of a scene that remain in the memory . . ." Mr. T. H. Sadler in "The Blue Book" Oxford. May '12' (*LN* 2:210).

[17] Joseph Conrad, *Tales of Unrest* (2012), 53; 'lay' is the reading of the typescript and Macmillan copyright edition; all other editions follow *The Savoy*, which printed 'lie'.

[18] Ford Madox Ford, Introduction to *The Sisters* (1928), 13.

[19] Merleau-Ponty, 'Cézanne's Doubt', in *Sense and Non-Sense* (1964), 19, original emphases.

to knowledge of the conditions of existence. This is the 'touching' which I explore. In the first full-length critical assessment of Conrad, Richard Curle wrote that 'Conrad's theory would seem to be this, that without atmosphere there can be no such thing as veritability';[20] and nothing less than 'truth' is the vital issue at stake for both writers. Hardy writes, 'in getting at the truth we get only at the true nature of the impression that an object, etc., produces on us' (*LW* 261). Analogously, six and a half years later, in the celebrated Preface to *The Nigger of the 'Narcissus'*, Conrad writes of 'bringing to light the truth' that 'Such an appeal to be effective must be an impression conveyed through the senses' (6).

Thus what Hardy and Conrad offer as novelists retains the reader upon a perceptual border where the presence, proportions and weight of the exterior and interior world are engaged as in contest, one aptly expressed by the physiologist and philosopher James J. Gibson in *The Senses Considered as Perceptual Systems*:

> Within limits, you can concentrate either on the edge of the table, say, or on the dent it makes in *you*. It is as if the same stimulating event had two possible poles of experience, one objective and the other subjective. There are many possible meanings of the term *sensation*, but this is one: the detection of an impression made on a perceiver while he is primarily engaged in detecting the world.[21]

The many passages of being detected by the world while detecting the world make up much of what is examined in the novels to follow. A continual holding off from ready interpretation and from achieved mental knowledge keeps characters' inner lives, their thoughts and feelings, at a scrupulous distance from the reader. Rather than mastered coherent selves, they too are phenomena in an apprehended scene of which their own apprehension is not the totality of its contents, and they retain the impenetrability of the merely phenomenal.

I begin this study, as I see both Hardy and Conrad beginning their novelistic careers, with the physiological standpoint that yields phenomena to be described. The particular contribution to the issues of

---

[20] Richard Curle, *Joseph Conrad: A Study* (1914), 75.
[21] James J. Gibson, *The Senses Considered as Perceptual Systems* (1968), 99. W. R. Grove, explaining his new application of the term 'correlation' to physics, uses the same analogy: 'the finger cannot press the table without the table pressing the finger' (*The Correlation of Physical Forces*, 1850, 94).

novelistic description broached above comes in the form that I term 'scenic realism', which I explore in each of the following chapters. How novelistic description is tied to Victorian empirical science I propose more fully in Chapter 2, prior to analyses of a number of the major novels in that light. In their composition of moments, events and scenes (a term used incessantly by both writers), I argue overall that these novels develop a 'field' view of reality that, while not directly influenced by Faraday's 'lines of force' and Clerk Maxwell's electromagnetic field of the 1850s and '60s, corresponds in a non-scientific manner to the profoundly re-structuring vision of reality that emerges from late-classical physics.

*

Connections between the two writers were slight. Hardy and Conrad met only three times, at dinner parties in 1903, 1907 and 1920. A fourth, and much more picturesque, meeting conjectures them both sheltering from a Zeppelin attack on the floor of J. M. Barrie's flat in Adelphi Terrace in 1917 along with Galsworthy and Bennett, later to be joined by Shaw and Wells. Hardy told Virginia Woolf, 'We just heard a little pop in the distance. The searchlights were beautiful. I thought if a bomb now were to fall on this flat how many writers would be lost.'[22] However, these meetings did not produce a friendship, or even a literary acquaintanceship of a more limited kind: they never corresponded directly, and each mentions the other only twice in their respective collected letters, despite having friends in common, notably Sidney Colvin, John Galsworthy, George Gissing and Edmund Gosse. When Hardy says of Conrad, in conversation with Hamlin Garland in 1923, 'He is a great writer, a very great writer, but he is not English in any sense', is it praise or slight disparagement

[22] Virginia Woolf, *A Writer's Diary* (1953), 91. The evidence for this putative meeting, accepted by Ray, is dubious, and rests entirely with Barrie, and only then in the recollection of William Lyon Phelps. Phelps writes, 'suddenly a tremendous bomb fell from the sky and exploded on the pavement very close to their apartment', which conflicts with Hardy's account (see Ray, 'Hardy and Conrad'). Hardy merely records 'they had some interesting meetings with other writers' (*LW* 407), and Conrad's letters do not record the visit, nor the episode. Arnold Bennett ends his journal entry for Wednesday 25 July 1917, 'Later in the evening Barrie brought along both Shaw and the Wellses by phone. . . . The spectacle of Wells and GBS talking firmly and strongly about the war, in their comparative youth, in front of this aged, fatigued and silent man – incomparably their superior as a creative artist – was very striking' (*The Journals*, 1971, 412). It is scarcely credible that, were he present, Bennett would not have mentioned Conrad, whom he revered.

that he intends?²³ And while, in the same year, Conrad casts affectionate praise on Hardy in calling him 'the last of the Elizabethans', Hardy was also the occasion for revealing a continuing exasperation, as Conrad grumbled to John Sheridan Zelie: 'Why do people call me a writer of sea-stories? They do not call Mr Hardy "a writer of land-stories".'²⁴ In 1908 Conrad had complained to Galsworthy,

> I suppose there is something in me that is unsympathetic to the general public – because the novels of Hardy, for instance, are generally tragic enough and gloomily written too – and yet they have sold in their time and are selling to the present day. Foreignness I suppose. (*CL* 4:9)

Hardy owned ten of Conrad's works in his library at Max Gate, including five of the novels; Conrad had no Hardy in his library at Oswalds, though his correspondence shows acquaintance with *The Return of the Native* and *Jude the Obscure*.²⁵ Although Galsworthy said that Conrad liked Hardy's poetry, if they were acute and perceptive readers of each other's works this does not appear either in their conversation, in which Hardy praises only *The Arrow of Gold*, one of Conrad's less distinguished novels, or in their letters, where Conrad's appreciation of Hardy is only suggested in his exclamation to Cunninghame Graham about *His People* (1906), 'What a *Return of the Native* you have given us!' (*CL* 3:406). Hardy declined to write an article for the commemorative issue of *La Nouvelle Revue française* devoted to Conrad on his death in 1924.²⁶ It would seem hard to find two contemporary great writers less inclined directly to acknowledge one another.²⁷

In addition to the reticence about enjoying each other's literary company, Hardy, seventeen years Conrad's senior, retains for many a distinctly Victorian air at odds with Conrad's modern cosmopolitanism. In October 1915 Galsworthy wrote to Garnett, 'I went over and saw Conrad from Tunbridge Wells, thought him looking better than for a long time . . . . We recently made the acquaintance of Thomas Hardy: it was queer somehow, like stepping back into another age;

---

²³ Quoted in Martin Ray, *Thomas Hardy Remembered* (2007), 269.
²⁴ See Ray, 'Interviews and Recollections', entries 275, 287.
²⁵ See www.library.utoronto.ca/fisher/hardy, which provides a reconstruction of the contents of the Max Gate library. For Conrad, see David Tutein, *Joseph Conrad's Reading* (1990) and Hans van Marle, 'A Novelist's Dukedom: From Joseph Conrad's Library', *The Conradian* 16:1 (Sept. 1991).
²⁶ On 22 October 1924, according to Timothy Hands, *A Hardy Chronology* (1992), 193.
²⁷ Looking at the list of literary figures who visited Max Gate provided by Mark Ford, Conrad is conspicuous by his absence (*Thomas Hardy: Half a Londoner*, 2016, 260).

and yet he's still very much alive.'[28] Yet while the impact of modern London was more important for Conrad *imaginatively*, the significance of living in London from 1862 to 1867, and of partaking in both the fashionable and more humdrum aspects of metropolitan life then and thereafter, cannot be overestimated for Hardy, and marks him in some ways as a more modern figure in British society than the Polish *szlachcic* dwelling in Kent. Conrad was the more overpowered: as he says in his 1920 Author's Note to *The Secret Agent*, 'I had to fight hard to keep at arms-length the memories of my solitary and nocturnal walks all over London in my early days, lest they should rush in and overwhelm each page of the story' (7). Hardy, the more detached, spends his time in observation: page after page of *The Life and Work* carries vignettes of 'a distinctly modern juxtaposition', as he puts it (*LW* 135). Watching the Lord Mayor's show in Ludgate Hill in 1879, Hardy sees the crowd as 'a molluscous black creature having nothing in common with humanity, that takes the shape of the streets along which it has lain itself, and throws out horrid excrescences and limbs into neighbouring alleys' (*LW* 134). Yet, reading their novels, Galsworthy's impression that Hardy and Conrad come from different worlds is hard to dislodge. An explanation is that their fiction was almost entirely produced either side of the demise, in 1894, of the three-volume novel, when Mudie's and W. H. Smith both ceased purchasing for that market.[29] No one puts this difference between the two writers more winningly than the novelist H. E. Bates, who makes use of the conjunction, in 1895, of the publication of Hardy's last novel and Conrad's first to highlight changes in 'the whole fabric of the novel' to Conrad's advantage. In a chapter indicatively entitled 'Joseph Conrad and Thomas Hardy', Bates writes:

> their work in tone and artistry and feeling and setting belongs not only to different centuries but almost to different worlds, Hardy's to a world that often seems to us as unreal and dated and strange as a Victorian fashion-plate, Conrad's to a world as unreal and strange in a vastly different sense but as undated as the sea and the stars and the sunlight of which he wrote so well.

[28] Edward Garnett, *Letters from John Galsworthy 1900–1932* (1934), 221.
[29] In relation to serialisation and the single-volume novel, see the very interesting discussion of the implications of linear sequence and a 'field view' of reality in *The Woodlanders*, *Lord Jim* and *The Dynasts* by Linda K. Hughes and Michael Lund, 'Linear Stories and Circular Visions: The Decline of the Victorian Serial', in Hayles ed., *Chaos and Order* (1991).

For Bates, 'Hardy is the cart-horse, Conrad the race-horse' in a rather brilliantly written essay in which Hardy's laboriousness is largely the whipping boy for the greater excitement to be derived from Conrad's 'higher blood-pressure'. Bates is clear: 'Jude is the end of a phase; Almayer the beginning of one.'[30]

Almost as frequently as Virginia Woolf's oft-cited statement about December 1910, the year 1895 figures in histories of Modernism as a marker of cultural rupture.[31] In his 1930 Preface to the first volume of *A History of Our Own Times*, Ford Madox Ford wrote that 'The year 1895 seems a very good one with which to end a volume that is in effect an introduction to our familiar, if inchoate, modernity. It is really as if January 1896 marked the division between an irrevocable past and our own perpetually changing present.'[32] Even the Marxist Raymond Williams, no simple friend to Modernism, writes in a chapter called 'A Parting Of The Ways': 'But the date, 1895, can serve to indicate as well as single dates ever can a new situation in the English novel.'[33] John A. Lester in *Journey Through Despair* reinforces the divide between a Victorian and a *fin-de-siècle* outlook in his memorable characterisation of the change of temper which took place towards the end of the century, writing that 'man was called on to live not so much with a world of materialistic determinism, as with a world of chance and change within which man had now to grope his way in uncertainty'.[34] Lester's version of Hardy calls man to face his doom under the reluctantly raised but necessary banner of materialistic determinism; Conrad, on the other hand, is

---

[30] In Derek Verschoyle ed., *The English Novelists: A Survey of the Novel by Twenty Contemporary Novelists* (1936) 231, 241.

[31] The idea of rupture seems to be essential to Modernism's myth of its own origins. In *Modernism as a Philosophical Problem* (1991), Robert B. Pippin examines the period under the sub-heading, 'The "Culture of Rupture"', seeing 'the unavailability of any direct appeal to nature' as intrinsic to what is modern in the modern novel (35). More recently, Christopher Herbert in *Victorian Relativity* (2001), and Rick Rylance in *Victorian Psychology and British Culture 1850–1880* (2000), have been highly critical of Modernism's amnesia about its forerunners in Victorian thought. In *Perspectives* (2009), Linda Shires looks past the occlusions of 'the stereotypical rupture narratives about modernity', particularly in the visual arts. Peter Garratt's examination, in *Victorian Empiricism* (2010), of Victorian 'relational, sceptical and perspectivist thinking' is explicitly mobilised against 'modernism's own denial of its own historicity' (20).

[32] Ford Madox Ford, *A History of Our Own Times* (1989), 11.

[33] Raymond Williams, *The English Novel from Dickens to Lawrence* (1973), 119.

[34] John A. Lester, *Journey Through Despair 1880–1914: Transformations in British Literary Culture* (1968), 30.

Lester's hero, struggling to impose meaning on a world of flux. In its turn, this corresponds to Dennis Dean's succinct attributions, 'Hardy's stoic resignation' and 'Conrad's heroic resistance'.[35] Yet Lester's 'chance and change' are Hardy's words, as we have seen, and it is Hardy who says they 'are forced upon us'.

But even if we call into question the notion of Hardy as the last of the old, and Conrad the beginning of the new, it is clear that not only in the circumstances of their lives, but as novelists, Hardy and Conrad come from different traditions. Conrad's novels can be understood as a whole when he is seen as a novelist of romance and adventure,[36] in which his reading of Captain Marryat and Fenimore Cooper and, as a child, Garneray's *Voyages, aventures et combats, Gil-Blas, Don Quixote* and Hugo's *The Toilers of the Sea* (in his father's translation), were the most formative influences upon his subject matter.[37] His romantic nature was given a literary and national embodiment in reading aloud Mickiewicz and Słowacki in his childhood. Conversely, Hardy is a novelist of an English locality, in whom one senses that, in addition to the local speech of workfolk and the instructional language of John Cassell's 1852–54 weekly series *The Popular Educator*, it is Tate-and-Brady's hymns, traditional tunes and ballads, the Authorised Version and the Book of Common Prayer that are the most vital forces in creating a communal language centred upon home and Stinsford church. The significant later reading of both writers serves to intensify this fundamental difference. When Samuel Chew placed Hardy in a tradition that included the Brontës, George Eliot, Trollope and R. D. Blackmore, Hardy responded, 'Surely, if anybody, Fielding

---

[35] Dennis Dean, '"Through Science to Despair": Geology and the Victorians', in Paradis and Postlewait eds, *Victorian Science and Victorian Values* (1985), 128.

[36] See Andrea White, *Joseph Conrad and the Adventure Tradition* (1993), and Katherine Isobel Baxter, *Joseph Conrad and the Swan Song of Romance* (2010).

[37] Hardy never mentions having read Fenimore Cooper, while, as late as 1908, Conrad writes, 'He has been one of my masters. He is my constant companion' (*CL* 4:101). The visual and auditory scene of *The Deerslayer*'s Glimmerglass Lake (1841) is intensely present in *Nostromo*'s Golfo Placido; yet the writing, full of the patient tracking of air currents and 'concurrence(s) of extraordinary circumstances' (348), is frequently more reminiscent of Hardy: on a single page (304) we read the Conradian 'the scene was suddenly lighted ... by a flash', and the Hardyan 'The scene that was now presented to the observation ...'. At different points we are told of three characters in a boat 'using their senses differently' (154), and later of Deerslayer 'trusting to the single sense of hearing' (465). In the one case a pervasive influence, in the other, apparently not at all, Cooper's own highly atmospheric scenic realism of the senses is a now-neglected forerunner to that of Conrad and Hardy.

(whose scenes and characters are Dorset and Somerset) and Scott?'[38] On the other hand, in *Joseph Conrad, A Personal Remembrance*, Ford Madox Ford recalls, 'But that which really brought us together was a devotion to Flaubert and Maupassant. We discovered that we both had *Felicité*, *St.-Julien l'Hospitalier*, immense passages of *Madame Bovary*, *La Nuit*, *Ce Cochon de Morin* and immense passages of *Une Vie* by heart.'[39] To this broad divergence in formative reading, I would add that Conrad learned his literary English in great measure from Dickens, whose later public readings Hardy says he 'frequented' (*LW* 54), but whom he nowhere counts as an influence.[40]

And yet in terms of asserting literary stature, sounding the names of Hardy and Conrad together was certainly not unusual in their respective lifetimes.[41] The most well-known estimate from this period is that of Virginia Woolf. Her incomparable essays for the *Times Literary Supplement* and *The Athenaeum* find her pairing Hardy and Conrad on four occasions. In 1917 Dent re-issued 'Youth', and Woolf's review in the *TLS* contains the comment, 'But Mr Hardy and Mr Conrad are the only two of our novelists who are indisputably large enough to engage the services of a whole anthill [of critics].' For Woolf, it is the appeal of Conrad's early fiction that is the strongest; the heroic figures of the early stories are often 'the poorest and most apparently worthless', but also 'seem to have the most of nature in them; they have been overlaid by civilization and need the particular tests of nature to call them out'. This feeling resonates closely but not identically with what Lawrence says so brilliantly about Hardy's characters:

> The little fold of law and order, the little walled city within which man has to defend himself from the waste enormity of nature, becomes always too small, and the pioneers venturing out with the code of the walled city upon them, die in the bonds of that code, free and yet unfree, preaching the walled city and looking to the waste.[42]

---

[38] 17 September 1922 (*CL* vi. 156). And see Samuel Chew, *Thomas Hardy, Poet and Novelist* (1928), 81. Like Hidaka, Chew visited both Hardy and Conrad in 1922. In 1925 he won the *Saturday Review of Literature*'s prize for suggesting an ending for Conrad's unfinished *Suspense*.

[39] Ford Madox Ford, *Joseph Conrad, A Personal Remembrance* (1924), 36.

[40] See Yves Hervouet, *The French Face of Joseph Conrad* (1990), and Hugh Epstein, '*Bleak House* and Conrad', in Moore, Knowles and Stape eds, *Conrad: Intertexts and Appropriations* (1997).

[41] See John G. Peters ed., *Conrad in the Public Eye* (2008).

[42] Virginia Woolf, *Times Literary Supplement*, 20 September 1917, 451. D. H. Lawrence, 'Study of Thomas Hardy' (1914), in *Phoenix* (1970), 419.

Woolf is both novelists' memorialist, asked by the *TLS* to provide the commemorative article on each on his death, three and a half years apart. However, the manner in which she associates both novelists in an artistic alliance against 'Mr Wells, Mr Bennett and Mr Galsworthy', in her essay 'Modern Novels' in the *TLS* (expanded into 'Modern Fiction' for *The Common Reader*), is part of a living debate about the relation of aesthetics to reality. Beginning 'we reserve our unconditional gratitude for Mr Hardy, for Mr Conrad', Woolf goes on to disparage the labours of Wells, Bennett and Galsworthy in her questions, 'Is life like this? Must novels be like this?' Implicitly she suggests that it is the novels of Hardy and Conrad, in distinction, that have a capacity to represent life as it is truly experienced, for, as she so memorably puts it: 'Life is not a series of gig lamps symmetrically arranged: life is a luminous halo, a semi-transparent envelope surrounding us from the beginning of consciousness to the end.'[43]

Woolf becomes explicit, however, when she comes to Joyce's *Ulysses*, questioning 'for what reason a work of such originality yet fails to compare, for we must take high examples, with *Youth* or *The Mayor of Casterbridge*'. And the characterisation Woolf then offers, although focused upon Joyce, indicates what it is she so values in Hardy and Conrad:

> But it is possible to press a little further and wonder whether we may not refer to our sense of being in a bright yet narrow room, confined and shut in, rather than enlarged and set free . . . Is it due to the method that we feel neither jovial nor magnanimous, but centred in a self which, in spite of its tremor of susceptibility, never embraces or creates what is outside itself and beyond?[44]

Enlarged and set free by a rendering of scenes which include the observing self but are not exactly co-extensive with it, the reader of

---

[43] Virginia Woolf, *Times Literary Supplement*, 10 April 1919; *Collected Essays* (1966), vol. 4, 160. There is an echo here of Jude's first sight of Christminster, in which he sees 'not the lamps in rows . . . only a halo or glow-fog over-arching the place', which has been noted by Sheila Berger in *Thomas Hardy and Visual Structures*, 170. As Allan Simmons has noted in *Conrad's 'Heart of Darkness'* (2007), 27, Woolf's image also recalls the much discussed analogy in 'Heart of Darkness' in which, for Marlow, 'the meaning of an episode was not inside like a kernel but outside, enveloping the tale which brought it out only as a glow brings out a haze' (*Youth, Heart of Darkness, The End of the Tether*, 2010, 45).

[44] Woolf, *Collected Essays*, vol. 4, 162.

Hardy and Conrad is not confined to a depiction of mental contents, however subtle and extensive, but is placed vividly in touch with what is also outside and beyond. I take Woolf to be right in a most important way about what Hardy and Conrad both offer; and the issue of the part played by the senses in yielding an exterior world, or in imprisoning us in a necessarily detached and interior one of our own making, is recurrent throughout this book.[45] In examining what Hardy and Conrad *shared* in their inheritance from Victorian science, this study discovers connections in their prose fiction at least as important as the differences, and asserts a distinctive late-Victorian place for their novels which can also speak with peculiar urgency to the twenty-first-century reader.

*

Criticism that associates Hardy and Conrad is not lacking but it is not abundant. The recurring ground for comparison is the two authors' pessimistic outlook, in which the determinism perceived to direct Hardy's world is consistently seen as allowing less scope for meaningful human action than Conrad's uncertain universe offers to his protagonists. Beginning the comparative disparagement of Hardy, in 1915 Wilson Follett writes that Hardy creates 'a world framed to illustrate the incarnate principle of disaster', while Conrad finds 'a quite different irony, inherent in the very blankness of the wall man has to front, and the dignity of man himself, his undismayed strivings, his indomitable hopes, the lustre of his tragic triumphs'.[46] In the year of Conrad's death, the Scots poet Edwin Muir concluded his celebration of Conrad, the 'sincere sceptic' who has 'found two or three planks to put between him and the incommensurable', with the distinction that 'His hopelessness is not like Mr Hardy's, a hopelessness without bound; it is a sane hopelessness, a hopelessness full of courage.'[47] These antitheses still seem to hold: in 2009 Ludwig Schnauder writes, 'In contrast to Modernist writers such as Conrad, Hardy's perspective of [*sic*] the universe and

---

[45] For the growth of academic interest in the senses, see the works by Constance Classen (1993, 2014), C. Nadia Seremetakis (1994), Robert Jütte (2005), Mark M. Smith (2007), Fiona MacPherson (2011), and Martin Jay (2011), itemised in the Bibliography.
[46] Wilson Follett, *Joseph Conrad: A Short Study* (1915), 21.
[47] Edwin Muir, *Latitudes* (1924), 56.

of humankind seems monolithic, like a closed system ... Conrad's universe is not a closed deterministic system but open, indeterministic, and ultimately unknowable.'[48] Writers on Conrad use Hardy in order to promote Conrad as unbounded, modern, and dealing with radical unknowables, forgetting his much greater desire for absolutes, and that he was temperamentally far less equipped to deal with relativity than Hardy was. It is interesting that writers on Hardy do not use Conrad's romantic idealisation as applied both to the nature of women and to masculine romance to define by contrast Hardy's modern and unillusioned depictions of the scope of men's enterprises and the relations between the sexes. The sometimes brilliant early Hardy critic, Joseph Warren Beach, divides Hardy from Conrad on the very ground where I find the most vital and fruitful association is to be made:

> They ['these moderns', and *not* Hardy] rely more on impressions of the senses – on a mere succession of sensations – for rendering the psyche. Their idea is perhaps to make the effect at the same time more real and less sharply defined.... this method conforms to the actual thought-process, which is chiefly made up of items of sensation, rather than being a connected chain of logical reasoning.[49]

Without claiming him for Modernism, Hardy's exclusion from the greater reality achieved by modern methods of narration is being to some extent repaired by recent criticism.[50] What Elaine Scarry calls the 'reciprocal jostling with the world' that we read in Hardy has much in common with the saturation in Conrad of 'the thousand effluences of a world which comprehends us rather than that we

---

[48] Schnauder, *Free Will and Determinism*, 56, 57. The view is constant: Irving Howe in *Thomas Hardy* (1966) writes, 'Hardy was closer to Wordsworth than, say, to Conrad, for as novelist and poet he continued to attribute meaning to the universe' (24).

[49] Joseph Warren Beach, *The Twentieth Century Novel: Studies in Technique* (1932), 335.

[50] See the works by Elaine Scarry (1994), John Hughes (2011), William A. Cohen (2009) David Sweeney Coombs (2011), and David James (2010) itemised in the Bibliography. James writes of Hardy anticipating the impressionism of Conrad, while offering caveats in respect of this view. Michael Irwin gets to the point with characteristic directness: 'Most novelists are essentially concerned with what their characters do, say and think. Hardy's emphasis tends to be on what they (and with them his readers) see and hear' ('Seen in a New Light: Illumination and Irradiation in Hardy', in Mallett ed., *Thomas Hardy: Texts and Contexts*, 2002, 7).

comprehend', as Ramon Fernandez put it in 1924.⁵¹ And in setting Hardy's sensory impressionism in dialogue with Conrad's, an aim of my own study is to see further into the dimension they share, rather than those by which they contrast, by recovering something of the later nineteenth-century materialist sensibility which was so concerned with man's place in nature.

Some very fine critics in the post-war era of modern academic criticism have written substantially about both Hardy and Conrad separately, notably Morton Dauwen Zabel, Albert Guerard, Tony Tanner, J. Hillis Miller, Bruce Johnson, Ross C. Murfin, H. M. Daleski and Martin Ray.⁵² Guerard's book on Hardy becomes an ode to the necessity for Conrad, but it is interesting that the others, with the exception of Zabel, turned 'back' to Hardy after publishing on Conrad. More recent criticism that has followed Gillian Beer's and George Levine's examinations of the impact upon the novel of evolutionary biology and the physical sciences has also discovered a range of interesting relations specifically *between* the two writers.⁵³ But despite Levine's notion of a 'late-century realism' that comprehends Gissing, Hardy, James, Conrad and Moore, and Philip Weinstein's strong pairing of Hardy and Conrad under the rubric of 'Tragic Encounters', I doubt that it is 'generally recognised', as Jacob Korg more recently asserts, that it was 'Hardy and Conrad who brought about a fundamental shift' in the novel, towards 'a reality that is unknowable'.⁵⁴ It is still only *Jude*

---

⁵¹ Scarry, *Resisting Representation* (1994), 51. Ramon Fernandez, 'The Art of Conrad', in *Messages* (1927), 140. Originally published as 'L'art de Conrad', in the Conrad commemorative issue of *La Nouvelle Revue française* in 1924, its eight pages remain the finest single short exposition of the nature of Conrad's fictional art. Fernandez also contributed to the commemorative issues on Hardy's death of *La Revue nouvelle* (nos. 38–39, Jan–Feb 1928, 84–96). See Gerber and Davis, *Thomas Hardy, An Annotated Bibliography*, 290.

⁵² Apart from Martin Ray's numerous contributions, mainly biographical, to the *Thomas Hardy Journal* until his death in 2007, all the key works in question are itemised in the Bibliography.

⁵³ See in particular Gillian Beer, *Darwin's Plots* (1983), and *Open Fields: Science in Cultural Encounter* (1996); George Levine, *The Realistic Imagination* (1981), *Darwin and the Novelists* (1988), *Dying to Know: Scientific Epistemology and Narrative in Victorian England* (2002), and *Realism, Ethics and Secularism: Essays on Victorian Literature and Science* (2008). The work of Philip Weinstein (1984), Perry Meisel (1987), Daniel Schwarz (1989), Daniel Bivona (1990), James Krasner (1992), Jim Reilly (1993), Michael Valdez Moses (1995), Ursula Lord (1998), Jesse Matz (2001), Tim Armstrong (2005), John Glendening (2007) and Aaron Matz (2010) is itemised in the Bibliography.

⁵⁴ Levine, *The Realistic Imagination*, 6; Philip Weinstein, *The Semantics of Desire* (1984), 105–84; Jacob Korg, 'Hardy, Conrad and the Agnostic Novel', in Marroni and Page ed., *Thomas Hardy* (1995), 223.

that is considered comparable to Conrad's vision of a world without inherent or shareable meaning.[55] The present study argues not for a shift, but for a specific and pre-eminent *place* in late-Victorian culture for these two novelists, and one that is illuminated by considering their novels in relation to mid- and late-century developments in physiology and physics. Correlation is not causation, and this is not a study of influence, either of science upon literature, or of the writers upon each other; rather, it is an examination of compatible writing in an age of the observation of phenomena.[56] As such, much of the concern is with literary style. J. A. V. Chapple, who wrote much about literature and science, makes the claim which underlies this book with great clarity: 'Conrad's central flame', he writes, 'burnt more strongly in the oxygen of scientific thought.' This is even more demonstrably true of Hardy. Chapple goes on: 'Despite the rapid development during the century of new chemical, mathematical, and other symbolic languages, most of that thought was contained in texts that were themselves literary, addressed to the general reader.'[57]

Though not written explicitly to do so, *Hardy, Conrad and the Senses* directly answers the plea in Alice Jenkins's *Space and the 'March of Mind'* for 'detailed work (to be) done on the ways in which ideas related to field theory were spread through literary and other culture' in the later Victorian period.[58] Jenkins's contention is that *Middlemarch* 'is centrally concerned with methods of connection and means of transmission; and therefore that other texts with these concerns may also be suitable for investigation in the light of field theory, though their author lacked Eliot's scientific knowledge'.[59] Hardy and Conrad are here offered in just that light.

---

[55] For instance, see Daniel Bivona (1994), Barbara DeMille (1990) and Brett Neilson (2004), itemised in the Bibliography.

[56] In her important *The 'Scientific Movement' and Victorian Literature* (1982), Tess Cosslett writes: 'Of course, the question of "influence" between science and literature can work both ways: the scientists, *being Victorian writers*, will most probably be affected by prevailing literary values and styles' (5, my emphasis added). An interest in Victorian writing is what primarily connects my book to hers. A much more recent book in the field, Philipp Erchinger's *Artful Experiments* (2018), declares of geologists such as Lyell, and of other scientists, 'Literature, in the sense of writing, was part of their scientific work because much of their scientific work was carried out through writing' (5).

[57] J. A. V. Chapple, 'Conrad's Brooding Over Scientific Opinion', *The Conradian* 10:1 (May 1985), 67.

[58] Alice Jenkins, *Space and the 'March of Mind'* (2007), 25.

[59] Ibid., 207.

In his *Analysis of the Phenomena of the Human Mind* (1869), James Mill writes, 'The pleasures and pains of Hearing and Sight are remembered best of any. This gives them a higher value in life; the addition made to the actual, by the ideal, is, in their case, the greatest of all.'[60] This sentiment, and the idealist 'addition' which seems true to Hardy and Conrad, indicates why I have broadly divided this book into visible and auditory worlds. A further preoccupation involved in this division, which emerges fully in Chapter 5, is suggested by Robert Jütte when he quotes Marx: 'the eye and the ear – organs which take man away from his individuality and make him the mirror and echo of the universe'.[61] In the novels which follow, the conditions of life are faced with the alertness of the senses, the fortitude of the will, and the resourcefulness of the mind. In placing the emphasis on the first of these, the story I tell here is of the senses as agents of attachment and involvement, an account entirely in accord with the outlook of the American Pragmatist, John Dewey, in his declaration that 'The senses are the organs through which the live creature participates directly in the on-goings of the world about him.'[62] The constant struggle in the novels of Hardy and Conrad is not to allow the necessary and vivifying receptiveness of the senses to absorb one into the present moment, but to maintain the self-possession which enables one to negotiate the world. In a passage which will be quoted again, Gabriel Oak, in *Far From the Madding Crowd*, has been rescued from smoke fumes in his shepherd's hut by Bathsheba Everdene:

> He was endeavouring to catch and appreciate the sensation of being thus with her, his head upon her dress, before the event passed on into the heap of bygone things. He wished she knew his impressions; but he would as soon have thought of carrying an odour in a net as of attempting to convey the intangibilities of his feeling in the coarse meshes of language.[63]

---

[60] Mill, *Analysis of the Phenomena of the Human Mind* (1869), 8 (originally 1829).
[61] Karl Marx, *Collected Works* 1: 173, quoted in Jütte, *A History of the Senses* (2005), 17. For a recent discussion of the issues involved in classifying sense experience, see Fiona Macpherson 'Introduction: Individuating the Senses', in *The Senses* (2011), 3–43.
[62] John Dewey, *Art as Experience* (1934), 22. The whole of Dewey's first chapter, 'The Live Creature', is intensely relevant to my discussion. As much as. . . . Bohlman the Existentialism which has been persuasively claimed for each by Jean Brooks and Otto Bohlman, Dewey's Pragmatism, though more readily assimilable to Hardy, illuminates much in both authors.
[63] Thomas Hardy, *Far From the Madding Crowd* (ed. Blythe, 1978), 70.

In a cancelled passage from the manuscript of *Under Western Eyes*, the secret agent Razumov maintains his alertness in conversation with the revolutionary Sophia Antonovna:

> In his effort to keep always a moral footing in the shifting conditions of his existence even the word 'duty' passed through his mind. It passed through his mind in relation to his task which was to observe and to listen with complete self possession, and an ever-alert intelligence. (465)

Between this intense and delicate susceptibility of the senses, and the exactions of a world which demands we employ those senses for survival, are found the urgent springs of both these authors' fictions.

Chapter One

The Physiology of Sensation and Literary Style
Desperate Remedies and *The Rescue*

> In our usual observations on external nature our attention is so thoroughly engaged by external objects that we are entirely unpractised in taking as the subjects of conscious observation, any properties of our sensations themselves, which we do not know as the sensible expression of some individual external object or event.
>
> Hermann von Helmholtz, *On the Sensations of Tone as a Physiological Basis for a Theory of Music* (1862)

The word 'sensation' is to be found everywhere in Hardy's and Conrad's writing. In this chapter I try to show that reading their novels against nineteenth-century research into the physiology of sense reception and transmission makes visible a shared materialist basis in their literary styles, however different the finished picture of their fictions. In practice, the grammarian and schools' inspector J. D. Morell, who claimed in 1846 to have coined the term 'sensationalism' to characterize a major strand of nineteenth-century philosophy (he says he had previously tried 'sensualism', 'sensism' and 'sensationism'), rather deplored its 'cosmological tendencies', but in a way that points directly to the two novelists we are considering. Sensationalism, he says, 'always evinces a disposition more or less decisive to erect the idea of nature over that of God'.[1] A view of nature released from divine purpose

---

[1] J. D. Morell, *An Historical and Critical View of the Speculative Philosophy of Europe in the Nineteenth Century* (1846), x and vol. 2, 450. See also Sue Zemka, *Time and the Moment in Victorian Literature and Society* (2012), 20ff. Martin Bock was the first to propose the term 'sensationist' in discussing Conrad's fiction: see his 'The Sensationist Epistemology in Conrad's Early Fiction' *Conradiana* 16:1 (1984), 3–18.

promotes a view of man freed from notions of special creation, and the mid- and late-century attention to man as an evolving and adapting organism made sensation a prime feature in studies of physiology which reached an audience well beyond specialists in the field.[2] What D. W. Hamlyn characterizes as the 'epistemological and psychological atomism' of this tradition is mirrored in the item-by-sensory-item literary style of Hardy's and Conrad's novels.[3]

The nature and the implications of this literary style are the subject of my examination of two dissimilar novels, both of which have been discussed more for their problematic, rather than for their formative, contribution to their authors' development as writers of fiction.[4] *Desperate Remedies* (1871) was Hardy's first published novel; and *The Rescue*, largely written as 'The Rescuer' between 1896 and 1898, resumed in 1916, and published in 1920, cast a long shadow over Conrad's later writing. In *Desperate Remedies*, Hardy adopts many of the devices of the sensation novel so popular in the previous decade, while in *The Rescue* Conrad is knowingly working in the mode of the exotic adventure novel. But some years later Hardy muses, 'A "sensation-novel" is possible in which the sensationalism is not casualty but evolution; not physical but psychical', and in which 'the effect upon the faculties is the important matter to be depicted' (*LW* 213);[5] and Conrad writes to William Blackwood: 'Of course the paraphernalia of the story are hackneyed. The yacht, the shipwreck, the pirates, the coast – all this has been used times out of number', but also says, 'I wish to obtain the

---

[2] See, for instance, the writing about sensation by Alexander Bain (1855), Herbert Spencer (1867 [1855]), G. H. Lewes (1860 [1859] and 1879), Gustav Fechner (1860), Hermann von Helmholtz (1862), Bain's 1869 annotations to James Mill (1869), T. H. Huxley (2001 [1871 and 1879]), James Sully (1874), W. B. Carpenter (1874), Ernst Mach (1897 [1886]), G. T. Ladd (1887), William James (1890), Karl Pearson (1892), which are itemised in the Bibliography. Nicholas J. Wade's eight-volume *The Emergence of Neuroscience in the Nineteenth Century* (2000), reprints seminal chapters by Bell, Müller, Bain, Sherrington and others. See also the chapter on 'Victorian Psychophysiology', in Bruce Haley, *The Healthy Body and Victorian Culture* (1978), 23–45.
[3] D. W. Hamlyn, *Sensation and Perception* (1961), 148.
[4] John Bayley is an honourable exception. Bayley's *An Essay on Hardy* (1978) seems to me of a different order to most academic writing on Hardy.
[5] Richard Taylor, in *The Neglected Hardy* (1982), comments on Hardy's entry: 'Thus defined, every one of his novels is a sensation novel . . . He becomes increasingly an inward artist, celebrating individual lives; the real drama becomes cerebral' (13). I think the first part of this claim is absolutely right, but would dissent from 'inward' and even more so from 'cerebral'.

effect of reality in my story' (*CL* 1:381). Both novelists thus use their conventional occasions to explore profoundly the sensational constituents of experience – transmission, medium and reception – which belong also to the mid and late nineteenth-century scientific interest in sensation.

*

In prefaces added to later editions of *Desperate Remedies*, first published by Tinsley Brothers in 1871, Hardy claimed that 'this sensational and strictly conventional narrative' ('Wessex Edition', 1912) was written 'at a time when he was feeling his way to a method' ('New Edition', Ward and Downey, 1889). Yet, a few pages into the novel, Hardy presents an episode that struck at least one contemporary reader as showing 'talent of a remarkable kind – sensitiveness to scenic and atmospheric effects, and to their influence on the mind, and the power of rousing similar sensitiveness in his readers'.[6]

Ambrose Graye is supervising work on a church spire, while his daughter Cytherea, in the Town Hall below, waits for a reading from Shakespeare to begin, 'unknowingly stood, as it were, upon the extreme posterior edge of a tract in her life, in which the real meaning of Taking Thought had never been known'.[7] 'Taking thought' in this novel will more often mean being struck by strong sensations, but at this point the narrative unfolds its action with a distant mildness:

> That the top of this spire should be visible from her position in the room was a fact which Cytherea's idling eyes had discovered with some interest, and she was now engaged in watching the scene that was being enacted about its airy summit. Round the conical stone-work rose a cage of scaffolding against the white sky; and upon this stood five men – four in clothes as white as the new erection close beneath their hands, the fifth in the ordinary dark suit of a gentleman. (13)

The reader here is drawn on to compose what Cytherea sees by a syntactical arrangement bearing the seeming innocence of mere sequence: 'That the . . . was a fact which . . . and she was now . . . that was being . . .'. An activity which is not hers, but which can

---

[6] *Spectator*, 22 April 1871, in Cox ed., *Thomas Hardy: The Critical Heritage* (1979), 3–5.
[7] *Desperate Remedies* (2003), 13. The editor Patricia Ingham uses the original Tinsley 1871 three-volume edition as copy-text. Subsequent references are given parenthetically in the text.

only be placed before us as the discovery of her eyes – and thus *is* hers, and hers only – is 'being enacted' in the passivity of this sentence. What begins the sentence objectively as 'the top of this spire' becomes by its end the subjectively poetic 'airy summit'; and, as the first sentence constructs the process of watching, so the second, with its stone-work, cage and men, realises item by item what is placed in the picture.

The innovative aspect of the writing lies in the depiction of the space within which what happens occurs. Hardy draws attention to the conventional pictorial construction of the scene: 'The picture thus presented to a spectator in the Town Hall was curious and striking. It was an illuminated miniature, framed in by the dark margin of the window' (13–14). Yet even as the reader is directed to this retinal apprehension of events, and the focaliser's vision – that is, Cytherea's – is very definitely framed, the indefinite phrase 'a spectator' withdraws the sight from her exclusive possession, and the account recedes from visual definition not only in being curiously colourless for a picture, with its white sky and white clothes, but also because the tactile suggestion of 'close beneath their hands' is reprieved by the narrator's observation that this sharp, dark frame 'emphasised by contrast the softness of the objects enclosed' (14). Touch charges the available sensorium in the scene more sensuously than the striking detachment of Cytherea's 'listless and careless' watching; it ensures for the reader that the 'objects' of this silent visual event are *not* 'enclosed' in their visual frame but are 'being enacted' as items of sense impression, yet at an indeterminate distance from the observer's senses. That something unusually precise but spatially unplaceable was being written was apparent to the early *Spectator* reviewer, who was touched by 'the dreaminess of a scene, commonplace enough, but for its height and distance and silence'.[8]

Hardy prolongs this removal from restricted visual apprehension in the estranging paragraph which follows:

> The height of the spire was about one hundred and twenty feet, and the five men engaged thereon seemed entirely removed from the sphere and experiences of ordinary human beings. They appeared little larger than pigeons, and made their tiny movements with a soft, spirit-like silence. One idea above all others was conveyed to the mind of a person on the ground by their aspect, namely, concentration of purpose: that they were indifferent to – even unconscious of – the distracted world beneath them, and all that moved upon it. They never looked off the scaffolding. (14)

---

[8] Cox ed., *Critical Heritage*, 4.

If these 'seemings' belong strictly to the distracted consciousness of Cytherea, the action of this paragraph is to diffuse them beyond the visual framing of a focaliser. The formally-phrased 'engaged thereon' effectively does *not* specify the precise attachment of the men to the spire, and as much as objects in the eyes of the idly watching Cytherea they have become the property of a scene that, for all its suggested dimensions, is suspended 'indifferent', before 'ordinary human beings', 'a person on the ground', 'the distracted world'. The 'soft, spirit-like silentness' at the heart of the paragraph attenuates almost to ghostliness these already white figures, though the delicate attention of the beautiful and original phrase, quietly prolonging the sense of touch, carries with it an engagement that belongs more to the men's commitment to their work than to the sentiments of Cytherea as a daughter. In an episode about the purely sensory registration of an event as it unfolds, the reader finds that the deep interest of the writing gathers around the strange transmission of the scene, here presented in a significantly passive construction – 'was conveyed'. The 'one idea' of detaching self-absorption (of the men, but also of Cytherea), imbues the scene as a whole. The subject is not so much the registrations of consciousness – as it would be in James, or Woolf – but the vibrations in the ether (to use a term that would obtain for at least sixteen years after the novel's publication), the *relations between* things that make what is conventionally called 'atmosphere'. This sequence, like many others of sensuously heightened description in the novel, explores what the poem 'Self-Unconscious' (*Satires of Circumstance*, 1914) calls 'The moment that encompassed him', a moment vividly present to consciousness but one that is viewed as containing that consciousness, rather than contained within it.[9]

The episode completes itself, independent of Cytherea's raised interest, with a shocking but understated swiftness:

> She moved herself uneasily. 'I wish he would come down,' she whispered, still gazing at the sky-backed picture. 'It is so dangerous to be absent-minded up there.'
> When she had done murmuring the words her father indecisively laid hold of one of the scaffold-poles, as if to test its strength, then let it go and stepped back. In stepping, his foot slipped. An instant of doubling

---

[9] See Penelope Vigar, *The Novels of Thomas Hardy: Illusion and Reality* (1974), 64–71. The scene bears some striking resemblances, as J. B. Bullen has examined in *The Expressive Eye* (1986), to the episode as recounted in *Life* and *Work* of the sixteen-year-old Hardy viewing a hanging at Dorchester gaol from outside the family house at Bockhampton through a telescope.

forward and sideways, and he reeled off into the air, immediately disappearing downwards.

His agonised daughter rose to her feet by a convulsive movement. Her lips parted, and she gasped for breath. She could utter no sound. One by one the people about her, unconscious of what had happened, turned their heads, and inquiry and alarm became visible upon their faces at the sight of the poor child. A moment longer, and she fell to the floor. (14)

The fall has nothing to do with Cytherea: although we are brought oddly close to the physical embodiment of her whisper by the phrasing 'she had *done* murmuring *the* words', the sentence which runs her words directly into her father's distant indecisive action could not more effectively disconnect the two of them, leaving each in a remoteness painful to the reader but unfelt by either. The writing restricts itself to the notation of a trajectory in a geometric plane. Mr Graye's fall is confined to the declarative clause 'he reeled off into the air', almost lively but startlingly abbreviated, and what happens to him afterwards is merely registered as a removal from the visual frame, which must be Cytherea's but uncoupled from any Cytherea-consciousness. Thus the discomforting objectivity of the whole sequence is brought to a climax without any rhetorical intensification. The discomfort is the point because, of course, Mr Graye's fall precipitates a second one, Cytherea's fall into disenchantment, her father's 'absent-minded' departure precipitating the consciousness of unsupported adulthood. The knowledge put on with this fall is 'of that labyrinth into which she stepped immediately afterwards – to continue a perplexed course along its mazes for the greater portion of twenty-nine subsequent months' (13), which comprises the remainder of this carefully dated novel. In pointing to where Cytherea 'unknowingly stood' and where Ambrose Graye unknowingly stands on the scaffolding, Hardy subtly connects the two characters throughout the episode. 'A moment longer, and she fell to the floor' syntactically re-enacts 'An instant of doubling forward and sideways, and he reeled off . . .'. The scene places connection and disconnection between father and daughter as an event *between* them, 'sensational' in being an account almost entirely delivered upon the authority of the senses, with interpretation into feelings subordinated to a single adverb and adjective, 'uneasily' and 'agonised'. A paradigm passage for the registration of an unexpected scene as it reaches a perceiver through space is Strether watching Madame de Vionnet and Chad rounding the bend in the river in *The Ambassadors*. James writes, 'The air quite thickened, at their approach, with further intimations'; but that thickening is securely located in Strether's consciousness as a matter of his unfolding interpretation. My argument is that Hardy (and Conrad, as we shall see) is distinct from James exactly in his attention to the thickened air that constitutes the imagined dynamics of a scene rather than the contents of a perceiving mind.

However, the sequence extends to one further paragraph. While a recognition of Cytherea's ejection from childhood into a world in which she can be a 'poor child' no longer is the primary cognitive function of this subtly imagined episode, this is framed for the reader by an aesthetic effect more elusive yet even more memorable.

> The next impression of which Cytherea had any consciousness was of being carried from a strange vehicle across the pavement to the steps of her own house by her brother and an older man. Recollection of what had passed evolved itself an instant later, and just as they entered the door – through which another and a sadder burden had been carried but a few instants before – her eyes caught sight of the south-western sky, and, without heeding saw white sunlight shining in shaft-like lines from a rift in a slaty cloud. Emotions will attach themselves to scenes that are simultaneous – however foreign in essence these scenes may be – as chemical waters will crystallise on twigs and wires. Ever after that time any mental agony brought less vividly to Cytherea's mind the scene from the Town Hall windows than sunlight streaming in shaft-like lines. (14–15)

For Cytherea, the 'sky-backed picture' of the men on the scaffolding is *not* the one that will involuntarily accompany 'mental agony' in the times to come; this 'scene from the Town Hall windows' will remain just that, displaced by a process explicable as an impersonal chemical reaction for the far more mysterious sky-image of 'sunlight streaming in shaft-like lines' (15). The reader is left, at the chapter's end, with Cytherea's 'impression' and with a haunting repetition of the rhythmically memorable phrase, one that does not quite so clearly *symbolise* something as does the psychologically similar 'pond edged with greyish leaves' of Hardy's imagist poem 'Neutral Tones', written four years previously. The dynamic energy of 'streaming', and the geometric force of 'shaft-like lines', untranslatable, but hard, striking through the earlier softness, is what impresses itself upon our memory.[10] Havelock Ellis, who later will praise Conrad's 'oblique method of narration' which 'lends itself to a shimmeringly brilliant effect of prolonged sensation', offers in his early article 'Thomas Hardy's Novels' (1883), the clue to Hardy's presentation of mental contents here and in his succeeding novels: 'Generally, [Hardy] is only willing to recognize the psychical element in its physical correlative . . . . This dislike to use the subjective method or to deal directly with mental phenomena is a feature in Mr Hardy's psychology which left a strong mark on his art.'[11] 'Mark' is right: there is a gestural directness in the visual image as a spatial imprint upon the memory, which Havelock Ellis registers even as he officially recognises only a different sort of direct dealing with the mind.

*

We turn now to the strange spaces of *The Rescue* to see how Conrad's evocation of psychic phenomena is unexpectedly in accord with Hardy's physical depiction.[12] In his own first reference to *The Rescue*, contained in a letter to Garnett of 23–4 March 1896, Conrad humorously announces, 'I am looking for a sensational title', clearly using the word in its accepted literary, rather than scientific, sense (*CL* 1:268). However, it is a novel whose style is so saturated by the literary transcription of the phenomena produced by seeing, hearing and touching, that most of its pages describe sensory orientations in space and thus explore dimensions in which contemporary physics and physiology were also showing great interest. In *The Rescue* Conrad put a style created by 'an absolute truth to my sensations (which are the basis of art in literature)' – as he

---

[10] Glen Wickens offers a more certain interpretation, focusing on the 'rift in a slaty cloud': 'Unconsciously, she transfers the stonework that her father fell from to the sky. Nature appears as an aggressive, hostile environment', with 'the memory of the sunlight streaming in shafts, like the bars of the architect's scaffolding' ('Romantic Myth and Victorian Nature': *English Studies in Canada* 8:2, June 1982, 161). I am very nearly convinced by Wickens's vision, but find it finally more resolved than the uncertainty retained in Hardy's lingering repetition. John Bayley's brief, brilliant comment sees the scene in terms of the transmission of lines of force (*An Essay*, 128).

[11] Havelock Ellis, 'Mr Conrad's World', in *The Philosophy of Conflict* (1919), 254; 'Thomas Hardy's Novels', *Westminster Review* (April 1883), 175.

[12] I take the phrase from Katherine Baxter, 'The Strange Spaces of *The Rescue*', *The Conradian* 29:1 (Spring 2004), 64–83.

later claimed in his famous defence of his art to William Blackwood (*CL* 2:418) – in the service of a story in which absolute faith becomes more and more subject to sensational uncertainty. The theme of the novel, like that of *Desperate Remedies*, concerns the possibilities and dangers of enchantment, although Cytherea's fall into the brief hopes and constrictions of an English adulthood is a very different affair from the inability of Captain Lingard and Edith Travers, becalmed in shallow waters on the flat shores of Borneo, to face the dilemma of loyalty and betrayal that their fascination for each other creates. But an examination of debilitating passivity in the face of things is the mainspring of both novels. The action of *The Rescue* is primarily about inaction, as it progressively disarms the confident and adventurous sailor Lingard of the 'careless certitude' with which he handles his brig, 'as if every stone, every grain of sand upon the treacherous bottom had been plainly disclosed to his sight' (53), until he becomes a figure in the thick morning mist, repeatedly asking, 'Can one see any distance over the water? . . . Has anything at all been seen?' (437).[13]

In a sentence from the manuscript, sadly cut from *The Rescue*, the still-sunlit immobility of the very opening of the novel yields this sharp visualisation of the brig:

> On the clear whiteness of the decks – ruled by straight lines of black pitch between the narrow planks – the shadows, that in a moving ship are always so restless and responsive to every slight balancing of the craft lay now clearly defined as if painted by a steady brush.[14]

This is a world of definite dimensions and clear operations, from which the long opening sequence will extend itself uncertainly towards less easily drawn outlines. After this stasis in which the ship 'had hardly altered its position half a mile during all these hours' (5),

---

[13] All page references to *The Rescue* are to the Dent Collected Edition (1949). The critical stock of the novel is so low that there is no edition currently in print in the UK. As the point of this chapter is to focus on the early, formative, fiction, I have in practice quoted throughout the manuscript of 'The Rescuer', which was written between 1896 and 1898. I have, anachronistically, retained the Dent pagination so that readers can locate my quotations in an available text.

[14] 'The Rescuer' ms. Ashley 4787, p. 6. In 1921 Conrad wrote excitedly to William Rothenstein about the marine paintings of Hardy's Dorset acquaintance John Everett (1876–1949): 'they appeal to me because I have always been alive to the shadow-effects of the sails' (*CL* 7:372).

the first action of the novel is the appearance out of a still night in the South China Sea of Carter's small boat up against the brig *Lightning*, as Lingard and his unappreciative and very English first mate, Shaw, conduct a desultory conversation. The qualities that make this forty-five page sequence so distinctive in fiction and so typical of Conrad – the same scenic construction of narrative characterises the seemingly aimless talk of Peyrol and Réal as they watch the *Amelia* off the French coast in *The Rover*, written twenty-seven years later – also make it a little unshapely to set beside Hardy's brief symbolic episode. However, the way in which both writers eschew the perceiving consciousness in favour of attention to the elusive substance of the space in which perception is stimulated offers a startlingly similar aesthetic, one in which phenomena maintain an aloof independence pitched beyond character and personal consciousness.

Whereas Hardy's silent mime concerned itself with sight, Conrad's tense and still scene begins by concerning itself with sound. A tide-rip has just passed under the brig, leaving the vessel 'as motionless and steady as if she had been securely moored between the stone walls of a safe dock':

> 'Now this is very curious –' began Shaw.
> Lingard made a gesture to command silence. He seemed to listen yet, as if the wash of the ripple could have had an echo which he expected to hear. And a man's voice that was heard forward had something of the impersonal ring of voices thrown back from hard and lofty cliffs upon the wide emptiness of the sea. It spoke in Malay – faintly.
> 'What?' hailed Shaw. 'What is it?'
> Lingard put a restraining hand for a moment on his chief officer's shoulder, and moved forward hurriedly. Shaw followed, puzzled. The rapid exchange of incomprehensible words thrown backward and forward through the shadows of the brig's main deck from his captain to the lookout man and back again, made him feel sadly out of it, somehow. (25–6)

Nothing here can be laid hold of directly. The active presences in the scene are ungraspable, particularly by Shaw – the quality of stillness, the ripple, the empty air that might vibrate to an echo, faint voices, incomprehensible and 'thrown' words, the shadows. Apart from Lingard's hand, hard, definite surfaces are the property of simile, summoned solely to suggest their absence – 'the stone walls of a safe dock', 'hard and lofty cliffs'. A further removal into modal conjecture is created by the presentation of Lingard, who '*seemed* to listen' for a wash that '*could have had* an echo which he *expected* to hear'. And just as Hardy took the reader's precise and visual apprehension of the scene to an unlocatable region of softness, so Conrad's remarkable following sentence finds its effects beyond the contents of a particular participant's consciousness. The abrupt discontinuity between 'which he expected to hear' and 'And a man's voice that was heard' – from Lingard's active listening to a passive reception diffused vaguely 'forward' – meets an opposing tendency in the conjunction 'And', which suggests a continuity, a sequence, but one that belongs to the scene itself, not to Lingard's attentiveness to a different sound or Shaw's observations on the tide-rip. When this other echo does return, it is 'thrown back' from quite a different region than surrounds the becalmed brig, the alien note introduced to the scene by the 'impersonal ring', not of this man's voice, but that of its ancestry in a whole line of seafarers or coastwatchers, expanding the reader's mental picture to open upon 'the empty distances of the sea'. It seems fair to wonder where, so swiftly, we have been transported, a feeling that might find a temporary home with the puzzlement of the unattractive Shaw, as 'voices thrown back from hard and lofty cliffs' become in the next paragraph 'words thrown backward and forward through the shadows of the brig's main deck'. Yet Shaw is only interesting to us as a participant in a moment caught by ears and eyes, but whose dimensions are not entirely defined on a scale of human understanding. In the physics of this passage, communicative sound is not decoded but exists as a force in motion whose properties conjure an imagined remoteness and whose waves pass through shadows, temporarily leaving humanity at the margins, in the diminishing adverbs, 'faintly', 'sadly', 'somehow'. Conrad is less interested in the consciousness of his characters than in the dynamic, vibrating quality of the scene itself, of which they are a part.

Effects such as these are frequent in this long and unhurried opening sequence, immersing the reader in a succession of sensations that often frustrates quick comprehension of the direction of the action. Communication is rendered as a series of projections through a dense medium, which is the subject of the writing as much as the messages themselves. So the emergence into the novel of Carter, the young second officer of the stranded schooner *Hermit*, is conveyed by this passage of atmospheric disturbance:

> A lump of blacker darkness floated into his [Lingard's] view. From it came over the water English words – deliberate, reaching him one by one; as if each had made its own difficult way through the profound stillness of the night.

'What – ship – is – that – pray?'

'English brig,' answered Lingard, after a short moment of hesitation.

'A brig! I thought you were something bigger,' went on the voice from the sea with a tinge of disappointment in its deliberate tone. (28)

The material quality of spoken words is significantly insisted upon in a novel in which Lingard's 'word' to come to the aid of the Wajo royal claimants, Hassim and Immada, is embodied in a ring, and in which that word fails to materialise in action. And the material aspect of perception, too, is what Conrad's writing insists on, even when it is a state of mind that is the ostensible subject. A predilection for physiology often means that the images chosen to embody a mental response escape into writing whose life is quite other than analytic description. So Lingard's first uncertainties about the nature of the events among which he moves are revealed in his encounter with Edith and Martin Travers on board their yacht, which 'deprived him in a manner of the power of speech. He was confounded. It was like meeting exacting spectres in a desert' (122). Conrad does not describe Lingard's perception of the Traverses; rather, in a move typical of all his writing, to describe the *sensation* of being confounded by them, he leads away from perceptual verisimilitude, away from realistically accurate depictions of a seen surface, into stark and fantastic regions through the gateway of simile.

Jesse Matz takes up exactly this point, in his sustained and trenchant opposition to the reading of Conrad's art that I am here proposing, in order to assert that 'Conrad's Impressionism is no sensationism': 'When Conrad wants to "make you *see*", he wants less to devote writing to surfaces and sensations than to renew a classic mode of figuration: he is less concerned with something new than with the very familiar effects of *simile*.'[15] Conrad's obsession with simile (especially in the 'as if' form) proves Matz absolutely right in one sense; where he is wrong, I think, is to elide 'surfaces' and 'sensations': Conrad moves away from the surfaces of things perceived in order to write about what it feels like to have sensations. These lingering, and very often surreal, similes correspond in a conventional literary form to Nicholas Humphrey's sense, in his physiological discussion of what it is to have a sensation, 'that what constitutes the conscious present is largely the immediate sensory *afterglow* of stimuli that have just passed by'.[16] Conrad writes of *The Rescue*, as he now calls it, to Mrs A. E. Bontine, Cunninghame Graham's mother,

---

[15] Jesse Matz, *Literary Impressionism and Modernist Aesthetics* (2001), 141.
[16] Nicholas Humphrey, *A History of the Mind* (1992), 176.

that 'an inextricable confusion of sensations is of the very essence of the tale' (*CL* 2:122); and by not allowing, in this opening section, the separate sensory events to cohere for the reader into a unified understanding of the whole situation (something that *Nostromo*, almost notoriously, performs on a much larger scale), he keeps us close to what has 'just past by' rather than retrieving achieved perceptions that have become the mental possessions of his characters. Recently, Kay Young has written, 'Mostly a Hardy character exists in a mental landscape of "un-thinking consciousness" or "after-thought consciousness"': the similarity of conception is striking.[17]

In this first episode, the prominent though intermittent use of the acute and confident Carter as focaliser charts in miniature the dissolution of certainties in the larger action to come. Though young, Carter has a professional alertness admired by Conrad. The moments in which the reader sees with his eyes and hears with his ears, as here, down in the sea in the dark in the small gig being towed by the brig, afford a sharply realised succession of sensational experiences without the estranging 'as if', in the surface manner that would avoid Matz's strictures:

> He was going to repeat his hail for the third time when he heard the rattling of tackles followed by a heavy splash, a burst of voices, scrambling hollow sounds – and a dark mass detaching itself from the brig's side swept past him on the crest of a passing sea. For less than a second he could see on the shimmer of the night sky the shape of a boat, the heads of four men, the blades of oars waving about while being got out hurriedly. Then all this sank out of sight, reappeared once more far off and hardly discernible, before vanishing for good. (49)

Four bursts of sound, four fleeting shapes pressed on the eye, the dash playing its part in leading from one to the other without causal connection: the receptive Carter registers everything around him in its physical actuality. He interprets accurately: 'Why, they've lowered a boat!' But this is not exactly what the scene communicates to him, nor the totality of the effect Conrad aims for in the sequence:

> The conviction that the yacht, and everything belonging to her, were in some indefinite but very real danger, took afresh a strong hold of him, and the persuasion that the master of the brig was going there to help did not by any means assuage his alarm. The fact only served to complicate his uneasiness with a sense of mystery. (49)

---

[17] Kay Young, *Imagining Minds: The Neuro-Aesthetics of Austen, Eliot and Hardy* (2010), 139.

This is an intellection subsequent to the initial series of sensations, but not presented as freed from the physical quality of encounter, nor as secured knowledge. 'The fact' is a harbinger of 'mystery'; the series of definite impressions yield an 'indefinite' feeling of danger. Ian Watt's notion of 'delayed decoding' has too often and too readily been appealed to as an explanation for what Conrad's impressionism is seeking to do in scenes such as these. In practice, it only explains a few of the less interesting effects, where experience can be resolved *into* the code provided by the accepted verbal currency, such as the whizzing little sticks that become arrows in 'Heart of Darkness'. 'Delayed decoding' implies a destination for experience in the mind which, once reached, does away with the original phenomena of the experience by intellectual dematerialisation into mental terms – they have been 'decoded' (which implies, wrongly I think, that they were already in code). I do not think this accounts accurately for 'Why, they've lowered a boat!', neither for Carter's experience, nor for the reader's experience which is, taking the scene as a whole, to be still immersed in that which resists enciphering.[18] More convincing is Ramon Fernandez's insight that Conrad 'applies himself to seizing things at their birth . . . we undergo them before they can be defined'.[19] The term 'delayed *en*coding' would match better the 'undergoing', the true Conradian strife in representing experience, which Fernandez identifies.

Neither Conrad's character Carter nor his readers have much hold upon the larger picture of events: both he and we are kept close to a sensational foreground pressed upon us. While Hardy's episode ends hauntingly on an arresting and untranslatable image, Conrad's episode stays in the reader's memory for its cumulative unsettling unexpectedness which dwells in the 'afterglow' of what has just passed rather than moving the action onward. Carter's crew in their small gig, briefly illuminated, 'resembled the faces of interested corpses'. The bowman drops the light in the water and 'the darkness, seemed to rush back at the boat, swallowed it with a loud and angry hiss' (29). It is the water of course, not the darkness, that produces the hiss, yet the writing insists on the more disturbing sensation. This movement of the reader into spaces of uncertain dimension brought

---

[18] For an excellent discussion along these lines, see Bruce Johnson, 'Conrad's Impressionism and Watt's "delayed decoding"', in Murfin ed., *Conrad Revisited: Essays for the Eighties* (1985). See also – for the issue runs and runs – Johan Warodell's minute analysis in *The Conradian* 40:1, Spring 2015.

[19] Ramon Fernandez, 'The Art of Conrad' (1927), 144.

to us by sudden but indefinite contact is the product of a writer who strenuously casts his eyes and ears into every event in his novel, searching, almost desperately, for some further disclosure from the wavering surfaces he has imagined. When Edward Garnett praised this opening section, which Conrad had sent him in manuscript, as 'clearly and forcibly *seen*', Conrad replied, 'The progressive episodes of the story *will* not emerge from the chaos of my sensations. I feel nothing clearly' (*CL* 1:288). This loss of narrative momentum to the production of 'atmosphere', however, is not simply Conrad's inability to get on with the story. As he stated in his previous letter to Garnett, 'Here I have used up 103 pages of manuscript to relate the events of 12 hours. I have done it in pursuance of a plan . . . I would present to the reader the impression of the sea – the ship – the seamen' (*CL* 1:286), an impression whose disclosures remain strange visual and auditory phenomena rather than resolved understanding. The alertness of our senses is all we are possessed of, and they do not illuminate very far: so Shaw 'fell back into the immense silence of the world' (7), and Carter 'disappeared as if he had fallen out of the universe' (44). The sensation communicated to the reader is that of a sudden awareness of how unsupported we are in a cosmos silently indifferent to our pretensions.

*

Hardy's and Conrad's fictions work in the same border area as those scientists and physiological psychologists whose concern with sensation constituted such a typifying feature of mid- and late-century enquiries into human awareness. Heinrich Hertz put the issue compellingly:

> Outside our consciousness there lies the cold and alien world of actual things. Between the two stretches the narrow borderland of the senses. No communication between the two worlds is possible excepting across the narrow strip . . . For a proper understanding of ourselves and of the world it is of the highest importance that this borderland should be thoroughly explored.[20]

The research into specific 'nerve energies', initially of Johannes Müller and later of Hermann von Helmholtz, provided the observations that confirmed the implication of the Bell-Magendie law of 1822:

---

[20] Heinrich Hertz, keynote address at the Imperial Palace, Berlin, August 1891, quoted in David Bodanis, *Electric Universe* (2006), 98.

that it is the sensory responsiveness of the perceiver, rather than the properties of the perceived object, that determines our sense of what 'actual things' are.[21] In the words of Edwin Boring's 'simple restatement' of one of Müller's ten principles of 1838: 'The same stimulus acting on different nerves gives rise to different qualities; different stimuli acting on the same nerve give rise to the same quality. It is the nerve, not the stimulating object, that matters'.[22] This can be read as an invitation to solipsism; but, popularising the experimental work of Helmholtz, Fechner, Weber and others for a British audience, the physicist and psychologist James Sully writes in 1874 that, 'no number of such experiments as those here described can at all affect the question of the existence of an independent material world',[23] indicating that scientific sensationism did not threaten a sense of the reality of the external world, but rather that it investigated exactly how that reality was felt and known. Literary sensationism, equally, does not necessarily presuppose the evaporation of the material world in a private region of purely neurological exchange; rather, in its intense attention to the impact of sight, sound and touch, it conveys the almost invasive presence of that external world conducted through the membrane of the senses. But the ideal world of feelings and conceptions is not thereby abolished. As Sully says, the assumption underlying these physiological experiments 'is quite as susceptible of interpretation on the Idealist's theory as on the Realist's', which gives us a clue as to what sensationism represents for Hardy and Conrad – the site in which the continually conflicting impulses in their art can meet in a four-fold world of apprehensions, imaginings, circumstance and action.

This is not to say that Hardy's and Conrad's work bears exactly the same relationship to sensationist thought and, taking the hint from Sully, it is clear that Hardy is more the Realist, and Conrad the Idealist.[24] The point is that adherence to the testimony of the senses

---

[21] James J. Gibson, to whose idea of an active perceptual system as opposed to passive sense receptors the novels of Hardy and Conrad respond very well, mounts cogent objections to the Müller tradition. See *The Ecological Approach to Visual Perception* (1979), 115–16, 245–6.

[22] Edwin Boring, *Sensation and Perception in the History of Experimental Psychology* (1942), 71.

[23] James Sully, *Sensation and Intuition: Studies in Psychology and Aesthetics* (1874), 72.

[24] This despite the fact that Shelley was Hardy's favourite poet, while Keats was Conrad's.

does not require a denial of the shaping world within but, on the contrary, brings mood and temperament to bear upon the impact of external forces in its account of experience. Hardy's love of Crabbe, for instance, 'an apostle of realism who practised it in English literature three-quarters of a century before the French realistic school had been heard of' (*LW* 351),[25] is exactly in accord with this sort of conditioning of external nature, as poems such as 'Peter Grimes' and 'The Lover's Journey' readily show. His diary entry for 10 February 1897 declares, 'In spite of myself I cannot help noticing countenances & tempers in objects of scenery: e.g., trees, hills, houses' (*LW* 302). The claims of a subjective ideal construction impose themselves upon objective observation in such a way as to involve a human 'temper' in the representation of a scene. The struggle with such conflicting evidence and attitudes is entirely characteristic of the borderline of which Hertz writes.

Where this sort of subjectivity leaves the perceiver and the perceived scene is a prime concern of the remainder of this chapter – whether it delves inwards to render the external scene as a property of the mind alone, in a proto-modernist manner, or whether it gestures outwards to locate the sensing self, not as a cerebral receptacle, but as an embodied agent within a scene in which it participates. Writing of the mid-century period, Kurt Danziger suggests that this dichotomy was a feature of contemporary scientific study too: 'There were two areas of investigation in which the boundary between physiology and psychology was particularly unclear. One was the area of sensation. Studies of the sense organs were certainly physiological, but the activity of these organs involved the property of sensibility which was usually considered to be psychological.'[26] When Hardy, six years after writing *Desperate Remedies*, copies into his notebook from Comte's *Social Dynamics* (1876), '<u>Sensations</u> (obj.) <u>more vivid than recollections</u> (subj.) – In madness the reverse' (*LN* 1:74), and inserts the prompts that indicate immediate sensations are more objective than a pondered recall of events, he reveals a continuing adherence to a physiological basis in his understanding of human responses, and one in which sensations are part of our vital *connection* to the world around us rather than a portal to solipsism. The sense that we find so vividly in Hardy's novels that the whole organism is the

---

[25] For Crabbe as a 'greater influence on (Hardy's) realism than Zola', see *LN* 1:385.
[26] Kurt Danziger, *Naming the Mind: How Psychology Found its Language* (1997), 52.

responsive agent, and not just, or even primarily, the reflective and sequestering brain, is one that he shares with a celebrated precursor in the investigation of the borderland of the senses, the polymath G. H. Lewes. Lewes famously proclaims, '*It is the man, and not the brain, that thinks:* it is the organism as a whole, and not one organ, that feels and acts';[27] and we might compare Hardy's note for March 1890: 'A staid, worn, weak man at the railway station. His back, his legs, his hands, his face, were longing to be out of the world. His brain was not longing to be, because, like the brain of most people, it was the last part of his body to realize a situation' (*LW*, 234).[28] Two years later, in a chapter called 'The Organisation of Impressions', Lewes makes the point again: 'Thus physiology concurs with Common Sense in affirming that it is *we* who feel, *we* who think and will; not the brain, not any single organ, but the whole living organism.'[29]

More than twenty years before these statements from Lewes, his fellow empiricist and physiologist Alexander Bain published *The Senses and the Intellect* (1855), often credited as a founding text in English for the new science of psychology. Like Lewes, Bain does not accept a model that makes the brain the sole receptacle of knowledge. In a statement central to my understanding of Hardy and Conrad, he writes:

> The organ of mind is not the brain by itself; it is the brain, nerves, muscles, and organs of sense.... It is, therefore, in the present state of our knowledge, an entire misconception to talk of a *sensorium* within the brain, a *sanctum sanctorum*, or inner chamber, where impressions are poured in and stored up to be reproduced in a future day. There is no such chamber, no such mode of reception of outward influence.
>
> We must thus discard for ever the notion of the *sensorium commune*, the cerebral closet, as a central seat of mind, or receptacle of sensation and imagery.[30]

---

[27] G. H. Lewes, *The Physical Basis of Mind* (Second Series, 1877), 441.
[28] We find Samuel Butler continuing the debate in *Life and Habit* (1878), and showing the brain is not the only seat of consciousness, saying, 'it is within the common scope and meaning of the words "personal identity" ... that each individual may be manifold in the sense of being compounded of a vast number of subordinate individualities which have their separate lives within him' (124).
[29] G. H. Lewes, *Problems of Life and Mind* (Third Series, 1879), 76.
[30] Alexander Bain, *The Senses and the Intellect* (1855), 61.

We can contrast this approach to the inner self with the more famous statement of Walter Pater in the Conclusion to *The Renaissance*, one that haunts so much Modernist writing, in which 'the whole scope of observation is dwarfed into the narrow chamber of the individual mind'; and in his proximity to Bain, Hardy certainly follows the path less travelled by the major novelists of the next generation.[31] For them – though the question will be to what extent for *Conrad* – the subjectivity that leads to an art in which representation of the world can *only* be the impression made upon individual consciousness becomes almost axiomatic. Such a position finds influential correlation in the world of the empirical sciences in the very popular *The Grammar of Science* (1892) by Karl Pearson, professor of geometry, statistician, socialist, feminist, and later, sadly, advocate of eugenics.

Pearson's survey of the modern scientific temper is dedicated on almost every page to the proposition that all that science can verify of the external world is our sense impressions of it,[32] so that 'The stored effects of past sense-impressions form to a great extent what we are accustomed to speak of as an "external object." On this account such an object must be recognised as largely constructed by ourselves.' As we have seen, the idea of a storage-house in the brain for these effects has already been rejected by Bain, and the difference between them becomes clearer as Pearson becomes more eloquent:

> How close then can we actually get to this supposed world outside ourselves? Just as near as but no nearer than the brain terminals of the sensory nerves. We are like the clerk in the central telephone exchange who cannot get nearer to his customers than his end of the telephone wires ... Of that 'real' universe outside himself he would be able to form no direct impression; the real universe for him would be the messages which flowed from the ends of the telephone wires in his

---

[31] Walter Pater, *The Renaissance, Studies in Art and Poetry* (1986), 151. The 'Conclusion' was written in 1868. A perfect example of the mind conceived of as a private vessel for storing impressions that exist to be revisited is James's description of Fanny Assingham in *The Golden Bowl*: 'The crystal flask of her innermost attention really received it on the spot, and she had even already the vision of how, in the snug laboratory of her afterthought, she would be able chemically to analyse it' (208).

[32] This view Pearson shares with his mentor, Ernst Mach, who will feature significantly in Chapter 5, though with a different inflection.

office ... Messages in the form of sense-impressions come flowing in from that 'outside world' and these we analyse, classify, store up, and reason about. But of the nature of 'things-in-themselves' of what may exist at the other end of our system of telephone wires we know nothing.[33]

In contrast, Bain's picture of sensation and perception, which lays emphasis upon the activity of transmission, is one that promotes an engagement with a more directly stimulating world. It is outer-directed. On a page of *The Senses and the Intellect* headed 'Externality Implies Our Own Energy', Bain writes:

> If we were the subjects of purely passive sensation, – such sensations as warmth, odour, light, – apart from any movement of any active member whatever, our recognition of the external world might be something very different from what we now experience. The state of the consciousness would then, so far as we are able to imagine it, be of the nature of a dream, and our perception of the universe would be sufficiently represented by a theory of idealism.

Cytherea comes perilously close to such a condition – though, significantly, Hardy's narrator does not – in the chapter describing her father's fall from the tower at Hocbridge.

The result of such a passive withdrawal from life is finely rendered in Walter Pater's own novel, *Marius the Epicurean* (1885), a work that Conrad was 'licking (his) chops in anticipation' to read when Garnett sent it him in May 1897 (*CL* 1:355). The Cyrenaic section of Marius's development represents the most fully articulated sensationist philosophy in the Victorian novel, but it is one with a very different temper from Conrad:

> Conceded that what is secure in our existence is but the sharp apex of the present moment between two hypothetical eternities, and all that is real in our experience but a series of fleeting impressions:– so Marius

---

[33] Karl Pearson, *The Grammar of Science* (1892), 49 and 74. A clear literary correlate is Henry James's story, 'In The Cage' (1898). Michael Whitworth, in *Einstein's Wake* (2001), analyses Pater's relation to Pearson and 'the problem of solipsism posed by descriptionism', which is the term he prefers to sensationism (see 83–94). George Levine has a very extensive discussion of Pearson and Pater in *Dying to Know: Scientific Epistemology and Narrative in Victorian England* (2002). G. H. Lewes had previously disposed of the 'telegraphic wires' image of the nervous system as a 'misconception', a significant difference from Helmholtz; see *The Physiology of Common Life* (1860), vol. 2, 10.

continued the sceptical argument he had condensed, as the matter to hold by, from his various philosophical reading:– given, that we are never to get beyond the walls of this closely shut cell of one's own personality; that the ideas we are somehow impelled to form of an outer world, and of other minds akin to our own, are, it may be, but a day-dream, and the thought of any world beyond, a day-dream perhaps idler still . . . (84)

As well as the gloom of necessary incarceration – Pearson, in the *Grammar*, speaks of 'the impenetrable wall of sense impressions' (82) – such a philosophy also lends itself to a more comfortable sheltering from the exertions of physical *work* demanded of so many characters in Hardy's and Conrad's novels. 'The matter to hold by' for Marius is derived from reading and argument; and 'ideas', 'mind', 'day-dream' and 'thought' all give a uniformly mental reading at some removal from whatever sensations might have reached the inner sanctum from the outer world.[34] Conrad is much more physical: his friend Arthur Symons reports, 'he vibrated to every sensation',[35] and in his fiction we find an acute awareness of the subjectivity of the senses, but not one that *reduces* the external world to mental phenomena, or finds in an internal life a substitute for the unknowable independent existence of the world 'out there'. For characters in Conrad, as so clearly in Hardy, the world discloses itself most vividly as a result of walking through it, sailing upon it, scrutinising it from odd angles, listening to it with alert attention, or negotiating its surfaces in some physical exploit.[36] They do not sequester themselves in the enclosure of the telephone exchange office, in which Pearson sits solipsistically, the counterpart in science to Pater in aesthetics. The image that best

---

[34] Gowan Dawson very helpfully sites *Marius* amidst the scientific debate between materialism and idealism conducted in contemporary intellectual journals: 'Walter Pater's *Marius the Epicurean* and the Discourse of Science in Macmillan's Magazine: "A Creature of the Nineteenth Century"', *English Literature in Transition* 48:1 (2005). Benjamin Morgan gives a very different account of *Marius*, and of Pater in general: 'Marius finds community with materiality and energy . . . Paterian pulsations drive outward to a world of substance' (*The Outward Mind*, 2017, 169, 172).

[35] Arthur Symons, *Notes on Joseph Conrad* (1925), 14.

[36] Clementina Anstruther-Thomson, writing in collaboration with Vernon Lee, reflects upon standing still in a landscape: 'we had expected to see the landscape better, but in fact we see it worse . . . . our weight, which had been partly handed over to the outer world while we swung along from one foot to the other, has returned in full, and oppresses us' (*Beauty and Ugliness*, 1912, 182). 'Partly handed over to the outer world' exactly makes the link between movement in the novels of Hardy and Conrad and their realism.

characterises Conrad's fiction is the one which he offers in his appreciation, 'Henry James' (1904), that of 'rescue work carried out in darkness against cross gusts of wind swaying a great multitude', a romantic picture of exposure, 'snatching vanishing phases of turbulence' in a physical activity exacted from the artist as he seizes hold of a world that he is a part of though not comfortingly at home in.[37] The intensity of Pater's cerebrally sealed sensitivity to sensation, in contrast, creates a psychological interiority never attained by Conrad, whose delineations do not seek out that entirely mental world.

I am thus arguing for an impressionism in early Conrad which renders the physics of the scene that contains the mind, rather than the psychology of the mind that contains the scene. This 'scenic realism' draws Conrad closer to the modernity of Hardy than the Modernism of James. The distinction is clarified by a description taken from the history of science rather than of literature, in Theo C. Meyering's discussion of Helmholtz's philosophical position in his far-reaching 1989 study *Historical Roots of Cognitive Science*. He writes of a transition in nineteenth-century thought,

> from austere systems of *materialism*, which demand that a satisfactory explanation subsume the laws governing all motion; via *sensationalism*, which demands that the intelligible world be reconstructed solely from indubitable sense-data as basic units; to *subjective idealism* and *solipsism*, in which all that is left of 'reality' is a single subject and his phenomenal world.[38]

From Almayer to Peyrol, Conrad portrays the temptation to withdraw into an ideal and solipsistic world that is independent of immediate externalities. But his sensationism (unlike Pater's) conceives of receptiveness and understanding as a continual process of exchange rather than as a raid whose haul is secreted within imprisoning walls; and the action of each novel is to disallow the main characters their desire to remain onlookers in an unassailed subjectivity. James and the later high Modernists undoubtedly find a finer language for the mind than Conrad, but it is at the cost of an attenuated external reality as sense-data yields to mental analysis of it behind the wall, as it were. Mental contents and thought are not often Conrad's subjects for sustained passages: it is the vibrations of a scene that he attends to more readily than those of the individual mind.

---

[37] Joseph Conrad, *Notes on Life and Letters* (1949), 13.
[38] Theo C. Meyering, *Historical Roots of Cognitive Science* (1989), 147.

In one of the most sustained Victorian definitions of 'sensation' – Bain's five-page note to the 1869 edition of James Mill's *Analysis of the Phenomena of the Human Mind* – Bain debates the outward and inward features that attach to this term. At one point he is quite definite:

> Another distinction between the Sensation and the Idea, is of the most vital importance. To the Sensation belongs Objective Reality; the Idea is purely Subjective. This distinction lies at the root of the question of an External World; but on every view of that question, objectivity is connected with the Sensation; in contrast to which the Idea is an element exclusively mental or subjective.[39]

In bringing a 'series of seemings' or a 'world of illusions' to the test of sensations rather than ideas in their writing, Hardy and Conrad give a fleeting substance to objective reality; and it is this statement by Bain which most clearly indicates why their novels are inclined to face the world without, while acutely aware of the nervous organisation within that orientates them to do so.

*

As this study progressively shows, to render 'the vibrations of a scene' requires an attention to the physics of the external world as well as to the physiology of the characters' senses. In the ten years preceding the writing of *Desperate Remedies* the major tendency in the world of physics was the transformation of questions of force, of attraction and repulsion, into questions of energy in an electromagnetic field. James Maxwell explained to Michael Faraday, 'Force is the tendency of a body to pass from one place to another', whereas 'Energy is the power a thing has of doing work arising either from its own motion or from the "tension" subsisting between it and other things.'[40] The idea of the conservation of energy, formulated by James Joule and William Thomson from 1847 onwards, represented a movement

---

[39] James Mill, *Analysis of the Phenomena of the Human Mind* (1869), 66.
[40] Letter to Faraday, 9 November 1857, quoted in Bruce Clarke, *Energy Forms: Allegory and Science in the Era of Classical Thermodynamics* (2001), 18. An accessible history of energy, electromagnetism and field theory can be found in Bruce J. Hunt, *Pursuing Power and Light* (2010), and a summary of the transition from forces to fields of energy by M. Norton Wise, 'Electromagnetic Theory in the Nineteenth Century', in R. C. Olby et al. eds, *Companion to the History of Modern Science* (1996), 342–56.

towards viewing all activity as part of an ecosystem; and while a great deal has been written on the importance of Clausius's 'entropy' and the Second Law of Thermodynamics for literature, and for the whole temper of the *fin-de-siècle*, it is arguably the First Law, that of the conservation of energy, which is the more important for Hardy as he explores what happens to that subsisting 'tension' of which Maxwell speaks. In practice, although he uses 'force' rather than 'energy', W. R. Grove, in *The Correlation of Physical Forces*, precedes Joule and Thomson when he writes:

> Now the view I venture to submit is, that force cannot be annihilated, but is merely subdivided or altered in direction or character.... Wave your hand: the motion, which has apparently ceased, is taken up by the air, from the air by the walls of the room, &c., and so by direct and reacting waves, continually comminuted, but never destroyed.[41]

This is profoundly Hardyan in feeling, in its attention to progressive diminishments but with a discernment of subsistence nevertheless. What so many readers of his novels disparage as wilful intervention of Fate is the exact observation of contingencies transferring their energies to situations in which probabilities are ignited. In *Desperate Remedies*, the whole of the chapter of the fire at the Three Tranters Inn, *From ten to half-past eleven, p.m.* (165–8), is devoted to the operation of the laws of physics in a contingent situation of a freshening breeze, introduced by a sentence which might stand as Hardy's signature throughout his fiction: 'A strange concurrence of phenomena now confronts us' (165).[42] As the American populariser of science, Edward Youmans, wrote in 1865 of forces, 'the moment they are determined to be indestructible, the investigator becomes bound to account for them', which, in its turn, suggests the scientific basis for the pedantic inductiveness of Hardy's early style in its compulsion to account for the transformation of energies as they pass between mental and physical events.[43]

---

[41] W. R. Grove, *The Correlation of Physical Forces* (2nd ed., 1850), 17. Grove wrote the lecture in 1846.
[42] Roy Morrell long ago disposed of the reading of Hardy as a determinist. He contrasts *Desperate Remedies* with *The Woman in White*, its supposed model, and uses the scenes of the two fires in particular to show the operation of contingency. See *Thomas Hardy: The Will and the Way* (1965), 55–8.
[43] Edward Youmans ed., *The Correlation and Conservation of Forces* (1865), Introduction, xiv.

Although, in *Desperate Remedies*, this will lead to the whole of its third volume becoming a species of crime and detective fiction, the first two volumes are lit by a scenic conception of narrative whose source of creativity is not ingenuity or invention but a vivid sense of the medium within which the flow of lives is conducted. In keeping with the First rather than the Second Law, energy is not lost but constantly converted. Without the intense lighting that suffuses the early boating scenes between Cytherea and Edward Springrove there would not be the electricity of the lightning-charged scene of Cytherea's meeting with Manston, a scene whose fascination is compounded by the intervening dazzling first vision of Miss Aldclyffe as 'a tall black figure standing in the midst of fire' (54), and the nighttime passions forced upon Cytherea in bed, accompanied by her acute registration of the ambient soundwaves conveying the death of Miss Aldclyffe's father – all of which are the connections conducting the unresolved passionate energies onwards, not as mere plot-sequence but as realisations of the phenomenon of transmission itself. 'Ideal conception' (27) infuses 'the more material media through which this story moves' (34) in ways that make the experience of reading sections of *Desperate Remedies* one of being magnetically drawn onwards into spaces in which never-to-be-spent energies, that have their origin in the brief, unconsummated passion between Ambrose Graye and Cytherea Aldclyffe, transform themselves into ever new forms.[44]

The luminous scenes at Creston begin with the energies released in reaction to Ambrose Graye's death. Cytherea advertises herself as 'desirous of meeting with an ENGAGEMENT as GOVERNESS or COMPANION' which 'seemed a more material existence than her own that she saw thus delineated on the paper' (22). What a material existence might consist of, for moments of sensation and emotion, for the trajectory of a life, is the novel's abiding concern, and throughout *Desperate Remedies* material existence is precarious: the remote deaths of the two fathers so strangely brought to the senses of eye and ear; the uneasy relation in which the apparently imperious Miss Aldclyffe stands to her own unexaminable life; the uncertainty of the material existence of the first Mrs Manston for much of the novel, and of Cytherea's existence as Mrs Manston; the debilitation of Owen and

---

[44] In her 'Early Hardy Novels and the Fictional Eye', Judith Bryant Wittenberg offers a compelling account of connection and transmission, featuring much of the same portions of text that I touch upon here, but in rather different psychoanalytic terms. See *Novel: A Forum on Fiction* 16:2 (Winter 1983).

the threatened existence of the Springroves; and, continually, the question of what material existence can be accorded to the love between Cytherea and Edward Springrove – all of these ask the reader to track the transmutation of energies, one thing becoming another, as much as the impact of substantial bodies upon one another.

In the scenes at Creston, Cytherea is more vibrantly alive than in any subsequent part of the novel, and the apprehension of the surrounding world is so intense as to convey her perceiving self only as constituted of the sensations created by outward forms. On the midsummer's day steamboat excursion that 'forms the framework of the next incident in the chain' (27), Owen leaves Cytherea in order to explore a medieval ruin while Cytherea 'remained where he had left her till the time of his expected return, scanning the details of the prospect around' (28). For the purposes of the narrative we need merely be told that she became so absorbed in the scene that she forgot the time; but the process of that 'scanning' is realised to the point of a disintegration of the subject self in the ambient vibrations and waves of sound and light that convey the external world to the senses:

> She turned her face landward, and strained her eyes to discern, if possible, some sign of Owen's return. Nothing was visible save the strikingly brilliant, still landscape. The wide concave which lay at the back of the cliff in this direction was blazing with the western light, adding an orange tint to the vivid purple of the heather, now at the very climax of bloom, and free from the slightest touch of the invidious brown that so soon creeps into its shades. The light so intensified the colours that they seemed to stand above the surface of the earth and float in mid-air like an exhalation of red. (28)

In that extraordinary sentence colour has become detached from material surfaces to become a property of the air only, released to become simply and purely itself – 'red' – the longest wavelength and lowest frequency of the very small visible spectrum that the human eye can accommodate. We are reminded of how Hardy's own atmospheric art is preoccupied with the quality that he claims is the painter Turner's chief subject, *'light as modified by objects'* (*LW* 225, Hardy's emphasis). What of Cytherea's consciousness of her own sensations? The paragraph goes on:

> In the minor valleys, between the hillocks and ridges which diversified the contour of the basin, but did not disturb the general sweep, she marked brakes of tall, heavy-stemmed ferns, five or six feet high, in a brilliant light-green dress – a broad riband of them with the path in their midst winding like a stream along the little ravine that reached to

the foot of the hill, and delivered up the path to its grassy area. Among the ferns grew holly bushes deeper in tint than any shadow about them whilst the whole surface of the scene was dimpled with small conical pits, and here and there were round ponds, now dry, and half overgrown with rushes.

The last bell of the steamer rang. Cytherea had forgotten herself, and what she was looking for. (28)

What constitutes Cytherea's material existence in this remarkable passage? If the reader at all retains a sense of her as a character separate from the landscape she is viewing, then we must note that her mental presence is only marked by the single verb of her own 'marking' of the ferns, immediately to be absorbed by qualities of size, dimension, colour and direction so that, in the winding and the delivery of the path, the activity described is not that of Cytherea's discerning eyes but of the path itself. Cytherea's very forgetting of herself is present as the life that thrills in lightwaves striking surfaces, her aroused participation in the *event* of the landscape. When Youmans, discussing the vast spaces traversed by light and the 'stupendous reach' of the law of the conservation of energy, memorably claims that 'Star and nerve-tissue are parts of the same system',[45] he might, six years later, have found a literary embodiment of that assertion in this passage, in which light revealing matter becomes what Cytherea *is*, briefly, in the creation of the event.

As so often, D. H. Lawrence points us towards something essential: 'In *Desperate Remedies* there are scarcely any people at all, particularly when the plot is working.'[46] Lawrence derides the novel's attempt to construct 'people' or, as his previous paragraph has it, 'distinct individuality', and, in so doing, hints that we might rather look for the unconscious energies that bind human and non-human as they urge themselves through material existence. So the ecstatic moment of the kiss between Edward Springrove and Cytherea in the boat on Lewborne Bay is depicted as partaking in the larger stasis and exchange of the moment: 'The gentle sounds around them from the hills, the plains, the distant town, the adjacent shore, the water heaving at their side, the kiss, and the long kiss, were all "many a voice of one delight," and in unison with each other' (47–8).[47] And when the sequence ends

---

[45] Youmans ed., *The Correlation and Conservation of Forces*, xli.
[46] D. H. Lawrence, 'Study of Thomas Hardy', in *Phoenix* (1970), 435.
[47] Glen Wickens examines the use of Shelley's 'Stanzas Written in Dejection' here ('Romantic Myth', 158–61). See also John Hughes, '*Ecstatic Sound*': *Music and Individuality in the Work of Thomas Hardy* (2001), 36.

with the retreat into despair and the reduction of Cytherea's advertisement to 'LADY'S MAID. Inexperienced.', her rejoinder to Owen, 'Yes, I – who am I?' (50), carries an unforced wider resonance deriving from the subtle examination of 'material existence' through the thirty pages preceding it.

Scene after scene is composed in this manner, not simply turning away from an analysis of thoughts in favour of a pictorial or symbolic representation of the subject's condition, but constructing that subject's existence and knowledge of the world from the physical qualities of the moment that travels through her. Although it is most prominent in the electric orchestrations of the episode in which Cytherea encounters Aeneas Manston for the first time – the 'extraordinary interval of melodious sound' (135) that closes Volume 1 – this sensationist epistemology generates several further scenes: Manston walking alone through fields and woods assailed by the 'flashing panorama of illuminated oblong pictures' of the passing train that bears his wife to Carriford (142–4); the late afternoon autumnal haze in which Cytherea, figured in the scene by the 'wailing gnats', blown on the breeze, that drift upwards against the relentless horizontals, acquiesces to Manston's attentions and does not withdraw her hand from his (216–17); the scenes of Cytherea's wintery marriage, culminating in the conversing of the inverted images of Cytherea and Edward Springrove on the flowing surface of a stream (237–41); the elaborate scene of Manston duping the postman on his rain-soaked round, with the intense sensational representation of his progress through paths and fields, maintaining him as a centre of radiant energy in its transformations (303–6); even the scurry of listening and following in the closing fifty pages, when 'Intentness pervaded everything; Night herself seemed to have become a watcher' (349). In each of these passages (the word is particularly appropriate), the attention of the writing is taken not by the mental interior, but by the scenic whole that conditions communication across surfaces. To diminish the medium into 'setting' misunderstands Hardy's sense of the human relation to environment. He writes in 1911, despite claiming it as 'not very intelligible', 'View the matrices rather than the moulds' (*LW* 383).

The clearest indication in *Desperate Remedies* of Hardy's conscious 'disproportioning' of his art towards a rendering grounded in sense impression lies in a moment in which Springrove leans upon the bars of a gate, 'surveying the scene before him in that absent mood which takes cognisance of little things without being conscious of them at the time, though they appear in the eye afterwards as vivid impressions' (192). Patricia Ingham, in her Oxford World's Classics edition (2003, 405n), notes that this is 'similar to a description of the lover Egbert Mayne in 'An Indiscretion in the Life of an Heiress',[48] as he goes to get a marriage licence "in that state of mind which takes cognisance of little things, without at the time being conscious of them, though they return vividly upon the memory long after" (Part II, ch.6)'. The change of 'mind' to 'mood', and 'vividly upon the memory' to the much more physical 'appear *in the eye* afterwards as vivid *impressions*' (my emphasis), as well as having that mood the product of 'surveying the scene before him', indicate how far Hardy's conception of a 'state of mind' at this stage of his career was moving towards a physical involvement in a scenic moment that is also active in producing consciousness. Such sensationism can, of course, be strained to an almost comic over-explicitness, as when Manston takes Cytherea into the church and, after an atmospherically-charged description of decay illuminated by evening light, Cytherea responds with '"What sensations does the place impress you with?"' (221). But Hardy's serious physiological preoccupation throughout the novel with fleeting impressions and passing sensations that attain some sort of 'material existence' is what stands revealed in this question, uttered in the face of 'the dank air of death which had gathered with the evening' (221). It is one that continues right up to Manston's strangely affecting final pronouncement before he hangs himself. It could almost have been written by Thomas Middleton:

> I am now about to pass into my normal condition. For people are almost always in their graves. When we survey the long race of men, it is strange and still more strange to find that they are mainly dead men, who have scarcely ever been otherwise. (370)

*

To render characters so extensively through mood and sensation can make them seem mere impressible surfaces, and human agency little more than reaction.[49] The American historian and diplomat Henry

---

[48] This story of 1878 incorporates and reconstructs much of Hardy's first novel, *The Poor Man and the Lady*, rejected by Macmillan in 1868.

[49] Mark Asquith, in *Thomas Hardy, Metaphysics and Music* (2005), takes something akin to this view: 'Hardy's characters being transformed into masks through which the wider process objectifies itself in a form of ventriloquism' (96).

Adams, in his 1903 autobiographical essay on the impact of Pearson's *The Grammar of Science*, expresses just such an awareness with exasperation: 'As for himself, according to Helmholtz, Ernst Mach, and Arthur Balfour, he was henceforth to be a conscious ball of vibrating motions, traversed in every direction by infinite lines of rotation or vibration.'[50] Hardy's descriptions court this physics and this physiology; but the study of disabling, even fatal, passivity which emerges from novel after novel shows his pained consciousness of exactly the human implication of this scientific determinism, and it is important to recall that *Desperate Remedies*' greatest rhetorical, as opposed to descriptive, moment sets itself against such self-subduing. Immediately after Cytherea's marriage to Manston, her brother Owen weakly tries to banish Springrove from her thoughts as 'a mean-spirited fellow', but, with a significant alteration from Wordsworth, 'her eye told of sensations too deep for tears' (235). Owen's citing of her 'duty to society' provokes Cytherea's thrilling speech of self-assertion and resistance:

> But ah, Owen, it is difficult to adjust our outer and inner life with perfect honesty . . . the many, and duty to them, only exist to you through your own existence . . . And perhaps, far in time to come, when I am dead and gone, some other's accent, or some other's song, or thought, like an old one of mine, will carry them back to what I used to say, and hurt their hearts a little that they blamed me so soon. And they will pause just for an instant, and give a sigh to me, and think, 'Poor girl', believing they do great justice to my memory by this. But they will never, never realize that it was my single opportunity of existence, as well as of doing my duty, which they are regarding; they will not feel that what to them is but a thought, easily held in those two words of pity, 'Poor girl', was a whole life to me; as full of hours, minutes, and peculiar minutes, of hopes and dreads, smiles, whisperings, tears, as theirs: that it was my world, what is to them their world, and they in that life of mine, however much I cared for them, only as the thought I seem to them to be. Nobody can enter into another's nature truly, that's what is so grievous. (236)[51]

There is an accent of the author's own conviction here, which carries the sense that this is the irremediable position for a philosophy

---

[50] Henry Adams, *The Education of Henry Adams* (1999 [1907]), 384.
[51] Compare Alexander Bain: 'Each man has the full and perfect knowledge of his own consciousness; but no living being can penetrate the consciousness of another.' *The Emotions and the Will* (2nd edn, 1865), 28. And see also Hardy's 1866 poem 'She, to Him II': 'your thin thought, in two small words conveyed, / Was no such fleeting phantom-thought to me, / But the Whole Life wherein my part was played'.

of knowledge grounded in a truth to our own sensations. And this anguish at an intrinsic condition of isolation is fundamental to Conrad too: it can be read more coldly, but at book-length, in *The Secret Agent*, or as concentrated succinctly by Marlow in 'Heart of Darkness', for whom one's own 'life-sensation' is incommunicable, and '"We live, as we dream – alone"' (70). Cytherea here voices a doubt, that is also Hardy's, as to how easy it is to fulfil Spencer's definition of the essential life of any organism – 'the adjustment of inner to outer relations'.[52] For her, as for all of us, the 'world' is a private matter of her own sensations, but it is also the public matter of being *in* the world and claiming what those sensations demand as imperative. 'Poor girl' recalls the designation of her as a 'poor child' as she faints on seeing her father plunge to death; and her efforts to escape this designation and live her adult life are scarcely aided by the 'respectable' Owen. Cytherea's 'grievous' feeling that we are fundamentally alone in this 'single opportunity of existence' to find our equilibrium corresponds to Hardy's own later declaration, in a letter to Roden Noel of 1892: 'if the body be only sensations *plus* perceptions & concepts . . . Each is, to all knowledge, limited to his own frame. . . . you cannot find the link (at least I can't) of one form of consciousness with another.'[53] This does not, however, leave Hardy, or Cytherea, in the solipsistic retreat from the world of Pearson or Pater's Marius: Hardy's letter to Noel is about *Tess*, which reminds us of the courageous humanity of his protagonists, that they are compelled to urge the claim upon them of their 'single opportunity', and are called upon to face the forces of nature, within and without, under the command of no other spirit than their own. And yet, as *Desperate Remedies* shows, the most intense moments of a person's life involve the dissolution of separate individuality, and to urge the claims of the 'self' is no self-evident course of action. This is also discovered by Tom Lingard in the dilemmas posed by *The Rescue*, to which we will turn.

*

When Youmans wrote in his Introduction to *The Correlation and Conservation of Forces*, 'Scientific enquiries are becoming less and less questions of matter, and more and more questions of force;

---

[52] Herbert Spencer, *First Principles* (2nd edn, 1867): *Collected Writings*, vol. V (1996), 486.
[53] CL i. 262. The whole letter is one of Hardy's most significant statements about metaphysics, consciousness and pessimism.

material ideas are giving place to dynamical ideas',[54] he succinctly provided the contemporary scientific correlate to what is so characteristic of much of Conrad's early writing: the construction of scenes that dramatise transmission in a force-field, scenes that are imbued with the physical as much as the social medium within which lives are lived.

In *The Rescue*, Conrad's attention to a human drama conveyed through straining after sights and sounds uncertainly apprehended across stretches of water renders transmission of energies as nearly always on the point of expiry in a nocturnal immobility. Conrad might well have been ruefully predicting his reader's experience when he describes Lingard's 'exiled' desire to restore Hassim and Immada to Wajo: 'he saw it all, shifting and indistinct like those shapes the strained eye of a wanderer outlines in darker strokes upon the face of the night' (195). But this impression of indistinctness (a repeated word in the novel) is very deliberately produced: as Conrad wrote to Blackwood on 6 September 1897, proposing the title *The Rescue* in place of 'The Rescuer', 'I also know what I am aiming at – and it is not pure story-telling.' What it *was*, Conrad asserts a month later to the patient and steadfast recipient of all of his trials over the novel, Edward Garnett: 'No analysis. No damned mouthing. Pictures – pictures – pictures' (*CL* 1:382, 392). It is the quality that Edwin Muir saw as characteristic of Conrad: 'Mr Conrad writes in pictures, for the pictures come, and what he shows us is not action, but a progression of dissolving scenes, continuous and living, which in the end reflect action and give us a true apprehension of it.'[55] Conrad put it another way: 'I wish to obtain the *effect* of reality in my story' (to William Blackwood, *CL* 1:381, my emphasis). In his practice of this declaration, Conrad constructs *The Rescue* out of fifty-three separately visualised scenes, twenty-seven of which are set at night, including the whole of Part III, 'The Capture', and all but the last scene of Part IV, 'The Gift of the Shallows', that make up the centrepiece of the six-part novel. The point is that in only eight of these scenes does Conrad *not* make the qualities of light and sound, and the human action of seeing and hearing, more often in conditions of obscurity rather than disclosure, essential features of the scenic composition.

[54] Youmans, *The Correlation and Conservation of Forces*, xii.
[55] Edwin Muir, 'A Note on Mr Conrad', in *Latitudes* (1924), 50.

The insistence is remarkable, and probably to some readers, wearying. Neil MacAdam, in Somerset Maugham's story of the same name, asserts 'There's no one who got atmosphere like Conrad'; but Maugham also allows Darya Munro a passionate outburst: 'That stream of words, those involved sentences, the showy rhetoric, that affectation of profundity . . . false, false, false.'[56] As Paul Wiley wrote more than fifty years ago, 'No critic is likely to recommend *The Rescue* to a reader seeking for the best approach to Conrad's art', being 'overcharged with operatic atmosphere'; yet he holds to 'The conviction that *The Rescue* is the most representative, if not the most popular of Conrad's novels', a feeling I share.[57] *The Rescue* is full of an atmosphere that operates as a generative force for narrative. The presence of the night is everywhere pressed upon the reader: Carter mounting to the deck of the brig is suffused in 'a darkness that had become impenetrable, palpable, and stifling'; an immense cloud is 'arrested' above; and the single source of light is a gleam, 'faint and sad, like a vanishing memory of destroyed starlight' (42).[58] That distantly violent elegy is consonant with the whole tone of the novel, and presages the account of Lingard's romantic heroism in his memorable visit to the lightning-struck shore of Wajo, where the writing kinetically demands of the reader an almost muscular holding-on as 'at every dazzling flash, Hassim's native land seemed to leap nearer at the brig – and disappear instantly as if it had crouched low for the next spring out of an impenetrable darkness' (79).

The central drama of *The Rescue* takes place in the immobilised aftermath of that glamorous exploit in Wajo, in a darkened stillness that offers up action only as a romantic story. Conrad procures that reigning immobility, symbolised by the Travers's yacht stranded on the sandbank, from many quarters, not least Mrs Travers's silent, still reverie on deck in Part III, in which a vision of the unmoving spaces of the night 'stood arrested as if to remain with her forever' (151). Captured by a hallucination in which 'she saw herself, standing alone,

---

[56] Quoted in Norman Sherry ed., *Joseph Conrad: The Critical Heritage* (1997), 377.
[57] Paul L. Wiley, *Conrad's Measure of Man* (1954), 173–4. See also Donald Benson's discussion of the atmosphere of *The Rescue* as an 'ontological construct' in 'Impressionist Painting and the Problem of Conrad's Atmosphere', *Mosaic* 22:1 (1989).
[58] 'Destroyed' introduces far more agency into the physical ambience than the manuscript's original 'like a vanishing memory of departed starlight'.

at the end of time, on the brink of days' (151), she comes to a crisis in her life, still unmoving and unnervingly unmoved:

> And there was such a finality in that illusion, such an accord with the trend of her thought that when she murmured into the darkness a faint 'so be it' she seemed to have spoken one of those sentences that resume and close a life. (151)

Such an acknowledgment that to resume life can only be to close what we would want to mean by 'life', written in these mournful cadences, introduces sympathetically the elegiac note that clings to Mrs Travers throughout the novel. The faint 'so be it' is an agreement to abandon the ideal conception of herself and to perish into an unfeeling pragmatism, an internal adjustment of herself as subtle as could be asked from novelists of greater interiority than Conrad. It is the very opposite of Cytherea's impassioned plea. Yet this conclusive settlement has not been reached by self-examination, but by a hallucinatory picture that has led the reader to contemplate the vast universe beyond Mrs Travers rather than the small world within. Even in the most psychological of moments in *The Rescue*, Conrad apprehends a state of mind by how the external world presses invasively upon the senses.

Lingard's voice appeals to Mrs Travers from the surrounding dark: '"I made out your shape – on the sky"' (153). The loneliness, and the sense of being at the edge of the world yet susceptible to a desired appeal, is all very close to Conrad himself. *The Rescue* is infused with the sensation expressed so powerfully in Conrad's first wonderful letter to Cunninghame Graham, written exactly as he was struggling to compose 'The Capture' in August 1897:

> Most of my life has been spent between sky and water and now I live so alone that often I fancy myself clinging stupidly to a derelict planet abandoned by its precious crew. Your voice is not a voice in the wilderness – it seems to come through the clean emptiness of space. (*CL* 1:370)

There is a hope, a conviction of the solidarity of human hearts which might respond to such a voice, but in its whole conception *The Rescue* presents a visible and audible world always on the point of expiry, a state of entropy in which transmission is always doubtful. Signals of time and action are absorbed into the larger events of immobile airs and dying days; and this diminishment of human agency is merely part of a larger cycle:

> The sea vanquished the light. Soon only a vestige of the sun was visible far off like a red spark floating on the water. It lingered, and all at once – without warning – went out as if extinguished by a treacherous hand. (14)

Throughout the novel, footsteps are heard dying away; even the resonance of Lingard's words as he discloses his idealistic nature to Mrs Travers in the night is quelled as he glides away from the yacht's side and 'A rippling sound died out' (165). As a type of all these extinctions, when Lingard rows Mrs Travers from the yacht to the comparative safety of the brig,

> he had before his eyes the stern lantern expiring slowly on the abandoned vessel. When it went out without a warning flicker he could see nothing of the yacht. Not a trace of the stranded vessel's outline could his eye find on the smooth darkness. She had vanished utterly as a dream. (207)

Amidst these vanishings, the empiricism of young Carter as he seeks to understand where he is and what is going on is a significant entry point for the reader in a novel about the attempt to impose conceptions upon surfaces that both resist and absorb. (Mrs Travers is *aesthetically* right, later in the novel, to respond to Mr Travers's sole enquiry, 'Edith, where's the truth in all this?', with 'It's on the surface, I assure you. Altogether on the surface' (272).) So Carter's return to the deck of the *Lightning* lit by flares in the night, with news of the unaccountable disappearance of Mr Travers and his travelling companion Mr d'Alcacer, and his challenge to Lingard, 'but is it clear to you?', produces no analysis of thoughts and feelings, but rather this scene of darkness, volumes of air, and light, in which a reader places herself in the external spaces, leaving the internal ones objects of acoustic gesture in the characters' utterances:

> 'Clearer than daylight,' cried Lingard, hotly. 'I can't give up –'
> He checked himself. Carter waited. The flare bearers stood rigid, turning their faces away from the flame, and in the play of gleams at its foot the mast near by, like a lofty column, ascended into a great blackness. A lot of ropes ran up slanting into a dark void and were lost to sight, but high aloft a brace block gleamed white, the end of a yard-arm could be seen suspended in the air and glowing with its own light. The sky had clouded over the brig without a breath of wind – stealthily.
> 'Give up,' repeated Carter, with an uneasy shuffle of feet.
> 'Nobody,' finished Lingard. 'I can't. It's as clear as daylight. I can't! No! Nothing!' (155)

The mast and the ropes may seem pointless appendages, but without them there would be no scene, and the scene, with its sudden ability to create strange spaces, is Conrad's method of showing the dynamics that play between and around these characters as they try to gain mastery of a passage of life that is exerting its force upon them. While Carter waits for Lingard to complete his self-justification, it is the mast which assumes the active agency of the next sentence in a stately manner, a 'lofty column' as it 'ascended', whirling the eye up to aerial heights in the darkness. It displaces the horizontal human confrontation on the deck with a vertical perspective displaying briefly but steadily items from the tackle of the ship, their solidity 'suspended in the air' and dematerialised into light. Their kinetic energy presides over a scene of immobile expectancy: it is an effect which, in Ramon Fernandez's incomparable phrase for Conrad's sensational, saturating art, 'evokes, through the creation of the atmospheric image, the obscure birth of the event'.[59] The mechanics of cause and effect has given way to the inclusive energy of the field.

If we read the 'event' in *The Rescue*, or elsewhere in Conrad, as having its mysterious and 'obscure birth' solely in characters' minds, we misread Conrad and miss what links his fiction more to the art of Hardy than to that of James or Woolf. When the reader is returned to the human dimension of dialogue on the deck of the brig, Carter's 'Give up', and Lingard's barely intelligible 'Nobody . . . No! Nothing!' ask us less to construct convincing characters, each with a psychology formed of thoughts on their neural pathways, than to hear these adjurations and assertions as participants in the vibrations of a moment, invested with human significance, caught in its passage over a particular spot on the earth's surface. Conrad's excited response to Dr John McIntyre's Röntgen machine in Glasgow, as recounted to Edward Garnett in a letter of September 1898, lends support to the idea that he was composing *The Rescue* with a consciousness of wave theory and its implications for an artistic portrayal of human consciousness:

> in the evening dinner, phonograph, X rays, talk about *the* secret of the universe and the nonexistence of, so called, matter. The secret of the universe is in the existence of horizontal waves whose varied vibrations are at the bottom of all states of consciousness . . . *all matter* being only that thing of inconceivable tenuity through which the various vibrations of waves (electricity, heat, sound, light etc.) are propagated, thus giving birth to our sensations – then emotions – then thought. Is that so? (*CL* 2:94–5)

---

[59] Fernandez, 'The Art of Conrad', 140.

It would be extravagant to claim that *The Rescue* or any of the novels in this study seeks to *explain* the ever-elusive relationship between matter and consciousness, but each of them explores 'the varied vibrations . . . at the bottom of all states of consciousness' in an exposure of man to the indifference of earth, air and water that is distinctive in English fiction. For my argument that this distinctiveness reveals itself most clearly in relation to nineteenth-century materialist scientific thinking, it is worth saying that Conrad's 'sensations – then emotions – then thought' follows the 'sensation, thought, emotion, of the moment', of the Scottish philosopher Thomas Brown, in the terms which he bequeathed to the physiological psychologists who thread through my account, replacing the 'passions, affections and sentiments' of the previous era.[60] When Conrad asks 'Is that so?' he is asking with self-deprecating humour, 'Have I remembered my psychology text-books correctly?'

The agency of emotions and thought is always in question in *The Rescue*, especially when they find expression in words and, ultimately, in Lingard's given 'word'. The novelist's deepest anguish is whether *words* can make any impression, a hidden psychological foundation to the whole enterprise that we may surmise contributed to Conrad's difficulty in writing.[61] '"It's difficult to imagine that in this wilderness writing can have any significance"' (325), says Edith Travers at one point. In *The Rescue* words travel across water or out into the air with uncertain import and effect. In the remembered episode that precedes the main action of the novel, Hassim in his prau parts from the brig the following morning and shouts his invitation to come to Wajo:

> 'Come soon – lest what perhaps is written should come to pass!'
> The brig shot ahead.
> 'What?' yelled Lingard in a puzzled tone, 'What's written?'
> He listened. And as if floating over the water came faintly the words: 'No man knows!' (77)

What Hassim apparently demands is a freely-chosen decisiveness, but what hovers in the air is a teasing uncertainty between determinism and mystery. More than a communicative medium the air is a preserving

---

[60] See Thomas Dixon, *From Passions to Emotions* (2003), 121.
[61] I am borrowing here from Conrad's words, but diverting their application to himself. In the recently discovered draft of a synopsis for 'The Rescuer' he wrote: 'The psychological phenomena are the foundation of the structure – and being the foundation must remain out of sight. Only action shall be visible. I shall avoid analysis – ' (See Katherine Baxter, '*The Rescuer* Synopsis: A Transcription and Commentary', *The Conradian* 31:1, Spring 2006).

one, as words and feelings hang in its constantly evoked immobility. So Immada, standing on the deck of the yacht bewildered at the distraction of Lingard from their cause, 'whispered an appalled "Why?" so low that its pain floated away in the silence of attentive men, without response, unheard, ignored, like the pain of an impalpable thought' (137). What is almost thought is almost given embodiment as it is tracked in its scenic trajectory. *The Rescue* is at its best exactly when it is negotiating the obscure dimensions of the 'shadowy appeals made by life and death' (70) as they are sensed across water, across space, from the decks of boats. In the long letter about the novel sent as a proposal to Heinemann's partner S. S. Pawling on 8 November 1897 there is confirmation, in terms that Hardy would have understood, that this sort of scenic composition was indeed an aspect of Conrad's conception: 'I want the love story to be only like a subtle breath in the tale; something like a shadow or rather like the pervading tint of a landscape; like the tones of red and yellow in a wood, in autumn' (*CL* 9:54). Although Conrad in his later years might have deluded himself about how good a book *The Rescue* was (he hoped that its publication might help gain him the Nobel Prize), he was right that it was 'rather a big thing', as he wrote to the publisher F. N. Doubleday (*CL* 8:282), his most extensive exploration of human sensations as they mediate between ideal conceptions and a material universe.

Reading these early novels in company with the writing of the physiological psychologists who had recently preceded them doesn't necessarily make them better novels. But it does encourage a realisation that, in them, both Hardy and Conrad in their different ways were beginning an exploration of a thoroughly serious nature that would set the compass for their future fiction. Making their characters' relations so insistently a description of the medium in which energies are operating in a particular place at a particular moment, these novels take their part in the mid- and late-century revolutions in the understanding of the constitution of reality, as readily as they do in the established genres of so-called 'sensation', romance and exotic adventure fiction to which they have somewhat uneasily been assigned.

Chapter Two

Facing Nature

> A man said to the universe:
> 'Sir, I exist.'
> 'However,' replied the universe,
> 'The fact has not created in me
> A sense of obligation.'
>
> Stephen Crane (1899)

'The very ground-thought of Science is to treat man as part of the natural order' (*LN* 1:65): Hardy copied this axiom from John Addington Symonds's *Studies of the Greek Poets* into the literary notebook which he began in 1876. In his 'Author's Note' to *The Shadow-Line* Conrad repudiates supernatural explanation for phenomena and asserts, 'whatever falls under the dominion of our senses must be in nature'.[1] Neither writer was a systematic thinker about nature, and yet the concept and the term remain a pervasive preoccupation throughout their various kinds of writing. My concern is with the novels, but in this chapter I draw primarily on these other writings to bring to light attitudes to nature, and to the means of representing it, that lie implicit in the novels' artistry.

Conrad's 'facing nature', in his statement to Hidaka, is no more a comforting invitation to contemplate pleasing harmonies than is Hardy's requirement that 'Nature's defects must be looked in the face and transcribed' (*LW* 118). Whether viewed as static or dynamic, the Nature that these novels face belongs very much to nineteenth-century materialist conceptions, whose representative statement is that of J. S. Mill in 'On Nature' (1874). Mill declares, 'In sober truth,

---

[1] Joseph Conrad, *The Shadow-Line* (1917), 5.

nearly all the things which men are hanged or imprisoned for doing to one another, are nature's everyday performances . . . Nature impales men, breaks them as if on the wheel, casts them to be devoured by wild beasts, burns them to death, crushes them with stones like the first Christian martyr, starves them with hunger, freezes them with cold . . .'.[2] T. H. Huxley, in his brief 'Autobiography' (1889), offers his courageous materialistic and moral credo of 'the resolute facing of the world as it is, when the garment of makebelieve . . . is stripped off'.[3] Hardy inherits both of these views: thinking of Hegel, he writes, 'These venerable philosophers seem to start wrong; they cannot get away from a prepossession that the world must somehow have been made to be a comfortable place for man' (*LW* 185). He writes to Edward Clodd in 1902, 'The more we know of the laws & nature of the Universe the more ghastly a business we perceive it all to be – & the non-necessity of it' (*CL* iii. 5), and four and a half years later to Frederic Harrison, 'nature is *un*moral – & our puny efforts are those of people who try to keep their leaky house dry by wiping off the waterdrops from the ceiling' (*CL* iii. 231). He could almost be echoing Conrad, so consonant is the thought, though not exactly the tone, with the gloomy *hauteur* of one of Conrad's pronouncements to Cunninghame Graham:

> The mysteries of a universe made of drops of fire and clods of mud do not concern us in the least. The fate of humanity condemned ultimately to perish from cold is not worth troubling about. . . . In a dispassionate view the ardour for reform, improvement for virtue, for knowledge, and even for beauty is only a vain sticking up for appearances as though one were anxious about the cut of one's clothes in a community of blind men. (*CL* 2:17)

If man has any purpose in this spectacle it can only be to reveal by his irrelevancy the power of the Juggernaut-progress of Nature to no purposed end; as Hardy puts it in a comment on *Moments of Vision*

---

[2] J. S. Mill, 'On Nature', in *On Liberty and Other Essays* (1926), 159. Hardy quotes the opening sentence in an entry in his Literary Notebook (*LN* 1:152). Phillip Mallett points out what Hardy would have disagreed with in Mill's essay: 'Hardy and Philosophy', in Wilson ed., *A Companion to Thomas Hardy* (2009), 27–30. Daniel Schwarz claims, 'Hardy is the first English novelist who wholeheartedly rejects the conventional Christian myth of a benevolent universe' ('Beginnings and Endings in Hardy's Major Fiction', in Kramer ed., *Critical Approaches to the Fiction of Thomas Hardy*, 1979, 19).

[3] Charles Darwin; Thomas Henry Huxley, *Autobiographies* (1983), 109.

and Miscellaneous Verses, 'human beings are of no matter or appreciable value in this nonchalant universe' (*LW* 409).

We are in the territory traversed by the proponent of Darwin and of the Higher Criticism, D. F. Strauss, whose *The Old Faith and the New* was translated into English in 1873 by Mathilde Blind:

> Beside and behind the narrow border-land on which Nature gives him free play, she reserves to herself an enormous predominance, which, bursting forth unexpectedly, makes cruel sport of every human effort . . . This indifference of Nature to him, his constant dealing with a power which is alien to him, and to which he himself is alien, and with which, in a word, nothing can be done – this it is that man finds unbearable, against which his inmost being rises in resistance.[4]

Hardy and Conrad hold onto the sensations of human experience in the face of nature's indifference, an offer of solidarity (perhaps that is all that resistance can amount to) against an awareness of dimensions and forces that are 'unbearable' by the human species. Conrad writes to Cunninghame Graham, 'We can't return to nature, since we can't change our place in it' (*CL* 2:30), and Hardy proclaims parenthetically '[Nature's ignorance of the moral sense:-]' in his *'Poetical Matter' Notebook* (38). In Conrad, this tough-mindedness often makes for a deep attraction to solipsism, and yet he asserts that man has 'that share [in the world] which his senses are able to give him' ('Guy de Maupassant').[5] 'Share' is the recuperative term: Torsten Pettersson comments, 'Conrad's emphasis on the senses is an attempt to counteract such isolation rather than a variety of the Pateresque craving for getting as many pulsations as possible into the given time', a view consistently supported by the analyses I offer here.[6] Again in Hardy, the senses, which could be seen to confine all experience to that of single and separate bodies, make available a common share in earth's processes. In the great scene in *Tess*, at Flintcomb-Ash, where Tess and Marian, swede-picking, are like flies crawling on the surface of the earth while the rain drives through them, the attritional experience of their senses gives communicable value to these moments, 'a distinct modicum of stoicism, even of

---

[4] D. F. Strauss, *The Old Faith and the New* (1873), 110.
[5] Joseph Conrad, *Notes on Life and Letters* (1949), 25.
[6] Torsten Pettersson, *Consciousness and Time* (1982), 31. Pettersson's fine study makes the case for Conrad as having a philosophy. See 13–41 particularly.

valour' (361), rather than consigning them to inconsequence and the meaninglessness they have in a cosmic scale.[7]

Yet it is just such a cosmic scale which is a constant penumbra to the writing of both authors, and which gives their novels the distinctiveness claimed for them by this book.[8] Man is a part of the natural order, and there is nothing but the natural order, yet nature is massively indifferent to human life and aspirations. More, Nature is absurd. To continue Hardy's letter to Clodd, quoted above, 'As some philosopher says, if nothing at all existed, it would be a completely natural thing; but that the world exists is a fact absolutely logicless & senseless' (CL iii. 5). And Conrad goes further in ridding nature of its associations of nurture, in a vision apt to the century to come:

> There is a – let us say – a machine . . . . And the most withering thought is that the infamous thing has made itself; made itself without thought, without conscience, without foresight, without eyes, without heart . . .
> It knits us in and it knits us out. It has knitted time space, pain, death, corruption, despair and all the illusions – and nothing matters. (CL 1:425)

This well-known letter of 1897 to Cunninghame Graham finds a further echo in Hardy, in *The Dynasts*, with its image of the Immanent Will as 'a knitter drowsed / Whose fingers play in skilled unmindfulness'.[9] The Keatsian strain of this is sweeter and more human in its actions than the emphatic repetitions of Conrad's self-sufficient mechanism, but nature's 'unmindful' disregard is consistent in both authors in its refusal to pay the slightest heed to what it produces.[10]

---

[7] For a different account of Hardy turning to the senses to find 'a philosophical position other than [. . .] bleak determinism', see Benjamin Morgan's *The Outward Mind* (2017), 117–23. Morgan's subject is aesthetic perception, not the facing of nature, but his extended discussion of a Victorian '*outward turn*: an exteriorization of mind, consciousness, and the self into networks of matter, sensations, and objects' (6), is informed by the same physiological tradition as the present study.

[8] Anna Henchman's recent interesting *The Starry Sky Within* (2014) has chapters on De Quincy, Tennyson, Hardy and George Eliot, though she is more concerned with mental experience than I am here.

[9] Thomas Hardy, *The Dynasts* (Part First, 1904), 2.

[10] Redmond O'Hanlon offers an acute contrast between the two writers: 'So Hardy's universe is a simple negative mirror image of the providential one it replaces; whereas Conrad's is more advanced, unfamiliar, bearing little trace of the old metaphysical comforts – not even by their outraged denial. . . . Hardy never doubts the reality of his external nature . . . Conrad continually doubts the reality

However, an exclusive focus on pessimistic conceptions of nature etiolates the much richer representations that emerge from the novels rather than from the authors' stated ideas. There, the struggle for existence leads to expressions of the multiplicity and plenitude that have a presence in the human strife which it is the novels' business to show.[11] And the enrichment cast by the human mind is not slighted: the picture of man's relation to nature in the novels corresponds in this respect to the feelings of the physicist John Tyndall, often viewed as *the* arch-materialist, who concludes the first of his 1872 lectures on light:

> At all events, whatever Nature meant – and it would be presumptuous to dogmatize as to what she meant – we find ourselves here as the upshot of her operations, endowed with capacities to enjoy not only the materially useful, but endowed with others of indefinite scope and application, which deal alone with the beautiful and the true.[12]

This endowment is also an ineradicable aspect of the voice of the sceptical, disconsolate novels I examine in this study. A way of understanding this particular hue of late-Victorian materialism is again provided by Thomas Huxley, whom Hardy so much enjoyed reading:

> If the materialist affirms that the universe and all its phenomena are resolvable into matter and motion, Berkeley replies, True; but what you call matter and motion are known to us only as forms of consciousness . . . And therefore, if I were obliged to choose between absolute materialism and absolute idealism, I should feel compelled to accept the latter alternative.[13]

Although they evoke them with haunting power, Hardy's and Conrad's novels are *not* content simply with the phenomena of nature,

---

of his nature, "a vain and fleeting appearance" . . . Yet Conrad's nature, although unfamiliar to the "general public" and new in the English novel's development, is nevertheless as real and as soundly based in contemporary science as Hardy's; it is merely less visual, less accessible, reflecting the ideas of physics rather than biology' (*Joseph Conrad and Charles Darwin*, 1984, 16).

[11] The work of Gillian Beer and George Levine has been seminal in this regard. Phillip Mallett, in 'Noticing Things: Hardy and the Nature of "Nature"', explores the parallel between Darwinian abundance and the plotting of Hardy's novels (*The Achievement of Thomas Hardy*, 2000).

[12] John Tyndall, *Six Lectures on Light, delivered in America in 1872–1873* (1873), 39.

[13] T. H. Huxley, 'Bishop Berkeley on the Metaphysics of Sensation' (1871), in *Collected Essays*, vol. 6 (2001), 279.

but wish to reveal something 'underlying'. At the time of composing *The Woodlanders*, Hardy writes,

> After looking at the landscape by Bonington in our drawing room I feel that Nature is played out as a Beauty, but not as a Mystery. I don't want to see landscapes, i.e. scenic paintings of them, because I don't want to see the original realities – as optical effects, that is. I want to see the deeper reality underlying the scenic, the expression of what are sometimes called abstract imaginings. (*LW* 192)

And art for Conrad, in the Preface to *The Nigger of the 'Narcissus'*, attempts 'to render the highest kind of justice to the visible universe',

> by bringing to light *the truth*, manifold and one, *underlying* its every aspect. It is an attempt to find in its forms, in its colours, in its light, in its shadows, in the aspects of matter and in the facts of life, what of each is *fundamental*, what is enduring and *essential* – their *one* illuminating and convincing quality – the *very truth* of their existence. (5, my emphases)

All the complexities of Conrad's art are directed towards realising that last phrase: nowhere does he put more nakedly what his writing seeks to get at.

The 'optical effects' are very much to the fore in Conrad's account, but what is worth searching for is 'underlying' as for Hardy, the 'deeper reality' for one writer being 'the very truth' for the other. This is neither simple empiricism nor idealism; and in having Edred Fitzpiers examine a fragment of old John South's brain through a microscope, and exclaim laughingly in the face of Grace Melbury's surprise that he is 'endeavouring to carry on simultaneously the study of physiology and transcendental philosophy, the material world and the ideal, so as to discover if possible a point of contact between them' (*Woodlanders* 133), Hardy portrays a character lightly toying with what also preoccupied his own practice in writing novels.[14] Conrad is typically more forthright in a letter to

---

[14] George Wotton characterises Hardy's authorial position as arising from 'that unique conjunction of discourses that were elaborated in the terms of an idealist philosophy, an empiricist theory of knowledge, an altruistic ethics, an undogmatic theology and a reformist politics' (*Thomas Hardy: Towards a Materialist Criticism*, 1985, 6). Discussing G. H. Lewes in particular, Peter Garratt seeks to offer a richer account than the 'all too familiar dichotomy of idealism/empiricism, whose poles continue to organize our view of mid-nineteenth century culture' (*Victorian Empiricism*, 2010, 108).

their mutual friend Sidney Colvin (1 March 1917), when he states, 'But as a matter of fact all my concern has been with the "ideal" value of things, events and people. That and nothing else' (*CL* 6:40). However we understand the 'ideal' of Conrad's protestation, this is a different account from his empiricist assertions of absolute fidelity to sensations. Tyndall writes that 'Indeed the domain of the senses in Nature is almost infinitely small in comparison with the vast region accessible to thought which lies beyond them.'[15] Neither Hardy nor Conrad would have disagreed; what is remarkable about their novels is how far they adhere to the senses without imparting the feeling of a confinement to a purely personal nervous network. In part this is due to an infusion of the ideal; but in equal measure it is due to a strong material sense, which Huxley elsewhere articulates: 'the limits within which this mastery of man over nature can be maintained are narrow'.[16] Rather than belittling man in a pessimistic fashion, this awareness magnifies the scene within which mankind's struggles to exist are to be portrayed.

At the level of individual experience then, in their apprehensions of nature Hardy and Conrad take part in the oscillations between Real and Ideal that also preoccupy the interrelations of physiology and psychology from Alexander Bain to William James. At the level of a universal physics, a far more modern description of nature is apposite, that of Heisenberg in 'The Representation of Nature in Contemporary Physics':

> The familiar classification of the world into subject and object, inner and outer world, body and soul, somehow no longer quite applies, and indeed leads to difficulties. In science, also, the object of research is no longer nature in itself but rather nature exposed to man's questioning, and to this extent man here also meets himself.[17]

Both Hardy and Conrad situate their sensational fiction on that disputable border of inner and outer world, whose rigid classification has 'somehow no longer quite applie(d)' perhaps since the middle of

---

[15] John Tyndall, 'Radiant Heat and its Relations', 19 Jan 1866, in *Fragments of Science*, 74.
[16] T. H. Huxley, 'Prolegomena' to *Evolution and Ethics and Other Essays*, in *Collected Essays* vol. 9 (2001), 14.
[17] Werner Heisenberg, 'The Representation of Nature in Contemporary Physics', *Daedalus* 87:3 (Summer 1958), reprinted in Sally Sears and Georgianna Lord eds, *The Discontinuous Universe* (1972), 131.

the nineteenth century.[18] And as their fiction repeatedly shows, there can be no representation of nature without the representation of its human construction. Heisenberg later writes:

> When we speak of a picture of nature provided by contemporary exact science, we do not actually mean any longer a picture of nature, but rather a picture of our relation to nature. . . . Science no longer is in the position of observer of nature, but rather recognizes itself as part of the interplay between man and nature.[19]

The novel, with its ironic narrators and awareness of its own language, has been better than science in recognising its own implication in world-construction, as Hardy shows with quiet wit in *The Trumpet-Major*, set in 1804, when 'Bob's Matilda could not say much about the glamour of the hills' and so on, 'As Nature was hardly invented at this early point in the century' (99). What Heisenberg posits as the condition of the observer, the subject, and the object, in post-relativity descriptions of nature, is involved in the practice of two writers from an earlier period who did not consciously conceive of physics in other than Newtonian terms.

In the novels offered for study here the picture of the non-human otherness of nature, supportive of human life within very narrow margins, is simultaneous with the knowledge of 'nature' as an entirely human construction, the universe only visible as such by taking the impress of the minds which observe it.[20] To bring this issue within the compass of modern discussions, I want to adduce two thinkers whose concern with nature and its agency in human life is particularly applicable to reading Hardy and Conrad, Kate Soper and Jane Bennett. Nature, as Kate Soper writes in *What Is Nature?*, 'carries an immensely complex and contradictory symbolic load': it is 'the environment and its various non-human forms of life, but also the concept through which we pose questions about the more or less natural or artificial quality of our own behaviour and cultural formations'.[21] Distinguishing between 'nature endorsing' and 'nature sceptical' arguments, she writes,

---

[18] See Philipp Erchinger's commentary on John Venn (*Artful Experiments*, 2018, 43).
[19] Heisenberg, 'The Representation of Nature', 134.
[20] In terms of particle physics, the modern case for a very narrow range of conditions in which life as a whole can flourish is made in detail by Geraint Lewis and Luke Barnes in *A Fortunate Universe* (2016). The classic text that argues this issue is John D. Barrow and Frank J. Tipler, *The Anthropic Cosmological Principle* (1986).
[21] Kate Soper, *What Is Nature?* (1995), 2. See also her fine reading of Hardy's depiction of Egdon Heath, 214–15.

For while ecologists tend to invoke nature as a domain of intrinsic value, truth or authenticity and are relatively unconcerned with questions of representation and conceptuality, postmodernist cultural theory and criticism looks with suspicion on any attempt to 'eternize' what in reality is merely conventional, and has invited us to view the order of nature as entirely linguistically constructed.[22]

In fact, an effect of reading the novels looked at in this study must be to agree wholeheartedly with Soper's own declared position: 'I recognize, that is, that there is no reference to that which is independent of discourse except in discourse, but dissent from any position which appeals to this truth as a basis for denying the extra-discursive reality of nature.'[23] Because these novels remain so predominantly in the force-field of the surrounding world as it touches the senses, nature's presence and agency is not *displaced* by the immediate and intervening operations of the mind, as in the tradition of the psychological novel. This tendency to 'remain' takes us to Jane Bennett, and her theorising of 'vital materialism' in her influential study of ethics, *Vibrant Matter*. In acknowledging nature as a human production, she nevertheless asks for a 'delay' which 'might render manifest a subsistent world of nonhuman vitality',[24] which accords well with the manner in which the sensationist writing of Hardy and Conrad retains the reader in vibrant phenomenal encounter with the external world. Bennett's interest lies in 'that which refuses to dissolve completely into the milieu of human knowledge', and the attempt, 'impossibly, to name the moment of independence (from subjectivity) possessed by things, a moment that must be there, since things do in fact affect other bodies, enhancing or weakening their power'.[25] Not naming, but giving expression to that 'moment of independence' is what I show Hardy and Conrad as doing, their scenes always exceeding the construction and viewpoint of their characters' minds, leaving a residue, an event-in-the-world facing the reader.

*

Jane Bennett's ethical appeal for 'delay' to allow non-human vitalities to speak to human awareness conveniently sets up the considerations

---

[22] Ibid., 6.
[23] Ibid., 8.
[24] Jane Bennett, *Vibrant Matter* (2010), 17.
[25] Ibid., 3.

of the second part of this chapter, which are of a more aesthetic nature. That appeal is lightly brushed aside in a novel which bears comparison with *Far From the Madding Crowd* (the novel to be discussed next) in terms of the situation of a young widow, and in the characterisation of the heroine, Meredith's *Diana of the Crossways* (1885). That some of Meredith's artistic concerns are similar, though he largely repudiates Hardy's solutions, is evident in the letter that Diana, sketching her own literary composition, writes to her great friend Emma Dunstane:

> So with landscapes. The art of the pen (we write on darkness) is to rouse the inward vision, instead of labouring with a Drop-scene brush, as if it were to the eye; because our flying minds cannot contain a protracted description. That is why the poets, who spring imagination with a word or a phrase, paint lasting pictures.[26]

While Hardy would have assented to the Wordsworthian desire to 'rouse the inward vision', he joins Conrad rather than Meredith's Diana in seeking to 'arrest' (to use Conrad's word in the Preface to *The Nigger of the 'Narcissus'*) 'our flying minds', and asking us to dwell as if it were with the eye in 'protracted description'. Meredith himself throws off almost casually some notable descriptive moments, but it is not, for him, so central a means of presenting a convincing fictional world as it is for Hardy and Conrad. The remainder of this chapter, then, considers the *representation* of nature, and the meaning of so much 'delaying' description.

The mass of description which enters the novel from Flaubert onwards is an index of an increasing sense of loss felt throughout the century, a loss of contact with a self-evident exterior reality, directly apprehended and named. Natural description becomes a major part of a literary aesthetic when physiology, and later psychology, establish models of perception that create a strong sense of the bounded inner self, separate from a perceived 'outer' world; and when geology and evolutionary biology disclose that world as not made specifically to nurture mankind, but show extinction to be the likely end, confirmed by the dominant late-century interpretation of the Second Law of Thermodynamics. Description is the attempt to make up for this knowledge of our alienation – were it not so, then simple substantives would put the reader in direct contact with the surrounding world – and evinces a compelling desire to use signs to strain past the

---

[26] George Meredith, *Diana of the Crossways* (1885), 143.

limitations of those signs in order to convey a direct apprehension of the elusive quality of things themselves. It becomes imperative to give the reader the *sense* of things. It is striking that A. D. Nuttall says of this 'nostalgia for the object', as he calls it, that 'The modern hunger for vividness is a symptom of the epistemological *malaise*' (my emphasis), and he cites Hardy among the sufferers.[27] As Alan Spiegel says, 'Where an earlier novelist could simply *tell* his story, Flaubert must now *prove* it moment by moment, must provide a continuing demonstration of the palpable certainty of his characters and events.'[28]

In terms of how 'palpable' this proving is to be, it is a significant moment when G. H. Lewes replaces 'The science of the facts of Consciousness' with 'The science of the facts of Sentience' as his definition of psychology in *The Physical Basis of Mind* (1877).[29] The reader of Hardy and Conrad too will find that 'consciousness' is a word implying too much mental awareness, something too near thought, to convey how their characters 'face nature' in the fictional scenes in which they are always partly agents and partly impressionable recipients of vibrations. 'Sentience' is a much better word for what these

---

[27] A. D. Nuttall, *A Common Sky: Philosophy and the Literary Imagination* (1974), 262. Cedric Watts, citing Nuttall approvingly, notes: 'Conrad's work, with its extreme combination of solipsistic intuitions and descriptive concreteness, is a perfect illustration of this thesis' (*Conrad's 'Heart of Darkness': A Critical and Contextual Discussion*, 1977, 167).

[28] Alan Spiegel, *Fiction and the Camera Eye* (1976), 18. Spiegel sees Hardy as operating by 'scenography', and Conrad as operating by 'cinematography' (39ff). Georg Lukács' important 1936 essay, 'Narrate or Describe?' depicts the 'loss' that I have posited rather differently: 'Epic art – and, of course, the art of the novel – consists in discovering the significant and vital aspects of social practice. Description, as we have discussed it, becomes the dominant mode in composition in a period in which, for social reasons, the sense of what is primary in epic construction has been lost. Description is the writer's substitute for the epic significance that has been lost' (*Writer and Critic*, 1978, 126/7). Lukács' hostility towards description takes Flaubert, Zola and Naturalism as its main targets. His celebration of dramatic method as the 'correct' way to represent the activity of life sees description, on the contrary, as capable of producing only 'still life'.

[29] G. H. Lewes, *Problems of Life and Mind* (1879), 7, originally published as *Physical Basis of Mind*. Michael Kearns's *Metaphors of Mind in Fiction and Psychology* (1987), concentrates on Eliot and James as novelists who find 'a way to understand and represent the life of the mind' (134), and makes scant reference to Hardy or Conrad – which makes my point. Vanessa Ryan has recently updated this position, claiming that 'the nineteenth century "psychological novel" puts into question the interiority of "inner" thoughts and feelings' (*Thinking Without Thinking in the Victorian Novel*, 2012, 24).

figures are accorded and what the narrator is animated by, though an awkward term for normal English use, carrying with it more of the laboratory than of the earth and air and seas that rouse its activities. Sentience is the basis for the 'scenic realism' which I propose as the particular form which marks the contribution of Hardy and Conrad to the swelling of novelistic description in the age of the observation of phenomena. It asks for a responsiveness to atmospheres and vibrations, a bodily cosmic awareness, such that the components of a scene as a *whole*, including human consciousness, infuse the rendering of moments as they pass. The written scene that results thus belongs neither entirely to a personal inner conception, nor entirely to a visible external social or physical reality, but to the moment in which those two coalesce to realise themselves as an event.

In this 'picture of our relation to nature', as Heisenberg put it earlier, neither of these novelists is a 'naïve' realist. To the strain that persists in scientific materialism which cannot entirely let go of the sense of something *behind* the phenomena of nature, is added a different sort of philosophical idealism, that of knowing that the world cannot be other than our own conception of it. *We* make the world we are in or, as William James puts it, 'each of us literally *chooses*, by his ways of attending to things, what sort of a universe he shall appear to himself to inhabit'.[30] Hardy says, as early as 1865, 'The poetry of a scene varies with the minds of the perceivers. Indeed, it does not lie in the scene at all' (*LW* 52), and a series of entries in the *Literary Notebooks* made in 1912 show him continuing to ponder the nature of nature and its representation in art. The most interesting of these, copied down without further comment but with underlinings in pencil, is identified by Hardy only as 'B. de Casseres on Fornaro. (Italian Painter)',[31] part of which runs:

> Shakespeare, wrong and banal in so many things, never said anything sillier than when he counselled the artist 'to hold the mirror up to nature.' <u>There is no such thing in art as nature, nor is there a mirror in the human mind. There are nothing but illusion, deformation and bias. Art is the record of a temperament, atrabilious or ethereal,</u> phlegmatic or ecstatic. 'Nature' is an illusory play of light and shadow on a perpetual changing network of nerves. And the 'mirror' that we are told to hold up to 'nature' is a hurrying torrent of feeling and thought. (*LN* 2:215)

---

[30] William James, *Principles of Psychology* (1890), vol. 1, 424 (James's emphasis).
[31] Benjamin de Casseres wrote for the *New York Times Book Reviewer*, contributing a review of Ezra Pound in 1920.

We must be wary of thinking that, because he copied it down, this represents Hardy's own attitude; but we have already seen how appealing to Hardy (and to Conrad, whom it virtually echoes) would be 'Art is the record of a temperament', and the idea of a simple mental 'mirror' does not survive his various statements about nature and realism. The sentence that follows about 'an illusory play of light and shadow' reads like a Conradian version of Walter Pater, with nature converted into nervous energy. The external world becomes the property of an onlooker because it can never be *known* as anything else, a 'viewing position' recognised everywhere in their fiction by Hardy and Conrad.[32] Although I argue strongly that this dematerialisation of nature into a personalised transaction between nerves and brain is *not* the 'nature' the novels leave us with, their art of fiction is informed by an acute sense that the world can only be known by knowers. But the distinctive shared position of Hardy and Conrad is that this knowing is not, primarily, mental contemplation. As the proponent of 'enactive' cognition, Alva Noë, puts it: 'The seeing does not happen in the head. Rather, the experience is achieved or enacted by the person. We do it *in the world*.'[33]

The withdrawn contemplative world of Pater's *Marius* has already been posited in the previous chapter in contrast; yet because his aesthetic writings were so clearly influential upon both Hardy and Conrad, Pater asks for a further moment of consideration in a discussion of the writers' realism. Hardy's *Literary Notebooks* reveal his careful reading of Pater's 'Essay on Style' (1888), about how style controls the 'flood of random sounds, colours, incidents, [which] is ever penetrating from the world without' to form the mental landscape within. Pater's regard for the artist's 'peculiar sense of fact' is echoed in many ways by both novelists, as is his claim, 'For just as in proportion as the writer's aim, consciously or unconsciously, comes to be the transcribing, not of the world, not of mere fact, but of his sense of it, he becomes an artist, his work *fine* art.'[34] And from the essay on Wordsworth (1874) Hardy underlines 'this art of impassioned contemplation', a phrase

---

[32] I take the term from *Viewing Positions* (ed. Linda Williams, 1995) which contains the influential essay by Jonathan Crary, 'Modernizing Vision', in which he claims that Johannes Müller's work on specific nerve energies replaced the 'camera obscura model of vision' in the 1820s and '30s to form 'a new type of observer'.

[33] Alva Noë, *Varieties of Presence* (2012), 114. See Jonathan Kramnick, *Paper Minds* (2018) for a sympathetic application of Noë's enactive account of perception to literature, mainly of the eighteenth century, which has considerable affinities with the present study.

[34] Walter Pater, *Appreciations, With an Essay on Style* (1907), 9.

which introduces a passage on the artist's aim that closely prefigures Conrad's Preface to *The Nigger of the 'Narcissus'*:

> Their work is, not to teach lessons, or enforce rules, or even to stimulate us to noble ends; but to withdraw the thoughts for a little while from the mere machinery of life, to fix them, with appropriate emotions, on the spectacle of those great facts in man's existence which no machinery affects . . .[35]

This desire to stand aside and contemplate is strong, particularly in Conrad. But just as *Victory* (1915) acts as a scathing critique of exactly such a withdrawal, so all of the novels I consider here produce a very different appeal from Pater's assurance that 'all disinterested lovers of books' find in art 'a refuge, a sort of cloistral refuge, from a certain vulgarity in the actual world. A perfect poem like "Lycidas" . . . has for them something of the uses of a religious "retreat".'[36] Certainly Conrad will attribute to Mrs Gould a consciousness that 'There was something inherent in the necessities of successful action which carried with it the moral degradation of the idea' (*Nostromo* 521), but no reader would turn to *Nostromo* to escape the actual world's vulgarity. Hardy's and Conrad's fiction offers neither contemplation nor retreat. The exterior world is not subdued into a mental possession as it is by Pater, but retains the independent material contours it has for those who have physically to work in it.

Idealist by temperament, in an age of empirical phenomenalist science, Hardy and Conrad developed a compatible awareness of their 'peculiar relation to realism', as George Levine says of Hardy.[37] Defining their shared position further, we can set against George Eliot's well-known statement in 'The Natural History of German Life', that 'Art is the nearest thing to life; it is a mode of amplifying experience', the continuation of the statement from Hardy's *Life and Work* begun earlier:

> Art is a disproportioning – (i.e., distorting, throwing out of proportion) – of realities, to show more clearly the features that matter in those realities, which, if merely copied or reported inventorially, might possibly be observed, but would more probably be overlooked. Hence 'realism' is not Art. (*LW* 239)

---

[35] Ibid., 62. For 'impassioned contemplation' see the interesting chapter by Stephen Arata, 'The Impersonal Intimacy of *Marius the Epicurean*', in Ablow ed., *The Feeling of Reading* (2010).
[36] Pater, *Appreciations*, 18.
[37] George Levine, *The Realistic Imagination* (1981), 234.

Comparably, in March 1902, Conrad wrote to Arnold Bennett to praise *A Man from the North* (1898), but also to say 'the die has not been struck hard enough .... What it wants is a more emphatic modelling; more relief': 'I would quarrel not with the truth of your conception but with the realism thereof. You just stop short of being absolutely real because you are faithful to your dogmas of realism. Now realism in art will never approach reality' (*CL* 2:390).[38] For Hardy the 'Art of novel-writing' is 'an observative responsiveness', as he puts it in 'The Science of Fiction' (1891), one that arises from a sensibility which trusts its own feeling about things: 'A writer who is not a mere imitator looks upon the world with his personal eyes and in his peculiar moods' ('The Profitable Reading of Fiction', 1888).[39] Conrad expresses the same attitude in the heightened rhetoric of the Preface to *The Nigger of the 'Narcissus'*, in which all art is viewed as 'the appeal of one temperament to all the other innumerable temperaments' (6), and the task for the novelist 'is to hold up unquestioningly, without choice and without fear, the rescued fragment before all eyes and in the light of a sincere mood' (7).

Hardy writes that a reader should seek 'a composition based on faithful imagination, less the transcript than the similitude of material fact', and then use his own insight to 'catch the vision which the writer has in his eye'.[40] The physiological cast in that phrase is one which this study emphasises throughout, while appreciating that 'vision' necessarily incorporates an ideal realm:

> A sight for the finer qualities of existence, an ear for the 'still sad music of humanity', are not to be acquired by the outer senses alone, close as their powers in photography may be. What cannot be discerned by eye and ear, what may be apprehended only by the mental tactility that comes from a sympathetic appreciativeness of life in all its manifestations ...[41]

– this, says Hardy in 'The Science of Fiction', is the gift that the reader seeks in a novelist. 'Mental tactility' is a moral quality, arising

---

[38] For Bennett, 'Never in prose literature was such a seer of beauty as Thomas Hardy' (article on Meredith's death for *The New Age*, 27 May 1909). His appreciation of Conrad was acute: he writes to H. G. Wells after he had read *The Nigger of the 'Narcissus'* in 1897: 'Where did the man pick up that style, and that *synthetic* way of gathering up a general impression & flinging it at you?' (*"My Dear Friend", Further Letters to and about Joseph Conrad*, ed. Knowles, 2008, 3).
[39] Michael Millgate ed., *Thomas Hardy's Public Voice* (2001), 109 and 86.
[40] Ibid., 80.
[41] Ibid., 109–10.

as it does from a sympathy with all expressions of life; the extraordinary phrase conjures *touching* as a direct capacity and process of the mind, a mind that will not let go of the delicate touch it extends to the world. Unlike the scientific realist, such a novelist 'may not count the dishes at a feast, or accurately estimate the value of the jewels in a lady's diadem; but through the smoke of those dishes, and the rays from these jewels', Hardy says, he will perceive and convey the paradox of lasting truths about the fleetingness of human life. It is in such a transitory medium, of course, that we find Hardy's own atmospheric art of scenic realism, whose mental tactility educates the eye and ear to attend to a scene not in the manner of an inventory, but to respond to the human experience which inhabits its lights and shadows and reverberations.[42]

An equivalent statement of artistic intent to Hardy's could be found in several of Conrad's essays and letters; the most illuminating in this instance necessitates quite a long quotation from an Author's Note, written in 1920, to the collection of short stories *Within the Tides* (1915). It is a note which could stand in front of all of Conrad's writing. Considering the relation between his imaginative work and a life 'far from being adventurous in itself', Conrad is drawn into discussing the romantic nature of his outlook:

> Even now when I look back on it with a certain regret (who would not regret his youth?) and positive affection, its colouring wears the sober hue of hard work and exacting calls of duty, things which in themselves are not much charged with a feeling of romance. If these things appeal strongly to me even in retrospect it is, I suppose, because the romantic feeling of reality was in me an inborn faculty. This in itself may be a curse but when disciplined by a sense of personal responsibility and a recognition of the hard facts of existence shared with the rest of mankind becomes but a point of view from which the very shadows of life appear endowed with an internal glow.[43]

---

[42] In proposing 'scenic realism' for Hardy I am varying the 'Romantic-Realism' that Hugh Walpole attributed to Conrad in 1916 (*Joseph Conrad*, 117), in which he was preceded by Richard Curle (*Joseph Conrad: A Study*, 1914) and followed by Ruth Stauffer (1922). For Peter Widdowson, anti-realism is 'the core of Hardy's fictional aesthetic' (*Hardy in History*, 1989, 164); but Tim Dolin's recent re-assessment of Widdowson proposes instead for Hardy a 'progressive realism' ('On Hardy's Realism, Again', in Simon Barker and Jo Gill eds, *Literature as History*, 2010, 50). 2016 and 2017 have seen books proposing 'telegraphic realism' and 'worldly realism'. My phrase bears no connection to Henry James's 'scenic method'.

[43] Joseph Conrad, *Within the Tides* (1978), 9.

Although Conrad is typically more personal and expansive than the self-veiling Hardy, the value accorded to 'the sober hue of hard work' is Hardy's 'sympathetic appreciativeness of life in all its manifestations'. In fact the deep and important contrast between Conrad and his master Flaubert lies in exactly what he shares with Hardy: a sympathy and value for physical labour, a sense of 'the hard facts of existence shared with the rest of mankind' which endows 'with an internal glow' all aspects of life, just as Hardy, looking 'Nature's defects' in the face, seeks there a 'hitherto unperceived beauty' (LW 118). Flaubert's desire to make a novel out of nothing is not Conrad's, nor Hardy's.

Conrad then turns to writing:

> But the origin of my literary work was very far from giving a larger scope to my imagination. On the contrary the mere fact of dealing with matters outside the general run of everyday experience laid me under the obligation of a more scrupulous fidelity to the truth of my own sensations. The problem was to make unfamiliar things credible. To do that I had to create for them, to reproduce for them, to envelop them in their proper atmosphere of actuality. This was the hardest task of all and the most important, in view of that conscientious rendering of truth in thought and fact which has always been my aim.[44]

To seek 'truth' in an *'atmosphere* of actuality' more than anything indicates the affinity of Hardy and Conrad in their relations with literary realism. Like Hardy's 'smoke' and 'rays', Conrad appeals to 'colouring' and 'shadows'. And, as always, both writers leave the reader uncertain whether 'existence' and 'actuality' is *in* the scene or is a condition applied *to* it. The 'romantic feeling of reality' is a colouring of reality according to temperament and mood, but its typical action is to cast the self out into the exterior world, rather than to draw in that world as a retrieved item for mental inspection. Indeed, J. Hillis Miller makes explicit the subtle association between Hardy and Conrad in their particular sort of spectatorship, each finding in writing a stay against the drift of suicidal withdrawal:

> Just as Conrad, after his experiences in the Congo could no longer live an active life as a seaman, but turned to writing as the only safe way of being related to the truth of life, so Hardy's lifelong commitment to writing seems to have been a strategy for dealing with the situation in

---

[44] Ibid., 10.

which he found himself. . . . Neither man could continue to 'look on and never make a sound' [*Victory*]. Spectatorship is still a mode of involvement. The watcher is still vulnerable to the beckoning solicitations of the world.⁴⁵

Neither the analysed moral world of George Eliot's novels, nor the mental world of Henry James's, the scenic realism of these novels is broader and less cerebral in its appeal to faculties of awareness other than those of thought. Its scope has been boldly grasped in two enduring critical statements about man's incorporation in nature and his resistance to it in these novels, a theme that runs through every chapter of this book. In the first general survey of Conrad's work in the English press, Edward Garnett wrote of his faculty for 'flashing a scene or episode upon us'.⁴⁶ His later review of *Nostromo*, 'Mr. Conrad's Art', for *The Speaker*, 12 November 1904, extends this insight:

> The critic, pressed for an explanation of Mr. Conrad's special power by which he accomplishes artistic feats beyond his rivals, may boldly declare that he has a special poetic sense for *the psychology of scene*, by which the human drama brought before us is seen in its just relation to the whole enveloping drama of Nature around, forming both the immediate environment and the distant back-ground. In Mr. Conrad's vision we may image Nature as a ceaselessly-flowing infinite river of life, out of which the tiny atom of each man's individual life emerges into sight, stands out in the surrounding atmosphere, and is lost again in the infinite succession of the fresh waves of life into which it dissolves. The author's pre-eminence does not lie specifically in his psychological analysis of character, but in the delicate relation of his characters to the whole environment – to the whole mirage of life in which their figures are seen to move.⁴⁷

Garnett's characterisation of Conrad's art completely wins my assent and underpins much that forms this study. The more recent statement, by Gilles Deleuze and Claire Parnet, goes considerably further than Garnett in undoing what generally passes for 'character' in fiction, part of a discussion in which Deleuze laments the way French novelists tend to reduce life to 'something personal':

> Take as an example the case of Thomas Hardy: his characters are not people or subjects, they are collections of intensive sensations, each is such a collection, a packet, a bloc of variable sensations. There is a

---

⁴⁵ J. Hillis Miller, *Thomas Hardy: Distance and Desire* (1970), 31/32.
⁴⁶ 'Mr Joseph Conrad' in the *Academy* of 18 October 1898, unsigned.
⁴⁷ In Norman Sherry, *Joseph Conrad: The Critical Heritage* (1997), 175.

strange respect for the individual, an extraordinary respect: not because he would seize upon himself as a person and be recognised as a person, in the French way, but on the contrary because he saw himself and saw others as so many 'unique chances' – the unique chance from which one combination or another had been drawn. Individuation without a subject. And these packets of sensation in the raw, these collections or combinations, run along the lines of chance, or mischance, where their encounters take place – if need be, their bad encounters which lead to death, to murder. Hardy invokes a sort of Greek destiny for this empiricist experimental world. Individuals, packets of sensations, run over the heath like a line of flight or a line of deterritorialization of the earth.[48]

The picture of the self here is not of personality and an essential continuity, but one of a sensory openness to the collisions of chance intersection, in which the individual him/herself is merely, but wonderfully, a chance of life. This artistic conception of a character's being as 'event', a series of events that flash upon the reader the reality of an existence within the natural order, emerges from a feeling of solidarity with individual organisms caught in the toils of circulating systems for which their self-conception unfits them. In Hardy it is the poignancy of the scattering of 'unique chances' upon contingency, in Conrad it is the disaster of the irremediable, that makes their representation of existence so compelling for the reader.

In a remarkable note towards the end of his *'Poetical Matter' Notebook*, Hardy writes,

> ? Moods towards Nature.
> [I think of her pathetic patience, her mismated beings, her misplanted seeds, her destroyed fruit. Still she plods on. Her illogical want of foresight in so creating that she cannot save both the lion & /his prey/ be merciful to his prey. Till she seems a pale-faced seampstress, shop-confined, who never weeps nor smiles. (73)

'Mismated', 'misplanted', 'destroyed': so much of Hardy's fiction is here. The vision of nature plodding on and taking up her being as a 'shop-confined' seampstress certainly belongs to the 'personal eyes' of Hardy and not of Conrad; in Conrad, 'a pathetic immobility of patience' (*Nostromo* 88) is the mien of the peasant population of Costaguana in *Nostromo*, not of nature herself. Conrad is

---

[48] Gilles Deleuze and Claire Parnet, *Dialogues* (1971), 40.

more absolute, drawn to the hard edge of statement: 'Our captivity within the incomprehensible logic of accident is the only fact of the universe', he writes to the publisher T. Fisher Unwin in 1896, a truth that if 'fearlessly faced' becomes 'an austere and trusted friend' (*CL* 1:303). Thus Virginia Woolf penetratingly says that in Hardy's novels 'there is always about them a little blur of unconsciousness, that halo of freshness and margin of the unexpressed', but of Conrad that his power came from something 'drastic' in him.[49]

---

[49] Virginia Woolf, 'The Novels of Thomas Hardy' (1928), *Collected Essays* (1966), vol. 1, 258; 'Joseph Conrad' (1924), *Collected Essays*, vol. 4, 303.

Chapter Three

The Visible World

> The sun on falling waters writes the text
> Which yet is in the eye or in the thought.
>
> Gerard Manley Hopkins (1864)

1 Fiction and Physics: Appearances in the Light

Far From the Madding Crowd and *Lord Jim*

On 18 October 1912 the publisher Martin Secker wrote to Conrad's literary agent, J. B. Pinker, 'A book on Joseph Conrad by Edward Thomas does not appeal to me, I'm afraid. I feel rather opposed to book about living writers, however eminent, though I am making an exception myself (justifiable, I think) in the case of Hardy.'[1] What a loss! For among other things it is Edward Thomas who helps to prise our understanding of the visual art of Hardy and Conrad away from the contemplative interior world of Walter Pater that has been alluded to. In a book published by Secker the following year, whose dedication is to Conrad, Thomas discusses how often the word 'picture' is used in *Marius the Epicurean*: 'Even "noble pain and sorrow" seem as a picture to him. The result of this spectator's attitude is that Pater sometimes forgets that the thing seen is not a picture.'[2] The pictorial

---

[1] The book in question was Lascelles Abercrombie's *Thomas Hardy: A Critical Study* (1912). I owe knowledge of this letter to the indefatigable researches of Mary Burgoyne.
[2] Edward Thomas, *Walter Pater: A Critical Study* (1913), 149. For Pater's pictorialism, see Benjamin Morgan, *The Outward Mind* (2017), 149–73, in particular his discussion of 'The Child in the House' as 'a point of origin for modernist literary impressionism' (152).

'thing seen', in the novels discussed in the present study, is made subsequent to the action of seeing the world in a flowing ambience of light, through characters who are walking, sailing, riding, peering, glimpsing, glancing, inspecting, hanging on – in other words, in all the temporary and unsettled states of engagement with the terrestrial world that demand they deploy body and senses for life, as it were. Yet light itself, the medium in which we see, is too rarely addressed in the extensive critical attention devoted to the visualised features and visualising activity in Hardy's and Conrad's writing.[3] As the influential Cambridge astronomer and physicist, James Jeans, wrote, 'we do not see a chair, but the event of daylight or electric light falling on a chair',[4] and it is the eventful quality of seeing in the light, and what the light discloses, that constitutes the particular focus of this more extended two-part chapter.

In *The Senses and the Intellect*, Alexander Bain designates light 'the most inscrutable of natural agents', yet a scrutiny of 'the information in the light', to use James J. Gibson's phrase, is exactly what Hardy and Conrad foreground in their writing with an insistence matched only by Faulkner, by Virginia Woolf in intensity but not in extent, and, later, by Elizabeth Bowen.[5] Particularly striking in Bain's account of 'the sensation of mere *light*' is a sense of pleasure: 'In clear strong sunshine, filling the entire breadth of the eye and freshly encountered, there is a massive powerful influence of pleasurable elation, acutely felt.'[6] A similar pleasure lends a vibrancy to the visual experience found in the novels of Hardy and Conrad, such that neither writer is signed up to the literary aims of Robert Louis Stevenson as he expressed them in a letter to Henry James (copied by Hardy into his notebook): Stevenson welcomes James's remarks on 'the starving of the visual sense' and declares, '1st War

---

[3] J. B. Bullen's *The Expressive Eye* (1986) has rightly been the most influential study, followed by Sheila Berger, *Thomas Hardy and Visual Structures* in 1990. However, two more recent essays move the interest to light itself: Michael Irwin, 'Seen in a New Light: Illumination and Irradiation in Hardy', in Mallett ed., *Thomas Hardy Texts and Contexts*, 2002, and Ruth Yeazell, 'The Lighting Design of Hardy's Novels', *Nineteenth Century Literature* 64:1, 2009. Donald Benson's four articles, cited in the text and the Bibliography, remain the most significant commentary on light in Conrad, along with Susan E. Cook, 'Nostromo's Uncanny Light', *Conradiana* 44:2/3 (2012).
[4] James Jeans, *The New Background of Science* (1933), 11.
[5] For Woolf and light, see Rachel Crossland, *Modernist Physics* (2018), 19–32, 61–2.
[6] Alexander Bain, *The Senses and the Intellect* (1855), 213 and 233. James J. Gibson, *The Senses Considered as Perceptual Systems* (1968), 54.

to the adjective. 2nd Death to the optic nerve.'[7] For Hardy and Conrad, the readiness of the optic nerve to receive the ingress of light irradiates their novels from first to last.[8] From 'The bloom and the purple light (that) were strong on the lineaments' of Edward Springrove and Cytherea Graye in Lewborne Bay, whose reflected rays sent from the seabed 'a silvery and spangled radiance upwards to their eyes' (*Desperate Remedies* 47), to the 'school of mackerel (which) twinkled in the afternoon light' glimpsed beyond the mourners carrying Avice Caro's coffin in *The Well-Beloved*, taking the eye to the 'vast spread of watery babble and unrest' beyond the graveyard (234); from 'the crude blaze of the vertical sun, in that light violent and vibrating, like a triumphal flourish of brazen trumpets' in which Kaspar Almayer watches the departing figures of his daughter Nina and Dain Waris (*Almayer's Folly* 194), to a moment amid all the watchings and sightings in *The Rover*, in which Peyrol 'saw (Arlette) appear, with nothing but the sky full of light at her back' (40) – from first to last, in these novels, light as an active agent expands attention from the mental drama to the local and planetary circumambience in which it participates. What I show in this chapter, then, is that the scenic spaces opened for the attention of the reader are vitiated if read only as physics, or only as physiology; only as external enveloping reality, or only as a set of associations made within a bounded mind and body. The novels of Hardy and Conrad characteristically locate themselves, very often outdoors, in a collision-place between personal concerns and impersonal forces, in which characters' senses are compelled into awareness of the surrounding energy-field – a concept made widely available through the dissemination of James Clerk Maxwell's physics in the 1860s.

The theory of light as transverse waves, demonstrated by Thomas Young in 1803, and replacing Newton's view of light as a particle or corpuscle, dominated all thinking about light throughout the nineteenth century. Perhaps the key moment in the idea of light that pervades the novels we are considering arrives with Maxwell's statement in 1862 that, 'We can scarcely avoid the conclusion *that light consists in the transverse undulations of the same medium which is the cause of electric and magnetic phenomena*' (Maxwell's italics), and thus again in 1864, 'light is an electromagnetic disturbance

---

[7] One of seventeen entries from *The Letters of Robert Louis Stevenson*, ed. Sidney Colvin (1899) in *LN* 2:136–8.
[8] 'He actually excites the optic nerve', writes Richard Curle (*Joseph Conrad*, 1914, 3).

propagated through the field according to electromagnetic laws'.[9] Einstein describes how one of the later results of conceiving of light as waves was to focus attention on what once had been thought of as empty now as a *medium*:

> Thought only began to take a new turn with the wave theory of light and the theory of the electromagnetic field of Faraday and Maxwell. It became clear that there existed in free space states which propagated themselves as waves, as well as localized fields ... they invented a medium pervading the whole of space, on the model of ponderable matter – the ether.[10]

The 'universe' thus attended to was one *between* and *involving* what had previously been considered separate and self-sufficient entities. Einstein and Infeld, discussing Maxwell's field theory in *The Evolution of Physics*, put the matter with a clarity that allows of application beyond electromagnetism: '*it is not the charges nor the particles but the field in the space between the charges and the particles which is essential for the description of physical phenomena*' (original emphasis).[11] And it is not only in the novel, in which the increased significance given to atmospheric description is palpable from the 1860s onwards, that this contemporary re-imagining of surrounding space is given expression. Painting, too, relocates its 'description of physical phenomena': in this period, instead of a focus upon separate figures there is a development of attention to the spaces between them, to the point where in Whistler's work there is no empty space.[12]

---

[9] James Clerk Maxwell, 'On Physical Lines of Force' (1861–2), *Scientific Papers* (1890), 500; 'Dynamical Theory of the Electromagnetic Field' (1864), 535.

[10] Albert Einstein, 'Maxwell's Influence on the Evolution of the Idea of Physical Reality' (1931), in *Ideas and Opinions* (1994), 307.

[11] Albert Einstein and Leopold Infeld, *The Evolution of Physics: Growth of Ideas from Early Concepts to Relativity and Quanta* (1938), 307. See also H. A. Lorentz in his Rede Lecture of 1923, *Clerk Maxwell's Electromagnetic Theory*, in which he attributes progress in scientific understanding to fixing 'attention on the intervening medium, localizing the energy in it and considering it as the seat of momenta and stresses' (20).

[12] I record the view of Caroline Arscott, curator at the Courtauld Institute, London, in conversation during the conference 'Psychology and Aesthetics in the Nineteenth Century', Senate House, London, 9 October 2010. See also, Betsy Cogger Rezelman, 'Discovering the Scientific Frame of Mind in the Late-Victorian Artistic Experiments of James McNeill Whistler and Stanhope Forbes', *Australasian Victorian Studies Journal* 2 (1996), and her discussion of Whistler, Forbes and the 'atmospheric envelope', particularly 144–6.

If, in Conrad's childhood and Hardy's youth, physics began to reconceive light as the visible radiation of the electromagnetic spectrum, the physiological medium *within* was undergoing changes too. How, where and as what the external world is seen is a question for biology, physiology, physics and philosophy with a long history of disagreement,[13] but an empiricist consensus formed in the second half of the nineteenth century that followed the researches of Hermann von Helmholtz. Helmholtz's most important statements for my present purpose occur at the end of 'The Sensations of Sight', a lecture from the 1860s collected in *Popular Lectures on Scientific Subjects*:

> This part of our enquiry has shown us that the qualities of these sensations [of sight] can only be regarded as *signs* of certain different qualities, which belong sometimes to light itself, sometimes to the bodies it illuminates, but that there is not a single actual quality of the objects seen which precisely corresponds to our sensation of sight.[14]

This view of the intervening and transformative status of vision – that vision produces signs requiring mental interpretation – was the dominant optical theory of the later nineteenth century, with Helmholtz's work popularised by John Tyndall, James Sully and W. K. Clifford in the *Fortnightly Review* and elsewhere.[15] (*Lectures on Scientific Subjects*

---

[13] A good history is offered by David Park, *The Fire Within the Eye: A Historical Essay on the Nature and Meaning of Light* (1997). Rudolph Arnheim, *Visual Thinking* (1970), and James Elkins, *The Object Stares Back: On the Nature of Seeing* (1996) are both stimulating on the psychology of sight.

[14] Hermann von Helmholtz, *Popular Lectures on Scientific Subjects* (1893), vol. 1, 263. Helmholtz's *Physiological Optics* (3 vols) was published in 1867. The experimental work on sensation by Johannes Müller set the direction and the assumptions for Helmholtz and others. He writes: 'In our intercourse with external nature it is always our own sensations that we become acquainted with, and from them we form conceptions of the properties of external objects, which may be relatively correct' (*Elements of Physiology*, vol. 2, Book Fifth (1840–43), in Nicholas Wade ed., *The Emergence of Neuroscience in the Nineteenth Century* vol. 4. (2000), 1068).

[15] In the famous 'Belfast Address' to the British Association for the Advancement of Science in 1874, John Tyndall proclaimed, 'That anything answering to our own impressions exists outside of ourselves is not a *fact*, but an *inference*, . . . Our states of consciousness are mere *symbols* of an outside entity which produces them and determines the order of their succession, but the real nature of which we can never know' (*Fragments of Science*, 1879, 57). W. K. Clifford, in *Seeing and Thinking*, four lectures given at Shoreditch Town Hall in 1879, says, 'the only thing quite certain is that our sensation of seeing a thing does not correspond to the picture made on the retina, but to something that is the mere sign of that picture' (67).

is the book that Nancy Lord hurriedly chooses from the shelves of the public library in Teignmouth in order to impress Lionel Tarrant in Gissing's *In the Year of Jubilee*.)[16] When Helmholtz reviews what is revealed in progressing from mere anatomy to the activity involved in visual perception, he drives home the point that can be seen to be a scientific basis for a pervasive feeling shared by Hardy and Conrad:

> The inaccuracies and imperfections of the eye as an optical instrument, and those which belong to the image on the retina, now appear insignificant in comparison with the incongruities which we have met with in the field of sensation. One might almost believe that Nature had here contradicted herself on purpose, in order to destroy any dream of a pre-existing harmony between the outer and the inner world.[17]

Knowing only the information delivered by the afferent (input) nerves to the brain, we are always, by constitution, at an interpretative remove from the external world, what we *see* being not an image on the retina but a reconstitution of externalities from electrical charges in the visual cortex. There is an estrangement inherent in the most immediate and familiar of our relationships, that which is provided by sight. Helmholtz dashes the longing for 'pre-existing harmony', for 'natural' relationship, even when we are at our most unpremeditated and involuntary. How different from Wordsworth's intention in *The Excursion* (1814) to show 'How exquisitely the individual Mind / . . . To the external World is fitted . . . / The external World is fitted to the Mind' (Preface, 63–8). Much later in the century, far from such assurance, Hardy and Conrad share a more Helmholtzian legacy of alienation. Swithin St Cleeve declares to Lady Constantine, 'whatever the stars were made for, they were not made to please our eyes. It is the same in everything; nothing is made for man' (*Two on a Tower* 28). Stein ruminates in the presence of Marlow:

> 'Sometimes it seems to me that man is come where he is not wanted, where there is no place for him; for if not, why should he want all the place? Why should he run about here and there making a great noise about himself, talking about the stars, disturbing the blades of grass? . . .' (*Lord Jim* 158)

---

[16] The Jubilee year was 1887. Tarrant finds a paragraph of Helmholtz pretty heavy going and entertains Nancy with 'La Belle Dame sans Merci' instead.

[17] Helmholtz, *Popular Lectures*, vol. 1, 263.

In an indifferent universe, spectacularly revealed to human enquiring eyes, everything fails in the end to guarantee for the characters in these novels a natural and given place in the light.

My contention is, then, that the visual scenes which are so striking a feature of Hardy's and Conrad's writing encompass in many and different ways the conflicting indications that emerge from later nineteenth-century physics and physiology, one of which confirms direct involuntary participation in physical processes, the other of which requires indirectness and re-presentation to mediate any engagement with the surrounding world. We do not know whether our apparently immediate perceptions confirm a place within the world or one uniquely distinct from it. A sense of disjunction features as a recognisable aspect of mid-century Victorian culture, with its yearning to activate a disconnected 'buried life'; and a growth of interest in describing a sequestered interiority contributes progressively to the investigation of subjectivities of all kinds in the following decades, a development which the novels of Hardy and Conrad both take part in and, typically, resist. In this respect, the physicist and mathematician Ernst Cassirer's discussion, *Substance and Function* (1910), offers a good indication of preoccupations in scientific thinking that are coincident with the emergence of literary modernism: 'What needs explanation is not the fact that we go from the inner to the outer, – for the absolutely "inner" is a mere fiction, – but how we are led to regard certain contents of the original external world as finally "in us".'[18] Novels offer evocation rather than explanation; and to understand Hardy's and Conrad's investigations of how the external world is felt to be 'in us', essentially, how we *see*, we should return to the epistemological sensationism that continues to be their artistic guide in attaching their characters to the world they inhabit. The 'explanation' of Thomas Brown, Alexander Bain's precursor as the professor of moral philosophy at Edinburgh, is thoroughly relevant: 'It is evident, that . . . the real object of sense is not the distant object, but that which acts immediately upon the organs, – the light itself, not the sun which beams it on us.'[19] No comment could come closer to what Hardy and Conrad seek to portray in their luminous evocations, which is not so much how the world is 'in us', as how we are 'in it'. If we cannot get beyond the matrix in which our perceptions

---

[18] Ernst Cassirer, *Substance and Function and Einstein's Theory of Relativity* (1923), 288.

[19] Thomas Brown, *Philosophy of the Human Mind* (1820), quoted by Edward S. Reed, *From Soul to Mind* (1997), 65.

are made, their novels seem to say, then let us at least examine that medium minutely. How light makes and reveals a visible world to human perceptions is a preoccupation of almost every page.

The key novels to discuss are *Far From the Madding Crowd* and *Lord Jim*. They are analogous works in their authors' careers, for each their fourth published novel, and the one in which a previously announced fictional territory is given definitive form. *Far From the Madding Crowd* employs the term 'Wessex' for the first time, and its brilliantly-lit depiction of daily agricultural work and a woman's room for manoeuvre in a rural community become, for Hardy, reiterated themes. *Lord Jim* is a study of an individual's ideal conception of himself, refracted through the eyes of a narrator continually seeking to interpret what he sees and through modes of enquiry that presage Conrad's various complexities of 'telling'. Both novels are preceded by an elegy conceived in pictorial form. In the declaration of *Under the Greenwood Tree* as 'A Rural painting of the Dutch School' Hardy places a frame upon events 'less than a generation ago', as he tells us on the novel's opening page.[20] Conrad comments to Arthur Quiller Couch on *The Nigger of the 'Narcissus'* that 'it has been my desire to do for seamen what Millet ... has done for peasants' (CL 1:430).[21] But the framed genre-painting is now too definite and complete. As Wilhelm Worringer wrote in 1908, clearly revealing the influence of the physiology of his age, 'Nothing gives us a more uncertain report of the material individuality and closed unity of a thing than optical perception.'[22] Optical perception is everywhere in Hardy and Conrad precisely because they are interested in that uncertain report; in *Far From the Madding Crowd* and *Lord Jim* the 'closed unity' of Bathsheba and Jim and their personalities and histories, indeed that of Marlow himself, proves elusive, and it is in the observation of how different lights fall upon such figures that these novels are made.

*

In 'The Profitable Reading of Fiction' (1888) Hardy maintains a relationship between the investigative action of the eye and the properties of light that is ideal in conception but empiricist in application. In the essay this light comes from within: a writer's 'representations of life'

---

[20] See Tim Dolin in his Introduction to the 1998 Penguin edition (xxiii).
[21] See Allan Simmons's discussion of the novel as 'narrative painting' in his Introduction to the 1997 Everyman edition (xxv–xxx).
[22] Wilhelm Worringer, *Abstraction and Empathy* (1997), 38.

are 'construed, though not distorted, by the light of the imagination', a light which 'can throw a stronger irradiation over subjects already within [the reader's] ken'. A writer's 'fictitious narrative' aspires to be 'an illuminant of life'.[23] The emission theory of light upon which the metaphor depends, though scientifically moribund by the nineteenth century, has the virtue of discovering a reality outside the perceiver's mind in which it is possible to share, rather than secreting vision away in an inner chamber. Reading *Far From the Madding Crowd* in this spirit discovers repeatedly the extraordinary attention that Hardy gives to the medium of light within which the eye makes its explorations.

The most remarkable of these lit moments occurs late in the novel on the day of the Greenhill sheep fair, when the apparently drowned Troy has returned to Weatherbury as part of a circus troupe in the guise of Dick Turpin. Bathsheba enters the show-tent to find herself, seated alone in a reserved seat, the object of 'many eyes . . . turned upon her' (402):[24]

> Once there, Bathsheba was forced to make the best of it and remain: she sat down, spreading her skirts with some dignity over the unoccupied space on each side of her, and giving a new and feminine aspect to the pavilion. In a few minutes she noticed the fat red nape of Coggan's neck among those standing just below her, and Joseph Poorgrass's saintly profile a little further on.
>
> The interior was shadowy with a peculiar shade. The strange luminous semi-opacities of fine autumn afternoons and eves intensified into Rembrandt effects the few yellow sunbeams which came through holes and divisions in the canvas, and spirted like jets of gold-dust across the dusky blue atmosphere of haze pervading the tent, until they alighted on inner surfaces of cloth opposite, and shone like little lamps suspended there.
>
> Troy, on peeping from his dressing-tent through a slit for a reconnoitre before entering, saw his unconscious wife on high before him as described, sitting as queen of the tournament. He started back in utter confusion . . . here was Bathsheba in her own person; and the reality of the scene was so much intenser than any of his prefigurings. (403)

---

[23] Michael Millgate ed., *Thomas Hardy's Public Voice: The Essays, Speeches and Miscellaneous Prose* (2001), 114–20 *passim*.
[24] All references to *Far From the Madding Crowd* (1874) are to the Penguin English Library edition, 1978, ed. Ronald Blythe, which takes the 1912 Wessex Edition as copy-text. Significant variants found in the Smith, Elder first book edition, 1874, are noted in the footnotes.

What is the second paragraph doing here? In the movement from what Bathsheba sees to what Troy sees, it is not possible for a reader to sustain this as Bathsheba's focalisation beyond the first sentence, 'The interior was shadowy with a peculiar shade.' We cannot believe that it is she who inspects the 'dusky blue atmosphere of haze' and the sunbeams that traverse it with the delighted imaginative tracking that can see them spirting, alighting and shining as enacted in the extraordinary second sentence. But the scientific 'luminous semi-opacities' suggests that the physics underlying the description of the 'few yellow sunbeams' in fact fits well the nostalgic mood aroused by the whole scene. The contest for an explanatory theory of light had largely been won by the undulatory or wave theory by the early 1830s,[25] so there is something deliberately backward-looking in Hardy's sunbeams here that so clearly recall an eighteenth-century corpuscular or projectile theory. A compatible late expression of this view can be found in John Herschel's 1833 description of the medium 'as consisting of innumerable distinct vibrating parcels of molecules, each of which parcels, with a portion of the luminiferous ether included within it . . . constitute[s] a distinct compound vibrating system'.[26] In fact Hardy might have read conflicting accounts in, for instance, Richard Potter's textbook of 1859 that continued to support the idea of light as 'luminous corpuscles . . . flying off in *surfaces, sheets or shells*', and in Eugene Lommel's promotion of the by then accepted ideas of light as 'an undulatory movement' of transverse waves in a medium of ether in his more broadly popular book *The Nature of Light* of 1875.[27] Whatever theory Hardy held to, if any, his humorous observation of the sunbeams' passage across the tent advances to a remarkable degree the sense of light as an entity in itself, independent of any significant object that it is allowing the reader to visualise.

In the ocular drama, strictly conceived, the paragraph is redundant. Yet, with little penetration allowed into the mental world of Hardy's characters, the exigency of living is made remarkably visible

---

[25] See, for instance, Mary Somerville's often-reprinted *On the Connexion of the Physical Sciences* (1834), 181–95.

[26] *Philosophical Magazine* 3, 410, quoted in G. N. Cantor, *Optics After Newton: Theories of Light in Britain and Ireland 1704–1840* (1983), 163.

[27] Richard Potter, *Physical Optics or the Nature and Properties of Light. Part II: The Corpuscular Theory of Light, Discussed Mathematically* (1859). Eugene Lommel, *The Nature of Light with a General Account of Physical Optics* (1875). See also the undecided G .H. Lewes in *The Physiology of Common Life* (1860), contemplating 'that objective something, whatever it may be, which we call Light . . . undulating ether, or luminous corpuscle' (vol. 1, 227).

to us by the immersion of the reader in the atmosphere in which things in those lives are seen. So, here, when we pass to Troy's vision of things, 'the *reality of the scene*' (my emphasis) is indeed 'intenser', in our reading, for having been drawn through a trajectory larger than that managed by his consciousness: one of repeated contemplative experience ('The strange luminous semi-opacities of fine autumn afternoons and eves'), that expands time and space and then contracts attention upon the particularities of 'holes and divisions in the canvas' and 'inner surfaces of cloth', to close upon the small tenderness of 'little lamps suspended there'. This is not the light of fresh morning with which the novel opens; there is a retrospective air to the 'afternoons and eves', and the 'little lamps' hint at evening, an intensely sad sensation for the reader who recalls that Bathsheba is only in her early twenties. The reality of the scene for the reader certainly includes this psychological world that exceeds the impression made upon Troy and the 'unconscious' Bathsheba, but it is simultaneously expanded to an impersonal event in the world of physics that encompasses this human drama and renders it the more poignant.

The aim of a novel that takes its action so much from the action of the eye might be presumed to be to make the reader see what the characters see. But the scenic realism of *Far From the Madding Crowd* is not concerned *absolutely* with the vision produced in or by a particular viewer's 'eye', but with the visual declaration of the whole lit scene. Hardy is a great novelist of situation and condition, rather than of psychology, and we should read him scenically.[28] To illustrate this necessitates a long and uninterrupted quotation, and one so filled with reference to eyesight that it might be called upon to stand against my argument.[29] It is the famous passage in the first chapter, to return to the freshness mentioned above, in which Gabriel sees a wagon coming down a hill before him with a young and attractive woman sitting on top:

> Gabriel had not beheld the sight for more than half a minute, when the vehicle was brought to a standstill just beneath his eyes . . . .
> The girl on the summit of the load sat motionless, surrounded by tables and chairs with their legs upwards, backed by an oak settle, and

---

[28] Many disagree. See Rosemary Sumner, *Thomas Hardy: Psychological Novelist* (1981), a book which I find very appealing in many of its readings; and Paul Kirschner, *Joseph Conrad: The Psychologist as Artist* (1968).

[29] And frequently has been, by such fine Hardy readers as Penny Boumelha, Judith Bryant Wittenberg, Judith Mitchell and Linda Shires, concerned to explore and to excoriate the 'male gaze'.

> ornamented in front by pots of geraniums, myrtles and cactuses, together with a caged canary – all probably from the windows of the house just vacated. There was also a cat in a willow basket, from the partly-opened lid of which she gazed with half-closed eyes, and affectionately surveyed the small birds around.
>
> The handsome girl waited for some time idly in her place, and the only sound heard in the stillness was the hopping of the canary up and down the perches of its prison. Then she looked attentively downwards. It was not at the bird, nor at the cat; it was at an oblong package tied in paper, and lying between them. She turned her head to learn if the waggoner were coming. He was not yet in sight; and her eyes crept back to the package, her thoughts seeming to run upon what was inside it. At length she drew the article into her lap, and untied the paper covering; a small swing looking-glass was disclosed, in which she proceeded to survey herself attentively. She parted her lips and smiled.
>
> It was a fine morning, and the sun lighted up to a scarlet glow the crimson jacket she wore, and painted a soft lustre upon her bright face and dark hair. The myrtles, geraniums, and cactuses packed around her were fresh and green, and at such a leafless season they invested the whole concern of horses, wagon, furniture, and girl with a peculiar vernal charm.[30] What possessed her to indulge in such a performance in the sight of the sparrows, blackbirds, and unperceived farmer who were alone its spectators – whether the smile began as a factitious one, to test her capacity in that art – nobody knows; it ended certainly in a real smile. She blushed at herself, and seeing her reflection blush, blushed the more. (53–4)

If this undoubtedly starts as what Gabriel sees, the joyousness in the writing soon exceeds the sobriety of that young man's eye, and the sight becomes the property of the uncontained richness of a spring morning scene, not of a purposive personal gaze.[31] It could be argued that Hardy has composed a pictorial exhibit of Bathsheba, framed for Oak's reception, but too many of the details have their own speaking life to be components of a watching consciousness: we are not interested in Oak's gaze (to which Hardy will return us shortly) but in the girl and everything on the wagon. The 'tables and chairs with their legs upwards', the precise position of the oblong package, the 'small swing looking-glass', the pots of

---

[30] 'a peculiar charm of rarity' (Smith, Elder, 1874).
[31] Fredric Jameson in his recent reading of Zola says that narrative can achieve 'a kind of stereoscopic view' which 'tends to release its sensory material from any specific viewer or individual human subject, from any specific character to whom the function of observation has been assigned' (*The Antinomies of Realism*, 2013, 56).

'myrtles, geraniums, and cactuses packed around' the girl, are each detailed to carry forward their independent existence even as they are also seen items. The comment of the psychologist R. L. Gregory is apt here when he says, 'Objects are far more than patterns of stimulation: objects have pasts and futures.'[32] We see this when we consider that the literary prototype for Bathsheba on the waggon is Hetty Sorrel admiring herself in the looking-glass in chapter 25 of *Adam Bede*. Hardy's art is quite different from Eliot's. We know exactly what Eliot's narrator thinks of Hetty's little flight of fancy, but Bathsheba's actions, unlike Hetty's, are not a decipherable code for Hardy's narrator to practise upon. The 'small swing looking-glass' on the waggon is lit by an independent existence while Hetty's 'small red-framed shilling looking glass, without blotches' functions as a vehicle for commentary.[33] More than in Conrad, whose objects tend to exist in a sensational present cut off from past or future, Hardy suggests the continuity of objects beyond their phenomenal present appearance.

In the Bathsheba extract, then, what Gabriel sees is 'something perceived but not made over' as a property of his consciousness.[34] The irony of the cat's affectionate survey is assuredly not the stolid Gabriel's;[35] and Hardy's care for Bathsheba rather than for Oak here leads him beyond Gabriel's field of cognition to 'She turned her head to learn if the waggoner were coming.' As 'her eyes crept back to the package' the reader's attention is not returned to Gabriel's eyes upon her but traverses the few inches across the items on the wagon; 'her thoughts seeming [to Gabriel?] to run upon what was inside it' is a mental addition which I doubt any reader makes. We are in the familiar Hardyan territory of events to be observed by *an* observer rather than the observation of them by *this* observer. When Bathsheba surveys herself and 'parted her lips and smiled', the transaction is a close-up between herself and the mirror, not between a distant Gabriel and herself. In a number of ways, the scene is out of his range. In the delighted expansion to the whole scene of the

---

[32] R. L. Gregory, *Eye and Brain* (1966), 8.
[33] George Eliot, *Adam Bede* (1859), 223.
[34] From Tony Tanner's far-reaching essay 'Colour and Movement in Hardy's *Tess of the d'Urbervilles*', *Critical Quarterly* X (1968), 219–39.
[35] Judith Bryant Wittenberg disagrees when she writes, 'the more libidinal moments of peeping which immediately follow are portended by the cat ... the cat's gaze, though idle, is unquestionably predatory, like the male gaze' ('Angles of Vision and Questions of Gender in *Far From the Madding Crowd*', *The Centennial Review* 30:1, 1986, 27). This ignores the information that the cat is female.

next paragraph, the language is not accommodated to Gabriel's consciousness, and the scene is written as a production of the light, not of his eye, a display to other productions of the morning which results in 'nobody['s]' knowledge. The 'unperceived farmer' is accorded no more significant sentience than the sparrows and blackbirds. A dozen years later, Hardy's notebook entry for 3 January 1886 states, 'My art is to intensify the expression of things, as is done by Crivelli, Bellini, &c. so that the heart and inner meaning is made vividly visible' (*LW* 183). What Hardy makes so visible here is decidedly not Bathsheba's heart and inner meaning, nor Gabriel's sexual appetite, but the vivid, varied life in the expressive face of the morning.

The unconstrained fullness of the writing – as different from the 'eruptive nature' of previous 'voyeuristic moments' in Hardy as it is from Conrad's squeezed concentration – arises at least in part from things seen as an event in themselves and not as contained in the observer's eye.[36] And where the activity of the prying eye *is* the issue, it is often not under cerebral or mental direction. At the end of the next chapter, having got Oak to peer down at Bathsheba and her aunt through a hole in a shed, Hardy writes, 'In making even horizontal and clear inspections we colour and mould according to the wants within us whatever our eyes bring in' (64). This is one of those moments where we can see the tendency of Hardy's art towards the physiological, for the earlier incarnation of this sentence is the observation in *A Pair of Blue Eyes*, as Knight is suspended one eighth of a mile above the sea which appears to be his 'funeral pall': 'We colour according to our moods the objects we survey' (216). Now, in his next novel, 'moods' has become the more fundamental 'wants within us', and the mental control (appropriate to Henry Knight) exercised in 'objects we survey' is overtaken by the more urgent physical appetite of 'whatever our eyes bring in'.[37] What gives the opening chapter of *Far From the Madding Crowd* its vitality is an escape from mental containment, and an independence of life that Gabriel, we are led

---

[36] The quoted terms are those of Judith Bryant Wittenberg, writing about *Desperate Remedies* and *A Pair of Blue Eyes* in 'Early Hardy Novels and the Fictional Eye', *Novel* 16:2 (Winter 1983).

[37] In *Middlemarch*, which was serialised throughout 1872, 'Our moods are apt to bring with them images which succeed each other like the magic-lantern pictures in a doze' (1912, vol. 1, 297). It would be of interest to know whether Hardy read this before writing *A Pair of Blue Eyes* or before *Far From the Madding Crowd*, prefiguring as it does elements of both of the quoted sentences. Eliot's masterful sentence ends with Dorothea seeing St Peter's in Rome as 'a disease of the retina'.

to think, can appreciate but that he cannot read. Bathsheba's self-delighting 'real smile' defeats the attempt to 'colour and mould' it as the product of another's eye. Initially, the narrator colludes with Gabriel's 'cynical inference' in saying 'Woman's prescriptive infirmity had stalked into the sunlight, which had clothed it in the freshness of an originality' (54), but by the end of the paragraph this is adjusted to 'She simply observed herself as a fair product of Nature in the feminine kind . . . the whole series of actions was so idly put forth as to make it rash to assert that intention had any part in them at all' (55). The actions given to the light are not drawn tightly into an interpretive web ('retina' is derived from *rete*, the Latin for a net); for to agree, with Gabriel, that 'Vanity' accounts for what we have read is, like the hungry retina, to miss most of what lights the chapter.[38] And that is not so much a male desire for possession, as a self-rejoicing completeness radiated by 'the whole concern of horses, wagon, furniture and girl'.

Gabriel's own examination by means of light is altogether stranger. Shortly after this survey of Bathsheba and, indeed, his proposal to her, his hopes of being an independent farmer are dashed by his young sheepdog driving his flock of ewes to its death over the brow of a chalk pit:

> Oak raised his head, and wondering what he could do, listlessly surveyed the scene. By the outer margin of the pit was an oval pond, and over it hung the attenuated skeleton of a chrome-yellow moon, which had only a few days to last – the morning star dogging her on the left hand. The pool glittered like a dead man's eye, and as the world awoke a breeze blew, shaking and elongating the reflection of the moon without breaking it, and turning the image of the star to a phosphoric streak upon the water. All this Oak saw and remembered. (87)

But this is not self-examination: while the reader can easily find a correspondence in the scene to Gabriel's presumed state of almost suicidal despair in the 'dead man's eye' and the 'attenuated skeleton', there is no encouragement to interiorise or see the scene as reflected in Gabriel's eye. In contradiction to the narrator's statement at the end of chapter 2, the impersonal light of the scene prevails over the temperament reading it. The reflection does not turn a face towards

---

[38] 'Only about ten percent of the light reaching the eye gets to the receptors, the rest being lost by absorption and scattering within the eye before the retina is reached.' Gregory, *Eye and Brain*, 19.

Gabriel (distanced throughout as 'Oak') but towards the moon. Akin to a Wordsworthian moment of admonishment, the extension of the final clause to the distant morning star, and the stretching of its refracted form in water to an elemental streak, enlists a non-human physics to enlarge the operations in the scene far beyond Gabriel's consciousness. Against such exposure to cosmic transformation, the simple gravity of the final sentence, so different in its rhythm, asserts its ethic of human endurance; that Hardy does not seek to convey what Gabriel *understands* from this eidetic experience ensures, for the reader, that it propagates an apprehension of the larger universe rather than being contained within the eye.

Light is the constantly-observed medium for the eye in the great afternoon, evening and night sequence of the sheep-shearing, the supper, Boldwood's declaration and the encounter with Troy (chapters 22–24); but the striking chapter of Sergeant Troy's sword exercise, 'The Hollow Amid the Ferns', is where light makes its strongest intervention in the drama. Bathsheba is transfigured at the hands of Troy, whose sword wields light as in a primal act of re-creation:

> 'Is the sword very sharp?'
> 'O no – only stand as still as a statue. Now!'
> In an instant the atmosphere was transformed to Bathsheba's eyes. Beams of light caught from the low sun's rays, above, around, in front of her, well-nigh shut out earth and heaven – all emitted in the marvellous evolutions of Troy's reflecting blade, which seemed everywhere at once, and yet nowhere specially. These circling gleams were accompanied by a keen rush that was almost a whistling[39] also springing from all sides of her at once. In short, she was enclosed in a firmament of light, and of sharp hisses, resembling a sky-full of meteors close at hand. (239)

Dazzling light 'shut(s) out earth and heaven' for Bathsheba, obliterating former life and creating for her a new 'firmament'. Significantly, the reader is kept to Bathsheba's sensations of the transformed *atmosphere* – only in the final paragraph of the chapter, where we are told that the 'minute's interval' in which Troy kisses her 'enlarged emotion to a compass which quite swamped thought' and released 'a liquid stream' (242), are we given a representation of the transformation experienced *within*. As readers, we are more

---

[39] 'These circumambient gleams were accompanied by a keen sibilation that was almost a whistling' (Smith, Elder, 1874). This attention to the surrounding atmosphere and sound is diminished by the later more conventional phrasing.

in the visionary and sounding air than we are in Bathsheba's mind. While we are positioned by the prepositional clauses to experience what she experiences – 'in front of her', 'seemed everywhere . . . yet nowhere', 'from all sides', 'close at hand' – what Hardy gives is not exactly, or simply, her point of view: 'Beams of light' and 'circling gleams', not Bathsheba's perceptions, are the grammatical subjects of two successive sentences, and this optical terminology is extended to physics in 'emitted', mathematics in 'evolutions', and astronomy in 'firmament' and 'meteors'. The enlargement created by such a language makes figures of the air the dimension of our reading, rather than the nerve ends of Bathsheba's subjectivity. The writing displays a highly charged field within which all relations are excited; we could contrast, as Bathsheba later does, the low-energy field that surrounds Boldwood's life, in which things take up fixed positions and are frozen there without oscillation, variation or adaptation.

If a new-born, sexually alive young woman has been disclosed to herself, it is at the cost of that self-possession which is Bathsheba's most inspiring feature, declared in her stirring 'I shall be up before you are awake; I shall be afield before you are up; and I shall have breakfasted before you are afield. In short, I shall astonish you all' (133). That such a loss is figured as inherent in the moment of greatest pleasure accorded Bathsheba in the novel might be taken as expressing Hardy's Manichean view that life's vital demand of sex destroys life's equally vital demand to maintain individual identity. My point, however, is that it is an event which has a life in the novel beyond the individual sensational record. Hardy earlier writes of Gabriel's rescue by Bathsheba's prompt action from suffocation in his unventilated shepherd's hut:

> He was endeavouring to catch and appreciate the sensation of being thus with her, his head upon her dress, before the event passed on into the heap of bygone things. He wished she knew his impressions; but he would as soon have thought of carrying an odour in a net as of attempting to convey the intangibilities of his feeling in the coarse meshes of language. (70)

The terms of this delicate, luxuriating but almost anguished observation lead to the heart of this study of Hardy and Conrad, prefiguring as they do Marlow's explanation of his narrative style in *Lord Jim*: 'I am trying to interpret for you into slow speech the instantaneous effect of visual impressions' (42). Impressions, of which sensation makes us viscerally aware, are the means of knowing our contact with the world; yet 'the event' has an existence beyond that which subjectivity perceives, which belongs to another order of event in the vibrations of energy that constitute the world's spectacular process. 'The event' and 'his impressions' are not synonymous. Of course, Hardy here has Gabriel think exactly the opposite, that the event dies with the individual sensational record of it, and that 'intangibilities of feeling' are incommunicable, a pained reflection familiar to the Modernism that derives from Walter Pater. But in the *novel* it is not exactly so, for there is available to the reader a comprehensiveness beyond the impressions and the fortunes of the individual characters, and one which does convey the odours precisely because of an ironic awareness of the nets, and because the participants in a scene do not simply lock it up in their own sensory systems, but contribute to the visual, aural and tactile field in which they participate. As the modern physicist Eric Schneider puts it, 'No organism is isolated; all are thermodynamically connected.'[40]

Examinations in their various forms, each individually lit, become a motif that connects different scenes in the novel. The same hollow amid the ferns, in a very different season, provides a paired chapter after Bathsheba has fled from Troy's heartless '"You are nothing to me – nothing"', uttered before Fanny Robin's opened coffin. Again, what Hardy writes is not exactly a scene of *self*-examination, but one in which Bathsheba is drawn out of herself and into the processes of the world immediately around her. In comparison to the earlier episode of the sword exercise, the first quality to strike the reader is a clarity and distinctness in things heard and seen that belongs to 'a freshened existence and a cooler brain' (362). Each individually identified, the characteristic utterances of sparrow, finch, robin, squirrel and ploughboy build up a world outside Bathsheba, enquired into, providing orientation. She 'could just discern in the wan light of daybreak a team of her own horses' (363), but Bathsheba's discernment makes each action of the horses a clear moment of visual attention: 'She watched them flouncing into the pool, drinking, tossing up their heads, drinking again, the water dribbling from their lips in silver threads' (363). This visual care for each ordinary item of the unfolding morning not only confers upon them an independent non-instrumental existence,

---

[40] Eric D. Schneider and Dorion Sagan, *Into the Cool: Energy Flow, Thermodynamics and Life* (2005), 295. This is not anachronistic, but derives from Faraday's 1850s conception of a force-field, of which William Berkson says, 'any material body in a force-field has its configuration of forces altered as a result of the field, of which it is part' (*Fields of Force*, 1974, 72).

but *receives from them* in consequence a confirmation of creaturely participation in a world with its own processes.

In contrast to the 'luminous streams' of Sergeant Troy's earlier '*aurora militaris*' (240), the natural morning light discloses in an extraordinary and grotesque manner the 'nursery of pestilences' (363) which the months' transformations have made of the hollow. The morbidity of this naturalistically depicted Slough of Despond, with its fantastic scarlet and saffron fungal outgrowths, comes in part from Bathsheba's eye, both fascinated and repelled, still under the influence of night terrors from which the fresh morning is only slowly extracting her. But also the blooming pestilence of the swamp is undoubtedly *there*, an inescapable feature of the transformations of the exterior world that must be faced – like the revelations of Troy's life and the nature of her marriage. The flag plant at the side of the hollow is seen to have 'blades' which 'glistened in the emerging sun, like scythes' (363) in the same spot that Troy's sword-blade had executed 'circling gleams' in the 'low sun's rays' 130 pages previously. With witty irony Bathsheba advises Liddy, in marriage, to 'Stand your ground, and be cut to pieces. That's what I'm going to do' – a conscious echo of Troy's challenge to her in the dazzling sword exercise. In fact, what saves Bathsheba from all that is implied by the swamp is not a resolve arrived at by thought, nor the immediate demands of the outside world, but something both more subtle and more convincing: she hears a boy passing who is trying to learn the collect by repetition of each word, and the narrator's comment is, 'In the worst attacks of trouble there appears to be always a superficial film of consciousness which is left disengaged and open to the notice of trifles, and Bathsheba was faintly amused at the boy's method, till he too passed on' (364). To be saved from destructive introspection by a faculty declared to be a 'superficial film', 'disengaged' from inner, and therefore to modern thinking real, anguish, is also to be thereby 'open', capable of noticing 'trifles' and to be 'faintly amused' by the merely contingent. All of this places Hardy's reader in a world conceived more physiologically than psychologically, a lit world of contact.

Ian Gregor says that Bathsheba 'half-realises' the significance of her night by the swamp.[41] We can say with more certainty that what Hardy depicts is a state of unarticulated, somatic, knowledge, rather than one that is cerebral and conceptualised. The most affecting moment in the novel is one in which understanding is a visual event

---

[41] Ian Gregor, *The Great Web: The Form of Hardy's Major Fiction* (1974), 54.

which is preserved pictorially but not elaborated into a verbal realisation or a lesson.[42] Liddy seeks out Bathsheba who tries to warn her not to cross the swamp, but as she has lost her voice in the night atmosphere her words do not carry to Liddy's ears:

> Liddy, not knowing this, stepped down upon the swamp, saying, as she did so, 'It will bear me up, I think.'
>
> Bathsheba never forgot that transient little picture of Liddy crossing the swamp to her there in the morning light. Iridescent bubbles of dank subterranean breath rose from the sweating sod beside the waiting-maid's feet as she trod, hissing as they burst and expanded away to join the vapoury firmament above. Liddy did not sink, as Bathsheba had anticipated. (365)

Irresistibly, a moral reading connects Bathsheba's never forgetting with 'All this Oak saw and remembered' (87). Yet the engraving upon memory is different, and that has much to do with the word 'transient'. Gabriel's is a solitary self-communing; 'that transient little picture of Liddy' rhythmically projects outwards, towards the girl crossing the swamp, rather than draws inwards, as in Gabriel's act of self-command. The permanence of 'never forgot' is countered by a more fluid, a more airy, notion of things passing: Liddy's little transit across the swamp, the brief passage of the picture that recurs to Bathsheba's inward vision, the course of a life crossed by the course of another's, something lightly-drawn and fitting the moment-by-moment nature of a life sensed in its shifting uncertainties – these suggestions in the cadence of the sentence mark the quality of the remembrance as peculiarly Bathsheba's, as that of a joy-seeking vigour that the novel chastens and stills.

But the novel is not as schematic as to insist only upon a contrast in Bathsheba's and Gabriel's sober coming to terms with themselves in the dawn. In a strikingly analogous moment in the great scene of the storm, the beleaguered Gabriel protecting Bathsheba's and Troy's barley ricks is vouchsafed a momentary picture in a flash of lightning:

---

[42] Helmholtz writes: 'In addition to the kind of knowledge that works with concepts and therefore is capable of being expressed in words, there exists yet another area of representational competence, which combines only sensory impressions that cannot immediately be expressed in words. In German we call it *das Kennen*' (*Vortrage und Reden*, vol. 1, 358, quoted in Theo C. Meyering, *Historical Roots of Cognitive Science*, 1989, 195).

What was this the light revealed to him? In the open ground before him, as he looked over the ridge of the rick, was a dark and apparently female form. Could it be that of the only venturesome woman in the parish – Bathsheba? (307)

What the light reveals is one of the fundamental actions of a Hardy novel. The 'morning light' discloses not only Liddy, but also, in true Hardyan manner, the gaseous bubbles displaced by Liddy's feet. They have their transit, their moment of expansion too, their processes in the transference of energy, alongside the pressing human concerns.[43] Hardy offers us a little picture, certainly, a small figure in a landscape, but it is a landscape in the terms proposed by Robert Macfarlane in his celebration of walking and Edward Thomas, *The Old Ways*:

> I prefer to take 'landscape' as a collective term for the temperature and pressure of the air, the fall of light and its rebounds, the textures and surfaces of rock, soil and building, the sounds (cricket screech, bird cry, wind through trees), the scents (pine resin, hot stone, crushed thyme) and the uncountable other transitory phenomena and atmospheres that together comprise the *bristling* presence of a particular place at a particular moment.[44]

*

The figure who strains most towards a *psychological* study in the novel is Boldwood, and one episode in particular points up the debate about whether the intense visualisation in Hardy's novels is the expression of the eye/I that sees, or whether it is a *visibility* accorded by the impersonal forces of light. The chapter's title, 'Effect of the Letter – Sunrise', projects both possibilities. As Boldwood thinks at night about Bathsheba's valentine, with its inscription 'Marry Me', that he has placed 'in the corner of the looking-glass' (150), Hardy's narration moves as close as it does in this novel to free indirect

---

[43] A comparison of this scene with two others that must have contributed to its literary conception shows how far Hardy keeps to the world as observed through the sensations, as opposed to the moral, transcendental and more psychological dimensions that could have been extracted therefrom. See Ch. XXXVII, 'The Journey in Despair', in George Eliot's *Adam Bede*, and Ch. XLII, 'Nature Speaks', in George Meredith's *The Ordeal of Richard Feverel*, both published in 1859.

[44] Robert Macfarlane, *The Old Ways: A Journey on Foot* (2012), 255.

speech to render Boldwood's thoughts, which operate like an inner eye, imaginatively creating a 'vision of the woman writing':

> Somebody's – some *woman's* – hand had travelled softly over the paper bearing his name; her unrevealed eyes had watched every curve as she formed it . . . Her mouth – were the lips red or pale, plump or creased? – had curved itself to a certain expression as the pen went on . . . (150)

These obsessive recreations are the reflections, cast upon an as-yet unknown woman's form, of the disturbance effected upon Boldwood's conception of himself: 'her brain had seen him in imagination the while. Why should she have imagined him?' (150). That the re-visioning of *himself* is the fundamental process at work that Hardy seeks to portray, is confirmed by the position of the valentine in the corner of the looking glass, leading to the moment in which 'he caught sight of his reflected features, wan in expression, and insubstantial in form. He saw how closely compressed was his mouth, and that his eyes were wide-spread and vacant' (151).

In this interior night-time scene, this new awareness of self is made visible by light which is itself reflected, not transmitted directly from its source, described with remarkable attentiveness:

> The moon shone to-night, and its light was not of a customary kind. His window admitted only a reflection of its rays, and the pale sheen had that reverse direction which snow gives, coming upward and lighting up his ceiling in an unnatural way, casting shadows in strange places, and putting lights where shadows had used to be. (150)[45]

The indirectness of this 'weird light' as it is called subsequently, and the distancing effect of the detached language and somewhat clinical observation of the cause of its pallor, all collide unsettlingly with a strong invitation to the reader to draw into Boldwood's mind here, beginning with the personal present of 'to-night', and finding in the unaccustomed angles and changed places of the light in the room a correlation for this unique psychological moment of unsettlement in the fixed and unbending man's life. It will not surprise us to read, four short chapters later, that women had been 'remote phenomena' to Boldwood: 'they had struck upon all his senses at wide angles' (168). The suggestive 'putting light where shadows had used to be' concluding the paragraph, and after which he jumps out of bed to inspect the letter again, reads as Boldwood's own access to feelings

---

[45] 'reversed' for 'reverse', 'phenomenal' for 'unnatural' (Smith, Elder, 1874).

previously hidden from him as he stares up at the ceiling sleeplessly. Vision, both for Boldwood and for the reader, in this episode is specular, that is, gained only from reflected light. It displays in concentrated form how Hardy's pictures of people in their moments of crisis do not open an inner world of thoughts, but keep to surfaces that connect his characters to the forces that surround them.

Rosemary Sumner sees in this scene 'an astonishing insight into a disturbed personality' but that 'the method of largely external description of behaviour used later in the chapter does not sustain this insight wholly effectively'. She aligns Hardy with Lawrence, but finds he falls short of the famous depictions of Mrs Morel shut out in the garden or 'Anna Victrix' in *The Rainbow*, as the method finally 'is not adequate for exploring Boldwood's unconscious'.[46] She is right in that the disclosure of an inner world is more limited than in Lawrence; but in Hardy the scene does not exist to display the forces in the individual, it exists to display the forces in the scene that include the individual. Regarded in this light, the chapter's later evocation of the bleak dawn over the fields deliberately seeks, after the containment of the night room, a more distanced perspective on the lonely figure assumed into the new day that must be lived. The morning scene is neither a transcript of the vision secreted in Boldwood's inner world, nor entirely a 'disproportioning' of the external world created by his disturbed mind: it is the picture of an estranging scene caused by the changed sources of light in sunrise over snow, an apprehension of the disconcerting newness and exhaustion in things that includes the condition of Boldwood's 'listless[ly] noting' (151) rather than proceeds from it. There is no warmth or animation, rather a sense of vacancy: 'the only half of the sun yet visible burnt rayless, like a red and flameless fire shining over a white hearthstone' (151). These are not Boldwood's thoughts, though the reader is free to associate such a vision with the newly revealed emptiness of his domesticity. Equally, Boldwood is not shown as finding any correspondence between himself and 'the wasting moon, now dull and greenish-yellow, like tarnished brass' (151), nor even depicted as looking at it, but the failure of illumination cast upon the scene is consonant with the single, rather disengaged, human consciousness included in it. What Boldwood's eyes *do* see is recorded with such striking detachment, yet minute precision – the glazed surface of the snow, bristling grass-bents encased in icicles, birds' footprints 'now frozen to a short permanency' (151) – that a reader might think that these are no

---

[46] Sumner, *Psychological Novelist*, 54.

longer a landowner's proprietorial eyes 'bringing in' and colouring such details with any sense of ownership or connection, precisely because there is no personal interpretation of the visual evidence in any way. Boldwood is mentally absent from the empty scene – very much of it, and not of it. While we gain no further insight into the internal and unconscious forces that are the cause of this displacement, as a depiction of the *effect* of the previous night's re-visionings Hardy's method of creating an external visual scene with no accompanying explicit comment about the psychology behind the viewing eye is an arresting one, exposing the visual subjectivism of the earlier part of the chapter to the impersonal light of day.[47]

While Hardy's presentation of Boldwood mainly sees him trapped within the eye's subjectivity, Bathsheba more frequently is seen as an object in the light. In the climactic scene in which Boldwood's threats prompt her clandestine night-journey to Troy in Bath, Bathsheba is first seen setting out for Yalbury after a small thunder-shower: 'before her, among the clouds, there was a contrast in the shape of lairs of fierce light which showed themselves in the neighbourhood of a hidden sun' (256). As Boldwood says when they unexpectedly encounter each other, 'Our moods meet at wrong places' (259): and the reading of *Far From the Madding Crowd* that I offer here is one that sees it as lighting the places at which moods meet – and only thus, indirectly, the moods themselves. A comment by Terry Eagleton is highly appropriate for Boldwood in this situation: 'For Conrad, and in a different way for Hardy, men and women view reality perspectively, from the standpoint of their own brooding obsessions, and the resultant clash of these multiple versions of the world is known as tragedy.'[48] *Far From the Madding Crowd* is a marvellously restless, glinting interplay of comic and tragic. The end of the chapter sees another of those places, lit to show a vaster perspective: after her unsought, sustained confrontation with Boldwood, the 'lairs of fierce light' are gone and the distracted Bathsheba is less a woman

---

[47] Another snow scene that, in its stylised detachment, contrasts notably with the subjective colouring of vision allowed to the Boldwood scenes is chapter 11 in which Fanny tries to converse with Troy in the barracks: 'This person was so much like a mere shade upon the earth, and the other speaker so much a part of the building, that one would have said the wall was holding a conversation with the snow' (136). This erasure of human individuality is an extreme instance of a style that makes the actors part of an impersonal drama. Hardy adopts it for Fanny throughout.

[48] Terry Eagleton, 'The Flight to the Real', in Ledger and McCracken eds, *Cultural Politics at the Fin de Siècle* (1995), 190.

in command of house and land and her journeys, than a moment of mortality exposed to remote space, whose illuminations have nothing to do with earth:

> Then she sat down on a heap of stones by the wayside to think. There she remained long. Above the dark margin of the earth appeared foreshores and promontories of coppery cloud, bounding a green and pellucid expanse in the western sky. Amaranthine glosses came over them then, and the unresting world wheeled her round to a contrasting prospect eastward, in the shape of indecisive and palpitating stars. She gazed upon their silent throes amid the shades of space, but realized none at all. Her troubled spirit was far away with Troy. (264)

Unlike the earlier description of 'the roll of the world eastward' (58) that the reader associates with Gabriel on Norcombe Hill, the picture here is of being propelled by an 'unresting world' in the face of remote bodies that are 'indecisive', 'palpitating' and undergoing 'throes' of an unimaginable kind. In Hardy, vision is temperamental, and Bathsheba is unable to see the grandeur of the cosmic spectacle because of her all-too-human preoccupations; but the novel also proposes a depiction of troubled humanity, constantly revolved, seen in the light of explosions on distant suns. In *Far From the Madding Crowd* Bathsheba is her most exposed representative.

*

In *Lord Jim*, references to the inquisitive eye are as ubiquitous as they are in *Far From the Madding Crowd*. If Jim is not subject to the 'tickling effect' of 'rays of male vision' (*Madding Crowd* 67) in the same way as Bathsheba, he is certainly the object of a sustained scrutiny through the eyes of many witnesses as to just what can be the 'truth' of a chief mate who has jumped from his ship to leave eight hundred passengers sailing on to an unshared fate. And in no novel more than *Lord Jim* does Conrad express that idealising yearning for the *underlying* truth of things that I alluded to in Chapter 2. As frequently as Bathsheba, Jim is seen as an object in the light; but light as a medium in *Lord Jim* takes on a more metaphysical dimension than in Hardy's display of physics. It becomes associated with the quest for a single unifying truth, an idea deeply appealing also to many of those Victorian physicists whose theories and experiments would seem to modern eyes to be dethroning Newton and God equally. Thus much of the light that will preoccupy us in the following section will be, if not exactly a mental production, associated with psychic need. The evidence of a few pages' reading shows that *Lord Jim* is a much more psychological novel than *Far From the Madding Crowd*: we are held in Marlow's *mind* more than is the case for any character in Hardy's novel. Yet Ian Watt is right when, in his discussion of *Lord Jim*, he writes, 'Conrad stands outside the main tradition of the novel of character; or at least his primary interest is not the detailed psychology of the nature, development, and relationships of individual personalities.'[49] In keeping with this view, what follows does not attempt any direct reading of Jim but sees *Lord Jim* as an enquiry into the question, 'in what illuminating medium can the truth of another's humanity – and perhaps one's own – be found?'

The process of the first half of the novel is Marlow's own account of his enquiry into what lies behind the 'facts' of Jim's jump to save himself from the apparently doomed *Patna*. Conrad's conception of the Jim who reveals himself to Marlow is inseparable from Marlow's action of trying to envision Jim's nature, and finding himself with a 'capricious, unconsolable, and elusive spirit that no eye can follow', and with loneliness (not only Jim's, but also his own) as 'a hard and absolute condition of existence' (137). Primarily, Marlow is left with a fragmentary series of briefly illuminated displays:

> The views he let me have of himself were like those glimpses through the shifting rents in a thick fog – bits of vivid and vanishing detail, giving no connected idea of the general aspect of a country. They fed one's curiosity without satisfying it; they were no good for the purposes of orientation. Upon the whole he was misleading. (62)

It is not that Jim is deceptive. What we are offered in *Lord Jim* is a series of scenes in which 'Jim' is coterminous with Marlow's investigations and yet always eludes the results of those investigations. The inviting glimpses do not yield communicable insights (not, that is, until Stein's later designation of Jim as 'romantic'); the reader remains with the glimpses rather than what they are glimpses *of*. They bring out the thickness of fog and the moment in which rents shift rather than a knowledge of Jim's psychological state, for there is no 'Jim' that the novel can deliver other than his phenomenal presence displayed before Marlow. The epistemology of a novel which, like the scientific investigations of Poincaré and Ernst Mach (and J. B. Stallo before them), locates knowledge of reality in the relations *between* things, forbids it, and leaves the reader instead with the poignancy

---

[49] Ian Watt, *Conrad in the Nineteenth Century* (1979), 169.

of 'only a speck, a tiny white speck, that seemed to catch all the light left in a darkened world ... And, suddenly, I lost him ...' (253).[50] The novel frequently promises epiphany, only for such 'moments of vision' not to expand into disclosures of Jim himself.[51]

Towards the end of the long section in the Malabar House (taking from chapters 7 to 13 in the telling), in which, against a night 'glittering and sombre' (64), Jim stumbles through his sometimes compulsive, sometimes hesitant account of the *Patna* incident, chapter 12 typically opens,

> All around everything was still as far as the ear could reach. The mist of his feelings shifted between us, as if disturbed by his struggles, and in the rifts of the immaterial veil he would appear to my staring eyes distinct of form and pregnant with vague appeal like a symbolic figure in a picture. The chill air of the night seemed to lie on my limbs as heavy as a slab of marble.
>
> 'I see,' I murmured, more to prove to myself that I could break my state of numbness than for any other reason. (104)

Any 'seeing' done by Marlow here does not have Jim for its object so much as the ambience of what passes between and surrounds them to make up the whole scene. Between Marlow and Jim lies 'the mist of his feelings' – 'immaterial' in that it is composed of feelings, but metaphorically material in that it is an obscuring mist, in which shifts and rifts can be discerned. In Conrad's description here, a potent *betweenness* is effected in the strange modality of 'he *would* appear to my staring eyes . . .'. Not only does this contribute to the layers that fill the space between Marlow and Jim introduced by the consistent turn in the writing towards simile – 'as if disturbed', 'like a symbolic figure', 'as heavy as a slab of marble' – it also makes the space dense with repetition, as a single moment (he

---

[50] Katherine Baxter points out how different is this last glimpse of Jim from Marlow's original memory (in chapter 16, 135) of his final vision of Jim, 'in all his brilliance. That was my last view of him – in a strong light, dominating, and yet in complete accord with his surroundings' (*Joseph Conrad and the Swan Song of Romance*, 2010, 45).

[51] See Allan Simmons, '"He was misleading": Frustrated Gestures in *Lord Jim*', *The Conradian* 25:1 (Spring 2000), for an examination at the level of individual sentences of how the narrative is composed of 'anticipatory gestures that ... frustrate the interpretive quests they invite the reader to follow' (39). Writing of Hardy's titles, Dennis Taylor says, 'Even the unexceptionable *Moments of Vision* sounds differently with Hardy than with Conrad', *Hardy's Literary Language and Victorian Philology* (1993), 252.

appeared) attracts to itself the sum of repeated moments of perception ('he would appear') in an uncertain, disconcerting stretching of time. Against the receding indefiniteness of Jim's appeal, 'the chill air' in its physical embodiment as 'a slab of marble' offers the relief of touch, however unconsoling. The extent to which the three sentences of the paragraph have *not* shown the reader Jim, but have explored the crowded perceptual space between Jim and Marlow, is remarkable.

In Hardy's manner, many of Conrad's figures, too, are enlarged by being seen alone in the cosmos. After another 'glimpse through a rent in the mist', chapter 11 in the Malabar House opens with one such moment:

> The dim candle spluttered within the ball of glass, and that was all I had to see him by; at his back was the dark night with the clear stars, whose distant glitter disposed in retreating planes lured the eye into the depths of a greater darkness; and yet a mysterious light seemed to show me his boyish head, as if in that moment the youth within him had, for the last time, gleamed and expired. (100)

The reader here is briefly loosed beyond Marlow's immediate consciousness by the beguiling physics of the stars' glitter 'disposed in retreating planes' which, with a sudden emotional darkening, 'lured the eye into the depths of a greater darkness'. This is not so much what Marlow sees, as what *is*, in which all that is human becomes lost. Whether the light that shows Jim's head in a small apotheosis against this darkness comes from the dim candle, or from the stars' distant glitter, or from Marlow's mind, is left vaguely 'mysterious'; but the reader finds in the 'boyish head' and 'the youth within him' a hope of innocent vitality to counter the depth into which he has been 'lured'. This sustains itself until the final poignant phrase of the sentence, which then rebounds upon the reader with quite the opposite vision, that Jim's youth – or is it Marlow's hope? – had 'in that moment . . . for the last time, gleamed and expired'. At the end of the previous chapter Jim had just, somewhat obliquely, intimated to Marlow that he had contemplated suicide in the lifeboat with the three other deserters, and 'in that moment' would seem to be the moment of that disclosure; but it is important not to lose the visual element of a momentary gleam and expiry, in the sense that it is the *sight* of Jim's youth and the extinguishing of it, something that catches the light and then falls into darkness, that remains the mode of his presentation from beginning to end.

The reason for this lighting of Jim is that Marlow requires an ideal and symbolic form of vision to defend against a corrosive invasion of the senses that his openness to impression leaves him a prey to. In this, more than in anything else, he is Conrad's surrogate in the text. At its most benign, Marlow's receptivity records the mere contingency of a world that is not subject to any inherent moral order. Thus, walking to the court, he sees the street-life around him as a 'damaged kaleidoscope', suggesting a Hardyan malfunction of a design in which random shapes should fall into a beautiful symmetry, with the eye searching the visible scene in expectation of pleasing coherence only to be met with 'jumbled bits' (121).[52] But vision for Marlow can be more discomforting than this, brought home forcibly within a few pages of his appearance in the novel when he sees the abrupt departure of the German skipper in a gharry to avoid the court proceedings:

> The little machine shook and rocked tumultuously, and the crimson nape of that lowered neck, the size of those straining thighs, the immense heaving of that dingy, striped green and orange back, the whole burrowing effort of that gaudy and sordid mass, troubled one's sense of probability with a droll and fearsome effect, like one of those grotesque and distinct visions that scare and fascinate one in a fever. He disappeared. I half expected the roof to split in two, the little box on wheels to burst open in the manner of a ripe cotton-pod – but it only sank with a click of flattened springs, and suddenly one venetian blind rattled down. His shoulders re-appeared, jammed in the small opening; his head hung out, distended and tossing like a captive balloon, perspiring, furious, spluttering. (40–1)

The beauty of Jim's lit boyish head is needed to stand against all this. Conrad gives to Marlow such a Dickensian visionary intensity here that it is the vibrating field itself, even more than items in the visual field, which returns upon the reader so forcefully. The extraordinary succession of verbs and noun phrases, which do not merely describe the German skipper but transmit an activity *given off* by him that 'trouble(s) . . . probability', creates for the reader a sense of relentless exposure to an unstoppable pantomime. We might be swallowed up by this; it is a display from which one must retreat for shelter in order to recover proportion.

---

[52] The kaleidoscope was invented in 1814 by Eoin Cussen and patented in 1816 by David Brewster. N. Katherine Hayles proposes the kaleidoscope as her metaphor for the nature of knowledge, as 'the language of cause and effect is inadequate to convey the mutuality of the interaction' (*The Cosmic Web*, 1984, 20).

We are thrown forward to that tragic moment when Jewel recounts the death of her mother, and 'the passive irremediable horror of the scene' is such as to drive Marlow 'out of that shelter each of us makes for himself to creep under in moments of danger'. But he allows this 'view' of the world's 'vast and dismal aspect of disorder' only for a moment:

> I went back into my shell directly. One *must* – don't you know? – though I seemed to have lost all my words in the chaos of dark thoughts I had contemplated for a second or two beyond the pale. These came back too very soon, for words also belong to the sheltering conception of light and order which is our refuge. (236)

The manifest *un*truth that Marlow offers ironically, that the world presents 'as sunny an arrangement of small conveniences as the mind of man can conceive' (236), is the necessary illusion that those 'in the ranks' live by. Conrad's own disbelief in a universal condition conferring light and order is affirmed in a letter to Edward Noble of 1895:

> Everyone must walk in the light of his own heart's gospel. No man's light is good to any of his fellows. That's my creed from the beginning to end. That's my view of life – a view that rejects all formulas, dogmas and principles of other people's making. These are only a web of illusions. (CL 1:253)

Such scepticism is a familiar aspect of nearly all of Conrad's writing; yet *Lord Jim* subjects this jauntiness to a sad and searching examination conducted in all sorts of light and shadow. Conrad's statement to Noble is consciously illusion-free; the novel, five years later, requires disillusion to be lit by romantic hope.

The attempt to give definition to the truth of things means that a great deal of the novel inhabits the shadows, often invested with a romantic glamour, where truth might hide, wary of revealing its form. When Jewel explains to Marlow that she 'didn't want to die weeping' (235) like her mother, and that she had 'urged Jim to leave her' (234) for his own safety,

> She fell at his feet – she told me so – there by the river, in the discreet light of stars which showed nothing except great masses of silent shadows, indefinite open spaces, and trembling faintly upon the broad stream made it appear as wide as the sea . . . . they came together under the

shadow of a life's disaster like knight and maiden meeting to exchange vows amongst haunted ruins. The starlight was good enough for that story, a light so faint and remote that it cannot resolve shadows into shapes, and show the other shore of a stream. (234–5)

In this light vision is romantic, and a 'broad stream' carries a beckoning assurance when 'the other shore' cannot be seen. A 'discreet light' maintains the statuesque chivalry of what is acknowledged to be merely 'that story', yet its circumspect care of the lovers barely masks the primary meaning of the alternative, 'discrete' – that such a light keeps Jim and Jewel separate from what surrounds them in the shadows, which the fuller light of day will resolve into shapes that demand to be recognised.[53]

*

Marlow acknowledges that his own desire for light and order is a 'sheltering conception' and a 'refuge'. A very powerful nineteenth-century fiction which literally connected light and order was that of the ether, a conception required by the undulatory view of light as travelling in a medium, and also one which maintained an idea of an ordered and unified universe. *Lord Jim*'s preoccupation with light, and the different longing of both Jim and Marlow for an ordered and visible intelligibility to connect the worlds of action and essence, encourage a reading that associates the novel with late-century conceptions of the ethereal medium. In their popular *The Unseen Universe*, which ran to fourteen editions between 1874 and 1888, the physicists Balfour Stewart and Peter Guthrie Tait maintained that 'the scientific mind is led from the visible and tangible to the invisible and intangible', and they saw the ether as the vehicle or agent for this journey of transformation. For them the ether was the manifestation of 'an invisible order of things'.[54] The extraordinarily widespread appeal of such a notion becomes apparent when we read in *The Art of Creation* (1904), by the socialist Edward Carpenter who could not have been more different from Stewart and Tait in every respect, that

---

[53] William Freedman writes, 'The flight to Patusan, as the novel's play of light makes clear, marks a turning away from harsh if flickering vision to a more protective haze' (*Joseph Conrad and the Anxiety of Knowledge*, 2014, 86).
[54] Balfour Stewart and Peter Guthrie Tait, *The Unseen Universe, or Physical Speculations on a Future State* (1886), 154, 199.

'there is inevitably a vast unity underlying all . . . and in that thought there is liberation, in that thought there is rest'.[55] The vain but never abandoned attempt to find peace in the intangible runs throughout the visible worlds of *Lord Jim*.

The idea of a medium necessary for the propagation of light became one of the most consistently defended notions in physics from the 1830s through to Einstein's 1905 Special Theory of Relativity, and even beyond, because the ether came to represent the material form of a deeper truth that physics itself could provide in the face of so many of its own disintegrating observations.[56] Long after the second Michelson-Morley experiment of 1887 failed to discover any ether-resistance to the motion of the earth, we can find ether celebrated as the material manifestation of a unified purpose in creation by a scientist such as Oliver Lodge, whose popularising 1909 book, *The Ether of Space*, is advertised in Harper's Library of Living Thought as 'Advocating the view which makes the Ether not only all pervading but substantial beyond conception – the most substantial thing – perhaps the only substantial thing in the material universe.' Lodge's governing idea is the need for a connecting medium, which is the title of one of his chapters, and its existence becomes the guarantee of a divinely inspired order, a feeling he impresses upon his readers by directly quoting an eloquent testament to ether by Maxwell himself:

> The vast interplanetary and interstellar regions will no longer be regarded as waste places in the universe, which the Creator has not seen fit to fill with the symbols of the manifold order of His kingdom. We shall find them to be already full of this wonderful medium; so full, that no human power can remove it from the smallest portion of space, or produce the slightest flaw in its infinite continuity.[57]

A fine account of how ether carried with it a metaphysic, even as it was presented as a purely physical explanation for the propagation of light, has been offered by Donald Benson, in '"Catching Light":

---

[55] Edward Carpenter, *The Art of Creation: Essays on the Self and Its Powers* (1904), 34.
[56] Even Faraday, whose concept of lines of force did not require the medium of an ether, reversed his view to admit of an ether in 1862. The thoroughly empiricist Sylvanus Thompson, in his Christmas 1896 lectures on light at the Royal Institution, finds ether a necessary concept: he says, 'Waves of light . . . must be waves of *something*', but confesses, 'If you ask me what the ether is made of, let me frankly say I do not know' (*Light Visible and Invisible*, 1897, 108).
[57] Oliver Lodge, *The Ether of Space* (1909), 104.

Physics and Art in Walter Pater's Cultural Context', a discussion of force and ether as two of the nineteenth century's sustaining fictions:

> What all nineteenth-century ethers do have in common is a capacity to mediate between material and immaterial – whether the immaterial be spatial void, human consciousness, or supernatural spirit.... Ether, in short, is the perfect fiction of continuity, with respect to matter and space, to causation, and, ultimately, to conscious and spiritual experience.[58]

In short, just as it conveys light, ether is the perfect medium in which to convey truth.[59] It is not possible to judge what Conrad himself, in his own search for truth, knew or thought. In his Preface to Richard Curle's *Into the East* (1922), he writes of the earth in modern times 'girt about with cables, with an atmosphere made restless by the waves of ether', but the spirit of this is rhetorical rather than scientific.[60]

Light and order come under examination before Marlow's enquiries and Jim's attempted explanations. The 'truth' of the *Patna*'s journey, her 'onward motion'

> imperceptible to the senses of men as though she had been a crowded planet speeding through the dark spaces of ether behind the swarm of suns, in the appalling and calm solitudes awaiting the breath of future creations (22)

appears very different by night and by day in the entranced description in chapters 2 and 3 of her progress towards the Red Sea. In the scorching light of day, the *Patna* is

> enveloped in a fulgor of sunshine that killed all thought, oppressed the heart, withered all impulses of strength and energy. And under the sinister splendour of that sky the sea, blue and profound, remained still, without a stir, without a ripple, without a wrinkle – viscous, stagnant, dead. (18)

---

[58] In George Levine ed., *One Culture: Essays in Science and Literature* (1987), 149. Benson's essays, itemised in the Bibliography, deserve to be much more influential than they are in appreciations of Conrad. For various theories of ether, see G. N. Cantor and M. J. S. Hodge eds, *Conceptions of Ether 1740–1900* (1981). For a discussion of attempts to construct a mechanical model of ether, see Berkson, *Fields of Force*, 256–68.

[59] See Hans Blumenberg's historical account of 'Light as a Metaphor for Truth' (1957), in David Levin ed., *Modernity and the Hegemony of Vision* (1993).

[60] Joseph Conrad, *Last Essays* (2010), 67.

The picture is not one of energy exchange but of an entropy in which vast power empties life of its vibrations as the *Patna* 'left behind her on the water a white ribbon of foam that vanished at once, like the phantom of a track drawn upon a lifeless sea by the phantom of a steamer' (18). But after the punishing exposure to light, 'The nights descended on her like a benediction' (18). Detail by detail in chapter 3, the progress of the *Patna* is redrawn: so at night the wake of the ship, instead of vanishing at once in the glare of days that disappeared 'one by one into the past, as if falling into an abyss' (18), is given five lines of description until it 'calmed down at last into the circular stillness of water and sky with the black speck of the moving hull remaining everlastingly in its centre' (19). It is, notably, a world of seemings, in which the stars 'seemed to shed upon the earth the assurance of everlasting security' and 'The propeller turned without a check as though its beat had been part of the scheme of a safe universe' (19); and in the long, mesmerising paragraphs of the next five pages the benediction given is conferred by exactly the longed-for feeling of unity of the ether scientists, with 'assurance' and 'everlasting' as its watchwords.[61]

In *Lord Jim* this security is rendered as illusion, most obviously because of 'the coming event', but equally because it is associated with Jim's exalted conception of himself which he reads in a given, naturalised relationship to nature:

> Jim on the bridge was penetrated by the great certitude of unbounded safety and peace that could be read on the silent aspect of nature like the certitude of fostering love upon the placid tenderness of a mother's face. (19)

The description by day has been of anything but a fostering love and placid tenderness, yet Jim's anthropocentric reading of the relief offered at night engenders 'something like gratitude for this high peace of ease and sky' (21), a secular providence which permits him dreams 'of valorous deeds ... imaginary achievements': 'They were the best parts of life, *its secret truth*, its hidden reality' (21, my emphasis). This sense of a harmonious wholeness which confers peace is what Jim will later depict himself as recovering in Patusan, where 'peace' is a recurrent word in Jim's talk. Rather than ask the reader to find this 'hidden' truth and reality in a mental interior, the novel persistently

---

[61] For nineteenth-century physicists' view of the unity of nature, see Iwan Rhys Morus, *When Physics Became King* (2005), particularly 54–86.

gestures outwards, here towards a version of *The Unseen Universe* in which Jim's thoughts are conceived – by himself – as inseparable from energies dedicated to an everlasting existence in an invisible order of things.

The impossibility of a mechanical model of the ether, on which Maxwell, Thomson, Lodge and others spent so much energy, was foretold by H. A. Lorentz's 1895 paper, 'Toward a Theory of Electrical and Optical Phenomena in Moving Bodies'. Reducing all explanations of phenomena to mechanics is the most typical mind-set of the Victorian period, and Lorentz's abandonment of Newtonian mechanics as an all-encompassing methodology signals the end of Victorianism quite as indicatively as any other of the writings of 1895. And *Lord Jim*, equally, finds itself having to abandon the ether-longing of Jim, the desire for unity, correspondence and harmony that Marlow shares but cannot maintain. The desired continuity between matter, consciousness and universal energy ends where the plot of the story begins, in the rupture of Jim's jump:

> he looked into the open palm for quite half a second before he blurted out –
> 'I had jumped . . .' He checked himself, averted his gaze. . . . 'It seems,' he added. (88)

For all the enquiring subtlety that will surround this moment, its unique angularity as it announces itself in these five discrete clauses (consider the divergent verbs: 'jumped', 'checked', 'averted', 'seems', 'added') remains an irreducible quantum not to be accommodated by any theory of continuity. From this point, Jim himself begins to wonder in what light – about which he had been so naïvely certain – his life will be lived: 'There was no going back. It was as if I had jumped into a well – into an everlasting deep hole . . .' (88). And for Marlow, in what medium the truth of the *Patna* affair will appear, and in which the truth of Jim will become visible, is the question that dictates the form of his remembrance of the unfortunate, self-regarding, young man, 'one of us'. This attempt to articulate the truth of an existence – Jim, in court, 'wanted to go on talking for truth's sake' (29) – cannot be achieved by the scientific approach of a minutely careful chronological account of what happened as an event unfolded: for Conrad, as he expresses it in his 1901 letter to the *New York Times* about *The Inheritors*, science 'is not concerned with truth at all, but with the exact order of such phenomena as fall under the perception of the senses'

(*CL* 2:348). Despite the overwhelming importance to Conrad of the evidence of the senses, the 'truth' of human experience eludes 'exact order'. In his essay on *Lord Jim*, Benson casts Conrad as 'A writer of metaphysical vision in an age of spatial and material crisis', who 'faced the same task as the physicist, to construct a cosmos in accord with new knowledge and new uncertainties'. He says, 'The result is no simple translation of the cosmos of ether physics . . . but it is clearly an expression of the same crisis that informed this physics.'[62] In finding a form in which to express and attempt to resolve this crisis, Conrad's fiction finds new ways to combine the physical and the psychological more readily than his conscious adherence to a Newtonian physics would have suggested.

We do not learn exactly what happens to the *Patna*. In keeping with the epistemology of a novel which can be read according to Newtonian mechanics and also according to a theory of energies in a field, we are offered two impressions of the event, both suspended in simile. The hull 'seemed to rise a few inches in succession through its whole length, as though it had become pliable'; and, alternatively, it was 'as though the ship had steamed across a narrow belt of vibrating water and of humming air' (26). Both accounts decompose into sensational terms the conceptual quality of 'fact' demanded by the Court of Inquiry, with simile the means that leaves open to question the nature of matter and its contact. The second displaces the idea of physical contact altogether; as so often in *Lord Jim* – and these are the last words of the account of the *Patna*'s voyage – the reader's senses are left fathoming a medium rather than closing upon an object. Such an account of reality asks for a countervailing truth to rescue the wholeness of life from a disintegration that leaves nothing to believe in. In *Lord Jim* the counter-force lies in another visual medium, in the truth that becomes visible in the other-worldly lighting of dream.

*

The advocate of following the dream in *Lord Jim* is Stein, who can accurately diagnose Jim's case because he, too, is 'romantic'. Marlow's visit to Stein is one of the high points of scenic imagination in Conrad and, like the Malabar House episode, it is a scene

---

[62] Donald R. Benson, 'Constructing an Ethereal Cosmos: Late Classical Physics and *Lord Jim*', *Conradiana* 23:2 (Summer 1991), 138.

which pays intense attention to the lights and shades of an interior, yet which suggests vast distances beyond. In both instances, the enclosed setting befits a mental effort to penetrate inwards towards an understanding of an enigma, Jim, and to puzzle over 'What's good for' his case. This withdrawal from showing directly what natural light displays, opting instead for an indirect and reflective psychology of interior illumination, has its precedent in Hardy's treatment of Boldwood at night in his room, as we have seen. Yet in this most intellectual of scenes in *Lord Jim*, the lighting of rooms, passageways and mirrors is not only, or even primarily, a metaphor of cerebral activity, and it becomes, in a remarkable manner as much as Stein's famous prescription, the 'meaning' of the episode.

Stein's memorable answer to his own question, 'How to be', is delivered from a 'shapeless dusk', beyond 'the bright circle of the lamp' where he has taken the butterfly case to replace it among the *Coleoptera*. The dematerialisation that takes place in the dim far spaces of the room lends Stein's pronouncement something of a hieratic quality: 'His tall form, as though robbed of its substance, hovered noiselessly over invisible things'; but, particularly, it is 'as if these few steps had carried him out of this concrete and perplexed world' (162). The shelter afforded by this retreat into the shadows enables Stein – the irony must be evident – to deliver his credo of courageous engagement:

> 'Yes! Very funny this terrible thing is. A man that is born falls into a dream like a man who falls into the sea. If he tries to climb out into the air as inexperienced people endeavour to do, he drowns – *nicht wahr?* . . . No! I tell you! The way is to the destructive element submit yourself and with the exertions of your hands and feet in the water make the deep, deep sea keep you up.' (162)

Man is born into a medium that of itself is not a providential home, the medium of human consciousness, the dream of ourselves that self-awareness requires. The attempt to live as if this condition were natural, 'to climb out into the air', is what drowns our senses with a deceptive at-homeness: it is exactly the state of being which, as we have seen, Jim breathes in chapter 3, and which makes him so unfit for the contingent conditions of living in the world. Stein is as romantic as Jim, but his vision of 'how to be' is quite opposite to Jim's naturalisation of his day-dreams as continuous with a universal physical reality. What Stein advocates is a strenuous attentiveness to our own awareness, to the conceptions of the world *we make* out of what is delivered by our senses; it is a vision that offers no relief, as, although we have no alternative but to pursue the dream of ourselves, it will not find us a place at home in nature. Far from any priestly assurance, such as Yeats draws for himself 'Once out of nature' in Byzantium, Stein's is a vision committed to the effort it takes to make an impermanent stay for the duration of our life *in* nature. It agrees with Conrad's letter to Cunninghame Graham: 'old life is like new life after all – an uninterrupted agony of effort'. Conrad goes on to write, 'fidelity to nature would be the best of all . . . if we could only get rid of consciousness' (*CL* 2:30). It is not man's place, Stein seems to suggest, to be granted satisfying and effortless natural presence, but rather unwearied exertion to keep alive the truths born of consciousness in a medium that must eventually destroy us.[63]

However, convincing as Stein's words are when uttered in the semi-darkness, the sturdy muscularity of his advice dissolves when he 'suddenly appeared in the bright circle of the lamp': 'the austere exaltation of a certitude seen in the dusk vanished from his face . . . The light had destroyed the assurance which had inspired him in the distant shadows' (162–3). And the effect of Stein's pronouncements casts both Marlow and the reader into a more doubtful region altogether, a 'vast and uncertain expanse' in which a 'charming and deceptive light' seeks to obscure what are really 'pitfalls' and 'graves' with a poetic 'dimness'. In this pivotal chapter of the novel, it cannot be doubted that Conrad has invested a great deal in Stein's idealism and Marlow's idealism; but the fictional procedures of subjecting such idealism to the demands of imagining *the scene* exacts from Conrad a truth to sensation which makes light an ineluctable and impersonal agent in offering more questionable shapes than either Stein or Marlow intend. In practice, Stein's romantic redrawing of life with an 'impalpable poesy' (the archaism a comment in itself) leaves an extraordinary picture out of 'Childe Roland' before Marlow's

---

[63] Bruce Johnson's account compels assent: 'What Stein's advice suggests . . . is that the man who recognises his contingency, his moment-to-moment formlessness, pursues the ideal as an expression of his humanity . . . To pursue the ideal as one's already innate essence [the position Johnson claims that Jim holds] is not to *pursue* it at all' (*Conrad's Models of Mind*, 1971, 60). Johnson credits Robert Penn Warren's 1951 reading (in the Introduction to the Modern Library *Nostromo*, xxi–xxiii) as 'the definitive explanation'. It is in this Introduction that Penn Warren parallels Conrad's 'Scepticism, the tonic of minds, the tonic of life, the agent of truth – the way of art and salvation' to Hardy's 'if way to the Better there be, it exacts a full look at the Worst' (xxvi).

mind, a desolate plain 'circled with a bright edge as if surrounded by an abyss full of flames' (163). For Marlow this threatening vision, rather than any suggestion about what Jim should do, forms the sensational reality of the moment.

Failing to locate any practicalities in their talk, the two men prepare for sleep, and what performs itself before Marlow's eyes is an effect as specular as the weird reflections in Boldwood's room at night, and, as in that scene, visits an external light upon mental preoccupations:

> We passed through empty dark rooms escorted by gleams from the lights Stein carried. They glided along the waxed floors, sweeping here and there over the polished surface of the table, leaped upon a fragmentary curve of a piece of furniture, or flashed perpendicularly in and out of distant mirrors, while the forms of two men and the flicker of two flames could be seen for a moment stealing silently across the depths of a crystalline void. (163–4)

The light and the mirror have more substance than the two men. While the men are momentary figures 'stealing silently' across the face of a mirror as if they should not be there, the candlelight continuously fabricates the event in a succession of verbs as active as those that wield the light from Sergeant Troy's blade: 'escorted', 'glided', 'sweeping', 'leaped', 'flashed'. If the mirror is 'void' it also has 'depths', while the men are depthless 'forms'. The reader is removed from a world of conscious human intention to one of the action of light upon surfaces, and the two protagonists are reduced to passing phantoms by physical processes of reflection, not depicted pursuing their mental reflections.[64]

In a novel which brings into question everything that passes before the senses, this climactic scene then proceeds to offer the strangest and most ambiguous of resolutions as Marlow seeks to pass beyond the excitations of sense into certainty. In this luminous medium that attenuates human embodiment to 'forms', far from 'the clashing claims of life and death in a material world' (165) which have silenced belief in Jim's existence, Stein's insistence that it is Jim's romanticism that makes him exist for them provokes the novel's long-promised epiphany – or, at least, a promise of it. Marlow's difficulty at that

---

[64] The description at this point revisits aspects of that early and undervalued story of lights, shadows and mirrors, 'The Return'. See Joseph Conrad, *Tales of Unrest* (2012), particularly 108–12, 146–7.

moment in believing in Jim's existence is broken through. He is not exonerated for actions aboard the *Patna*, but

> his imperishable reality came to me with a convincing, with an irresistible force! I saw it vividly, as though in our progress through the lofty silent rooms amongst the fleeting gleams of light and the sudden revelations of human figures stealing with flickering flames within unfathomable and pellucid depths, we had approached nearer to absolute Truth, which, like Beauty itself, floats elusive, obscure, half submerged, in the silent still waters of mystery. (164)

This offers to see Jim 'vividly', though what is seen is decidedly more Platonic than those glimpses of Jim in rents in the mist at the Malabar House. His reality is now 'imperishable', freed from the conditions of material life, and seen in consequence of a postulated approach ('as though') nearer to 'absolute Truth' than heretofore, an approach only known as a specular effect in a passage towards veiled abstractions. Although the sensationist mode – this is what it *felt* like – prevails over the explanatory – this is what I *saw* – the reader is left at the end of this sentence far removed from the seeing and hearing demanded by the material world. The vision described, as opposed to that which we are told of, is not of Jim himself but of a condition *in which* his 'reality' might truthfully be seen.[65] And it is telling, as a comment on just how close any of us can come to knowing the living reality of another, as Cytherea Graye had lamented, that the episode ends upon Stein going back to his butterflies, specimens of perfect beauty and adaptation, that have been killed to be admired by those who can never simply *be*.[66]

Despite the many ways in which *Lord Jim* brings into question a single impersonal 'truth', the hard and absolute purity of 'absolute Truth' *remains* appealing to Conrad, even if all he can give us is a sensation of the light in which it might reside. It represents something his temperament desires far more than Hardy's does, to whose

---

[65] With characteristic clarity, Tony Tanner explores 'truth' in a different manner in one of the essential articles on *Lord Jim*: 'Butterflies and Beetles – Conrad's Two Truths', *Chicago Review* XVI (Winter–Spring 1963). His exploration of 'man as butterfly, man as beetle' leads him to the conclusion that '*Lord Jim* is a prelude to profound pessimism . . . that there might be absolutely no meaning at all to be found.'

[66] See Katarzyna Sokołowska's discussion of 'spectre and shadow imagery' in which 'Conrad plays with Platonic mimesis only to refute the very core of Plato's philosophy', in *Conrad and Turgenev: Towards the Real* (2011), 80–90.

physiological vision W. K. Clifford is closer when he writes, 'instead of contemplating an eternal order, and absolute right, we find only a changing property of a shifting organism'.[67] Accordingly, *Far From the Madding Crowd* is far more than *Lord Jim* about accommodation to changing circumstance, the world offering only relative happiness. There are casualties. In our last sight of Bathsheba, a shawl over her head at her door – 'now only three or four-and-twenty' (463) – she is silent while jokes are made about husbands and wives: 'Then Oak laughed, and Bathsheba smiled (for she never laughed readily now)' (465) are the last, saddening, words about her. The rays of the couple's lantern fall upon a group of local fellows and their antique instruments – how different from when the rays from Bathsheba's dark lantern 'burst out' to disclose Troy, 'brilliant in brass and scarlet' (214). Marlow's (and I would say, Conrad's) investment in the ideal and the absolute is very much higher, and correspondingly in *Lord Jim* the sense of loss is more starkly complete. Marlow's final offering of a sight of Jim is in fact an erasure of any continuing existence in the world's light: 'he passes from my eyes like a disembodied spirit astray amongst the passions of this earth – ready to surrender himself faithfully to the claim of his own world of shades' (313). Reversing Marlow's last words in 'Heart of Darkness', the light has been too bright altogether.

2 Searching Space

A Laodicean and 'The End of the Tether'

To take further an enquiry into what 'seeing' actually entails in Hardy and Conrad, this second section examines more briefly how two under-regarded middle-period works portray the negotiations between the eye and a scene disclosed to it. *A Laodicean*, Hardy's eighth novel, and one of his least read, is his most quizzical and perplexed enquiry into the 'bringing-ins' of the eye. 'The End of the Tether', written in 1902 in the aftermath of *Lord Jim* and 'Heart of Darkness', constitutes Conrad's most concentrated examination of the nature of vision. It is not coincidental that the rather doubtful heroes are in the one case an architect and in the other a sea captain; that the spaces they both scan professionally to yield

---

[67] W. K. Clifford, 'Cosmic Emotion' (*Nineteenth Century*, October 1877), in *Lectures and Essays* (1901), vol. 2, 279.

precise measurement open uncertainly upon indeterminate dimensions; that in both works the opportunities and displacements of a modernised life are a central concern. Taken together, they show how both novelists seek direct visual engagement with the world to determine meaning, but find, ruefully, the indirections by which insight arrives.

*

The idyllic romance of Paula Power and George Somerset, two modern minds engaged in the appreciation and accommodation of the past in the restoration of Stancy Castle, looks fairly set for a joyful consummation by the end of Book One of *A Laodicean*. But this is the story of a deferred, deflected, sabotaged love-suit which, in practice, requires six Books to achieve its happy, but more provisional, conclusion. This elaboration is very much the product of the uncertainty of sight – and sightings – itself. Looks given and received on entrance and departure, looks out of windows and across vistas, peerings in through windows and apertures, the appearance of people and actions deduced from 'insufficient data' giving rise to 'mere conjecture' (40),[68] such recurrent visual activity suspends the defended uncertainty of Paula's heart and the designs upon it in a medium traditionally associated with clarification and insight, but in which nineteenth-century physiology had discovered subjectivity, distance, and separation from the object in the ocular frame.

As with Volume 3 of *Desperate Remedies*, the underrated second half of the novel generally receives little attention, regarded as just the tired unravelling of the complications of the plot, and to be accounted for by Hardy's illness at the time.[69] Much of Books Four and Five unfolds a continental travelogue, in which Somerset trails after the restless and undecided Paula, each always missing direct sight of the other, with the comic pleasure for the reader in seeing the positions 'inversely imitated' (397) in Book Six. Amid all the incident, there is a brief, stiller, scene which displays how something seen

---

[68] Thomas Hardy, *A Laodicean* (1991). Edited by Jane Gatewood, this edition uses as its copy-text the three-volume edition published by Sampson Low in 1881, which is helpful in revealing Hardy's original impulses in composition.

[69] So Michael Millgate says the novel becomes 'a fairly disastrous failure'. He sums up a widespread feeling about the novel in concluding that Hardy's ambitions for *A Laodicean* were 'completed in (such) weary despair' (*Thomas Hardy: His Career as a Novelist*, 1994, 166/173).

does not always resolve itself into conceptual understanding, but is retained in the visual field as an untranslatable phenomenon. Paula and her much-loved companion Charlotte find themselves in 'an old-fashioned red hotel at Strasburg' overlooking the Kleber Platz. Book Five opens:

> The whole square, with its people and vehicles going to and fro as if they had plenty of time, was visible to Charlotte in her chair; but Paula from her horizontal position could see nothing below the level of the many-dormered housetops on the opposite side of the Platz. After watching this upper story of the city for some time in silence, she asked Charlotte to hand her a binocular lying on the table, through which instrument she quietly regarded the distant roofs.
> 'What strange and philosophical creatures storks are,' she said. 'They give a taciturn, ghostly character to the whole town.'
> The birds were crossing and recrossing the field of the glass in their flight hither and thither between the Strasburg chimneys, their sad grey forms sharply outlined against the sky, and their skinny legs showing beneath like the limbs of dead martyrs in Crivelli's emaciated imaginings. The indifference of these birds to all that was going on beneath them impressed her: to harmonize with their solemn and silent movements the houses beneath should have been deserted, and grass growing in the streets. (297)

Paula's position involves her intently in the 'upper story' of city life and also cuts her off from its more familiar sights and sounds. Time is stretched out to most uncity-like dimensions throughout the passage as distance attenuates any display of purpose by the Strasburg citizens, who seem to move '*as if* they had plenty of time'. This is an effect enhanced by the silence, which is initially Paula's as 'she quietly regarded the distant roofs' (a quiet regard being the least hurried of looks), but which then is seen to emanate from the birds themselves in 'their solemn and silent movements'. The slow silence finally locates itself in the visually imagined thought, presumably Paula's but not confined to her, of depopulated streets that time themselves to the growth of grass. In the temporal extension created by the unfolding of these steady sentences, it is the strange philosophical birds that hold the visual attention, their 'sad grey forms' and 'skinny legs', engraved with a weight of human suffering which retains a pictorial self-sufficiency rather than being illustrative of Paula's thought-process. Any implied extension of Paula's feelings from sadness to pain, or intellectual contrast between her uncommitted heart and martyrdom for an exacting faith, has to contend with the birds' aloof 'indifference', which remains the most lasting impression made upon Paula and the reader.

What does Paula see? Her own emotional emaciation, or a desired indifference that, despite her perceived Laodiceanism, is contrary to her nature? Somerset's apparent indifference to her, gambling at the Monaco tables as she thinks, or his hither and thither loneliness? To read the framed picture symbolically in this manner seems invited, but it is an intrusion upon the containment of the storks within 'the field of the glass', a self-enclosed completeness which Hardy does not let slip over the next page and a half, when they fade, silently and unremarked, from the account. The storks are not there to illustrate the cast of Paula's mind; they are another illustration of how things in Hardy, as I have already quoted Tony Tanner as saying, are 'scrupulously watched in (their) otherness, something perceived but not made over'.[70] The irreducible storks that remain in the visual field of the glass are the sign of a discomforting distance between the self and the world which most of the novel explores in the vein of rather pained romantic comedy.[71]

From the outset, *A Laodicean* concerns itself with how the observing eye is itself subject to the light that it scans. The initial 'spectacle of a summer traveller from London sketching medieval details' (9) is evoked as a 'brilliant chromatic effect of which he composed the central feature' (7), and a chapter which promises to describe the 'tall mass of antique masonry' that George Somerset is sketching, foregoes representing that solidity in favour of representing the light in which both young man and battlemented parapet are 'fired to a great brightness by the uninterrupted solar rays, that crossed the neighbouring mead like a warp of gold threads' (7). The absorption of Somerset as an effect of the scene continues as he 'remained enveloped in the lingering aureate haze' (9) sketching till nightfall. Somerset is like Clym Yeobright in that 'he had more of the beauty – if beauty it ought to be called – of the future human type than of the

---

[70] Tanner, 'Colour and Movement in *Tess*', 219. See also Mark Simons, 'Hardy's Stereographic Technique', *Thomas Hardy Journal* 13:3 (1997). He argues that in adopting the technique of the stereograph, Hardy 'could create an alternative space/time in his readers' imaginations . . . an accentuated middle ground for the viewer to roam through and investigate' (70).

[71] A much more dramatic appearance in 'the field of my glass' is that of the heads surrounding Kurtz's compound that make Marlow 'throw my head back as if before a blow' in Conrad's 'Heart of Darkness' (103), posing disturbing questions about mankind's relation to nature in another mood entirely.

past' (8); and yet it is sight more than thought which is emphasised in that he has 'a too dominant *speculative* activity in him' (8, my emphasis). Somerset's 'modern malady of unlimited appreciativeness' (12) is, we are told, an incapacity to make up his mind such that 'He wished that some accident could have hemmed in his eyes between inexorable blinkers' (12).

This insistence upon ambient light and the curious eye soon lends the writing its own quality of speculation, catching something of the voyeurism which piques Somerset's interest as he peeps in upon the chapel where Paula Power is undergoing a baptism ceremony of total immersion, and where he searches from the lit surfaces inside the building an intelligible narrative for the proceedings:

> Between the minister and the congregation was an open space, and in the floor of this was sunk a tank full of water, which just made its surface visible above the blackness of its depths by reflecting the lights overhead. (15)

The hostile otherness given to this tank is created by an imagination moving among indeterminate planes and uncertain volumes into which human immersion is demanded by the ceremony: 'space', 'sunk', 'full', 'surface', 'blackness', 'depths', 'reflecting', 'overhead' – so many words here require visual readjustment that the effect is vertiginous. For the subject of this immersion to emerge as a young woman in a virginal white gown suggests a cruel erotic coercion as the potent, if unarticulated, force uniting the items taken in by Somerset's eye. Somerset's sympathetic interest in the figure of Paula is not exempt, as it moves from 'all that could be *gleaned* of her' (17, my emphasis) from the surface allowed to the eye, to the divination of 'a clandestine, stealthy inner life' living behind her 'repression of nearly every external sign of (that) distress' (17). Paula's refusal to enter 'that dark water' (18) and her withdrawal to the vestry is followed not only by a lacerating sermon on her Laodiceanism, but also by the eyes of the whole congregation that, 'one and all, became fixed upon that vestry-door as if they would almost push it open by the force of their gazing' (19). While the sermon continues, 'For Somerset there was but one scene: the imagined scene of the girl herself as she sat alone in the vestry' (20), a visual penetration that substitutes a private space for the public spectacle that had entertained the eye previously. Aware, when he goes to visit the castle the next day, that 'he had already through his want of effrontery lost a sight of many interiors' (24), Somerset's sexual curiosity is aroused and rewarded by finding himself in Paula's private set of chambers and able to look into her bedroom and let his eyes take note of the intimate things therein.

As well as Stancy Castle itself, another building to which Hardy draws attention is Paula's thoroughly modern gymnasium. Elaborately, Hardy contrives to have Paula watched by an older, womanising suitor, Captain De Stancy. Having him peeping in upon 'a sort of optical poem' (172) of Paula's callisthenics, Hardy creates a direct parallel and antithesis to the scene in the chapel. If the Baptist chapel is the scene of Paula's public oppression and subsequent rejection of submission to the patriarchal word, her gymnasium is designed to be the scene of her private untrammelled feminine self-expression, displayed before her aunt and her friend Charlotte rather than before the congregation led by the severe minister, Mr Woodwell. Yet both scenes are presented as spaces subject to the survey of unseen watchers, the second even more so, since De Stancy's son, William Dare, and Somerset's rival architect Havill, stand watching Captain De Stancy watching Paula, and 'could almost see the aspect of her within the wall, so accurately were her changing phases reflected in him' (174). The passage of Paula's 'phases' to the exterior and then to another's body, a man's, is disturbing: with the reader's complicity, walls are disassembled to allow a visual access that is a violation. What De Stancy sees is the eroticism of Paula's 'undulating in the air', her 'gyrations' and 'absolute abandonment to every muscular whim', receiving an even greater charge from the 'noonday sun ... irradiating her with a warm light that was incarnadined by her pink doublet and hose, and reflected in upon her face' (173). This scene in particular illustrates James Elkins's contention that 'Looking is hoping, desiring, never just taking in light, never just collecting patterns and data. Looking is possessing or the desire to possess ... Those appetites don't just accompany looking: they are looking itself.'[72] And Hardy artfully ends the chapter on a note that is soft and visually lustrous, in which Paula displays herself as Ariel asleep in a cowslip's bell (these are also the last words of the second Book): 'she flung out her arms behind her head as she lay in the green silk hammock, idly closed her pink eyelids, and swung herself to and fro' (174). Yet Elkins's comment on the astringent quality of seeing reveals at a profound level what has happened in this scene: 'And so looking has force: it is sharp,

---

[72] James Elkins, *The Object Stares Back: On the Nature of Seeing* (1996), 27.

it tears, it is an acid. In the end, it corrodes the object and observer until they are lost in the field of vision. I once was solid, and now I am dissolved: that is the voice of seeing.'[73]

*

In the most joyful part of *A Laodicean* it is not too extravagant to say that the medium searched by various eyes is light as modified by love.[74] The party which Paula holds at the castle is the occasion of a brief summer storm in which she and Somerset watch

> the rain streaming down between their eyes and the lighted interior of the marquee like a tissue of glass threads, the brilliant forms of the dancers passing and repassing behind the watery screen, as if they were people in an enchanted submarine palace. (121)

That the enchantment is with each other is soon confirmed by an intimate verbal exchange; however, graceful ease in the possession of the enchanted palace is a gauzy romance from which Paula will always be divided, and the sight retains its fairy-tale evanescent otherness, not to be incorporated in Somerset and Paula's subsequent history. In fact, Book One ends two pages later with Somerset entertaining the 'phenomenal agonies and questionable delights' (123) that prove to be his sensational experience for most of the novel. The counterpart and exact opposite to the garden party scene is played out in Book Four in Nice, where Somerset impulsively follows Paula, pricked on by the presence there of his rival, De Stancy:

> Northern eyes are not prepared on a sudden for the impact of such images of warmth and colour as meet them southward, or for the vigorous light that falls from the sky of this favoured shore. In any other circumstances the transparency and serenity of the air, the perfume of the sea, the radiant houses, the palms and flowers, would have acted upon Somerset as an enchantment, and wrapped him in a reverie; but at present he only saw and felt these things as through a thick glass which kept out half their atmosphere. (280)

---

[73] Ibid., 45.
[74] Such an idea is familiar from Donald Davie's famous 'Hardy's Virgilian Purples' (*Agenda* 10:2–3, 1972), where he claims, 'the purples which prink the main as seen from Beeny Cliff are the spiritual light of sexual love' (140).

The transmissiveness (as Hardy puts it in *Tess*) of the earlier English scene has evaporated in the harder Mediterranean light; Somerset is unable to breathe the atmosphere of the enchantment that the sentence insistently proposes for him, as the 'tissue of glass threads' has become an insulating 'thick glass'. He fears that 'under this crystalline light' as a 'solitary unimportant man in the lugubrious North' he will 'have faded from her mind' (280). What Paula's mind is, the subject of the novel as declared in its title, is archly (some readers feel) withheld from Somerset and from the reader; so, as in a guided tour, we receive a lot of what Somerset sees while we want to know *her* view. Yet this design upon us does not only provide the pleasing discomfort of comic misprision: the picaresque second half of the novel gains a measure of unity when seen as an exploration of the subjectivity of vision as an inescapable condition, one whose very immediacy simultaneously puts us at a remove from a shared verifiable world.

It is as if Hardy wishes it were not so, and that what we see arises directly and reliably from unmediated encounters with our visual environment. He borrows a phrase taken from his recent reading of Leslie Stephen's essay, 'The Moral Element in Literature', published in *The Cornhill* in January 1881, in which Stephen asserts that the novelist reveals 'truths (*pace* Bain) capable of being proved by direct intuition . . . so far as we are in sympathy with him, the proof – if it be a proof – has all *the cogency of direct vision*' (*LN* 1:136, my emphasis). Hardy introduces the phrase into *A Laodicean* in conjunction with the photographer William Dare, the character whose professional skill in manipulating visual appearance is at the root of the novel's plot of intrigue and deception. Dare's alteration of a photograph of Somerset, to make him look to be an habitual drunkard, makes interference in direct vision a significant complication in the misapprehensions that keep Paula and Somerset apart. Paula and Charlotte are deceived by the photograph, for, 'To them that picture of Somerset had all the cogency of direct vision' (320). Similar to Conrad's appeal to 'Direct vision of the fact' in 'Autocracy and War' (1905),[75] the force of the memorable phrase carries with it an authorial plea for 'direct vision', for vision as information, almost as a moral good; however, the complication of simple directness is, in practice, exactly what Hardy's novel practises in scene after scene, as it subjects this desire for immediate visual revelation to odd frames

---

[75] Joseph Conrad, *Notes on Life and Letters* (1949), 84.

and angles, impediments and delays, that correspond to the indirectness, as we have seen, of Helmholtz's physiological optics.

We are not privy to the visions in other people's minds, and the negotiations between imagination and verification necessary to discover how others see us, the world, their own position in it, is what the process of all the tracking and the errors in the second half of *A Laodicean* explores. Somerset thinks at one point, 'He was only her hired designer' (280), and the question of through what lens he is seen, that of architect or lover, becomes the trope that governs the sight-seeing plot through a dozen European tourist centres. It falls to Paula, finally, to free Somerset from his subjective misperceptions by direct word ('if you want to marry me as you once did, you must say so; for I am here to be asked' (417)), and thus to allow the suggestion of love that wavers uncertainly in appearances to be acted on. It is significant that, later, Paula is firm in her resolution to get married to Somerset before returning to England and the still-potent attractions of medievalism in the castle of the De Stancys. It is even more significant that, after the fire which destroys it, the castle is not restored, and that the reader is not invited to see a solid remodelled structure but an uncertain space into which hasty plans for a modern future are projected. In an addition in 1912 to the Preface, Hardy recognises that in this 'Story of To-Day', as he subtitles the novel, solid matter appears to dissolve in the bright light that conveys it to the subjective eye, a decomposition that Conrad uses richly and centrally in 'The End of the Tether'. Using another reference to *The Tempest*, Hardy says that the 'sites, mileages, and architectural details' of *A Laodicean* are 'but the baseless fabrics of a vision'; and however carefully he observed exactly these verifiable features to generate the novel, Hardy's emphasis as he looks back upon it is surely right. Scanning the life that appears before her, Paula will finally describe herself as '"one of that body to whom lukewarmth is not an accident but a provisional necessity, till they see a little more clearly"' (428). That 'provisional necessity', rather than the acquisition of some hard-won insight in the manner of her Victorian forebears, makes her one of Hardy's most engagingly modern heroines.

*

The searching eye is never merely quiescent in these novels and stories, and Conrad in particular subjects it to the strains of exposure to the light. In fact, the way these fictions answer the charge of passivity that can be levelled against sensationism is perfectly expressed by Theo Meyering when he describes Helmholtz's 'unusual theory of unconscious inferences':

> His theory holds that the percipient is not stripped of all activity while merely inertly interacting with a surrounding medium of mechanical energies. Rather, the percipient is regarded as an active participant in the perceptual process and as gradually 'tuning in' to the unknown structures of the surrounding world. Thus he can do more than merely absorb whatever comes his way through experience as well as being conditioned by it. He can also break through the walls of his 'intraphenomenal prison' and genuinely *learn* from experience by means of creative activity and intelligent experimentation.[76]

In the novels we are discussing, response to an accretion of sensations represents this gradual 'tuning in' – often more abruptly in Conrad – which permits a breaking out of the Paterian prison, in a manner consistent with other branches of enquiry that seek objective forms and explanations for subjective experience. Conrad's 'The End of the Tether' presents the reader with extended examples of just such 'tuning in', but also of a rather more violent and revolutionary breaking through of the walls than Meyering's 'learning' suggests.

'The End of the Tether' is the novella which completes the volume *Youth: A Narrative and Two Other Stories* (1902), the second of which is 'Heart of Darkness'. It immerses the reader from the very beginning in a visual field in which the fall of light upon surfaces, and upon the eye itself, retains a significance which is only slowly unfolded through the length of the tale:

> For a long time after the course of the steamer *Sofala* had been altered for the land, the low swampy coast had retained its appearance of a mere smudge of darkness beyond a belt of glitter. The sunrays fell violently upon the calm sea – seemed to shatter themselves upon an adamantine surface into sparkling dust, into a dazzling vapour of light that blinded the eye and wearied the brain with its unsteady brightness.
> Captain Whalley did not look at it. (129)

The capacity of the eye to survey the scene is repudiated here by a violent falling, shattering and blinding, leaving only a faded afterimage, 'a mere smudge of darkness', as its possession. And then we might wonder why, in a spirit quite contrary to the 'tunings in' mentioned above, we are told so categorically that 'Captain Whalley did not look at it.' The precise way in which it emerges, with prolonged

---

[76] Meyering, *Historical Roots of Cognitive Science*, 123.

uncertainty for the first-time reader and for the participants in the tale, that this is the story of a sea captain who is losing his sight, accounts for its unremitting attention to the visual realm. A man of grand self-conscious rectitude, Captain Whalley's continuing to command a ship while going blind, in order to provide for his daughter, is the moral dimension of a tale whose social context is the colonial development of Singapore into an aggressive and soulless modernity.[77] I want here to examine contrasting kinds of vision which the tale offers in two episodes, and which culminate in absolute and sudden revelations that contrast with the indeterminacies of *A Laodicean* and the attractive provisionality on which that novel ends.

Captain Whalley's long walk through the streets of modern Singapore, having sold his barque, the *Fair Maid*, and beset with a sense of his own marginality, is an exercise in the experience of ocular bewilderment. Disclosures of light are full of activity not rendered as passing through Whalley's senses: almost as an automaton, Whalley crosses the indigenous part of town where the threat of 'cavernous lairs' and the 'looming' cable tramway, the enticements of overflowing merchandise, a sunset that can 'take' the street 'from end to end' (140) and light falling on faces, backs, moustaches – none of these advance upon Whalley as they do so readily for the reader. He has no agency in constructing a narrative or meaning, and, reaching the government quarter, the vision of the empty elegance of modernised Singapore achieves a comic climax as Whalley's walk dissolves into an extraordinary, silent, slow-motion parade of carriages 'along the newly opened sea-road' (147). If *A Laodicean* is concerned, literally, with what substance modernity is to be made from, this sequence in 'The End of the Tether' exhibits the material substance of those who have profited by the modernisation of Singapore, viewed not by the embodied eye of Whalley or another observer, but held suspended in the evening light and as seen by the nerveless camera-eye of the narrator which both enlarges and removes depth simultaneously:

> The wheels turned solemnly; one after another the sunshades drooped, folding their colours like gorgeous flowers shutting their petals at the end of the day . . . and the motionless heads and shoulders of men and women sitting in couples emerged stolidly above the lowered hoods – as if wooden. (147)

---

[77] See J. H. Stape, 'Conrad's "Unreal City": Singapore in "The End of the Tether"', in Gene M. Moore ed., *Conrad's Cities* (1992), and A. M. Purssell, '"The End of the Tether": Conrad, Geography and the Place of Vision', *The Conradian* 33:2 (Autumn 2008), 30–43.

Conrad's incessant simile-making freeze-frames these products of the light into a procession of mannequins, the 'gorgeous flowers' contributing the reverse of natural vitality as they are tidied away for the night. The animation given to this almost funereal scene, which prefigures the great cab-ride of chapter 8 of *The Secret Agent* in its rendering of forward motion as an endlessly-replayed immobility, is provided by the lone carriage of the governor which 'fled along in a noiseless roll':

> The landau distanced the whole file in a sort of sustained rush; the features of the occupants whirling out of sight left behind an impression of fixed stares and impassive vacancy; and after it had vanished in full flight as it were, notwithstanding the long line of vehicles hugging the curb at a walk, the whole lofty vista of the avenue seemed to lie open and emptied of life in the enlarged impression of an august solitude. (148)[78]

This wonderful flourish of the Conradian grotesque achieves its peculiar absence of tactile hold upon the reader because it twice asserts 'impression' without providing an impact upon the senses. The 'fixed stares and impassive vacancy' of the four members of his Excellency's family hover like the Cheshire Cat, except resolutely unsmiling, as important life departs with them to confer a speciously august pall upon the scene for having passed through it. Enlargement is, indeed, empty.

When Whalley looks up, what *he* sees is quite different from this surreal filmic unspooling. 'Swept out of the great avenue by the swirl of a mental backwash', Whalley's vision is of

> muddy shores, a harbour without quays, the one solitary wooden pier (but that was a public work) jutting out crookedly, the first coal-sheds erected on Monkey Point, that caught fire mysteriously and smouldered for days, so that amazed ships came into a roadstead full of sulphurous fog, and the sun hung blood-red at midday. (149)

Precise and full, Whalley has constructed a narrative from what was once so vividly seen which re-embodies the past in his present mental vision; as in Hardy, subjective vision, threatened though it is by

---

[78] Conrad has developed the nerveless style of this sequence from the similar episode of carriages stuck in a traffic jam in his favourite French novel, Flaubert's *L'Éducation sentimentale*.

temperamental distortion, is finally the guarantee of the solidity of external material reality precisely because of that temperamental contact. What is implied and then made explicit is that to see fully, with comprehension, is to *evoke*:

> In this evocation, swift and full of detail like a flash of magnesium light into the niches of a dark memorial hall, Captain Whalley contemplated things once important ... he stopped short, struck the ground with his stick, and ejaculated mentally, 'What the devil am I doing here!' (149)

This is the first of three occasions in 'The End of the Tether' in which a creative reconstitution achieved by mental vision, rather than a merely correct interpretation of what is conveyed in the light falling upon the retina, leads to a true understanding of things. Magnesium, used in flash photography, is highly reactive and burns with an intense white flame: Whalley's visionary moment of self-knowledge is a sudden flare of light recovering lost memories. Jay B. Losey's description is apt here: 'Memory, not reason, aids in the transcription of Conrad's delayed epiphanies – ones arising from the memory of a prior event or experience, not in itself an epiphany.'[79] Although Losey does not refer to 'The End of the Tether', this conveys the dramatic arc of the novella in which the review of a whole life, by eyes unable or unwilling to see exactly what is in front of them in the present, produces a flash of insight that entirely revisits what being in this present moment means. The value that Conrad places upon the brevity and immediacy of such an experience is suggested by a letter of several years earlier to Edward Garnett, about rewriting 'Karain' under the sting of Garnett's criticism:

> the full comprehension of what you objected to came to me like a flash of light into a dark cavern. It came and went; but it left me informed with such knowledge as comes of a short vision. The best kind of Knowledge because the most akin to revelation. (*CL* 1:343)

Knowledge as revelation demands the recasting of a story in quite a different light.

'The End of the Tether' conducts a dialogue about seeing, knowing and understanding that draws all of the story's characters into

---

[79] Jay B. Losey, '"Moments of Awakening" in Conrad's Fiction', *Conradiana* 20:2 (Summer 1988), 92.

its scanning of visual fields. In the various modes of seeing the world that Conrad attributes to his characters, the almost silent Serang is accorded by far the greatest certitude that what he sees corresponds to the material reality of things:

> The record of the visual world fell through his eyes upon his unspeculating mind as on a sensitised plate through the lens of a camera. His knowledge was absolute and precise . . . He was not troubled by any intellectual mistrust of his senses. (172–3)

Conrad makes clear that the Serang has very deliberately detached his ocular life from his inner thoughts for the sake of mere survival. In him, vision leads to cognition with mechanical accuracy because the economics of his life (and this is a story essentially about money, an untouchable five hundred pounds) dictates the exclusion of the knowledge of uncertainty. The Serang has most perfectly adapted himself to his circumstances, and is the fittest to survive in a tale that in its exploration of the survival or extinction of self-esteem on the part of all involved, evolves from light touches of comedy to the darkest tragic vision.

*

The second 'illuminating moment' in the tale belongs to its arch-empiricist, the chief mate Sterne – though it does not exactly arise from his 'weeks of watchful observation' (181). In Conradian epistemology, for all the attention to vision, it is conviction rather than induction which leads to what we 'know'. For the reader, though, Sterne's 'discovery' arises from a passage through a remarkable visual sequence of four pages of the most sustained evocative writing in all Conrad's fiction. It follows 'the usual track of the *Sofala*' (182) through a 'reef-infested' region at the mouth of Pangu Bay, as if we were watching through Sterne's eyes from the deck of the ship, yet with an intensely imaginative attention to the surfaces of water and rocks that quite exceeds his utilitarian scrutiny, one which is 'always . . . on the look out for an opening to get on' (180). The play of wind and light reveals a cluster of rocks,

> crumbs of the earth's crust resembling a squadron of dismasted hulks run in disorder upon a foul ground of rocks and shoals . . . like anchored rafts, like ponderous, black rafts of stone . . . squat domes of deep green foliage that shuddered darkly all over to the flying touch of cloud shadows . . . (182)

Despite the wealth of language, this is a place of such desolation that 'the lives of uncounted generations had passed it by' (182) to become the haunt of seabirds 'emitting a strident and cruel uproar' (183). Unknown as yet, and the reason for the narration's visionary evocation, this will be the site – if only we could see it! – of the novella's dénouement. In reading, the passage does its work proleptically in darkly and ironically prefiguring the shipwreck of the tale's end and, as an unrecognised prelude to his discovery, in making Sterne *see*:

> it had been like a revelation to behold for the first time the dangers marked by the hissing livid patches on the water as distinctly as on the engraved paper of a chart ... a clear day, just windy enough for the sea to break on every ledge, buoying, as it were, the channel plainly to the sight; whereas during a calm you had nothing to depend on but the compass and the practised judgement of your eye. (185)

Thinking, indifferently enough, about eyesight and the knowledge it contains or fails to convey, for Sterne these 'were the very last moments of ease he was to know on board the *Sofala*' (186).

My point is, more broadly, that the attention to seeing does not place the reader in a mental interior. Not so much the workings of awareness – that, in Sterne's immediate case, is to come – but the conditions in which a viewer receives images of the world, and the conditioning of 'things themselves' by the medium they inhabit, is here the subject of the writing. Though psychology is involved, this scenic realism draws us, rather, out to the realm of physics. Such a preoccupation with between-ness, with the medium through which things are seen and heard – the so-called 'atmosphere' widely praised in both novelists from the outset – is entirely of a piece with a physics of electromagnetic fields, discussed in Chapter 2, and aphoristically summed up by Donald Benson as 'dematerializing substance while substantiating the immaterial'.[80] This is vividly enacted in the modality with which the passage through Pangu Bay in calmer weather is conceived:

> On such days the luminous sea would give no sign of the dangers lurking on both sides of her path. Everything remained still, crushed by the overwhelming power of the light; and the whole group, opaque in the sunshine – the rocks resembling pinnacles, the rocks resembling spires,

---

[80] Benson, 'Constructing an Ethereal Cosmos', 135.

> the rocks resembling ruins; the forms of islets resembling beehives, resembling mole-hills; the islets recalling the shapes of haystacks, the contours of ivy-clad towers – would stand reflected together upside down in the unwrinkled water, like carved toys of ebony disposed on the silvered plate-glass of a mirror. (184–5)

As so often in Conrad, light does not gently illuminate; it exercises a violent downward force, stilling movement and reducing large forms to reflected 'toys'. It transforms substance – successively imaged as 'the rocks', 'the forms of islets', 'the islets' – into shapes conceived by eyes squinting into the fierce sunlight: pinnacles, spires, ruins, beehives, mole-hills, haystacks and ivy-clad towers. The English landscape that materialises from a reef in the Malacca Strait is formed from inland scenes in the imagination of homesick British seamen, the immaterial made substantial – yet the effect of this 'resembling' and 'recalling' is not to invite a reader into a conceptualising mental space, but to place her in that vibrating space between the eye and the rocks as they shift their forms in an insistence upon an exchange in the realms of physiology and physics. A multiplicity of resemblances is finally stilled to a single image that renders the islets remote and strange in form and texture. The effect is not like that of looking at a picture in its frame, but of being drawn out to an encounter in an indeterminate space with forms that seem to have come adrift from their referents plotted on charts and maps. In *Science and Hypothesis* (1905), Henri Poincaré wrote, 'The aim of science is not things themselves but the relations between things: outside those relations there is no reality knowable.'[81] The knowable reality left with the reader of this paragraph in 'The End of the Tether' is not that of 'the things themselves' but of what Poincaré later terms 'the images that we are forced to put in their place' by the process of seeing.[82]

Evidence in 'The End of the Tether' is inconclusive and belongs to the realm of suggestion. When the *Sofala* traverses Pangu Bay at night,

> All would be still, dumb, almost invisible – but for the blotting out of the low constellations occulted in turns behind the vague masses of the islets whose true outlines eluded the eye amongst the dark spaces of the heaven [*sic*]. (183)

---

[81] Henri Poincaré, *Science and Hypothesis* (1905), xxiv.
[82] Ibid., 161.

'"What the eye has seen is truth!"' declares Arsat passionately in 'The Lagoon',[83] but in 'The End of the Tether' the eye is inadequate, and 'vague masses' only give an impression of their dimensions by what is 'occulted', the astronomical term carrying with it a suggestion of the mysterious and unexplained, secreted in 'the heaven'. It is at this point, too, that other eyes than those on board the *Sofala* radically change the sightlines of the story: 'Sometimes there were human eyes open to watch them come nearer . . . the eyes of a naked fisherman in his canoe . . . A few miserable, half naked families' (183). For these people the *Sofala* is no more real than a 'monthly apparition'; and the activities of their own lives, seen with such beautiful precision, leave the reader quite uncertain about the medium within which they are conducted: 'and the men seemed to hang in the air, they seemed to hang enclosed within the fibres of a dark, sodden log, fishing patiently in a strange, unsteady, pellucid, green air above the shoals' (184). In something of the manner of Paula's storks, these figures visit a story in which they are not required, briefly to transform the reader's sense of where life is carried on and what it can be known to be:

> their lives ran out silently . . . the unbreathing, concentrated calms like the deep introspection of a passionate nature, brooded awfully for days and weeks together over the unchangeable inheritance of their children . . . (184)

Yet 'The End of the Tether' is exactly about lives running out and the inheritance of children; 'the brown figures stooping on the tiny beaches' (184) bear the burden of nature and the 'unchangeable inheritance' that it visits upon their children in a manner that rebukes those who trust in Providence, wills, solicitors or the Manila lottery. In a way that echoes 'Heart of Darkness', the previous tale in the volume, a far greater sense of reality is conveyed by this evocation of their presence than belongs to the carriages and avenues of Singapore.

The seeing that the reader has undergone in this passage out of Pangu Bay brings existence in wind and water vividly before us – but still as something *looked at*; and it has not provided the insight that Sterne seeks. When that revelation arises from something Sterne has seen a hundred times before, the prompt for understanding is not visual. It comes from language, from 'the fancifulness of the

---

[83] Conrad, *Tales of Unrest*, 160.

comparison' that he applies to Captain Whalley and the Serang, who are 'never far apart; a pair of them, *recalling to the mind* an old whale attended by a little pilot-fish' (187, my emphasis). Seeing, if we mean comprehension, depends not so much upon the lens as upon the 'sensitized plate' upon which the light falls, receptors sensitised by culture, inheritance, language, by immediate circumstance, so that 'seeing', for all the impression that we have of it as an instantaneous, naturally given event, has its narrative.[84] For Sterne,

> His captain on his bridge presented himself naturally to his sight. How insignificant, how casual was the thought that had started the train of discovery – like an accidental spark that suffices to ignite the charge of a tremendous mine! (186)

The narrative that transforms a 'sight' into a 'discovery' lasts a full two pages, and culminates in exploring 'the ideas evoked by the sound, by the imagined shape of the word pilot-fish' (187). In a further letter to Garnett two days after the one already quoted about 'short vision', Conrad writes excitedly about the sort of experience he here gives to Sterne:

> Where do you think the illumination – the short and vivid flash of which I have been boasting to you came from? Why! From Your words, words, words. They exploded like stored powder barrels – while another man's words would have fizzed out in speaking and left darkness unrelieved by a forgotten spurt of futile sparks. An explosion is the most lasting thing in the universe. It leaves disorder, remembrance, room to move, a clear space. (*CL* 1:344)

While erosion and abrading belong to Hardy's fictional world, latent combustion is a fundamental condition in Conrad's novels. Sterne feels 'he could blow him [Whalley] up sky-high with six words' (190). And what lasts in reading Hardy's novels are the figures, forms and ways of life that have endured hard treatment, while what lasts from Conrad's novels are the irremediable moments of explosive clearance and evacuation.

Conrad's examination in 'The End of the Tether' of the limited capacity of the eye to see the truth of things is directly complementary

---

[84] Biology confirms the relative unimportance of the lens in the process of seeing. In modern biological terms, seeing happens in the primary visual cortex, a plate of 200 million cells, 2mm thick, with a surface area of a few square inches.

to its scorn of the notion of Providence, which Whalley trusts to light his way. Whalley's Gloucester-like claim to his friend, the refined Van Wyk, that 'You begin to see a lot of things when you are going blind' (223), is only partly borne out by the story. Hans Blumenberg, in his 1957 survey, 'Light as a Metaphor for Truth', describes the medieval 'small room and monastic cell, places where the truth is openly present, an indication that now everything can be expected *from within* . . . caves and chambers in which one can *wait* for the light' (his emphasis).[85] This powerful tradition of chastened introspection operates in Austen, Eliot and James but, I suggest, is almost repudiated by the two writers who attend most to the eye, Hardy and Conrad, in whose fictions illuminating truth is forcibly borne in upon characters from without.[86] And Captain Whalley will need something more external to him than 'the illuminating moments of suffering' to alter course: we are told that 'he came to cling to his deception with a fierce determination to carry it out to the end' (240). When the distance-receptor of sight has failed, Whalley must be assailed more closely and more violently to be enabled to see.

In the complex and incident-packed climax to the lengthily-unfolded tale, it is the fall of the owner/chief engineer Massy's lead-weighted jacket, which 'struck the deck heavily with a dull thump' (244), that produces the elucidation which can only come (when sight guarantees nothing) from the absolute verification of touch: 'Captain Whalley fell on his knees, with groping hands extended in a frank gesture of blindness. They trembled, these hands feeling for the truth. He saw it. Iron near the compass' (244). His first 'frank gesture' for many pages produces the truth of Massy's machinations to hole the ship and collect the insurance money. However, Whalley's final 'flash of insight' (246) does not illuminate; it merely confirms that 'The light had ebbed for ever out of the world' (245), as he perceives that his own dishonest course has inextricably entangled himself with the criminal designs of Massy.

Blumenberg concludes his great encomium on the metaphoric values that have been attributed to light: 'Light remains what it is while letting the infinite participate in it; it is consumption without loss. Light produces space, distance, orientation, calm contemplation; it is the gift that makes no demands, the illumination capable

---

[85] Blumenberg, 'Light as a Metaphor for Truth', 38.
[86] In this regard, the capacity to direct their lives by inner reflection make Elizabeth-Jane and Emilia Gould unusual in Hardy's and Conrad's respective fictional worlds.

of conquering without force.'[87] If the eye, as we have seen, is the agent and creature of appetite, light is here offered as the plenitude where the spirit can range without consuming, where dimension can be understood without a coercive teleology. It is an idealisation without which neither Hardy nor Conrad would have produced the novels they did; but these same novels show that what the human eye in practice does with the limited visible spectrum on which it can seize leaves its owners yearning into the light for something of greater promise. To have taken two fictions with a comic resolution by Hardy, and two tragic ones by Conrad, has perhaps placed that promise apparently closer to hand for the characters who operate within the rich visual observation of Hardy's novels than for those who fall within the compass of Conrad's more astringent visual imagination. It is a promise latent in light's powers of enabling, revealing, and conferring a natural and delighted place for the human eye within an intelligible and purposive world; but in none of these novels is the imagined covenant fulfilled.

---

[87] Blumenberg, 'Light as a Metaphor for Truth', 38.

Chapter Four

An Audible World

> the means of access, the media through which the impressions of light and sound are received, ether in the one case, air in the other, constitute a fundamental difference in the sort of material, so to speak, which the external world presents to the two higher senses.[1]
>
> Edmund Gurney, *The Power of Sound* (1880)

In *The Soundscape* Murray Schafer writes, 'The eye points outward: the ear draws inward. It soaks up information. Wagner said: "To the eye appeals the outer man, the inner to the ear."'[2] Just as the previous chapter showed Hardy and Conrad exhibiting light as entity, agent and medium, this chapter examines varied uses of sound in their fiction. However, there are some interesting contrasts in physics and physiology between sound and audition that locate this enquiry in a distinctly more contested dimension than its visual equivalent. A recent book by the acoustic scientist Seth Horowitz designates hearing 'the universal sense', and asserts how much older and more fundamental it is than the other senses. Hearing operates four and a half times faster than sight even though light is 900,000 times faster than sound through air.[3] And yet, despite the speed and precision of hearing, to sound belong the issues of location, transmission and constitution that make its airborne condition mysterious and so often suggestive of a hidden 'within' from which it emanates and to which,

---

[1] The modern physics of this difference is succinctly explained by Frank Wilczek, *A Beautiful Question: Finding Nature's Deep Design* (2015), 157/8.
[2] R. Murray Schafer, *The Soundscape: Our Sonic Environment and the Tuning of the World* (originally published as *The Tuning of the World*, 1977) (1994), 11. More recently, the social anthropologist Tim Ingold has advanced cogent objections to the concept of 'soundscape', in *Being Alive* (2011), 136–9.
[3] Seth Horowitz, *The Universal Sense: How Hearing Shapes the Mind* (2012).

slowly, it travels. As Don Ihde puts it in *Listening and Voice*, 'An inquiry into the auditory is also an inquiry into the invisible.'[4] This mysterious invisibility in the power of sound provided, in the nineteenth century, a continuity with those qualities ascribed to the ether which were prominent in the previous chapter. Wordsworth's 1828 poem, 'On the Power of Sound', opens

> Thy functions are ethereal
> As if within thee dwelt a glancing mind,
> Organ of vision![5]

not only attributing to the ear a swift independent intelligence with which to unite the furthest reaches to an understanding 'within', but also in its glance, and in the apostrophe itself, ennobling the ear by conferring upon it the capacity for 'vision'. The ambitious empiricism of John Tyndall, in the first of his popular series of lectures, *Sound* (1867), sets out a programme literally to envision the medium the ear 'sees' when he proposes, 'we must endeavour to form a definite image of a wave of sound'.[6] Picturing a wave of sound is what both Hardy and Conrad often do, entering thereby a disputed territory, in which what is fleeting seeks by the very power of its invisibility to extend its domain to a more lasting permanence than the simply visible.[7]

Works already discussed show us both writers giving visible form to sound in ways that are characteristic of their differences, but which also establish a significant similarity. They like to release sounds from their sources to observe the aerial and temporal flight of phenomena in ways that unsettle habitual relations. The church clock in Weatherbury strikes eleven, and after the distinct whirr and click of the clock-work in the empty air,

> The notes flew forth with the usual blind obtuseness of inanimate things – flapping and rebounding among walls, undulating against the scattered clouds, spreading through their interstices into unexplored miles of space. (265)

---

[4] Don Ihde, *Listening and Voice: Phenomenologies of Sound* (2007), 51.
[5] Wordsworth, *Poetical Works* (1965), 185. The poem was set to music as a cantata by Arthur Somervell in 1894.
[6] John Tyndall, *Sound* (5th edition, 1893), 5. Tyndall venerated Wordsworth, fervently quoting 'Tintern Abbey' to close the famous 'Belfast Address' of 1874.
[7] Gillian Beer suggests a historical sequence in nineteenth-century idealisations of light and sound, in which 'Sound began to assume the status as ideal function that sight had earlier held' ('Authentic Tidings of Invisible Things', in Jay and Brennan eds, *Vision in Context*, 1996, 91).

The ungainly aerial journey of these acoustic individuals transports the reader into dimensions far from their parochial origins in *Far From the Madding Crowd*. Lingard, in *The Rescue*, listening from his brig for a sound of oars in the surrounding darkness, gives his order to the Serang to 'have the hands turned up':

> Suddenly, above the dull and confused noises a long shrill whistle soared, reverberated loudly amongst the flat surfaces of motionless sails, and died out, gradually as if the sound had escaped and gone away, running upon the water. (26)

Nothing anchors the weirdness of the sound to a definite point of production or human purpose, and finally it is released somewhat humorously into its own activity of 'running upon the water'. As in so much of Hardy too, the changed and enlarged sense of space that the reader is left with directs attention to the dynamics of energy in a medium more immediately than to changed states of consciousness in characters. And for all the precise observation devoted to these acoustics, something indeterminable remains which seems to be in the nature of the medium. We hear this in Tyndall's *Sound*, where the confident definition of sound with which he opens his lectures reveals the ontological uncertainty that persists behind declared empirical certainties: 'The sound of an explosion is propagated as a wave or pulse through the air. This wave impinging upon the tympanic membrane causes it to shiver, its tremors are transmitted through the drum to the auditory nerve to the brain, where it announces itself as sound.'[8] A definition that concludes with 'sound' being 'announce[d]' in the brain starts with 'The *sound* of an explosion' already announced, leaving it entirely unclear as to *where* 'sound' is, and *what* it is. One might reflect that 'to make you hear' will always involve the writer and the reader in entities and dimensions more doubtful even than those which pertain 'to mak[ing] you *see*'.

Whether in an English village or market town, on board ship or in a small Malay settlement, Hardy and Conrad both find their fictional beginnings in worlds in which an audible summons or voice of command can impose its presence upon the imagined aerial dimension. Alain Corbin's outstanding study of acoustic ambience in nineteenth-century France, *Village Bells*, provides a rich social counterpart to the fiction of both writers. When Corbin suggests that 'bells shaped

---

[8] Tyndall, *Sound*, 43.

the habitus of a community or, if you will, its culture of the senses. They served to anchor localism, imparting depth to the desire for rootedness and offering the peace of near, well-defined horizons', it provokes the realisation that such a conserved space is always receding or threatened in Hardy's novels.[9] Hardy rarely locates the intensity of his drama at the centre of communities, but more frequently on those horizons from which characters sometimes listen for the sounds of a settled life left behind, those margins to which Boldwood or Henchard or Winterborne or Tess are impelled. At the end of *Jude*, 'The bells struck out joyously; and their reverberations travelled round the bedroom';[10] to the reader positioned by Jude's coffin these Remembrance Week celebrations sound only the note of exclusion, one that had a complex resonance throughout Hardy's own life. The 'culture of the senses' from which Conrad draws so much of his earlier fiction has its origins elsewhere, with the effect of a more radical estrangement from 'well-defined horizons'.[11] The most penetrating and the most lasting sound of Conrad's life reached his ears early in the voyage of the *Mont-Blanc* in December 1874, when, as he says in *The Mirror of the Sea*, 'I listened for the first time with the curiosity of my tender years to the song of the wind in a ship's rigging':

> The monotonous and vibrating note was destined to grow into the intimacy of the heart, pass into blood and bone, accompany the thoughts and acts of two full decades, remain to haunt like a reproach the peace of the quiet fireside, and enter into the very texture of respectable dreams, dreamed safely under a roof of rafter and tiles. (153)

Written when he was forty-seven, a year after he had completed his labours on *Nostromo*, these lines recall the soundmark of an earlier professional life that persists to disturb Conrad's middle age.[12] The legacy of that former life is not envisaged as the outspread calm of

---

[9] Alain Corbin, *Village Bells: Sound and Meaning in the Nineteenth-Century French Countryside* (1999), 96.

[10] Thomas Hardy, *Jude the Obscure* (ed. Sisson, 1984), 490.

[11] No commentary, however, explains with such clarity and feeling the rural silences that pervade *The Rover*, with its post-Jacobin setting in 1804, as Corbin's account of the historical rupture of the Revolutionary years enacted in the silencing of church bells.

[12] A soundmark, to recur to Murray Schafer's terms, is a sound 'specially regarded or noticed by people in that community' (*The Soundscape*, 11).

something looked back upon, but as the 'spoil' of a handful of letters of recommendation written by shipmasters:

> They rustle, those bits of paper – some dozen of them in all. In that faint, ghostly sound there live the memories of twenty years, the voices of rough men now no more, the strong voice of the everlasting winds, and the whisper of a mysterious spell, the murmur of the great sea, which must have somehow reached my inland cradle and entered my unconscious ear.[13]

When contemplating his own experiences it would seem, rather than remembered sights, it is remembered sounds that stir Conrad to an awareness of what his life has been, in a vocabulary of voices, whispers and murmurs, familiar from his fiction.

Hardy and Conrad are distinguished as novelists for their interest in the constitution of sound itself.[14] Part of the appeal is that sound, in its temporal and impermanent nature, questions ontological certainty. As the philosopher Mark S. Muldoon says memorably of auditory qualities, 'They only exist in going out of existence.' He continues, 'By their very nature, auditory qualities are impermanent and do not qualify as particulars in a classical atomistic sense. They do not fall into the Newtonian world view with its logic of solid bodies.'[15] Hardy and Conrad consciously adhere to Newtonian laws, but also express a counter-intuition of a world of energies and fields. It is as if, in fictional writing, both writers want to hold on to these sounds by giving them location and particular form, even as they are ever becoming different forms of motion. With the moon shining through the window after the long scene of the two Cythereas in bed together in *Desperate Remedies*, the younger woman recalls to her vision an earlier moonlit scene, 'But sounds were in the ascendant that night. Her ears became aware of a strange and gloomy murmur' (86). The nomination of 'sounds' at the beginning of the sentence, and the angular adverbial phrase 'in the ascendant', makes 'sounds' starkly the subject here, with physics becoming physiology

---

[13] Joseph Conrad, *The Mirror of the Sea & A Personal Record* (1988), 110.

[14] Michael Irwin's chapter, 'Noises in Hardy's Novels', in *Reading Hardy's Landscapes* (2000), 37–61, offers an excellent survey of the novels' representation of 'Hardy's instinctive interest in sound for its own sake' (61). I don't know of an equivalent survey yet published on Conrad.

[15] Mark S. Muldoon: 'Silence Revisited: Taking the Sight out of Auditory Qualities', *Review of Metaphysics* 50:2 (1996), 279.

in the progression of subject to 'Her ears' in the succeeding sentence. There follow two pages of minute dissection of just-audible phenomena as Cytherea 'was in the mood for sounds of every kind now, and strained her ears to catch the faintest, in wayward enmity to her quiet of mind' (86). Her efforts to interpret and visualise the source of these noises is written so that it is the auditory scene, not Cytherea's mental state, that is the subject of the chapter, permitting Hardy's description to reveal a fundamental difference between sight and sound – that we treat sounds other than voiced language and music as the *sign* of something rather than the thing itself.[16] This characteristic of our hearing becomes the subject of a tense moment in Conrad's collaboration with Ford Madox Ford, *Romance* (1903). A chapter we know Conrad to have written, opens, 'Silence, stillness, breathless caution were the absolute conditions of our existence',[17] and concerns the attempt by the central pair, John Kemp and Seraphina, to escape by boat in thick fog to an English ship out in the bay whilst in the vicinity of an unseen cluster of enemy boats. They have little idea where they are in the fog, when suddenly the brigands' leader, Manuel, blows a shrill whistle:

> We are always inclined to trust our eyes rather than our ears; and such is the conventional temper in which we receive the impression of our senses, that I had no idea they were so near us. The destruction of my illusory feeling of distance was the most startling thing in the world.

In comparison to the Hardy passage, Kemp's observation here moves the attention to an analysis of sensational reception: as we have observed before, while Hardy so often concerns himself with a feeling out into the world, Conrad more frequently dramatizes an impact in the other direction, as the exterior world assails his characters' senses. Both writers concede the 'conventional' primacy of visual over auditory interpretation while placing their characters in an auditory world, one that amplifies problems in the theory of sound that are even more disputed today than they were in the nineteenth century – direction, location and loudness.

---

[16] It will be appreciated that the argument is different from that of the previous chapter, which suggested that what Helmholtz and others had shown to provide *signs*, that is, sight, is generally taken to present the thing itself.
[17] Joseph Conrad and Ford Madox Hueffer, *Romance* (1909), 229. The later quotations are drawn from pages 238 and 239.

From the mid-century, when scientific accounts began to dissolve matter and force into energy, and Newton's instantaneous action-at-a-distance was replaced by temporal transmission through a medium, an intense interest in *medium*, to which Hardy's and Conrad's novels so distinctively belong, encouraged a view of sound not as an entity but, like light and heat, a mode of motion. As with light and vision, it would appear that the 1860s was a decisive decade, seeing not only Tyndall's lectures, published in 1867, but also Helmholtz's *On the Sensations of Tone* in 1862, which received wide dissemination through references in periodical literature.[18] Two broad theories of sound and hearing competed during this period – as they continue to do. The older view, derived from Locke, is that sound is a secondary property of objects, like colour, shape and size. This position continues to have its proponents, notably Robert Pasnau, who writes,

> we should think of sounds as existing within the object that 'makes' them. (Strictly, on my view, we should say that objects *have* sounds.) Instead of identifying sound with the vibration of air molecules (or any other medium), I propose identifying sound with the vibrations of the object that has the sound.[19]

Pasnau characterises as 'the standard view' of science a theory of sound as longitudinal pressure waves which directly opposes this 'property view', and which is clearly to be associated, in the Victorian period, with Helmholtz, Hertz, Tyndall, James Sully and many others. Most modern philosophies of sound – for example, those of Matthew Nudds, Roy Sorenson and Brian O'Shaughnessy – embrace a wave theory that sees motion through time as essential to their accounts: at an extreme, Nudds claims, 'According to common sense tutored by science, sounds just are travelling waves.'[20] It is difficult to align Hardy's or Conrad's writing fully and precisely with either the 'property view' or the 'wave view'; like many writers on sound they are, in fact, eclectic, and different passages imply different conceptions. But what is clear is that both were writing during a period

---

[18] Mark Asquith has provided us with an invaluable analysis of nine leading periodicals' contribution to the culture of the senses in the auditory sphere (*Thomas Hardy: Metaphysics and Music*, 2005, 9–11).
[19] Robert Pasnau, 'What Is Sound?', *Philosophical Quarterly* 49:156 (1999), 316.
[20] Matthew Nudds and Casey O'Callaghan eds, *Sounds and Perception: New Philosophical Essays* (2009), 7.

when interest in sound was moving from its production and transmission to its reception.[21] One of Helmholtz's most significant series of experiments, reported in *On the Sensations of Tone*, was to show that each filament in the fibres of Corti (discovered in the cochlear partition in the inner ear by Alfonso Corti in 1851) is 'a tiny resonator each one tuned to a different frequency' as Georg von Békésy later summarised it, affirming that 'The resonance theory of Helmholtz is probably the most elegant of all theories of hearing.'[22] The reduction of the world to the perceptions of an organism, so typical of a century whose new science is that of psychology, finds its auditory complement in very specific research into the ear: as Békésy says, 'By the end of the nineteenth century many theories had arisen regarding the process of hearing, and attention had become focused upon the hair cells and their enclosing structures.'[23] 'The process of hearing', as delicately recorded in the novels of Hardy and Conrad as the process of seeing, draws inward to such minutiae; but the intense interest in *transmission* which so distinctively characterises these novels means that the exterior world is not attenuated in presence or importance as it is in the hushed world of a more complete sensationist, such as J. K. Huysmans, whose hero Des Esseintes, in *À Rebours*, avers 'Nature has had her day.'[24]

On the Sensations of Tone pursues for several pages a delightful and very Hardyan evocation of 'mutually overtopping and crossing' waves of the sea 'viewed from a lofty cliff', by which Helmholtz leads us to his central point about audition:

> But the ear is much more unfavourably situated in relation to a system of waves of sound, than the eye for a system of waves of water. . . . The ear is therefore in nearly the same condition as the eye would be if it looked at one point of the surface of the water through a long narrow tube, which would permit of seeing its rising and falling, and were then required to undertake an analysis of the compound waves. It is easily seen that the eye would, in most cases, completely fail in the solution of such a problem.[25]

---

[21] For an extended discussion of this tendency, see Benjamin Steege's fine study of attention, *Helmholtz and the Modern Listener* (2012), especially 60ff.

[22] Georg von Békésy, *Experiments in Hearing* (1960), 404.

[23] Ibid., 14. Between 1924 and 1928 Békésy subjected Helmholtz's theories in this area to further experiment, finding that his mentor's readings of frequency did not stand scrutiny.

[24] J. K. Huysmans, *Against the Grain* (1969; *À Rebours*, 1884), 22.

[25] Hermann von Helmholtz, *On the Sensations of Tone as a Physiological Basis for the Theory of Music* (1998), 44/5.

But Helmholtz also calculated that human hearing extends over a range of nearly ten octaves; while the very small visible spectrum of the electromagnetic field only permits to human sight a span equivalent to one octave, if calculated in the same way according to frequency.[26] This way of seeing the perceptual situation for eye and ear is very much to the point for a study of two novelists whose visual sense is readily appreciated, but whose auditory sense draws fewer comments.[27] Helmholtz's attitude to the ear's achievements is echoed by Tyndall when he considers its interaction with the aerial medium which bears 'sound':

> And the most wonderful thing of all is, that the human ear, though acted on only by a cylinder of that air, which does not exceed the thickness of a quill, can detect the components of the motion, and, by an act of attention, can even isolate from the aerial entanglement any particular sound.[28]

Such 'auditory scene analysis', to use the title of Albert S. Bregman's influential technical study, places the listener in an arena which asks of his faculties question after question: 'How many people are talking? Which one is louder, or closer? Is there a machine humming in the background?'[29] Despite the frequent accuracy of the answers, uncertainty is the familiar aspect of auditory experience – and that, of course, is its attractiveness to writers who explore how man seeks to locate and define himself amid the impersonal forces of the world. The auditory scenes in Hardy and Conrad reach as deeply into a sensational experience of the world as do their visual scenes, are more unsettling, and, like the ear itself, less easily closed. Sight places a scene in front of the viewer; hearing immerses the listener in it as it surrounds him in the air. If sight is, as the last chapter suggested, frequently corrosive, the circumambient sounds of these novels take possession of the whole organism more completely.

---

[26] See John Henshaw, *A Tour of the Senses* (2012), 25.

[27] Among those who have discussed auditory qualities at some length are Michael Irwin (2000), John Hughes (2001), Mark Asquith (2005) in Hardy; Aaron Fogel (1985), Ivan Kreilkamp (1997), Patricia Pye (2007) and Adam Parkes (2011) in Conrad, all itemised in the Bibliography.

[28] Tyndall, *Sound*, 362. Helmholtz's and Tyndall's accounts of sound reception are made violently immediate by Conrad describing Martin Ricardo's whistle, 'which seemed to drive a thin, sharp shaft of air solidly against one's nearest ear-drum' (*Victory*, 317).

[29] The questions are taken from Bregman's delightful allegory of deciphering sounds by means of purely visual signals by the side of a lake: *Auditory Scene Analysis* (1990), 5–6.

I consider here first *The Return of the Native* and 'Heart of Darkness', both of which stand at the threshold of their authors' full expression of a tragic sensibility, each distinctively evoking an oppressively enveloping environment through auditory means. In contrast, I then take the percussive soundworld of *Nostromo* to explore how depiction of economic, social and political change generates a new auditory fabric of noise in Conrad's prose. *Nostromo*'s partner-novel in the construction of a dynamic civic world, *The Mayor of Casterbridge*, will feature in the next chapter to show the more psychological uses into which Hardy was led by his attention to audition.

1 Sonic Imaging
The Return of the Native and 'Heart of Darkness'

The first sounds positively impressed upon the reader of *The Return of the Native* arrive in chapter 2 through the silence that follows the good evening bidden between Captain Vye and Diggory Venn, as Venn leads his van along the lonely chalk road that branches across Egdon:

> There were no sounds but that of the booming wind upon the stretch of tawny herbage around them, the crackling wheels, the tread of the men, and the footsteps of the two shaggy ponies which drew the van. (14)[30]

It is almost ironic that a sentence devoted to the evocation of four finite sounds is introduced by the declaration 'There were no sounds', but the phrase plays its part in making these sounds the property of the scene rather than of the hearing of the two men who are in the midst of them. Hardy's summoning of auditory experience, without ascribing it to the acute hearing of his two characters, conveys simultaneously the intent identification and placing that sounds ask of listeners, and also their escape into suggestions that are not wholly placeable. While the 'crackling wheels' sharply concentrates the ear upon the precise sound of the moment, the felloes' bumping on the

---

[30] All references to *The Return of the Native* are to the 1990 Oxford World's Classics edition, edited by Simon Gatrell. The copy-text for this edition is the surviving manuscript and the revisions incorporated into the Smith, Elder first edition of 1878.

chalk surface of the road, the 'booming wind on the stretch of tawny herbage' provides an ever-surrounding keynote that amplifies the scene outwards, rather than bears down upon the men absorbed in it.[31] The 'footsteps' of the ponies suggests something more humanly and delicately picking its way among the chalk scree than the deliberate and dogged 'tread' of the men. In an unremarkable sentence, Hardy brings before the reader the precisions and indeterminacies of the auditory world, an acute sensory registration and an impersonal extension to an indefinite cognitive horizon that permits the novel to replay gestures familiar since antiquity and yet also exhibit a fine particularity. So, after a few unreported remarks, Captain Vye and Diggory Venn slip back into silence again and continue walking together as 'in these lonely places ... contiguity amounts to a tacit conversation ... where not to put an end to it is intercourse in itself' (14). Such a studied care of formal statement, at a deliberate idiomatic distance from the two characters, leaves the reader with the substance of the silence as some sort of elusive entity rather than with any knowledge about the characters themselves. To be left between immediate phenomena and custom (the next chapter is called 'The Custom of the Country') is so often the effect of this novel.

In the novel's encompassing auditory realisation, custom visits the heath with a different music from that with which it is invested by wind and vegetation, though one that is intimately related. The Fifth of November festival, the mumming, and the August 'gipsying' at East Egdon are full of the sounds of human jollity and resistance to the surrounding sameness and indifference that ultimately reduces voices to silence and habitation to grassed-over mounds.[32] This is the joy of sheer noise: there is no appeal to permanent moral values, just as there are no normative modes of living the novel is committed to. Timothy Fairway whirls Susan Nunsuch, 'a woman noisily constructed', over the sparks of the dying bonfire:

> The chief noises were women's shrill cries, men's laughter, Susan's stays and pattens, Olly Dowden's 'heu-heu-heu!' and the strumming of the wind upon the furze-bushes, which formed a kind of tune of the demoniac measure they trod. (33)

---

[31] Murray Schafer's term: 'the keynote sounds of a landscape are those created by its geography and climate: water, wind, forests, plains, birds, insects and animals' (*The Soundscape*, 9).

[32] It is well known how important for Hardy was his reading of E. B. Tylor's *Primitive Culture* (1871). Andrew Radford explores this in *Thomas Hardy and the Survivals of Time* (2003), 28.

The noises sound out on the night, finding brief concordance with the under-drone which is also their antagonist, and their meaning is simply this assertion of a clamour to match briefly the enduring note of attrition.[33] The 'yell for yell' traded with 'a westerly gale' by the seamen of the *Narcissus* represents an ethic that can be adhered to, the work of getting the ship through; but one cannot *live* a 'demoniac measure', and the attempt to wrest a living from the unyielding ground of the heath (as opposed to wringing out 'a meaning from our sinful lives' as *The Nigger* has it, more metaphysically (129)), which is embodied in 'Wildeve's Patch', sounds out a different and more subtle relationship between the heath and its human inhabitants.

Thus when Mrs Yeobright and Thomasin approach the Quiet Woman after the postponed marriage,

> The water at the back of the house could be heard, idly spinning whirlpools in its creep between the rows of dry feather-headed reeds which formed a stockade along each bank. Their presence was denoted by sounds as of a congregation praying humbly, produced by their rubbing against each other in the slow wind. (44)

This rare and haunting acoustic simile quietly concentrates a sense of the always present, always receding quality of keynote sounds. The reader is led beyond the two women's immediate presence in the scene as auditory focalisers to a more intense but less determinately placed sense of *listening*, in which the narrator's role in what 'could be heard' has been characterised comprehensively by J. Hillis Miller in *Thomas Hardy: Distance and Desire*:

> At a distance in time and yet present as the events occur, a cold observer, spatially detached, seeing without being seen, and yet at the same time able to share the feelings of the characters, see with their eyes, and hear with their ears – a paradoxical combination of proximity and distance, presence and absence, sympathy and coldness, characterizes the narrator whose role Hardy plays . . . . This odd form of inherence in the world . . . is present in one form or another in every paragraph Hardy wrote.[34]

---

[33] See Mark Asquith's examination of this scene and the songs sung in it by Grandfer Cantle (*Metaphysics and Music*, 107–10).

[34] J. Hillis Miller, *Thomas Hardy: Distance and Desire* (1970), 55–6. Another brilliant characterisation of Hardy's narrator which is apt here is that of John Bayley: 'his presence is the reverse of a *persona*: he is a landscape of kinds of mutually oblivious intentness, constituting his intellectual being, his *animula*' (*An Essay on Hardy*, 1978, 194).

It is present in this particular paragraph, above all, in the suggestiveness afforded by the phrase 'as of a congregation praying humbly' that exceeds the careful recording of what 'produced' it. While it contains a visual transference of the bowed heads of the reeds, its main effect is to lead beyond immediate visual equivalence to a sense of ordered submission and supplication conducted through the tradition of centuries of Christian worship, quite at odds with the customary Promethean rebellion on Blackbarrow that Mrs Yeobright has just left. If the image of the congregation is an image of an accepted defeat for the spirit of cultivation in the face of the pagan tract, it also speaks of persistence, defensiveness and a sort of brotherhood as the rows of reeds 'formed a stockade' and rubbed 'against each other'. Sounds thus set up for the reader of *The Return of the Native* disturbances identical to those which trouble modern philosophies of sound, particularly those which question where sound is located and what it tells us about location. To know where the reeds' sound was 'produced' does not tell the reader where 'Their presence was denoted', where *that* sound is. But what Hardy's writing does do is to fasten upon the reader's ear the sensation of being in the air which conveys these sounds, here – as Conrad often does – by taking leave of naturalistic description and the expected auditory perspective.

However, just as 'To dwellers in a wood', as the opening phrase of *Under the Greenwood Tree* has it, 'almost every species of tree has its voice as well as its feature', so to dwellers on a heath sound as well as sight *can* produce 'intelligible facts regarding landscape' (*Native* 11). Whatever makes its way through the medium of an atmosphere is subject to scientific attention from Hardy: so, as the bonfire on Blackbarrow sinks low along with the other Fifth of November fires, the narrative comment claims that 'Attentive observation of their brightness, colour, and length of existence would have revealed the quality of the material burnt; and through that, to some extent, the natural produce of the district in which each bonfire was situate' (31).[35] In a moment that seems designed to provide a precise transfer to the auditory sense, Wildeve observes to Eustacia, 'How mournfully the wind blows round us now!'

> She did not answer. Its tone was indeed solemn and pervasive. Compound utterances addressed themselves to their senses, and it was possible to view by ear the features of the neighbourhood. Acoustic pictures were

---

[35] See Anna Henchman, *The Starry Sky Within* (2014), 136–42, for a very good account of the bonfires and the nineteenth-century visual science of spectroscopy.

returned from the darkened scenery: they could hear where the tracts of heather began and ended; where the furze was growing stalky and tall; where it had been recently cut; in what direction the fir-clump lay, and how near was the pit in which the hollies grew; for these differing features had their voices no less than their shapes and colours. (84)

The modality in the phrase 'it was possible' extends the occasion of this hearing to countless other moments of standing in the middle of the heath. Eustacia and Wildeve may both profess their hatred of the heath, yet the paragraph reveals how attuned they are by it to an acute receptivity. But for all the precision of information that matches what is revealed to the surveying eye, there is a different quality to the orientation which is well captured by Steven Connor writing about the difference between sight and sound in *Dumbstruck*: 'A world apprehended primarily through hearing, or in which hearing predominates, is much more dynamic, intermittent, complex, and indeterminate. Where the eye works in governed and explicated space, the ear imparts implicated space.'[36] That access to a sensory reception which is both intermittent and multi-directional is perfectly represented in the syntax of Hardy's long sentence, with its five short gusts of information asking auditory readjustment on the part of the reader. Hardy's 'acoustic pictures' have, of course, occasioned a great deal of comment, but Connor's incisive final insight about imparting 'implicated space' returns us to the complete statement, 'Acoustic pictures were returned from the darkened scenery', with an enhanced feeling of the echo-sound of return through intervening darkness proposing the opening of the auditory field upon imagined space. As Don Ihde says, 'The field is what is present, but present as implicit ... The field is the specific form of "opening" I have to the World.'[37]

Hardy manages this aural 'opening' upon the world in ways that are outlandish and yet are close to Helmholtz's celebration of the ear's ability to summon so wide a vision through so small an orifice. The whole episode of the meeting of these heath-listeners is itself listened to by Diggory Venn, both comically and somewhat sinisterly having crawled close enough to overhear by completely covering himself in turves 'as though he burrowed underground' (81) and become the ears of the heath itself. When he emerges after Eustacia and Wildeve have departed and walks back across to his cart, his spirits 'perturbed to aching' (85) on behalf of Thomasin, Hardy continues to insist upon

---

[36] Steven Connor, *Dumbstruck: A Cultural History of Ventriloquism* (2000), 18.
[37] Ihde, *Listening and Voice*, 73.

the embodiment of sound in air in a manner that brings the reader bizarrely close to the material process of the reddleman's muttered threat: 'The breezes that blew around his mouth in that walk carried off upon them the accents of a commination' (85). These small but frequent occasions when hearing, or sound itself, is called into more than usual prominence do not direct the plot of *The Return of the Native*, which is more determined by the impulses expressed in the courses that feet take upon Egdon's paths; however, they make the air breathed on Egdon dense with possibility and uncertainty, without which the plot of intersections and conjunctions might have become diagrammatic.[38]

The most celebrated and extended evocation of sounds borne upon the Egdon breeze is occasioned by Eustacia, waiting upon the bank at Mistover Knap to hear whether her brightly burning bonfire has summoned up Wildeve to her on what should have been his wedding day. William Cohen begins his beautifully observed examination of the scene by stating, 'While Clym is principally associated with vision and its failures in the novel, Eustacia is often linked to hearing.'[39] In fact, Hardy's manuscript entitles chapter 6 'Old chords are effectively touched',[40] though the revision towards the optical in the more familiar 'The Figure against the Sky' shows Hardy's concern to impress upon the reader the visual organisation of an extraordinary opening sequence which extends itself over eight chapters. But at this point the geometric conception of Eustacia as 'the pivot of this circle of heath-country' (54) gives way to a less defined one of her as an aural conduit as Hardy conjectures, 'It might reasonably have been supposed that she was listening to the wind' (54). That familiar modality, used by Hardy to preserve the sense that as interior networks of thought and feeling people can only be guessed at, is the prelude towards a means of drawing inwards towards Eustacia that deliberately resists inwardness, and that secures our ear for the *scenic* moment, leaving Eustacia herself distant.

The wind 'laid hold of the attention. The wind, indeed, seemed made for the scene, as the scene seemed made for the hour' (54). As a

---

[38] The most significant single term in the novel is 'course(s)', and much attention is devoted to following paths across the heath: 'the whole secret of following these incipient paths . . . lay in the development of the sense of touch in the feet, which comes of years of night-rambling in little-trodden spots' (57). See Robert Macfarlane, *The Old Ways* (2012), for the idea of 'footfall as knowledge'. He traces the verb *to learn* back to *liznojan*, 'to follow or to find a track' (31).
[39] William Cohen, *Embodied: Victorian Literature and the Senses* (2009), 94–8.
[40] See the facsimile edition by Simon Gatrell (1986), 72.

way of approaching Eustacia's innermost feelings, then, Hardy takes the intriguing and troubling uncertainties of sound itself – location, travel through the air, source – to trace a particular note back to its tiny and remote origin, through three paragraphs that begin by registering a special tone that 'could be heard nowhere else':

> Gusts in innumerable series followed each other from the north-west, and when each of them raced past the sound of its progress resolved into three. Treble, tenor, and bass notes were to be found therein. The general ricochet of the whole over pits and prominences had the gravest pitch of the chime. Next there could be heard the baritone buzz of a holly tree. Below these in force, above them in pitch, a dwindled voice strove hard at a husky tune – which was the peculiar local sound alluded to. Thinner and less immediately traceable than the other two, it was far more impressive than either. In it lay what may be called the linguistic peculiarity of the heath; and being audible nowhere on earth off a heath, it afforded a shadow of reason for the woman's tenseness, which continued as unbroken as ever. (55)

In two ways this description is intent upon an attention very much of its time. Undoubtedly, it rests upon a wave theory of sound, such as that proposed by Helmholtz and popularised by Tyndall, in which sound is always conceived of as a motion of the air.[41] The gusts of wind *are* the sound, as the sound of each gust's progress is what is heard and analysed into notes to become the vocalisation of the landscape. Helmholtz writes, 'The motions proceeding from the sounding bodies are usually conducted to our ear by means of the atmosphere. The particles of air must also execute periodically recurrent vibrations, in order to excite the sensation of musical tone in our ear.'[42] And this final phrase indicates a second way in which Hardy's description is pre-modernist: the conversion here of sound to music is entirely in accord with the many pages spent by Helmholtz and Edmund Gurney in distinguishing between music and mere noise,

---

[41] See 'Analogy in the Theory of Undulations', in William Stanley Jevons's *The Principles of Science* (1874), for a contemporary discussion of the use of waves as an analogy, and its success as an explanatory tool, which shows how it became the dominant mode of description for sound (originally by Newton) and then light and heat (vol. II, 293–7).

[42] Helmholtz, *On the Sensations of Tone*, 13. James Clerk Maxwell in The Rede Lecture at Cambridge for 1878 praises *On the Sensations of Tone* in a metaphor that is striking in the light of Hardy's novel of the same year: 'Helmholtz, by a series of daring strides, has effected a passage for himself over the untrodden wild between acoustics and music' (*Nature* 18:449, 6 June 1878, 163).

to the elevation of the former. In practice, however, 'treble', 'tenor', 'bass', 'chime', 'baritone' and 'tune' could stand as Hardy's rebuke to Gurney's strict interpretation of musical embodiment in his assertion that, 'Among the sounds of inanimate nature, though many of them are agreeable and impressive, there is not a vestige of form, scarcely even a vestige of the tone-material out of which forms are built.'[43] The emergence of musical form and the patient auditory tracking of its constitution to material substance is exactly what Hardy is describing here. The suggestion of song in 'a dwindled voice strove hard at a husky tune' will be made explicit in the next paragraph, in the most memorable phrase of the whole passage. Though thin, this sound is 'impressive' in the contemporary scientific use of the word, and, in a novel whose first visual statement is the chapter heading 'A Face on Which Time Makes But Little Impression', the reader waits to feel the acoustic impress of this small indigenous sound.

The next two paragraphs, in which we do so, are among Hardy's great achievements in the novel in their simultaneous listening outwards towards an acoustic horizon, and inward to the touched interior of a single organism. The aerial retention of the material basis of sounds, and the successively deeper apprehension into which the listener is drawn, is carried on a rhythmic prose in which each sentence casts forward to a new sensory experience without abandoning the basis of an almost scientific explanatory discourse:

> Throughout the blowing of these plaintive November winds, that note bore a great resemblance to the ruins of human song which remain to the throat of fourscore and ten. It was a worn whisper, dry and papery, and it brushed so distinctly across the ear that, by the accustomed, the material minutiae in which it originated could be realized as by touch. It was the united products of infinitesimal vegetable causes, and these were neither stems nor twigs, neither leaves nor fruit, neither blades nor prickles, neither lichen nor moss.[44]
>
> They were the mummied heath-bells of the past summer, originally tender and purple, now washed colourless by Michaelmas rains, and dried to dead skins by October suns. So low was an individual sound from these that a combination of hundreds only just emerged from silence, and the myriads of the whole declivity reached the woman's ear

---

[43] Edmund Gurney, *The Power of Sound* (1880), 39.
[44] The Wessex Edition of 1912 reads, 'neither stems, leaves, fruit, blades, prickles, lichen, nor moss' (105), which is a distinct improvement, dispensing as it does with the impeding 'neither . . . nor' and the fussy binaries (though the ear could be supposed to be distinguishing between like materials), to create a forceful list.

but as a shrivelled and intermittent recitative. Yet scarcely a single accent among the many afloat to-night could have such power to impress a listener with thoughts of its origin. One inwardly saw the infinity of those combined multitudes: one perceived that each of the tiny trumpets was seized on, entered, scoured and emerged from by the wind as thoroughly as if it were as vast as a crater. (55)

Like Eustacia, we attend to distance and to nearness, to what is 'dwindled' and yet has unique acoustic power. Many lexical items convey a receding diminishment: 'ruins', 'worn', 'minutiae', 'infinitesimal', 'washed colourless', 'dead skins', 'so low', 'only just emerged', 'shrivelled and intermittent'; yet if we strain after these small remainders, there is also a burgeoning that fills the ear in 'so distinctly', 'could be realised', 'the united products', 'hundreds', 'myriads of the whole declivity', 'power to impress', 'infinity', 'multitudes' and the vigorous verbs that take us to 'vast as a crater'. But more potent than this dense counter-suggestiveness in the denotative vocabulary is the way that each sentence projects forward – 'It was a worn whisper . . . It was the united products . . . and these were' – until, with almost a triumph in the recovery of 'the material minutiae', the reader is released from 'neither . . . nor' into the next paragraph's definite 'They were the mummied heath-bells of the past summer'. The writing has so musically involved the reader in this auditory reach after the origins of this 'dry and papery' sound, and made it so palpable to the sense of touch, that when its 'accents' are finally transformed into a simultaneous vision of 'combined multitudes' of heath-bells and the intimate yet harsh scouring of single bell-heads, we are indeed impressed 'inwardly' by this frail sound. William Cohen suggests that the 'desiccated heath-bells . . . are themselves described as if they were little ears',[45] which helps to explain an identification between the listeners (Eustacia, the narrator, the reader) and the tiny dried yet persistent husks of a season that is past, because they have undergone the same experience.

There is a poignancy in the relation of the two dimensions summoned by this 'dwindled voice' on the wind – the one, seasonal, returning, composed of myriads, the other, momentary, individual, and complete, the single trumpet seized and scoured. Partaking of both, the reader thinks of Cytherea's plea for individual existence, which is Eustacia's and all Hardy's heroines' too. In a corresponding manner, sounds embody two different relationships to the universe:

[45] Cohen, *Embodied*, 96.

the sense that things once spoken have always a lasting presence; yet, once spoken is also to be lost and past. This is captured evocatively in two contrasting statements by Jonathan Rée in his historical and philosophical excursion into language, deafness and the senses, *I See A Voice*; writing about his childhood, and finding hearing different from the other four senses, he says:

> Sounds seemed to me to be nature's waifs and strays: they did not fit into the familiar world of physical things, and they could not be tracked down by my other senses either. After hatching in the dripping tap or ticking clock, they plunged into empty space, fanning out through the room, passing my ears on the way, and then, spreading through the rest of the house, growing weaker and weaker all the time, and then the garden, the sky, the moon, becoming more diluted, mile after mile, year after year; but never, I supposed, reaching any absolutely definitive end.

This is Hardyan in its phenomenology, and Dickensian in its narrative, plunging fantastically after the intangible passage of sounds into an unteleological eternity in which, once uttered, sounds may attenuate but are undying absolutes. Conversely, Rée the mature philosopher reflects,

> If there are such things as natural symbols, then sounds are surely the natural symbol of transience and the lostness of past time. They are essentially evanescent, an exact correlative of wistfulness and poignant regret, not to mention sentimentality. They seem to be nature's way of mourning, and in the inevitable metaphor, they are born only to die away.[46]

Instead of speaking of eternal preservation, this casts sound as a reminder of the irretrievability of every moment, the opposite face of the irremediable nature of our expressed being. It is not too fanciful, I think, to suggest that Rée's two evocations are a faint echo of the laws of the conservation of energy and of entropy, between which late-century thinkers found so much cause for hope and despair.

What is so interesting in this regard about Hardy's evocation of the heath-bells is that the auditory horizon is not brought close: if the sound they muster *belongs* to the visible topography of the heath, it is also *released* by it. These 'mummied heath-bells' are

---

[46] Jonathan Rée, *I See a Voice: A Philosophical History of Language, Deafness and the Senses* (1999), 19 and 23.

brought visually to some form of definition, but it is one that is produced imaginatively by the sound of the wind that has seized upon and scoured them, and thus they retain for the reader an indeterminate place in the auditory field, rather than a finite position in a visual one. It is in this way that they can plausibly be joined by Eustacia's sigh: 'Thrown out on the winds it became twined in with them, and with them it flew away' (56). This is not a depiction of a forward-projected cry; volition plays no part in its constitution, and as the narrator goes on to say in his most scientifically detached manner, 'in allowing herself to utter the sound, the woman's brain had authorized what it could not regulate' (56). While the visual field, as Ihde reminds us, 'displays itself with a definite *forward oriented* directionality' – we see what is before us – the auditory field is different, for, 'as a field-shape, sound *surrounds* me in my embodied personality'.[47] So Eustacia's sigh, which does not begin and end with the event of a sounded passage of air through her lips, but starts earlier in the psychic process and ends later in the cosmic one, having no shape in itself can be 'twined in' with the surrounding field, itself spatially indeterminate.

Eustacia's utterance has a continuing presence in the atmosphere, for, with the winds, 'it flew away': it is lost and not lost. Throughout *The Return of the Native*, and nowhere more than here, Hardy's presentation of the auditory world bears resemblance to one aspect of the thought of the mid-century Cambridge mathematician and founder of computer science, Charles Babbage, in *The Ninth Bridgewater Treatise* (1837). In his ninth chapter, 'On the Permanent Impression of our Words and Actions on the Globe we Inhabit', Babbage's primary assertion is that 'The pulsations of the air, once set in motion by the human voice, cease not to exist with the sounds to which they give rise.' In Babbage's cosmology, were our senses and mathematical knowledge far finer, we 'could trace every the minutest consequence of that primary impulse', which leads to his memorable vision of resonance:

> Thus considered, what a strange chaos is this wide atmosphere we breathe! Every atom, impressed with good and with ill, retains at once the motions which philosophers and sages have imparted to it, mixed and combined in ten thousand ways with all that is worthless and base. The air itself is one vast library, on whose pages are for ever written all that man has ever said or woman whispered. There, in their mutable but

[47] Ihde, *Listening and Voice*, 75.

unerring characters, mixed with the earliest, as well as with the latest signs of mortality, stand for ever recorded, vows un-redeemed, promises unfulfilled, perpetuating in the united movements of each particle, the testimony of man's changeful will.[48]

It would be extravagant to claim that this is exactly the physics of *The Return of the Native*, and yet Egdon is a closed system from which nothing escapes; Eustacia's sigh flies away with the wind, but that wind isn't seen to dissipate elsewhere, and for Clym the later parts of the novel resonate with words said. When Clym whispers, '"O, my mother, my mother: would to God I could live my life again, and endure for you what you endured for me!"' (388), it is an utterance that in the novel's acoustic circulation attaches itself to the mournful sounds of the Egdon winds.

In the poem 'A Kiss', a kiss is now 'One of a long procession of sounds / Travelling aethereal rounds / Far from earth's bounds / In the infinite'. But just as a harmonious ethereal infinite fails to manifest itself in *Lord Jim*, so there is no aerial restorative in *The Return of the Native*, though an atmosphere that is resonant with the prosaic sounds of human and natural life persists. A Babbage-like consciousness informs the poignancy of the late picture of Clym, returned to Blooms-End after the breach with Eustacia, yet ever listening for her:

> When a leaf floated to the earth he turned his head, thinking it might be her footfall. A bird searching for worms in the mould of the flower-beds sounded like her hand on the latch of the gate; and at dusk, when soft strange ventriloquisms came from holes in the ground, hollow stalks, curled dead leaves, and other crannies wherein breezes, worms, and insects can work their will, he fancied that they were Eustacia standing without and breathing wishes of reconciliation. (331)

The acuteness of Clym's hearing is matched by the immediacy of his desire to transform the aerial presence of the small activities around him to the palpable sensation of Eustacia's foot, hand and breath. Of course, nobody comes: the homely courses of the novel are recalled to the reader as pages earlier read and enjoyed, but which cannot be revisited with quite the same sensation. But rather than the blank misgivings that will later rend 'The Voice' – 'Or is

---

[48] Charles Babbage, *The Ninth Bridgewater Treatise*, facsimile of the second edition (1838), 8–14 *passim*.

it only the breeze in its listlessness / ... You being ever dissolved to existlessness'[49] – the novel allows to Clym a gentler auditory reminder of Eustacia on the Fifth of November: 'Echoes from those past times when they had exchanged tender words all the day long came like the diffused murmur of a sea-shore left miles behind' (332). While Babbage's 'vast library' suggests that sounds can be retrieved and the impulses behind their formation re-inspected, the contrasting sadness inherent in Hardy's conception of auditory convalescence lies in that transformation of tender words to a 'diffused murmur ... left miles behind'. The accuracy of Hardy's ear for the open sounds of a shoreline fronting the sea reminds us that we are inland now and dipped beyond that auditory horizon. Barbara Hardy has a wonderfully phrased observation that is apt here: 'nothing could be less like Wordsworth's memorial consolations than Hardy's sad shafts of recollection'.[50]

*

While light poignantly displays to the reader's vision the symbols that tell the story – the figure against the sky, the weird reddleman, the closed door and Clym's furze-hook, the silver burnished heron – it is through sound that the reader is incorporated into the heath's atmosphere and that the novel exerts its claustrophobic power.[51] And the journeys of sound over the surface of Egdon make of Hardy's characters *inhabitants*, an idea important to Hardy's fiction, more so than to Conrad's with its recurring shadow of exile. In *The Return of the Native*, readers and characters dwell amidst its material topography in a peculiarly unrelieved manner, and the climactic chapter of the novel, whose title 'Sights and Sounds Draw the Wanderers Together' makes the point, shows how human psychology is secondary to ambient phenomena in Hardy's melodrama:

> At this moment a footstep approached, but the light of the lamps being in a different direction the comer was not visible. The step paused, then came on again.
> 'Eustacia?' said Wildeve.

---

[49] Most editions of Hardy's poetry prefer his revision to 'wan wistlessness'. I don't. It weakens the harsher and more uncompromising quality of his first conception, and it changes the issue from her very existence to her capacity for knowing.
[50] Barbara Hardy, *Tellers and Listeners: The Narrative Imagination* (1975), 177.
[51] It was not until after I had written this chapter that I discovered David James' fine essay, 'Hearing Hardy: Soundscapes and the Profitable Reader' (*Journal of Narrative Theory* 40:2, 2010, 131–55), with which it has such a close affinity.

> The person came forward, and the light fell upon the form of Clym, glistening with wet, whom Wildeve immediately recognised; but Wildeve, who stood behind the lamp, was not at once recognised by Yeobright.
> He stopped as if in doubt whether this waiting vehicle could have anything to do with the flight of his wife or not. The sight of Yeobright at once banished Wildeve's sober feelings, who saw him again as the deadly rival from whom Eustacia was to be kept at all hazards. Hence Wildeve did not speak, in the hope that Clym would pass by without particular enquiry.
> While they both hung thus in hesitation a dull sound became audible above the storm and wind. Its origin was unmistakable – it was the fall of a body into the stream adjoining, apparently at a point near the weir. (354–5)

It is impossible to make convincing the notion that on such a night, in such a place, anyone would 'pass by without particular enquiry', or that the source of the 'dull sound' could be 'unmistakable' – except to someone who had been expecting it. However, what enables the passage to incise its scene in the reader's mind is exactly what connects Hardy's writing to the tradition of empirical science, a meticulous attention to its physical details presented as phenomena: a footstep and its progress, the fall of the light, what, in a moment of hesitation, becomes audible from the exterior world, its origin, its location. Sounds place a hearer within a scene more readily than sights do, which, rather, place a scene in front of us. The issue that this bears down upon is the *included* quality of the ear as it is incorporated into the production of sound, as opposed to the relatively excluded position in which the eye places a seer, whether the eye is that of a fictional participant or the mental eye of a reader. Nowhere is this plight of the excluded inhabitant made more painfully clear than in one of the novel's supreme moments of visual beauty, as Mrs Yeobright, exhausted in her retreat across the heath from the closed door at Alderworth, raises her eyes from the colony of ants at her feet to the life-giving atmosphere that now seems enticingly, hopelessly, distant:

> While she looked a heron arose on that side of the sky, and flew on with his face towards the sun. He had come dripping wet from some pool in the valleys, and as he flew the edges and lining of his wings, his thighs, and his breast, were so caught by the bright sunbeams that he appeared as if formed of burnished silver. Up in the zenith where he was seemed a free and happy place, away from all contact with the earthly ball to which she was pinioned: and she wished that she could arise uncrushed from its surface, and fly as he flew then. (278)

An opposing counterpart to the scouring of the wind suffered by each one of the heath-bell blooms, this passage stands as a longed-for expansion into freely directed motion released from earthly courses, as comprehensive as any symbolic vision in Conrad. Yet Mrs Yeobright is detached from the condition of the heron by exactly the visual means which displays its beauty. Sight is the objectifying sense that renders phenomena as completed objects: as Ihde says of Aristotle's visualism, 'The preference for vision is tied to a metaphysics of objects.'[52] So the heron, 'as if formed of burnished silver', is rendered an object of desire, complete in itself, 'up in the zenith' and not a sharer in the same aerial medium that gives a little breath to Mrs Yeobright's depleted condition.

In contrast, what the ending of the novel draws out is *in*completion, the condition of sound. The final glimpse forward to 'the career of an itinerant open-air preacher' (389) leaves the novel suspended in the medium in which utterance circulates, and allows, for the first time, sound to travel beyond the confines of Egdon. Clym speaks 'in a more cultivated strain elsewhere',

> from the steps and porticoes of Town-halls, from market-crosses, from conduits, on esplanades and on wharves, from the parapets of bridges, in barns and in outhouses, and all other such places in the neighbouring Wessex towns and villages. (389)

The repeated 'from' in these various locations offers to the mental eye the raised attitude of the speaker and the air into which his 'strain' is projected. We follow the material more than the intellectual substance of the opinions that 'occupy his tongue', in that 'some said that his words were commonplace . . . But everywhere he was kindly received, for the story of his life had become generally known' (390). Sound is more fitting than sight to yield the un-Aristotelian and unteleological conclusion to the novel which gives it its modern vibration. The visual display of Eustacia in death has the completion of a perfected form; but the final circulation of sound in the novel returns us to the story of unfinished life, as custody of the returned native's history and opinions inconclusively passes to the ears of others.

*

'Heart of Darkness' is 'one of Marlow's inconclusive experiences' (47), yet it, too, is a story to pass on, turned into a tale which would, its

---

[52] Ihde, *Listening and Voice*, 7.

author hoped, possess a quality causing it to 'hang in the air and dwell on the ear after the last note had been struck' (Author's Note 6).[53] Two features associate it with *The Return of the Native*. Both novels depict the circulation of sounds within a closed system, but with the comforting implications of recovery or restitution that Victorian readers could associate with the First Law of Thermodynamics (the Conservation of Energy) notably absent.[54] And while both novels navigate a visual as well as a sonic landscape, an inability to *see* is a shared central trope. Far more than in *The Return of the Native*, however, in 'Heart of Darkness' the orientation provided by sound becomes the means of a specifically human definition amid a fecund natural world.

Sound enters 'Heart of Darkness' very quietly. Marlow casts the whole of what he is about to tell ('the culminating point of my experience') as a peculiarly indistinct *visual* episode:

> It seemed somehow to throw a kind of light on everything about me – and into my thoughts. It was sombre enough, too – and pitiful – not extraordinary in any way – not very clear either. No. Not very clear. And yet it seemed to throw a kind of light. (48)

The subdued tenor of this circling statement, with its claim to 'a kind of light' surviving four negatives, makes cautious headway, like so much of the tale and the way it is recounted. The kind of light which Hardy suggestively employs for the opening of *The Return of the Native*, in which 'darkness had to a great extent arrived ... while day stood distinct in the sky', also gives way to the encroachment of the night with the same gradual inevitability of Marlow's progress 'deeper and deeper into the heart of darkness. It was very quiet there' (79). The introspective turn of the addition ' – and into my thoughts' of course marks a significant difference between the 'Ishmaelitish' tract of heath and Marlow's mental landscape of (self-) discovery disclosed to the reader of the respective novels.[55] However, both works

---

[53] The allusion is to Toni Morrison, *Beloved* (1987): 'It was not a story to pass on' (274). See Dorice Williams Elliott, 'Hearing the Darkness: The Narrative Chain in Conrad's "Heart of Darkness"', *English Literature in Transition 1880–1920* 28:2 (1985), 162–81.

[54] See Tina Young Choi, 'Forms of Closure: The First Law of Thermodynamics and Victorian Narrative', *ELH* 74:2 (Summer 2007), 301–22.

[55] And yet an entry in Hardy's notebook reads, 'Moralists assert that under every human breast there lies a tract of undiscovered country in comparison with which the unexplored solitudes of central Africa are but as a speck' (*LN* 1:134, quoted from 'The Mysteries of the Basement', *World*, 16 June 1880, 8, quotation with slight variation). We sadly don't know whether Hardy read 'Heart of Darkness'.

are notable for the manner in which their silent, visually-rendered opening panoramas slowly release a sound which will typify what is to come; and yet to turn from one text to the other is to move from sights and sounds as one might walk among them to the apparition of sights and sounds in a dream.

It is a full fourteen pages before the first evocation of a sound just makes itself heard as Marlow watches the coast of West Africa from the French steamer:

> There it is before you – smiling, frowning, inviting, grand, mean, insipid, or savage, and always mute with an air of whispering, Come and find out. (150)

This is typically disconcerting in the way in which it leaves the reader more conscious of a saturation of Marlow's sensations than quite what is 'before' him. Despite this, the seen, very fully with its eight intriguing and contrasting adjectives, precedes the heard, which is not a whisper but an unplaceable 'air of whispering' proceeding from muteness. Yet the whisper is important: this, the first imagined sound of 'Heart of Darkness', is the first of twenty-one uses of the word, as significant as Eustacia's analogously placed sigh is to *The Return of the Native*. The difference between a whisper and a sigh says much about the difference between the auditory dimension of the two works. A sigh is an exhalation, a respiratory motion 'expressing dejection, weariness, longing, pain or relief' (*OED*). A whisper projects and conceals all its activity among tongue, teeth and lips: it is full of intention, 'usually implying hostility, malice, conspiracy' (*OED*). Although a whisper foregoes the deep embodiment of a sigh, it carries the insinuating design upon a listener of a *voice*; and it is by a voice emanating with increasing insistence from the heart of darkness that Marlow's ear is captured, and through the beckoning of imagined sound that a reader of 'Heart of Darkness' is drawn to its most inward reaches.

'The voice of the surf heard now and then' as Marlow's steamer toils down the west coast of Africa 'had a meaning' (54); and the 'dull detonation' which aimlessly lays waste the ground near the company station has 'the same kind of ominous voice' as the French warship 'firing into a continent' (57). Thus both vital meaning and absurd meaninglessness have their voices in the tale. The scale is both tiny, as in the 'clink' in the links of the chain that binds the labourers to their servitude, or vast, as when Marlow approaches the grove of death:

> The rapids were near and an uninterrupted, uniform, headlong rushing noise filled the mournful stillness of the grove where not a breath stirred, not a leaf moved, with a mysterious sound, as though the tearing pace of the launched earth had suddenly become audible. (58)

In its slow, inexorable, yet sudden revelation of distance and force, in imagining sound for what is usually conceived as silent, this is the most vertiginous, unbalancing sentence in 'Heart of Darkness'. The fierce stripping away of normal atmospheric conditions that protect us from any sense of the physics of the spinning earth lends uncanny estrangement to the sudden declaration of where Marlow, in cosmic reality, is. Where Marlow *is*, is the story brought home to us if we read 'Heart of Darkness' as auditory exploration. Throughout, there is an uncertainty about the *location* of sound which persists right up to the whisper on the 'rising wind' in the absolutely still drawing-room of the Intended's apartment in Brussels at the end of the novel. Much of the novel is given to the sensation of encountering sounds wandering free of their origins in an oppressive space allotted to the European ear trying to make its habitation in front of an immensity of wilderness. The European 'pilgrims' remain trapped within the invasive atmosphere they have brought with them:

> The word ivory rang in the air, was whispered, was sighed. You would think they were praying to it. A taint of imbecile rapacity blew through it all like a whiff from some corpse. By Jove! I've never seen anything so unreal in my life. And outside, the silent wilderness surrounding this cleared speck on the earth struck me as something great and invincible, like evil or truth, waiting patiently for the passing away of this fantastic invasion. (65)

Where the word 'ivory' originates, at whom it is directed, recedes beyond the auditory compass to become an invisible prime-mover, as inherent in the air as a smell. With 'imbecile', 'unreal' and 'fantastic', Marlow seeks to hold himself free of this 'taint'; yet the capers of the trading invasion are also brought startlingly close in the darkness by the cynicism of the brickmaker, his fellow-listener in the night: 'I heard a scathing murmur at my ear, "Heap of muffs – go to"' (68).

The 'property view' and the 'wave view' of sound have both been briefly characterised for their dominant explanatory positions during the Victorian and Modernist periods. More recently, the contemporary philosopher of mind Casey O'Callaghan has proposed a third 'event view' which, as its name suggests, is congruent with the mode of reading Hardy and Conrad followed throughout this study, and which resonates with 'Heart of Darkness' in particular. He writes, 'sounds are events in which a wave disturbance is introduced into a medium'.[56] The reader is more conscious of the disturbance to the medium than of the precise source of the sound; this fits the experience of reading 'Heart of Darkness' with one's ears, which is to be assailed by auditory events whose origin and communicative intent is always unclear. As O'Callaghan writes at greater length:

> If perception is for revealing objects and their properties, and sounds seem among neither objects nor their properties, it is tempting to suppose that sounds are mysterious, ethereal, or otherwise questionable items of sense. If sounds as we perceive them do not exhibit the common marks of items in the material world, and if they are not obviously features of those items, that might encourage us to believe that sounds have no natural home in the world. That, in turn, may tempt us to understand sounds as having no place other than the mind.[57]

In practice, neither Conrad nor O'Callaghan falls to that temptation, though readers who sever Conrad from his materialist Victorian roots sometimes do. For both novelist and philosopher, sounds are *not* purely mental events, as it has been the argument of this study throughout to show. Yet O'Callaghan captures here something of the perceptual uncertainty that is so much the subject of 'Heart of Darkness', which he traces back to the fugitive and materially undecidable status of sound that asks us to approach it, in Hardy's phrase, as 'a series of seemings'.

As Marlow navigates up-river, it is through his account of ambient sound that he strives to communicate this uncertain orientation between human activity, its disturbance of a medium and its reception upon the senses, an account which registers the material world that he passes through as indistinguishable from its passage through him. It is worth looking at (listening to) this in some detail:

> The word ivory would ring in in the air for a while – and on we went again into the silence, along empty reaches, round the still bends, between the high walls of our winding way, reverberating in hollow claps the ponderous beat of the stern wheel . . . . We penetrated deeper and deeper into the heart of darkness. It was very quiet there. At night

---

[56] Casey O'Callaghan, *Sounds: A Philosophical Theory* (2007), 99.
[57] Ibid., 6.

sometimes the roll of drums behind the curtain of trees would run up the river and remain sustained faintly, as if hovering in the air high over our heads till the first break of day. Whether this meant war, peace or prayer we could not tell. (78–9)

Neither can a reader tell whether this is an impression *of* or an impression *upon*, a subjective expression of the sensation of hearing sounds during a progress up-river, or an objective account of how that movement and those sounds presented themselves to the senses. It is as if Conrad has placed Marlow in the narrow corridor afforded by the ear's aperture as envisaged by Helmholtz, but has granted him only the eye's capacities not the ear's: sound is prolonged and closed off, but not resolved into meaning or definition. Where exactly are the 'hollow claps' – on the surfaces of 'the high walls' or 'between' them, part of 'our winding way'? The contrasting definiteness and much lowered trajectory of the two sentences, 'We penetrated deeper and deeper into the heart of darkness. It was very quiet there', less sensationally concentrates a drama of human direction, but one that is no more conclusive. An unsettling iteration returns ('The word ivory *would* ring in the air'), more distantly now, as 'sometimes the roll of the drums . . . would run up the river' implies that what is known of sounds is the shape of a wave-front as it meets the conducting medium of air. Conrad conveys the ear's attempt to encompass and image that shape with a wonderful sense of how the assonantal possibilities of English – 'rem*ai*n sust*ai*ned f*ai*ntly' – bring upon the reader's mental ear the auditory tension between distance and persistence. And he then portrays the delicate effort of attention needed to assign a place to this unseen phenomenon through a succession of vowels contained by repeated aspirations that lift them into air: 'as if hovering in the air high over our heads'. The idea might come to mind that, for Conrad, sounds are symbolic embodiments of homelessness and exile. It is not so much, as O'Callaghan briefly entertains, that 'sounds have no natural home in the world', but rather, in the words from Jonathan Rée which I have already quoted, that they are 'Nature's waifs and strays'.

*

The climax of the suspension in sensory uncertainty which accompanies this journey into an interior arrives in the remarkable long paragraph that Conrad devotes to describing the evening and morning when, 'about eight miles from Kurtz's station', Marlow 'brought up in the middle of the stream' (83). A feeling of insulation is given the aspect of a deliberate exclusion from the truth of things all around them by the momentary lifting, the following morning, of the 'white shutter' of the fog before it 'came down again smoothly as if sliding in greased grooves' (83). A state of simultaneous sensory alertness and deprivation concentrates itself in a desire to *see*, which is denied, the only orientation being given suddenly by sound:

> I ordered the chain which we had begun to heave in to be paid out again. Before it stopped running with a muffled rattle, a cry, a very loud cry as of infinite desolation soared slowly in the opaque air . . . It ceased. A complaining clamour, modulated in savage discords, filled our ears. The sheer unexpectedness of it made my hair stir under my cap. I don't know how it struck the others; to me it seemed as though the mist itself had screamed, so suddenly and apparently from all sides at once did this tumultuous and mournful uproar arise. It culminated in a hurried outbreak of almost intolerably excessive shrieking which stopped short, leaving us stiffened in a variety of silly attitudes and obstinately listening to the nearly as appalling and excessive silence. (83–4)

Suffering from an absence of meaning communicated by their surroundings, Marlow and his companions suddenly find themselves subject to too much – twice we are told it is 'excessive' – as this unidentified collective voice suspends before them its 'complaining', 'mournful' 'desolation'.[58] The source of these sounds remaining hidden, they captivate the pilgrims by their activity as auditory events, a succession of seemingly uncompleted aerial transmissions, from a soaring which 'ceased', to 'a hurried outbreak' which 'stopped short'. Yet the human event eludes them. A recent discussion of 'auditory objecthood' is instructive here: the authors claim the visual system 'is generally concerned with *surfaces* of objects, not with the *sources* that illuminate them', but the auditory system 'is generally concerned with *sources* of sound . . . not with *surfaces* that reflect the sound'.[59] On this account, inherent in sound is an invitation to its source, yet Conrad has confined the European listeners to the surfaces of these sounds, as they announce themselves in the uncertain location of

---

[58] See Josiane Paccaud, 'Speech and the Nature of Communication in Conrad's "Heart of Darkness"', *The Conradian* 8:1 (Winter 1983), 45, for a discussion of the 'collective voice'.

[59] David Van Valkenburg and Michael Kubovy, 'From Gibson's Fire to Gestalts: A Bridge-building Theory of Perceptual Objecthood', in John G Neuhoffer ed., *Ecological Psychoacoustics* (2004), 117.

'the opaque air' or 'apparently from all sides at once'. Allowing the ear only the capacities of the eye intensifies to an almost intolerable degree an exposure to the spatial dimension of these sounds, but an inability to comprehend their invitation – their *human source*. So Marlow, left only with ambience, can only describe his unforgettable sensation of absurdity: 'the mist itself had screamed'.[60]

The violent sensational contradiction of this phrase, forcibly conflating a substance and an action that are in every way incompatible, marks an extreme in Marlow's phenomenal bewilderment. This is a tipping-point in the novel, beyond which Marlow's allegiance to a shared, communicable world is subject to a doubt from which return can only be made by a lie. Yet Marlow is able to hear in the desolate cry as recalled three pages later, 'the curious, inexplicable note of desperate grief' (86), an auditory knowledge, in the word 'grief', of kinship with a cultured human feeling. As Walter Ong writes: 'Sound binds interiors to one another as interiors.'[61] A claim has been made upon Marlow beyond the 'surface-truth' necessity of keeping his eyes fixed on the snags in the river. But it is from this point, the other side of a sensational rupture as it were, that Marlow begins to make a critical choice among his auditory nightmares. Despite his recognition in the scream of a 'sorrow', an 'unrestrained grief' and 'a great human passion let loose' (87), he listens for something else.[62]

For amid the hovering of faint drumming, the oppressive silence, the 'mournful uproar' and the 'savage clamour' of the soundscape of the novel, there is only one *voice* 'exclusively', as he says, which provides Marlow with a sense of direction in his journey. After the attack upon the steamer and the death of the helmsman, Marlow concludes that Kurtz too is dead and experiences a profound disappointment:

> I . . . became aware that that was exactly what I had been looking forward to – a talk with Kurtz. I made the strange discovery that I had never imagined him as doing, you know, but as discoursing. I didn't say to myself, 'Now I'll never see him,' or 'Now I will never shake him by the hand,' but, 'Now I will never hear him.' The man presented himself as a voice. (92)

[60] Of course, Munch's 'The Scream' (1893–1910) is the most famous visual attempt to represent the sound of desolation spatially that would be relevant to 'Heart of Darkness'.
[61] Walter J. Ong, *The Presence of the Word* (1967), 125.
[62] This is Conrad's racist culpability in Chinua Achebe's influential account.

Surrounded and assailed by the unfamiliar, the meaningless and seemingly absurd, the clue that guides Marlow is conceived as a voice to which he can listen. Mladen Dolar explains convincingly: 'what defines the voice as special among the infinite array of acoustic phenomena is its inner relationship with meaning. The voice is something which points towards meaning, it is as if there is an arrow in it which raises the expectation of meaning.'[63] For Marlow to hear Kurtz's voice would be not only to have the conspiracies of the Central Station explained, but also to understand something of the meaning of his own journey, to understand his captivation by that 'distinct glimpse' in which he 'seemed to see Kurtz for the first time', 'setting his face towards the depths of the wilderness, towards his empty and desolate station' (75). In practice, Kurtz has no wisdom retrieved from extremity that will convey to Marlow the meaning of his own life – far from it: Kurtz is an empty, self-obsessed sham. Yet it is *his* voice and no other that holds out the promise of some meaning to this, the defining if inconclusive, episode of Marlow's life. Thus the imperative that Marlow faces is to retrieve some meaning from the encounter with Kurtz that his concept of Kurtz *as a voice* has led him to expect.

Marlow is quite capable of being sardonic about Kurtz 'getting himself adored', and penetrating in his anatomy of Kurtz's 'deficiency':

> But the wilderness had found him out early and had taken on him a terrible vengeance for the fantastic invasion. I think it had whispered to him things about himself which he did not know, things of which he had no conception till he took counsel with this great solitude – and the whisper had proved irresistibly fascinating. It echoed loudly within him because he was hollow at the core. (104)

Kurtz is a vessel for the resonance and amplification of the 'whisper' that entered the novel many pages previously (these are the ninth and tenth occurrences of the word), its insinuating sibilance swelling a sentence which, semantically, diminishes Kurtz to an object of scorn, but which auditorily confers a grandeur upon him. And although Marlow is proof against Kurtz's words, the *whisper become a cry*, as we will see, possesses a power against which rationality is no defence. Conrad pondered incessantly the relation between the sound of a voice and the words it utters, as might be expected of a writer living so much by his ears, who for twenty years previously had heard all

---

[63] Mladen Dolar, *A Voice and Nothing More* (2006), 14. See also Sam Halliday, *Sonic Modernity: Representing Sound in Literature, Culture and the Arts* (2013), 36/7.

the accents of the world far from their native soil, and who was now himself a foreigner who had elected to become an English gentleman. His most explicit statement is the reflection at the opening of 'A Familiar Preface' to *A Personal Record*:

> He who wants to persuade should put his trust not in the right argument, but in the right word. The power of sound has always been greater than the power of sense. I don't say this by way of disparagement. It is better for mankind to be impressionable than reflective. Nothing humanely great – great, I mean, as affecting a whole mass of lives – has come from reflection. On the other hand, you cannot fail to see the power of mere words; such words as Glory, for instance, or Pity. (xi)

The irony here will be evident to anyone who has read *Nostromo*; yet the appeal in the power of sound is not dismissed as fraudulent and, significantly for 'Heart of Darkness', what preoccupies Conrad is the *effect* of the uttered word, the voice as it has become disembodied, an accent: 'For who is going to tell whether the accent is right or wrong till the word is shouted, and fails to be heard, perhaps, and goes down-wind, leaving the world unmoved?' (xii). For all the difference of ironic inflection in Conrad's voice, the concern with the aerial and mental medium within which sound resonates is as persistent as it is for Hardy. As a reflection upon the sonic drama created for Marlow, it points towards Marlow's choice: there is in the accent vibrating in Kurtz's voice, 'far off and yet loud like a hail through a speaking trumpet' (112), a sincerity preferable to the Manager's expediently correct, but cynical, condemnation of Kurtz's 'unsound method'. And, in preference to the general sorrow that he hears as diffused in the air, it is the single tone that Marlow selects as speaking to him.

*

The most celebrated moment of 'Heart of Darkness' has functioned in a variety of discourses as a prescient pre-echo to the sound of the century to follow:

> I saw on that ivory visage the expression of sombre pride, of ruthless power, of craven terror – of intense and hopeless despair. Did he live his life again in every detail of desire, temptation and surrender during that supreme moment of complete knowledge? He cried in a whisper at some image, at some vision, he cried out twice, a cry that was no more than a breath –
> 'The horror! The horror!'
> I blew the candle out and left the cabin. (117)

In this picture of a man who has hardened into what he has sold himself to ('that ivory visage'), phrase after phrase casts Kurtz as ridden with worldly vice. Yet the climactic 'that supreme moment of complete knowledge' has the heroic, ecstatic quality of the goal of a quest attained. In a rhetorical and elevating move, the deictic 'that' casts beyond the bounds of Marlow's question to a definite event; but a suspicion of Yeatsian sleight-of-hand lingers around it, and a less heightened sentence might have employed the indefinite article instead. Marlow's *need* to wring out a 'moral victory', as Vincent Pecora has put it (his emphasis), from Kurtz's shabby death can be found concentrated in this single word.[64] The distant vision towards which Kurtz's gaze has been directed ('some image', 'some vision') is brought inescapably within an immediate auditory compass, whose resonance surrounds and fastens upon both Marlow and the reader. Innumerable readings have been given of 'the horror', and it is not the point of this study to offer another one. But in trying to account for the persistence with which this utterance haunts Marlow, the manner in which his attention is claimed by Kurtz's voice demands consideration: 'He cried in a whisper . . . he cried out twice, a cry that was no more than a breath'. Steven Connor comments, 'A cry always seems in excess of the one from whom it issues, and in excess of the semantic content which it may have.' He extends this 'excess' to the issue that accompanies the portrayal of Kurtz: 'The cry – whether of anger, fear or pain – is the purest form of the compact between voice and power.'[65] Nowhere is Kurtz more powerful than in his end, as Conrad introduces into the novel's steadily accumulating 'whisper' the energy of Kurtz's cry, generated from sources beyond his wasted body.

Kurtz's vocalisation of 'complete knowledge' claims a loyalty deeper than 'a distant kinship affirmed in a supreme moment' (96), the deliberately close locution drawn from Marlow by the earlier death of his helmsman. It is (or should be) disturbing:

> He had summed up – he had judged. 'The horror!' He was a remarkable man. After all, this was the expression of some sort of belief. It had candour, it had conviction, it had a vibrating note of revolt in its whisper, it had the appalling face of a glimpsed truth – the strange commingling of desire and hate . . . . I like to think that my summing up would not have been a word of careless contempt. Better his cry – much better. (118)

[64] Vincent Pecora, '"Heart of Darkness" and the Phenomenology of Voice', *ELH* 52:4 (1985): 'Just as a reader might prefer to do, Marlow salvages, recuperates, discovers once again a victory in the midst of despair' (1008).
[65] Connor, *Dumbstruck*, 33.

Many readers have found 'The horror!' to be exactly that 'word of careless contempt' which Marlow disparages.[66] Yet it is the *cry* that Marlow emphasises, the cry which is the only assertion possible against the 'immense jabber, silly, atrocious, sordid, savage, or simply mean, without any kind of sense' (93) that a pessimistic late-Victorian sensibility makes of universal existence. The contrast that can be made with Eustacia Vye is instructive in estimating what Marlow makes of the vibrations of that 'note of revolt in its whisper'. As she sinks down into the heath, defeated by 'the cruel obstructiveness of all about her', '"I do not deserve my lot!" she cried in a frenzy of bitter revolt' (*Native* 341). This is the last speech Hardy gives her; but when we are invited to look at her in death, after her body has been dragged from the weir, it is 'as if a sense of dignity had just compelled her to leave off speaking' (361). The visual composition of a Eustacia more dignified in death than she had been in life offers its silent commentary on her ineffectual revolt; Marlow, on the other hand, wrests from Kurtz's miserable death an explicit assertion of victory, 'an affirmation', precisely because his cried and whispered revolt does *not* leave off speaking – it occupies the whole of Marlow's thoughts in the long paragraph after Kurtz's burial 'in a muddy hole', and its mockery persists under the details of Marlow's return to Brussels to sound again, unappeased, in the final episode.

But this 'moral victory' of revolt is Marlow's proclamation, not exactly Conrad's depiction. As Peter Brooks says, since 'summing-up . . . is unknowable in one's own life, it must be sought in the voice of another', and what the tale shows us, in practice, is not Kurtz's moral victory but Marlow's continuing dealings with the voice that he has sought in order to confer a meaning on his journey.[67] In the diminished soundscape, briskly told, of his return to Brussels, Marlow parades a sense of superiority over those who 'could not possibly know the things I knew' (119), a private, inner certainty derived from having heard Kurtz's voice. Marlow's account is that he possesses a visionary dark truth while the Intended, the mere product of her society, is bathed in the light of illusion. Yet, in an atmosphere in which 'the sound of her low voice seemed to have

---

[66] See, for instance, Peter Brooks, *Reading for the Plot: Design and Intention in Narrative* (1984), 250.
[67] Ibid., 252. For my understanding of the final scenes of 'Heart of Darkness', I am indebted in different ways to Peter Brooks and to Nina Pelikan Straus, 'The Exclusion of The Intended from Secret Sharing in Conrad's "Heart of Darkness"', *Novel* 20:2 (Winter 1987), 123–37.

the accompaniment of all the other sounds, full of mystery, desolation, and sorrow, I had ever heard' (124), the drama of the final scene shows both Marlow and the Intended equally as needing to wring some form of victory from the encounter. Marlow's sardonic irony, '"His end," said I with a dull anger stirring in me, "was in every way worthy of his life"' (125), is brought by the Intended to a coercive climax of explicitness in which audition is the subject of each utterance and each unvoiced comment:

> 'I think of his loneliness. Nobody near to understand him as I would have understood. Perhaps no one to hear . . .'
> 'To the very end,' I said shakily. 'I heard his very last words. . . .' I stopped in a fright.
> 'Repeat them,' she said in a heartbroken tone. 'I want – I want – something – something to – to live with.'
> I was on the point of crying at her, 'Don't you hear them?' The dusk was repeating them in a persistent whisper all around us, in a whisper that seemed to swell menacingly like the first whisper of a rising wind.
> 'The horror! The horror!'
> 'His last word – to live with,' she murmured. 'Don't you understand I loved him – I loved him – I loved him!'
> I pulled myself together and spoke slowly.
> 'The last word he pronounced was – your name.'
> I heard a light sigh and then my heart stood still, stopped dead short by an exulting and terrible cry, by the cry of inconceivable triumph and of unspeakable pain. 'I knew it – I was sure!' . . . She knew! She was sure. I heard her weeping; she had hidden her face in her hands. (125)

The previous chapter observed the visual density of space in *Lord Jim*; at the end of 'Heart of Darkness' space is dense with sound. All the previous whispers from the wilderness crowd into the persistent, swelling, rising repetitions that suffuse Marlow's senses: here and there, present and past, reverberate to a single whisper in a perpetually playing recapitulation. But this invisible fabric of sound does not operate like the fictional invisible ether as a materialisation of the inviolable unity of an authored creation; it acts, rather, as the ultimate agent of the fragmentation that creates separate listening selves, subjects of their own sensations as Pater and Pearson described. Marlow and the Intended both extort their own, unsharable, victories from their individual defeats. While the 'barbarous and superb woman', so far away, is able to withstand 'the flying terror of the sound' (115) when Marlow sounds his steam whistle in a pre-echo of a great acoustic moment to come in *Nostromo*, in pointed contrast the Intended is unable to hear the sound which, for Marlow, fills all the space in the Brussels' apartment. Yet structurally answering the desolation of the cry from the wilderness, the 'exulting and terrible cry' of the Intended, reinforced adjectivally four times over and reiterated with the assertion of the definite article, is as extravagant as any sound in the novel. However, the defeat inflicted upon Marlow, that of having to tell the lie that denies his loyalty to the truth he finds in Kurtz, is far from total. It is immediately erased by his return to his sardonic tone – 'She knew! She was sure' – an irony that preserves him intact from her emotionalism, and preserves intact the dark truths of the human heart for sharing with a different audience.[68]

An unsigned review of *Youth, a Narrative; and Two Other Stories* in *The Athenaeum* for 20 December 1902 reads, 'after turning the last page of one of his books we rise saturated by the very air they [his characters] breathed'.[69] The air of 'Heart of Darkness' is particularly heavy, laden with a burden that commentators ever since have been trying to re-express. The storyteller himself feels the burden: at one point Marlow breaks off to challenge his listeners, 'Do you see him? Do you see the story? Do you see anything?' (70). After a silence, Marlow resumes,

> 'Of course in this you fellows see more than I could then. You see me, whom you know....'
> It had become so pitch-dark that we listeners could hardly see one another. For a long time already he, sitting apart, had been no more to us than a voice. (70)

With a glimmer of humour, the dictum 'before all, to make you *see*' is given up in favour of a precarious trust in the auditory dimension. As Peter Brooks has brilliantly expressed it: 'One must tell and tell again, hoping that one's repetition will in turn be repeated, that one's voice will re-echo.'[70] Auden, too, said, 'All I have is a voice / To undo the folded lie', but in 'September 1, 1939' the 'ironic points of light'

---

[68] In terms of 'facing nature', it is illuminating to compare the interview with the Intended with Hardy's 1866 poem, 'Her Dilemma', particularly when accompanied by the illustration which Hardy provided for the first publication in *Wessex Poems*, 1898.
[69] Norman Sherry, *Joseph Conrad: The Critical Heritage* (1997), 138.
[70] Brooks, *Reading for the Plot*, 263.

are still to be discerned, allowing a certain brightness to his 'affirming flame', whilst Conrad's narrator is left looking only 'into the heart of an immense darkness'. Of course, to return to the 'Author's Note', Conrad was well aware of his progressive truancy from a primarily visual rendering in 'Heart of Darkness' in this attempt to make the air retentive and suggestive:

> There it was no longer a matter of sincere colouring. It was like another art altogether. That sombre theme had to be given a sinister resonance, a tonality of its own, a continued vibration that, I hoped, would hang in the air and dwell on the ear after the last note had been struck. (6)

Marlow declares he has found sincerity in Kurtz; and Conrad's earlier conception of his art is one which holds up 'the rescued fragment before all eyes and in the light of a sincere mood' (Preface to *The Nigger of the 'Narcissus'*, 7). However, 'Heart of Darkness', which is 'like another art altogether' in turning to the auditory, finds sincerity too finished and complete a position: so many of the words here – 'resonance', 'continued', 'hang', 'dwell', 'after' – like the novella's final scene, suggest an on-going activity afterwards, still seeking. Hardy's friend and not-too-distant neighbour, T. E. Lawrence, had an ear for that 'continued vibration'. Writing to F. N. Doubleday in 1920, he says,

> You know, publishing Conrad must be a rare pleasure. He's absolutely the most haunting thing in prose that ever was: I wish I knew how every paragraph he writes (do you notice they are all paragraphs: he seldom writes a single sentence?) goes on sounding in waves, like the note of a tenor bell, after it stops. It's not built on the rhythm of ordinary prose, but on something existing only in his head, and as he can never say what it is he wants to say, all his things end in a kind of hunger, a suggestion of something he can't say or do or think.[71]

Acknowledging that sound is always passing away, 'All his things end in a kind of hunger' memorably expresses the part-desire for insinuating sound and the part-horror of it. The unresolved antagonism keeps the 'suggestion' in the air.

---

[71] Owen Knowles ed., *'My Dear Friend'* (2008), 104. Lawrence met Conrad once, at the house of Hugh Walpole in July 1920. For Conrad and Lawrence, see Ton Hoenselaars and Gene Moore, 'Joseph Conrad and T. E. Lawrence', *Conradiana* 27:1 (Spring 1995), 3–20. In 1929, Lawrence tried unsuccessfully to get Jacob Epstein to do a commemorative bust of Hardy, which would have complemented the one of Conrad he had completed five years previously.

2 The Sound of History

Nostromo

While from its very opening, with the clouds hushing the Placid Gulf, much of *Nostromo* finds its life in the air, the note struck and its strident resonance demand a different auditory attention from anything met in this study so far. The strain of civic life in Sulaco, heard 'braying operatic selections on the plaza' (90),[72] competes with the more indigenous sound of the popular feasts held on the land just acquired by the Railway Company, and soon to be heard there no more,

> the dance music vibrating and shrieking with a racking rhythm, overhung by the tremendous, sustained, hollow roar of the gombo. The barbarous and imposing noise of the big drum, that can madden a crowd, and that even Europeans cannot hear without a strange emotion, seemed to draw Nostromo on to its source . . . (126)

This is not disdain for inept performance; what Conrad does with that we know from *Victory*: 'An instrumental uproar, screaming, grunting, whining, sobbing, scraping, squeaking some kind of lively air . . . The Zangiacomo band was not making music; it was simply murdering silence with a vulgar, ferocious energy' (69). Neither is it disdain for 'the primitive', such as can be found in the psychomusicology of Edmund Gurney, for instance. Although it is deemed 'barbarous', the commanding aerial presence released by the beaten skin of the gombo dramatises something that is thoroughly *contemporary* in the soundscape, produced in the conditions of racial, national, linguistic and class collision through which modern Sulaco is born. Both the music and the writing approach the condition that Luigi Russolo celebrated in *The Art of Noises: Futurist Manifesto* (1911), an art which 'seeks out combinations more dissonant, stranger, and harsher for the ear. Thus, it comes ever closer to the *noise-sound*.'[73] Even though Conrad as a listener to music would have shuddered with distaste at the '*6 families of noises* of the futurist orchestra' that Russolo proposes ('Roars, Explosions etc.'; 'Whistling, Hissing etc.'; 'Whispers, Murmurs etc.'; 'Screeching, Creaking etc.'; 'Beating on Metals, Woods etc.'; 'Shrieks, Howls etc.'), as an artist of modern life

---

[72] All references to *Nostromo* are to the 1947 Dent Collected Edition, a reprint of the 1923 Uniform Edition.
[73] Luigi Russolo, *The Art of Noises* (1986), 24.

he understands the distinction Russolo provocatively makes between noise and sound:

> Every manifestation of life is accompanied by noise. Noise is thus familiar to our ear and has the power of immediately recalling life itself. Sound, estranged from life, always musical, something in itself, an occasional not a necessary element, has become for our ear what for the eye is a too familiar sight. Noise instead, arriving confused and irregular from the irregular confusion of life, is never revealed to us entirely and always holds innumerable surprises.[74]

Hardy is more under the sway of sound as the musical 'something in itself' than Conrad. And Conrad seeks more strenuously than Hardy to pressurise the fabric of his prose with that present quality of 'arriving', and of the potential revelation of noise as Russolo describes it. In his Introduction to the unfinished *The Sisters* (1928), Ford Madox Ford points up this aspect of Conrad's prose, 'its one aim being to be interesting and to be interesting because of the quality of surprise' (25). In *Nostromo*, that surprise works on the ear of the reader to press close or withdraw to a distance with such rapidity that reading much of the novel has a precipitous and highly-strung quality to it, especially for those prepared to become immersed, even temporarily lost, through the inducements of the wittily mobile style.

The 'uproar' and 'unrest' provided by *Nostromo* (two of Conrad's favourite words, while 'conjunction' and 'courses' are two of Hardy's) is belied by the stately, and silent, unfolding of the visual scene of the novel's opening – a silence that stretches behind the busy action of the foreground, and one that I will return to in the next chapter. But it is, indeed, sound that announces the transformation effected by the extractive industries' material re-arrangement of the landscape, emptying the solitude of the San Tomé gorge of its 'paradise of snakes'. In the ever-present but generally unremarked keynote of the 'revolving turbine-wheels' of the mine, *Nostromo* exemplifies what Emily Thompson has written, that 'A soundscape, like a landscape, ultimately has more to do with civilisation than with nature, and, as such, it is constantly under construction and always undergoing change.'[75] For what is heard on those evenings when 'the ore shoots would begin to rattle' is the civilising 'desire' which Charles

---

[74] Ibid., 27.
[75] Emily Thompson, *The Soundscape of Modernity* (2002), 2.

Gould has heard in his imagination, which is now the 'accomplished fact' of the Occidental Province:

> The great clattering, shuffling noise, gathering speed and weight, would be caught up by the walls of the gorge, and sent upon the plain in a growl of thunder. The pasadero in Rincon swore that on calm nights, by listening intently, he could catch the sound in his doorway as of a storm in the mountains.
>
> To Charles Gould's fancy it seemed that the sound must reach the uttermost limits of the province. Riding at night towards the mine, it would meet him at the edge of a little wood just beyond Rincon. There was no mistaking the growling mutter of the mountain pouring its stream of treasure under the stamps; and it came to his heart with the peculiar force of a proclamation thundered forth over the land and the marvellousness of an accomplished fact fulfilling an audacious desire. (105)

This simple evocation of the flow of the silver ore is extraordinary in provoking far from simply the questions that continue to trouble and divide philosophers in the field of audition – where is this sound? what constitutes it? True to wave theory, the writing locates it in many places: between 'the walls of the gorge', 'upon the plain', 'in (the pasadero's) doorway' in Rincon, 'at the edge of a little wood just beyond Rincon', but also in the mountain, 'under the stamps'. On the other hand, a more fanciful propagation of this sound has it reaching 'the outermost limit of the province', suspended 'over the land', yet also located intimately in 'his (Gould's) heart'. So densely specified is its presence, the reader must share Charles Gould's sense that the harsh sound of silver production has penetrated the fabric of life in the Occidental Province to be a resident of the state with its own force of personality. To describe what this sound *is*, Conrad gives it animated qualities of shuffling, growling and muttering, embodies it as an object that can be sent out upon the plain and, conversely, as a subject with the independent intention to go out to meet Don Carlos riding at night. Equally, this sound is constituted of an ideal aspect in its imagined power in the minds of men – from the aural image of 'a storm in the mountains', to its transformation into 'a proclamation', and finally to its most abstract form as a marvel and a fulfilment. As such, the mental medium of perception and the material medium of mountain, plain and air, are so involved as here to embody that interpenetration of the material with the ideal which *Nostromo* in so many ways takes as its central subject.

The issues raised in the paragraph above resound in every corner of the novel. Aaron Fogel has memorably and succinctly summarised the dynamic of this by proposing that Part First of *Nostromo* 'sets up a contrast between nature as silence and history as noise'.[76] The thronging density recorded and transmitted by the surface of the text has engaged or bewildered readers since the novel's publication, placing them vividly 'in the thick of things', as Captain Mitchell would say, or merely confusing and overwhelming them. Though perhaps not quite 'annihilated mentally', the *Daily Telegraph* reviewer of 9 November 1904 seems not far from suffering the 'sudden surfeit of sights, sounds, names, facts, and complicated information imperfectly apprehended' (486) endured by Captain Mitchell's privileged passenger, as he writes, 'the beauty of the scene as a whole is lost, the sense of proportion is absent . . . detail absorbs the position of outline, which becomes impossibly blurred . . . his canvas is immense, and yet it is overcrowded'.[77] However, this visual assessment can be rewritten in terms of sound – or noise – in order to attend precisely to what the overcrowding produces in place of beauty, proportion and outline. The noise of history certainly blurs these things, just as it scatters the development of character into the contingency of events. The unruly, jostling aspect of Costaguana's civic life is its public gatherings and declamations, manufacturing a discourse of projected, official speech to which the individual inner life is lost.

So in Part Third, after Pedrito Montero's triumphant counter-revolutionary entry into Sulaco, his followers expect him 'to begin scattering at once some sort of visible largesse', but 'What he began was a speech' (389). No more than an expressive mime to the majority of the crowd, what is brilliantly captured is the transmission and 'decay' (as acoustic science terms it) of noise-sound in urban space:

The *vivas* of those nearest to the orator bursting out suddenly propagated themselves

> irregularly to the confines of the crowd, like flames running over dry grass, and expired in the opening of the streets. In the intervals, over the swarming Plaza brooded a heavy silence, in which the mouth of the orator went on opening and shutting, and detached phrases – 'The happiness of the people,' 'Sons of the country,' 'The entire world, *el mundo entiero*' – reached even the packed steps of the cathedral with a feeble clear ring, thin as the buzzing of a mosquito. (390)

---

[76] Aaron Fogel, *Coercion to Speak* (1985), 107.
[77] Sherry ed., *Joseph Conrad: The Critical Heritage*, 167.

The sporadic eruption of these little entities of sound observed in their birth, motion and expiry robs expressive language of coherent meaning, but leaves it a dangerous irritant on the body politic. The buzzing mosquito of Pedrito Montero recalls his opponent, that believer in parliamentary institutions, Don Justé Lopez, intoning the 'acceptance of accomplished facts' (the victory of the Monteros) in the Casa Gould, where 'the convinced drone of his voice lost itself in the stillness of the house like the deep buzzing of some ponderous insect' (367; see also 355 and 237). Thus what passes in the drawing room of the Casa Gould is equally exposed to a satirical ear, and can be raised in pitch, literally, towards hysterical absurdity:

> In the comparative peace of the room the screaming '*Monsieur l'Administrateur*' of the frail, hairy Frenchman seemed to acquire a preternatural shrillness. The explorer of the Capitalist syndicate was still enthusiastic. 'Ten million dollars' worth of copper practically in sight, *Monsieur l'Administrateur*. Ten millions in sight! And a railway coming – a railway! They will never believe my report. *C'est trop beau.*' He fell a prey to a screaming ecstasy, in the midst of sagely nodding heads, before Charles Gould's imperturbable calm. (199)

The near silence between Charles and Emilia Gould following this gathering of the Blancoist cabal is part of a pattern of acoustic shifts which point up the desperation heard in the timbre of all the foreground noise. In the larger, persistent, unresponsive silences of the novel, Conrad is continually alert to the quelling of such sounds by what he called in another context, 'an unresonnant (*sic*) medium' (*CL* 3:162).

In the early pages of *Nostromo* sound intrudes upon the quiet of Sulaco to bring the violent incursions of 'history' into the lives of the people and the province in a manner more closely pressing upon the senses than any we have yet examined. The description of the riot of the townspeople which covers chapters two, three and four shows the extent to which Conrad conceives such scenes in terms of an auditory field charged with movement in something of the manner that Russolo wished to incorporate into music. We experience the events of 'that day'[78] as a series of sound fragments uncertainly heard from the interior of the Casa Viola, where 'the first sounds of the riot' (18) have caused the staff to flee, leaving Old Giorgio, who 'had

---

[78] 2 May 1890, according to Cedric Watts. However, Conrad wrote to Edmund Gosse that the history is 'an achievement in mosaic . . . in the seventh decade of the nineteenth century' (*CL* 6:231).

disregarded the preliminary sounds of trouble' (16), and his family alone to face the looters:

> Bursts of great shouting rose and died away, like wild gusts of wind on the plain round the barricaded house; the fitful popping of shots grew louder above the yelling. Sometimes there were intervals of unaccountable stillness outside, and nothing could have been more gaily peaceful than the narrow bright lines of sunlight from the cracks in the shutters, ruled straight across the *café* over the disarranged chairs and tables to the wall opposite. (18)

The shifting, nearing, receding relations between things are, to this group of sheltering inmates, necessarily a matter of sound; the given, stable ground of things is visual, with the 'gaily peaceful' 'bright lines of sunlight' conveying the domesticity that usually reigns.

In the following paragraph, as we begin to make a sequence out of what had seemed random, we read,

> A sudden outbreak of defiant yelling quite near the house sank all at once to a confused murmur of growls. Somebody ran along; the loud catching of his breath was heard for an instant passing the door; there were hoarse mutters and footsteps near the wall; a shoulder rubbed against the shutter, effacing the bright lines of sunshine pencilled across the whole breadth of the room. (19)

The removal of any auditory horizon, and the effacement of the reassuring lines of sunlight, amplifies the obscure threat. Similar to many scenes of listening and interpretation of sound in Hardy, it stops us at the phenomenal quality of the event, with access to the individual apprehending *mind* suspended. However, by the end of the next paragraph the darkness of the room is 'alight with evil, stealthy sounds. The Violas had them in their ears as though invisible ghosts hovering about their chairs had consulted in mutters' (19). This final sentence is the first in the paragraph to make its grammatical subject the Violas and the physiological immediacy of the listening 'in their ears'. Yet, even here, the ascendancy of sound is maintained by a wonderfully grotesque example of Conrad's signature participial clause of resemblance ('as though invisible ghosts hovering . . .'), with its indeterminate status between sensation and conception the feature that makes it so attractive to its author. Only then is the reader finally led to a perception in the collective mind of the Violas, that these sounds are a subdued conversation 'as to the advisability of setting fire to this foreigner's casa' (19). For three paragraphs the reader has been held in the disputed airspace between the source of sounds and their reception; in the noise of historical events, the reader is held unusually fast to the sound itself before an explanation of the source or the mental perspective of a recipient is offered as relief.

When Giorgio concludes that 'These were not a people striving for justice, but thieves' (20), the enduring visual ground of his existence re-asserts itself with his glance at 'the coloured lithograph of Garibaldi in a black frame on the white wall; a thread of strong sunlight cut it perpendicularly' (21). Definite line and colour re-enter, and the picture removes the strife of history to a fixed and ideal distance, in whose illuminated figure the sound of the present is as nothing. For Giorgio, history is vision, not noise. But the chapter refuses the consolations of this idealism, summarily bringing the reader back to immediate contact with present events in the blows, snorting, tramping, striking, jingling and shouts that explosively pack the concluding paragraph to end on the stridently rising cadence of the 'Hola! hola, in there!' (21) of Nostromo's arrival. Anxiously contemplating 'the ever-enlarging vistas opening before me' of his 'largest canvas',[79] Conrad is repeatedly captured by the abrupt summons of disruptive sound.

*

As sight is inherently spatial, so sound is bound to duration. And as opposed to a musical tone, which 'strikes the ear as a perfectly undisturbed, uniform sound which remains unaltered as long as it exists', Helmholtz considered that *noise* is characterised by 'a rapid alternation of different kinds of sensation of sound'. Hillel Schwartz directly comments, 'It followed that noise was of the instant, while musical tones relied upon elongations of experience to be heard as uniform and undisturbed.'[80] The quality of the instant as apprehended in the disturbance made by noise is what is concentrated into the crowded foreground of *Nostromo*, contrasting with the spatial dimensions into which the novel widens and where sound is lost.

Part of the capaciousness of this extraordinary novel lies in its attention to the tiny as well as the vast, and the nature and impact of this 'instant' is illuminated by a materialist strain of thought about physical and mental shock which had weight in the second half of

---

[79] 'Author's Note' to *Nostromo* and to *The Secret Agent*.
[80] Both quotations in Hillel Schwartz, *Making Noise: From Babel to the Big Bang and Beyond* (2011), 326.

the nineteenth century. In discussing 'the individual sensations and emotions, real or ideal, of which consciousness is built up', Herbert Spencer in *The Principles of Psychology* arrives at the suggestion, 'It is possible, then – may we not even say probable? – that something of the same order as that which we call a nervous shock is the ultimate unit of consciousness.' The connection I am making is that, drawing upon Helmholtz's acoustic experiments, Spencer makes his way to the idea of nervous shock as the irreducible unit from which consciousness is compounded by considering units of *sound*: 'If the different sensations known as sounds are built out of a common unit, is it not to be rationally inferred that so likewise are the different sensations known as tastes, and the different sensations known as odours, and the different sensations known as colours?' In his determination to find the material constituents of consciousness, Spencer continues:

> Have we any clue to this primordial element? I think we have. . . . The subjective effect produced by a crack or noise that has no appreciable duration is little else than a nervous shock. Though we distinguish such a nervous shock as belonging to what we call sounds, yet it does not differ very much from nervous shocks of other kinds.[81]

Nearly twenty years later we find Bain giving a similar character to consciousness: 'The simplest term we can employ for a mental state is a *shock*; a word equally applicable to the bodily side and to the mental side.'[82] William James later demolishes Spencer's fundamentally atomic argument with his view of consciousness as 'a sensibly continuous stream', so influential for the literature of the early twentieth century. He casts Spencer and the sensationists as thoroughly misguided in following 'the Humian doctrine that our thought is composed of separate independent parts'. Our awareness seizes upon things not in fragments but as a whole, and it is the whole of our thought that does so: '*Whatever things are thought in relation are thought from the outset in a unity, in a single pulse of subjectivity.*'[83] However, as a mode of literary composition, not a

---

[81] Herbert Spencer, *The Principles of Psychology*, second edition (1870), vol. 1, 148, 151, 150.
[82] Alexander Bain, *Mind and Body* (1873), 40. See also Jill Matus, 'Emergent Theories of Victorian Mind Shock', in Anne Stiles ed., *Neurology and Literature 1860–1920* (2007), 163–83.
[83] William James, *Principles of Psychology* (1890), vol. 1, 237 and 278. It is, however, G. H. Lewes who introduces the phrase 'stream of consciousness' and 'stream of sensation' into discussions of mind well before James, with whom the idea has become associated: see *The Physiology of Common Life* (1860), vol. 2, 45, 47.

theory of mind, a general sense of bodily and mental awareness as made up of innumerable nervous shocks retained an attraction for Conrad, and in part accounts for the explosive presence of sound in his novels. It is while writing *Nostromo* that Conrad claims to Wells that 'for me, writing – *the only possible writing* – is just simply the conversion of nervous force into phrases' (*CL* 3:85), which asserts a startlingly material basis for composition.[84]

Nostromo's portrayal of history both invites and refuses the sweep of panorama because of the atomising attention to the small shocks that constitute and disrupt it. The paired scenes of departure from the port – that of the railway investor Sir John in Part First, and of Barrios, in order to secure Cayta for the Occidental province, in Part Second – are large outdoor scenes of moment in Sulaco's secession from Costaguana, which in our reading become an amalgamation of personal muttering, 'distant acclamations', 'crepitating noise', detonations and 'faint bursts of military music'. But what the earlier scene depicts in an amused and ironic manner has become 'a most desperate game', at least to Mrs Gould's mind, in the second. In each case Conrad has the returning Gould party pass the Casa Viola and exchange words with Giorgio. After the meeting with Sir John, Mrs Gould is able to reassure the old Garibaldino that his house will be safe from the changes to be wrought by the development of the railway. The return from the departure of Barrios is telling in its difference: it is the ironically offhand Decoud who converses with Giorgio, procuring only a bitter retort about 'the people' serving the interests of the Blancos. And, instead of the sound of the popular holiday, alluded to at the beginning of this section, in the midst of which Nostromo is hero, the later chapter concludes upon the sound which has replaced it upon the same patch of ground. It is the most striking phenomenal description in the entire novel.

> The bells of the city were striking the hour of Oracion when the carriage rolled under the old gateway facing the harbour like a shapeless monument of leaves and stones. The rumble of wheels under the sonorous arch was traversed by a strange, piercing shriek, and Decoud, from his back seat, had a view of the people behind the carriage trudging along the road outside, all turning their heads, in sombreros and rebozos, to look at a locomotive, which rolled quickly out of sight behind Giorgio Viola's house, under a white trail of steam that seemed to vanish in the breathless, hysterically prolonged scream of warlike triumph. And it was all like a fleeting vision, the shrieking ghost of a railway engine fleeing across

---

[84] Compare Bain: 'We assume, as a fundamental fact, that, with nervous action feeling begins' (*Mind and Body*, 52).

the frame of the archway, behind the startled movement of the people streaming back from a military spectacle with silent footsteps on the dust of the road. It was a material train returning from the Campo to the palisaded yards. The empty cars rolled lightly on the single track; there was no rumble of wheels, no tremor on the ground. The engine-driver, running past the Casa Viola with the salute of an uplifted arm, checked his speed smartly before entering the yard; and when the ear-splitting screech of the steam-whistle for the brakes had stopped, a series of hard, battering shocks, mingled with the clanking of chain-couplings, made a tumult of blows and shaken fetters under the vault of the gate. (171–2)

After reading this we must feel that, when Grant Allen writes in *Physiological Aesthetics* that 'auditory nerves are not liable to be scratched, burned, bruised, or attacked by chemical agents, but only to be wearied by over-use and jarred by discordant sounds', he gives only a faint notion of our susceptibility to the penetrating power of sound.[85] However, the astonishing 'hard, battering shocks' of the violent conclusion (one thinks of the 'frightful strident concussions' in the 'Coal Dust' chapter of *Women in Love*) should not deafen our senses to the uncanny synaesthesia of the phenomenal experience that precedes it, and which draws the arrival of the future upon a stunned present that already feels like the past. While the 'sonorous arch' of the old city gateway has been for three centuries resonating to the rounded rumbling of carriage wheels, a new sonic entity is scored as a bisecting horizontal, a 'shriek' and a 'scream', across the archway's 'frame' and across the familiar 'rumble' itself, as one sound is 'traversed' by another one pitched higher. Conrad's verb, in keeping with a classical mechanics of force, makes us view sound as action; yet as sound dissolves into vision, that singular force is reviewed as the more dispersed property of an energy field, mirroring a modern physics that just predates the action of the novel. The experience is doubly paradoxical: filled with velocity and wounding noise, this stilled moment is *seen* as in mime, one from which sound has departed; though conversely, and confoundingly, a trail of steam appears to vanish *sounded* in a breathless, hysterical scream. The senses cannot seize upon the substance that constitutes the moment which now possesses them. But when the material train returns shockingly upon us with the 'ear-splitting screech of the steam-whistle', the nerves, assaulted almost beyond bearing, in practice recover their accustomed afferent pathways to render an unequivocally auditory sensation.

[85] Grant Allen, *Physiological Aesthetics* (1877), 98.

An apt comment by Hillel Schwartz gives a historical context to this sensational and disorientating experience of history:

> acoustically the steam whistles gave a local twist to time and presence.... the twist in time produced by the steam-driven locomotives came from the relationship of listeners to sounds now crossing regularly in front of them at a velocity that had previously been witnessed only on the rarest of occasions: a person falling from a cliff, screaming; a meteor sizzling across the sky.[86]

This illuminates the aspect of visual revelation in Conrad's summons of this new sound, an eidetic and hallucinatory quality announced by the 'strange piercing shriek', which is elongated by a Doppler effect to a 'breathless, hysterically prolonged scream', then to re-realise itself as a fleeting and fleeing *vision*, an appalling 'shrieking ghost'. Passing, vanishing, then approaching, the reappearing ghost-train is ridden by a nerveless cipher, like a silent portent that then declares itself in irresistible waves of noise. Dr Monygham will, of course, give his celebrated judgement on the inhumanity of the progress instituted by 'material interests'; but, coming more than 300 pages earlier, this conjuring of the 'material train' impresses the same message in the vivid epiphany of the central sentence of this passage: 'And it was all like a fleeting vision, the shrieking ghost of a railway engine fleeing across the frame of the archway, behind the startled movement of the people streaming back from a military spectacle with silent footsteps on the dust of the road.' Tracking back from the sensory phenomenon of the 'fleeting vision', through the material embodiments of power (the steam engine, the archway, the military), the sentence ends with the age-old palpable reality of the silent footsteps of the people and the dust of the road. In the next chapter Decoud is granted the acuteness to analyse his auditory and spectacular experience in precisely the historical terms these juxtapositions suggest, when he declares 'This sound puts a new edge on a very old truth' (173). But already the train bisecting the archway of the conquistadors in the city walls, startling the silent people, is an emblem fit for the armorial shield above the arch, 'smoothed out as if in readiness for some new device typical of the impending progress' (173). But rather than a readable pictorial effect, the chapter closes by leaving such a 'tumult' of relentless metallic concussion resounding around us that any capacity to take hold of the scene in this way is, at least temporarily, obliterated.

[86] Schwartz, *Making Noise*, 318.

Inherent in Conrad's style is a registration of history as impact and collision clearing a space for some new apparition to materialise. It orientates towards a sensational present and an emergent future, and distinctively crowds out the melancholy note of elegy. It is not incidental that the *OED* entry for 'impression' commences 'L. *impressio* onset, attack', complementing the revelatory 'short vision' that is Conrad's favoured mode of perception, as we saw in the last chapter. And the idea of an 'onset style' is in accord with modern theories of audition that suggest the physiology of hearing is attuned to onset, focusing upon the initial portion of a signal rather than its continuation.[87] Such a mode of attention adopted as writing produces a sensational art of jolts and shocks, gusts and receding visions, employed to make 'history' a dramatic encounter. It contests the novel's other demonstration that, before all, history is discourse.

Nostromo's most startling and resonant depiction of being enveloped in the sound of history comes at the end of Part Third, chapter 4. In this chapter Charles Gould returns to his house in the early morning of 4 May after aiding the exodus of Blanco families from Sulaco, and awaits the triumphant entry into the town of Pedrito Montero who has crossed the Sierra in pursuit of the fleeing Ribiera after the battle of Socorro. Learning from Dr Monygham of the apparent deaths of Decoud and Nostromo, Gould imagines himself writing to Holroyd, 'I am forced to take up openly the plan of a provincial revolution' (379), and then continues to discuss quietly the current plight with Monygham and his wife. He is cut short:

> His voice was covered by the booming of the great bell of the cathedral. Three single strokes, one after another, burst out explosively, dying away in deep and mellow vibrations. And then all the bells in the tower of every church, convent, or chapel in town, even those that had remained shut up for years, pealed out together with a crash. In this furious flood of metallic uproar there was a power of suggesting images of strife and violence which blanched Mrs. Gould's cheek. Basilio, who had been waiting at table, shrinking within himself, clung to the sideboard with chattering teeth. It was impossible to hear yourself speak. (381–2)

This is sound as onslaught, bearing all before it, but also bearing all with it: the uncustomary cacophonous crash summons all of the members of the Gould household, 'mozos from the stable, gardeners,

---

[87] Steven Greenberg, 'Auditory Function', in Cocker ed., *Encyclopaedia of Acoustics* (1997), vol. 3, 123–30.

nondescript helpers living on the crumbs of the munificent house' (382), even down to the old gatekeeper, whose vivid witness of the execution by firing squad of Henry Gould, Charles's uncle and president of a separate Sulaco, forty-five years previously, takes up six lines of the description. This, too, is history suddenly displayed; in Conrad's abrupt and startling fashion, sound detonates the quiet order maintained by thick walls and floors to release vision, not of the welcome given to the new dispensation of Pedrito Montero, which waits for the next chapter, but, unexpectedly and paradoxically, of a past which encompasses the earliest reaches of the present political situation. Conrad widens and widens the sensational moment until the Casa Gould resonates to the experience of being engulfed by the tide of history. The chapter ends – the third time that Conrad auditorily suspends the reader in this way – 'The crockery rattled on table and sideboard, and the whole house seemed to sway in the deafening wave of sound' (383).

*

Soundwaves are the agitated fabric of *Nostromo*. Unlike the singular voice of Kurtz, drawing Marlow towards it in a search for meaning, the multiple voices of Costaguana radiate towards peripheries. For the novel's central episode, in which Nostromo and Decoud are pitched into the black night of the Placid Gulf with a consignment of silver, Conrad creates a totally auditory environment of straining ears and urgent whispers, in which 'the stillness was so profound that Decoud felt as if the slightest sound conceivable must travel unchecked and audible to the end of the world' (284). In a more sustained way than in any other novel transmission and collision are Conrad's concerns, which find their most heightened expression in the strange aerial dimension of the Gulf. Here the collision of Sotillo's troopship with the lighter bearing the silver is the central event in the plot, affecting everything that comes after it, and felt by Decoud as 'a crack of timbers and a staggering shock', and heard in a weirdly displaced manner as 'a strange and amazed voice cried out something above him in the night' (291). This voice is that of Hirsch, the Esmeralda hide-merchant who had been hiding in the lighter, and who is now clinging to the snagged anchor of Sotillo's vessel in a terrified attempt to escape the nightmare his own fears had flung him into. Hirsch's later role is to embody the most extreme case of what we find everywhere in the novel, that human sounds are the cries forced from men and women by the collisions of fixed ideas with unaccommodating realities, and of their own concept of themselves with that of others.

Sotillo has Hirsch appallingly tortured by strappado to wrench from him the truth about the silver, a truth in accord with Sotillo's obsessive desire to lay his hands upon the treasure. (It is fitting that these details are more than a hundred pages apart in the narrative, and that a reader has to force recollection through a welter of other events to feel she commands a coherent sequence that corresponds to this particular thread.) Leaving Hirsch strung up over a beam in the O.S.N. warehouse where he has billeted himself, Sotillo leaves the room:

> Hirsch went on screaming all alone behind the half-closed jalousies while the sunshine, reflected from the water of the harbour, made an ever-running ripple of light high up on the wall. He screamed with uplifted eyebrows and a wide-open mouth – incredibly wide, black, enormous, full of teeth – comical. (447)

The contrast between the pleasant, continuous 'ever-running ripple of light' and the heavily hanging agony in the room, wracked by the different continuousness of pain, is such that Hardy's eye and ear would make; but the unseemly zest with which the second sentence extends its lacerations through a parenthesis that cartoonishly thrusts Hirsch's mouth at us is purely Conradian. 'Comical' is the most unsettling single word in the novel, perhaps in all Conrad's fiction, finding out the reader's already felt reaction to Hirsch's screaming mouth and making us aware of our complicity in the hateful, laughing torture of the Jew. Conrad does not, however, leave Hirsch's screams as a postmodern device for robbing the reader of a standpoint for moral judgement; they are an audible reality of the Sulacan soundscape:

> In the still burning air of the windless afternoon he made the waves of his agony travel as far as the O.S.N. Company's offices. Captain Mitchell on the balcony, trying to make out what went on generally, had heard him faintly but distinctly, and the feeble and appalling sound lingered in his ears after he had retreated indoors with blanched cheeks. He had been driven off the balcony several times during that afternoon. (447)

Hirsch, so often paraded by the narration as a hapless and ridiculous victim, has the power to transmit the meaning of what is being done to him, even to Captain Mitchell, and one page later he will summon the physical and psychological force to project himself at his tormentor Sotillo at a visceral level even more somatically intimate than the yell of pain: 'with the sudden flash of a grin and a straining forward of the wrenched shoulders, he spat violently into his face' (448). Hirsch's precipitate action (it precipitates his immediate death) is launched from the novel's primary energy of jolting, surprising, forward movement and collision.

To close where the novel does, upon Linda's final cry from the lighthouse of the Great Isabel after she hears from Dr Monygham that Nostromo is dead, is to acknowledge the opposite movement, a final attempt to will a stilled fixity and permanence upon what is dynamic and always in flight. Mark Muldoon brings the sensory dimension of this into focus when he says, 'What is most difficult for philosophers to accept is the fact that auditory qualities are completely dynamic and hence imageless.'[88] This is a difficulty not only for philosophers, but for Linda Viola and for Conrad too. The final scene is composed of the shouts of Dr Monygham as he pulls into the Great Isabel on the police-galley, and the cries of Linda from the outer gallery of the lighthouse; yet a powerfully pictorialising demand is made upon this auditory flight. Linda whispers in the moonlight:

> 'I cannot understand. But I shall never forget thee. Never!'
> She stood silent and still, collecting her strength, to throw all her fidelity, her pain, her bewilderment, and despair into one great cry.
> 'Never! Gian' Battista!'
> Dr Monygham, pulling round in the police-galley, heard the name pass over his head. It was another of Nostromo's triumphs, the greatest, the most enviable, the most sinister of all. In that true cry of undying passion that seemed to ring aloud from Punta Mala to Azuera and away to the bright line of the horizon, overhung by a big white cloud shining like a mass of solid silver, the genius of the magnificent Capataz de Cargadores dominated the dark gulf containing his conquests of treasure and love. (566)

The aspect that retrieves for this passing cry a place of permanence is the turn to the visual image, and one whose spatial dimension has been there from the very beginning of the novel. Although Linda's cry that 'ring(s) aloud' is the subject of the novel's final sentence, its waves of sound are effectively lost and absorbed by the static and imposing vision of the 'big white cloud shining like a mass of solid silver' that now bars both entrance to and exit from the Gulf in eternal fixity. It is

---

[88] Muldoon, 'Silence Revisited', 279.

the visual image of the silver rather than the cry of love (even though that is the last word), upon which, I imagine, nearly every reader closes the novel. Strangely, we are brought back to Mrs Yeobright and the gloriously complete ensilvered heron 'up in the zenith'; for all that the deepest need in any Conrad novel is the imposition of a human voice upon silence, for his ringing close he could not quite trust to sound. But as readers, to have travelled by the aerial transmission of sound from the fastness of Egdon Heath to that of mountain-girt Sulaco, from one novel that could be seen almost to repel political history, to another which records it so acutely – and via a novella held in several ways to be the quintessential witness to its contemporary history – is to have been made to realise upon our senses how Hardy and Conrad are creatively associated in their turn to the auditory field to convey *activity*, the precursor to change.

Chapter Five

Identity and Margin

> On a bright summer day in the open air, the world with my ego suddenly appeared to me as *one* coherent mass of sensations, only more strongly coherent in the ego.
>
> Ernst Mach, *Contributions to the Analysis of the Sensations* (1886)

In *Helmholtz and the Modern Listener*, Benjamin Steege proposes that 'the project of organic physics' of the mid-nineteenth century incorporated 'the erasure from scientific discourse ... of the difference between forces internal to organisms and those external to them, between organic and inorganic, between living and dead'.[1] The project of the nineteenth-century novel, on the other hand (with a notable exception in *Wuthering Heights*), might be thought of as a definition of human identity more in line with physiology, with the operation of the senses patrolling the borders of subjectivity to provide a delineation between self and environment. This chapter, however, sees the mature fiction of Hardy and Conrad as exploring a point at which sensory experience creates a margin within which self and circumambient world are not so exclusively defined. In terms of the wider affiliations of this book, Alice Jenkins puts the matter very aptly:

> Field theory obliges us to be sceptical about beliefs in limits, in solidity, and in neutral space. In terms of fiction these are the beliefs that give rise to ideas about the self as a bordered atomic unit; about the boundaries of influence exerted by people on one another; and about the neutrality of the spaces in which they live. These beliefs appear to be fundamental to the realist novel.[2]

---

[1] Benjamin Steege, *Helmholtz and the Modern Listener* (2012), 68ff.
[2] Alice Jenkins, *Space and the 'March of Mind'* (2007), 207.

In *The Mayor of Casterbridge*, the strongly physiological cast of Hardy's conception of the self is by no means discarded, but the enlarged role given to interior mental space is also challenged in the novel by a different account of inhering in the world. *Tess of the d'Urbervilles* and *Nostromo* progressively widen this vision to offer the furthest reaches of Hardy's and Conrad's exploration of the relation between the individual sense-world and the larger processes that surround it. In different ways the conventional boundaries between 'inner' experience and that which is expressed in the 'outer' world are reimagined: the three books are their authors' supreme achievements in realising a world in which characters assert their existence, and to which, creatively and destructively, they lose it.

1 Inspection, Immersion

The Mayor of Casterbridge

At its centre, and radiating out to its final words, *The Mayor of Casterbridge* depicts two different ways of being in the world. Recurrent in Hardy is the portrayal of a young woman coming to awareness of herself at a moment of crisis. For Elizabeth-Jane this arrives in the poignant, brief chapter 18, which, with its corresponding following Henchard chapter, is a highlight in Hardy's portrayals in any of his novels of the individual human consciousness finding itself amid the larger movements of life. Through the importuning of sounds and sights, Elizabeth's night vigil by her dying mother's bedside becomes a self-interrogation:

> The latter sat up with her mother to the utmost of her strength night after night. To learn to take the universe seriously there is no quicker way than to watch – to be a 'waker', as the country people call it. Between the hours at which the last toss-pot went by and the first sparrow shook himself, the silence in Casterbridge – barring the rare sound of the watchman – was broken in Elizabeth's ear only by the time-piece in the bedroom ticking frantically against the clock on the stairs; ticking harder and harder till it seemed to clang like a gong; and all this while the subtle-souled girl asking herself why she was born, why sitting in a room, and blinking at the candle; why things around her had taken the shape they wore in preference to every other possible shape. Why they stared at her so helplessly, as if waiting for

the touch of some wand that should release them from terrestrial constraint; what that chaos called consciousness, which spun in her at this moment like a top, tended to, and began in. Her eyes fell together; she was awake, yet she was asleep.

A word from her mother roused her. (189)[3]

The loosening of Elizabeth-Jane's habitual careful defences is a movement inward, transforming surrounding sounds to insistent questions about things, and place, and self. While this indication of an inner landscape has incipient precedents in earlier Hardy, generally, as we have seen, the writing guards access to interiority, catching on the phenomena of the senses to leave the 'inner self' a presumption. Here, Elizabeth-Jane's awareness of time is, initially, presented neither as individual nor inwardly felt: she fulfils the country notion of a 'waker', whose lonely vigil is marked from without by the drunkard, the watchman and the sparrow lending their voices to a silence which belongs to Casterbridge. In fact, the subject of the unwinding central sentence is 'the silence in Casterbridge', not her; yet the action of the main clause brings extraneous sound boldly to her own sensational threshold, as this silence 'was broken in Elizabeth's ear', suddenly confining the reader to physiological space, and one that vibrates to a different time, 'ticking frantically'. 'Frantically', and then 'harder and harder', are the adverbial signs which move the reader into Elizabeth's subjective experience of time urged forward alarmingly, seconds treading on each others' heels until divisions of measurement collapse and 'it seemed to clang like a gong'. Physical space is filled by a single strident and summoning sound as the confusion of clock against clock promotes a comparably material explanation of unsynchronised sound; but this is simultaneously a mental space, with its suggestion of Elizabeth's distress and sense of isolation creating an experience of space and time which can only be represented by sounding the note of alarm.

The direction towards an unvoiced inner speech here takes Hardy further than his previous fiction in the correlation of physical sensation and mental awareness. For it is not that the one exactly gives rise to the other; in a beautiful simultaneity – 'and all this while the subtle-souled girl asking herself . . .' – Elizabeth-Jane's separate thinking

---

[3] All references to *The Mayor of Casterbridge* are to the Penguin English Library edition (1978), edited by Martin Seymour-Smith, which follows the Wessex edition of 1912.

being asserts itself, accommodating yet finding its feet, as it were, against the sensory flow. There is no further to go than this circulation of questions that encompass the profoundest doubts about identity and purpose, but which never leave the physical circumstance of the room and the candle staring back at her. Elizabeth's four 'whys' finally resolve themselves into a 'what', her awareness of a 'chaos called consciousness' giving her a perspective unmatched by any other character in the novel. But freed of constraint herself, motion now whirls within the still girl like a spinning top, and the direction and purpose of this awareness of self is explicitly questioned as to what it 'tended to, and began in'. The paratactic construction of the sentence, beginning with 'Why' and returning to 'began in', repudiates the possibility of arrival at an answer, and Elizabeth-Jane, though asleep yet certainly 'awake' in a new way, is not again in the novel given the unrestful privilege of such insight into the constitution of the mind.[4]

To show more completely how Hardy realises a *mental* perspective that is new in his work (as opposed to interesting camera-angles upon events), requires that we see this moment of Elizabeth's awareness more structurally, as the silent yet sounding centrepiece to an episode whose totality is framed strongly in visual terms. In the previous chapter Henchard has received a letter from Lucetta, which he looks at 'as at a picture, a vision, a vista of past enactments' (187). After Susan's death he again 'allowed his eyes to scan [a] letter' (195) somewhat distantly and carelessly, this time from Susan: '*Mr Michael Henchard. Not to be opened till Elizabeth-Jane's wedding-day.*' Reading the letter, which reveals Elizabeth's true paternity, leads to this:

> Her husband regarded the paper as if it were a window-pane through which he saw for miles. His lips twitched, and he seemed to compress his frame, as if to bear better. His usual habit was not to consider whether destiny were hard upon him or not – the shape of his ideas in cases of

---

[4] John Goode calls attention to 'the Paterian image' of consciousness here, and uses it to further his view of Elizabeth as 'modern' as opposed to Henchard's having 'a more primitive sense of "the scheme of some sinister intelligence"' (*Thomas Hardy: The Offensive Truth*, 1988, 85). In *Thomas Hardy: Distance and Desire* (1970, 3–6), J. Hillis Miller is outstanding on this scene. He says, 'the mind [is] still turned chiefly toward the outside world, still asking why things are as they are rather than why the mind is as it is' (5), while I would point to the final three clauses ('what that chaos . . .') to suggest that, for once, Hardy entertains that question.

affliction being simply a moody 'I am to suffer, I perceive.' 'This much scourging, then, is it for me?' But now through his passionate head there stormed this thought – that the blasting disclosure was what he had deserved. (196)

In its brevity and contrasting expansiveness that first sentence is among the great single sentences of Hardy's fiction. There is no special pleading for Henchard and we are given no special access to him: 'Her husband', the dispassionate steadiness of the verb 'regarded', the letter emptied of its intention as personal communication to become merely, yet materially, 'the paper' – all retain Henchard at a distance so characteristic in Hardy, not to be interfered with by a reader's emotional siding with him. And the simile extends the sense of an unalterable physical reality, a 'window-pane', through which no 'vista of past enactments' is displayed as a comfortable retrospective picture, but which is the means of a foreknowledge so sure that Henchard can lay it out in front of him in miles.

But, taken as a whole, the paragraph bears implications that move us beyond these immediate ironies of vision. Whereas Elizabeth-Jane's enlarged perception of life in the previous chapter took the form of a self-reflexive wonder about the nature of consciousness itself, Henchard absorbs his enlightenment in a physical reaction of bracing himself, familiar through repeated 'affliction'. Hardy does not take us into a reflective mind through free indirect speech when it comes to Henchard; rather, 'his ideas' are seen and heard as physical embodiments, having 'shape' and being uttered aloud as brief declarations. And when we are thrust into his thoughts, it is with a bodily violence that he is to be known and understood: we are not taken into his mind but 'his passionate head', through which 'stormed' a 'blasting disclosure'. That it is 'what he had deserved' is beyond the reader's anticipation and – so different from Eustacia's 'I do not deserve my lot!' (*Native* 421) – makes of Henchard, and exactly at this point, a compelling tragic figure matched only by Tess in Hardy's novels. This somatic knowledge of himself, experienced as reaction, not in repose, is a different model of self-knowledge from Elizabeth's silent wondering: while she embodies heroic observation, learning by watching, he is the figure of the heroic egotist, the protagonist for whom knowledge is visceral, a struggle played out in action. Henchard is precipitate, and the language that conveys his thought and action – often inextricably welded – is brief and direct; on the other hand, the slowing and deliberating factor in the narration belongs to Elizabeth, who, 'When she walked abroad',

> seemed to be occupied with an inner chamber of ideas, and to have slight need for visible objects. She formed curious resolves on checking gay fancies in the matter of clothes, because it was inconsistent with her past life to blossom gaudily the moment she had become possessed of money. (166)

The Paterian 'chamber' of her inner life is a place in which to manufacture sentences like the second, in which the details of phrasing and syntax in free indirect form convey the musing, self-conscious detachment which constructs the grammar and vocabulary of her ideas. Henchard, on the other hand, is somewhat like Conrad's Falk, of whom the narrator says that he was concerned to preserve something 'simple, natural and powerful . . . the five senses of his body'.[5]

*

These depictions of the differing mental life of Henchard and Elizabeth-Jane constitute the novel's explorations of that margin between a determination of human responses through sensation, and a mental independence allowing us to escape from such immediate compulsion, that so preoccupied the philosophers and scientists who began in the 1850s to transform physiology into the new science of psychology. The sequence of entries in Hardy's *Literary Notebooks* headed Notes in Philosophy (*LN* 2:108–14) shows him drawn to the same issues of objective and subjective reality, perception, the status of physical and mental phenomena, and the constitution of consciousness. Herbert Spencer features prominently, but it is the brief quotation from Alexander Bain that illuminates most clearly the interest that goes into the portrayal of mind in *The Mayor*: 'One substance with two sets of properties, two sides, the physical & the mental – a double faced unity' (*LN* 2:108).[6] In the *Macmillan's Magazine* article in which this first appeared, Bain's materialist endeavour is part of a much wider re-envisioning of man as an unprivileged part of Nature, and subject to its laws, that would have drawn Hardy's assent. Bain

---

[5] Joseph Conrad, *Sea Stories*, ed. Keith Carabine (1998), 117.
[6] From Bain's article first published as 'On the Correlation of Force and its Bearing on Mind' in *Macmillan's Magazine* 95 (September 1867), 373–83.

concludes that 'The line of mental sequence is thus, not mind causing body, and body causing mind, but mind-body giving birth to mind-body; a much more intelligible position.'[7] This view of mind and body as 'too intrinse t'unloose', as integrated receptive and expressive agents of an organism, finds concentrated artistic expression in the figure of Henchard; the view of the mind as less vitally linked to sensation, as a place of retreat for detached conceptualisation, is depicted in Elizabeth-Jane.

In fact we might consider that Elizabeth resolves Cytherea's great plea, and that she is the successful practitioner of the 'adjustment of inner to outer relations' which Spencer claims to be the fundamental process of living organisms,[8] an adjustment that Henchard, given no mental space in which to retire from the immediacies of sensation, reaction and emotion, tragically fails to make. For Elizabeth, 'an approach to equanimity' (251) is the reward for her capacity to reflect upon her own responses to having lost Henchard's paternal regard, and having lost Farfrae to Lucetta:

> She had learnt the lesson of renunciation, and was as familiar with the wreck of each day's wishes as with the diurnal setting of the sun. If her earthly career had taught her few book philosophies it had at least well practised her in this. (250)

It is difficult not to agree with Marjorie Garson that 'In her philosophy and in her deference to the claims of propriety Elizabeth-Jane is Hardy's own child.'[9] Through syntax ('it had at least well practised her'), Hardy quite deliberately makes Elizabeth's practice inseparable from what life has practised upon her: it lends the intimacy of an irony shared between writer and his fiction when writing of a character who is 'the nearest approach to the distinctly Hardyan point of view' in Michael Millgate's words, and a 'sour-puss' in David Musselwhite's.[10] And if Elizabeth is to be regarded as Hardy's model of success in Spencerian adaptation, then it is very much on the modest lines that Bain prescribes: 'The ideally best condition is a moderate surplus of pleasure – a gentle glow, not rising into brilliancy or

---

[7] Ibid., 375.
[8] Herbert Spencer, *Principles of Psychology* (1855), 486.
[9] Marjorie Garson, *Hardy's Fables of Integrity* (1991), 120.
[10] Michael Millgate, *Thomas Hardy: His Career as a Novelist* (1994), 253. David Musselwhite, *Social Transformations in Hardy's Tragic Novels* (2003), 79. Musselwhite has an excellent discussion of the presentation of Elizabeth-Jane (63–71).

intensity, except at considerable intervals (say a small portion every day), falling down frequently to indifference, but seldom sinking into pain.' A human organism in this sort of equilibrium with its environment might be faintly repellent in the conventionality of its mind. And we must think that, in fact, the mind is keeping a watchful eye over the body when Bain warns, 'Every throb of pleasure costs something to the physical system; and two throbs cost twice as much as one',[11] an almost comic utilitarianism which speaks to the puritan in Elizabeth that encourages her admiration of Farfrae. While Hardy shares some of Bain's ideas, the portrayal of Elizabeth-Jane clearly also functions as a critique of the narrowness of such a temperament.

How to read Henchard and Elizabeth-Jane receives further illumination when we turn to another, more renowned, contributor to contemporary discussions of mind, G. H. Lewes, and his writing about feelings and sensibility. For Lewes, the sensorium *'is the whole which reacts on the stimulation of any particular portion of that whole'*. It is 'the ideal conception of a *movable centre*. It is the organism conceived as reacting on the stimulation of its organs. Any one feeling is an attitude of the organism.'[12] Henchard is Hardy's embodiment of this vein of thinking in Lewes: 'any one feeling is an attitude of the organism' suggests so acutely the absolute quality of 'the momentum of his character' (263) precisely because it holds to an organic basis for sensibility. It is just what Farfrae cannot appreciate and that Elizabeth-Jane *does* appreciate about Henchard's final feelings, that they are 'a piece of the same stuff that his whole life was made of' (410), an 'attitude of the organism' that gives to each of Henchard's feelings a greater integrity, a more passionately-knit sensibility, than those of the wiser and more articulate characters who surround him. More than any other of his fictional creations, Hardy constructs Henchard to put readers in the presence of 'the whole which reacts on the stimulation of any particular portion of that whole'.

Lewes's metaphors for the mind are fluid, shifting and connective. In his seminal grouping of Bain, Spencer and Lewes, Rick Rylance draws attention to 'Lewes's deployment of images that suggest energy systems rather than fixed entities',[13] a characterisation of Lewes's approach to the material and the immaterial which strikes a note of accord with Maxwell's contemporary development of field theory.

---

[11] Bain, 'On the Correlation', 381, 380.
[12] G. H. Lewes, *Problems of Life and Mind* (Third Series, 1879), 76, 82, emphasis in original.
[13] Rick Rylance, *Victorian Psychology and British Culture 1850–1880* (2000), 309.

Hardy's depiction of feeling, thinking and action in *The Mayor of Casterbridge*, divided, I am suggesting, between the contrasting dispositions of Henchard and Elizabeth-Jane, finds its philosophical and physiological counterpart in Lewes's discussion of what he calls the Psychological Spectrum. Here he clarifies his two-fold vision of sentience:

> The Germans distinguish the directly excited feeling as 'the feeling in us' – *Empfindung*; and the indirectly excited feeling as 'the placing before us' – *Vorstellung*. We have no such happy terms, but Sensation and Image, or Idea, serve pretty well.
>
> The sensation, or presentation, is fitly considered *real*, because it has objective reality (*res*) for its antecedent stimulus. The *re*-presentation, whether image or symbol, is *ideal*, because its antecedent is a subjective state. Reality always indicates *that* antecedent which excites sensation when in direct contact with the sensory organism. Hence we say that a feeling is real when it is felt, ideal when it is only thought, not felt. To feel cold, and to think of cold, are two markedly different states.[14]

Hardy's art of 'disproportioning', of stylising reality to reveal intensely 'the features that matter in those realities' (*LW* 239), considers the difference between these two ways of receiving and facing life matters enough to conceive of them as different temperaments. This can be seen in *The Mayor* in the second great moment of sudden and shocking visual encounter in the novel that Henchard undergoes, and its contrast with a comparable moment for Elizabeth-Jane. As Henchard stands on the brink of Ten Hatches Hole, intending to do away with himself after Newson's return, his eyes find themselves detecting a shape 'which was that of a human body, lying stiff and stark upon the surface of the stream':

> In the circular current imparted by the central flow the form was brought forward, till it passed under his eyes; and then he perceived with a sense of horror that it was *himself*. Not a man somewhat resembling him, but one in all respects his counterpart, his actual double, was floating as if dead in Ten Hatches Hole. (372)

Although the effigy from the skimmity-ride is placed before him, Henchard's experience is of *Empfindung*, 'the feeling in us', the present reality of his sensation of seeing himself as 'it passed under his eyes' overwhelming the rational distinction between a perceiving *me*

---

[14] Lewes, *Problems of Life and Mind* (First Series, 1879), 149.

and perceived *it*. The object, after all, is a *re*-presentation, an idea of Henchard, but the directness of Henchard's identification of himself as a dead and drowned man makes it '*himself*'. Neither is his response made in the mode of thought, but is driven bodily, kinetically: 'He covered his eyes and bowed his head. Without looking again into the stream he took his coat and hat, and went slowly away' (372).

Elizabeth's moment of seeing herself re-presented is also a chastening one, but her experience corresponds very fully to *Vorstellung* as Lewes explains it. In order to understand Farfrae's feeling for her after the dance in the South Walk, 'that silent observing woman' (182) places before herself her own image:

> To solve the problem whether her appearance on the evening of the dance were such as to inspire a fleeting love at first sight, she dressed herself up exactly as she had dressed then – the muslin, the spencer, the sandals, the parasol – and looked in the mirror. The picture glassed back was, in her opinion, precisely of such a kind as to inspire that fleeting regard, and no more – 'just enough to make him silly, and not enough to keep him so,' she said luminously; and Elizabeth thought, in a much lower key, that by this time he had discovered how plain and homely was the informing spirit of that pretty outside. (183)

Henchard's effigy declares its corporeal reality to his 'eyes'; the 'glassed back' Elizabeth is a 'picture' subject to 'opinion', a representation to be mused upon and to be thoroughly understood. The principle of Elizabeth's existence is a bringing to conscious examination of every sensation and reaction. She accompanies herself with an internal commentary whose exact, knowing and just slightly pleased tone is given in the phrase that judges her pretty image to be 'precisely of such a kind': she makes her way in a life of thoughts that mediate between sensation and symbol. One section of *Problems of Life and Mind* is called 'The Logic of Feeling', another 'The Logic of Signs'. Rylance comments that 'The Logic of Feeling is the immediate sensory experience of the world. The Logic of Signs is the encoding or representation of that experience by language or other means' (291). While Henchard is dominated by the former, Elizabeth involves herself almost exclusively with the latter. As readers of novels, we spend a lot of time doing just what Elizabeth does, and often in search of a representation that conveys the intensity of a Henchard-like sensory experience but which, of necessity, cannot *be* it, and might well be said, in practice, to be a defence against it.

Elizabeth's dwelling *on* experience and Henchard's dwelling *in* it is the double aspect of consciousness that Hardy noted in Bain, and which Lewes characterises as a fluctuating and contingent state, divided between *'logical attitude'* and *'psychical mood'*. In Henchard, Hardy creates a figure dominated by *'psychical mood'*, conscious of a succession of 'vague massive feeling[s]', in Lewes's use of the term,[15] which direct 'the momentum of his character' as Hardy puts it. Elizabeth, on the other hand, has imbibed the *logical attitude*, attentive and perceptive, the model student. Her unrivalled power of observation – pin-point yet inclusive at the Three Mariners, both witty and divining at Lucetta's tea party in chapter 26, feelingly penetrative in perceiving Henchard's loneliness after Lucetta's death – is also a self-abnegation that holds her at a little distance from her acts of kindness. These contrasting aspects of psychological make-up are artistically enhanced as Henchard is so often surrounded by an auditory landscape, whilst Elizabeth, apart from the profound night-vigil stirring that we have already examined, is associated more with sight. Walter Ong, who is committed with a theological fervour to a sense that 'the sound world has depth, dimension, fullness such as the visual, despite its own distinctive beauties, can never achieve', offers an explanation that confirms this difference between Henchard and Elizabeth-Jane:

> That is to say, too, that sound and hearing have a special relationship to our sense of presence. When we speak of a presence in its fullest sense . . . we speak of something that surrounds us, in which we are situated. 'I am *in* his presence,' we say, not 'in front of his presence.' Being in is what we experience in a world of sound.[16]

Elizabeth-Jane places people and dilemmas in front her in order to appreciate and confront them, which is, inescapably, a visual action, with typically a 120 degree width of forward vision. Henchard, confronted visually by his effigy, does not exercise the objectifying, distancing function required by successful seeing, but subjectively sees '*himself*' because Hardy has orchestrated his presence by the weir-hole to place him *in* rather than *in front of* a scene:

> The wanderer in this direction who should stand still for a few minutes on a quiet night, might hear singular symphonies from these waters, as from a lampless orchestra, all playing in their sundry tones from near and far parts of the moor. At a hole in a rotten weir they executed a recitative; where a tributary brook fell over a stone breastwork they

[15] Ibid., 150.
[16] Walter Ong, *The Presence of the Word* (1967), 130.

trilled cheerily; under an arch they performed a metallic cymballing; and at Durnover Hole they hissed. The spot at which their instrumentation rose loudest was a place called Ten Hatches, whence during high springs there proceeded a very fugue of sounds. (371)

Significantly, the passage is not about Henchard: it is the *scene* which multiplies its surrounding presence as it fills with instruments of sound, and any 'wanderer' contained within it is tensed into a listening attitude. Ong claims that a listener is given 'an experience of living within events more intense than the experience' of a visualiser,[17] and here an auditory event waits for Henchard's immersion in the 'fugue'. It is this prior effect of *sound* that accounts for the remarkable force – both of Henchard's identification with the effigy and the reader's identification with Henchard – achieved in the very short paragraph of Henchard's visual encounter to come. He lives within events intensely and at times we accompany him into this event-like dimension. When, towards the very end of the novel, his zest for life has departed, 'He had no wish to make an arena a second time of a world that had become a mere painted scene for him' (395). Henchard is reduced to looking-on, having no energy to re-enter the circular arena within which events are sounded.

*

When Henchard finally leaves Casterbridge in the hopeless certainty of Newson's imminent reconciliation with Elizabeth, we see again the 'attitude of the organism', to borrow Lewes's wonderfully apt phrase, in contrast to the more adaptable sensibility of Elizabeth-Jane. The narration adopts her intense visual registration of his departure:

> She watched his form diminish across the moor, the yellow rush-basket at his back moving up and down with each tread, and the creases behind his knees coming and going alternately till she could no longer see them. (388)

The intent, sustained gaze upon the bodily movement of her father, as she still believes him to be, known through what he wears and carries, is as feeling a moment as any in Elizabeth-Jane's history, especially that 'coming and going' with its painful premonition of

---

[17] Ibid., 174.

the final stages of the novel. Despite, however, Elizabeth's 'seeing feelingly', the narrative goes on to occupy the space taken by the retreating Henchard in the evoked scene:

> He went on till he came to the first milestone, which stood in the bank, half way up a steep hill. He rested his basket on the top of the stone, placed his elbows on it, and gave way to a convulsive twitch, which was worse than a sob, because it was so hard and so dry.
> 'If I had only got her with me – if I only had!' he said. 'Hard work would be nothing to me then! But that was not to be. I – Cain – go alone as I deserve – an outcast and a vagabond. But my punishment is *not* greater than I can bear!'
> He sternly subdued his anguish, shouldered his basket, and went on.
> Elizabeth, in the meantime, had breathed him a sigh, recovered her equanimity, and turned her face to Casterbridge. (388)

From seeing at a distance, the reader is moved to intimacy with Henchard's bodily necessity for utterance of the pressures which propel him away from us. The brief phrases to declare his condition done, though without any sense of relief, he shoulders the burden of his consciousness and the scene closes around him. Hard and dry, 'sternly subdued', the demand upon Henchard's frame is one that almost cracks it. Elizabeth, on the other hand, can have no part other than to direct a sigh backward and to turn her face to her own future. 'Equanimity', which Henchard has never known, which Hardy, looking into his mirror, feels could be his were he other than he were, for Elizabeth-Jane is a recoverable commodity.[18] She is one who keeps life in front of her to look at it steadily, while for Henchard, but for the singular moment of seeing through the window-pane of Susan's letter, life exacts an entirely different physical stance – he is always in the midst of it. The measure of this difference is that 'the sympathy of the girl seemed necessary to his very existence' (376): he makes a claim upon Elizabeth and desires to be claimed in return. Nothing and nobody in Elizabeth's life is *necessary* to her, nor becomes so. Her 'lesson of renunciation', from a certain point of view so admirable, leaves her guiltless but bloodless.

Henchard's integrity, on the contrary, is one that is governed by the senses. The interview with Richard Newson sees him claim of the sale of his wife, 'I was not in my senses, and a man's senses are himself' (366). This has more than a touch of Hamlet's self-exculpation about

---

[18] Thomas Hardy, 'I Look Into My Glass', *The Complete Poems* (1988), 81.

it; but when, shortly after, 'Newson's shadow passed the window' having heard Henchard declare that Elizabeth-Jane is 'Dead likewise', Henchard, 'scarcely believing the evidence of his senses, rose from his seat amazed at what he had done. It had been the impulse of a moment' (368). 'The evidence of his senses' is precisely what is to be believed, and his lie to Newson, 'the impulse of a moment', has his whole desire for life behind it. And, whatever the moral judgement a reader applies to Henchard, we are completely convinced of his *existence*, that bare and irreducible word which so links Hardy to Conrad.

Henchard's extinguishing of his own existence is the painful subject of the closing pages of the novel – his return with the caged goldfinch and the spurning by Elizabeth-Jane, her remorse and his death in the bleak and dilapidated hut. Hardy makes singularly expressive two moments of silence after the noisy strife of the novel has died away. To Elizabeth's 'O how can I love as I once did a man who has served us like this!', at her marriage celebration, 'Henchard's lips half parted to begin an explanation. But he shut them up like a vice, and uttered not a sound. How should he, there and then, set before her with any effect the palliatives of his great faults . . .' (402). And the chapter ends with Henchard departing 'by the back way as he had come; and she saw him no more' (403), which proves, simply, to be the case. Why should this brief action, two short sentences, one of which draws towards utterance and the other of which repudiates it, be so moving? In part it is because of the poignant contrast with the assertiveness that Elizabeth has heard in Henchard over the course of the novel: the first time that she heard him, three hundred pages earlier after the dinner at the King's Arms, 'Henchard's voice arose above the rest' (103). And there is also an aspect which is intrinsic to any refusal to use the voice, that can be seen sharply against the eloquent claim made by Steven Connor in *Dumbstruck*:

> What a voice, any voice, always says, no matter what the particular local import may be of the words it emits, is this: this, here, this voice, is not merely *a* voice, a particular aggregation of tones and timbres; it is voice, or voicing itself. Listen, says a voice: some being is giving voice.[19]

If this account is accepted, it leads to the heart of what is so painfully affecting in Henchard's shutting of his lips and foregoing the opportunity to speak in his own defence. Connor attributes to the

---

[19] Steven Connor, *Dumbstruck: A Cultural History of Ventriloquism* (2000), 3.

voice 'persisting action ... that asserts this continuity and substance' of the self against the disintegrating forces that would leave any sense of self as a series of discrete moments. When Henchard part opens and then firmly shuts his lips, he asserts a decision to give up being, his silence announcing a cessation of the effort to maintain 'Michael Henchard' in the world of competing forces.

This self-conflicting abnegation is part of the rhythm of assertion and collapse that marks his history – but it is the final act of that drama. However, a self-silencing is not an erasure: the writing of 'Michael Henchard's Will' continues the tragic paradox of *The Mayor of Casterbridge*, of Henchard being visible as a powerful presence precisely as he seeks invisibility. Even as it casts his passing as invisible and inaudible, the successive injunctions, '& that ... & that' of his will make an indelible impression, demanding to be read according to the logic of their feeling. This transfer from the evanescence of voice to the permanence of writing marks, literally, a final paradox, that the demand for self-extinction is the supreme action of self-assertion in the novel: 'To this I put my name. MICHAEL HENCHARD' (409). The failure to leave his name embodied in Elizabeth-Jane here receives the counter-statement of the *individual* life: the childless hero, with no continuing history, falls back into obscurity, but with the page of his testament that he *had* a unique life asserted against the 'mindless rote' of morphology, and part of its record.

If Hardy's novels do not, finally, portray the rich and self-renewing profusion of Darwin's 'entangled bank' – increasingly they contemplate histories that crush and extinguish rather than sustain – there are figures in all the novels who are released into an aftermath that requires them to continue, and none bears more weight than Elizabeth-Jane. Hers is the second significant silence in *The Mayor*'s conclusion. Abel Whittle concludes his account of Henchard's death,

> 'But he didn't gain strength, for you see, ma'am, he couldn't eat – no, no appetite at all – and he got weaker; and today he died. One of the neighbours have gone to get a man to measure him.'
> 'Dear me – is that so!' said Farfrae.
> As for Elizabeth, she said nothing. (409)

When she does speak again, through tears, it is to regret her final unkindness to Henchard and to acknowledge 'there's no altering – so it must be' (410). Elizabeth's silence reciprocates Henchard's in refusing to fill the appalling moment with any claim upon it, allowing the meaning of Whittle's words, and then Henchard's writing, the time and space to establish themselves in her that their gravity demands. In this way Hardy persuades us of the reality of Elizabeth's inner life, a sphere uninhabited by Farfrae, which is offered by the novel as consolation for the destruction of Henchard's vitality. It is one that diminishes the life of the senses, whose appetite, as far as Elizabeth is concerned, is severely confined. Her most purely sensational moment, rather incidental in itself, significantly enough re-composes sound into sight. She and Lucetta have met by appointment below the churchyard wall, the other side of which Henchard has his corn-yard:

> Voices were borne over to them at that instant on the wind and raindrops from the other side of the wall. There came such words as 'sacks', 'quarters', 'threshing', 'tailing', 'next Saturday's market', each sentence being disorganized by the gusts like a face in a cracked mirror. (215)

By an unremitting watchful consciousness, Elizabeth is one who pieces together the contingent fragments as they fall upon her eyes and ears into a coherence that she can set before herself as a whole. The striking synaesthesia here, that by simile moves sound into sight, precisely indicates her primary action throughout the novel, which is to compose the different facets of life briefly disclosed to her into a single picture that can be 'glassed back', legibly.

The achievement of this patient and specular approach to the world around her is the subject of the final three paragraphs of the novel. This coda, that assumes so much importance in most readings of the novel, is strangely one that conducts both a contraction and an expansion. 'The secret (as she had once learnt it) of making limited opportunities endurable' envisages the possibilities of life in a very small compass; yet it is exactly in the contemplation of such realities that the movement towards expansion in the novel's conclusion finds its origin, in 'the cunning enlargement, by a species of microscopic treatment, of those minute forms of satisfaction that offer themselves to everybody not in positive pain' (410). The movement into the visual realm is not incidental: looking *at* life, rather than being surrounded *by* it in the manner of so much auditory experience, lends that distance in which a consciousness of the separation of the outer from the inner life arises. Elizabeth is Hardy's empiricist, building from small observations an 'unforeseen' coherence into the 'equable serenity' and 'unbroken tranquillity' that she is finally able to contemplate as her own life by the novel's end. And in closing the novel upon Elizabeth's Spencerian accommodation of the inner needs of the organism to its environment, Hardy tentatively asserts a value in *awareness* of what that inner life is and how it is secured when a spontaneously-sensed fullness of existence seems beyond one's compass. It is an awareness of minutiae which has much in common with the thinking pursued so finely by G. H. Lewes in his short chapter, 'The Inner Life', in *Problems of Life and Mind*:

> The Inner Life thus represents the whole of our experience. . . . If we understand that not a sunbeam falls upon a garden wall but the wall is altered by that beam; much more is it comprehensible that not a thrill passes through the body but our Sensorium is altered by it. The alteration may be evanescent and inappreciable, or it may persist in a more or less appreciable modification. To have once had a headache is to be so far modified that we can sympathise with the ache felt by some one else. . . . The sum of such traces is the Inner Life.[20]

Elizabeth provides a protective sense of in-dwelling by an awareness of the home she has made for herself in the inner life. Henchard, whose inner life is an immediacy not to be detached from a sensational present, unprotected, is of all the five protagonists who make a home in Casterbridge the most homeless.

2 Widening Margins

Tess of the d'Urbervilles and Nostromo

A high point of psychology among Hardy's novels, *The Mayor of Casterbridge* leaves us with the consolations, and with the diminishments, of the inner life. The wider horizons of *Tess of the d'Urbervilles* and *Nostromo* leave us less confined to human personality, and the second half of this chapter shows how both authors further explore immersion and ambience rather than introspection to produce their fullest depictions of existence. The movement that I trace in both novels is outward to an encompassing physics that surrounds the attitudes of organisms, whether of the labouring work-folk or of the body politic, one which ultimately recedes into the unperturbed and silent face of nature. The irony of humankind's self-importance in these all-absorbing dimensions is well caught by Hardy as he observes

---

[20] Lewes, *Problems of Life and Mind* (Second Series, 1879), 86.

the tipsy Trantridge crowd returning from the Chaseborough dance, in terms that are recurrent throughout this study:

> They followed the road with a sensation that they were soaring along in a supporting medium, possessed of original and profound thoughts, themselves and surrounding nature forming an organism of which all the parts harmoniously and joyously interpenetrated each other. (110)[21]

Conrad transfers the grandeur from befuddled minds to the scene itself as Giorgio Viola looks out upon the warring parties on the Campo:

> the movements of the animated scene were like the passages of a violent game played upon the plain by dwarfs mounted and on foot, yelling with tiny throats, under the mountain that seemed a colossal embodiment of silence. (27)

Human pretensions are not always the subject of so sardonic a perspective, and the amplitude of these two novels draw out their characters into a scenic grandeur larger than Hardy and Conrad summon elsewhere in their work. In *Tess* I attend to two broad phases that characterise opposed aspects of this movement; *Nostromo*'s striking soundworld has already been touched upon, and here I extend the ear to the silence that lies always behind it.

*

On the morning that Tess leaves for Trantridge to tend the fowls at 'The Slopes', we are told that she wakens before dawn, 'at the marginal minute of the dark when the grove is still mute, save for one prophetic bird' (89). Much of the novel takes place in those sensed but unreportable moments of transition when the margin between one state and another loses its identity as a mark of separation and becomes the conduit of continuity.[22] It is a time that the novel associates particularly with Tess herself who, wandering the woods alone during her pregnancy,

---

[21] References to *Tess of the d'Urbervilles* are to the 1978 Penguin English Library edition, edited by David Skilton, based on the *Wessex Novels* edition of 1912.

[22] Two studies that examine this acutely, though differently, are those by Jean R. Brooks in *Thomas Hardy: The Poetic Structure* (1971) (and see her chapter on *The Woodlanders*, entitled 'A Novel of Assimilation'), and Kathleen Blake, 'Pure Tess: Hardy on Knowing a Woman', *Studies in English Literature 1500–1900* 22:4 (1982).

> knew how to hit to a hair's-breadth that moment of evening when the light and the darkness are so evenly balanced that the constraint of day and the suspense of night neutralize each other, leaving absolute mental liberty. It is then that the plight of being alive becomes attenuated to its least possible dimensions. (134)

No novel of Hardy's grasps with so sensitive a touch all that is folded (it is one of the word's several meanings) into 'the plight of being alive', the wonderful directness of the phrase concealing the many strands plaited into 'plight' which the novel parts so sympathetically: peril, danger, risk, sin, offence, guilt, blame, undertaking, pledge, engagement, condition, health, mood, promise, to be bound to, to knit, to knot (*OED*, 1977). It is in these marginal moments that Tess's 'flexuous and stealthy figure became an integral part of the scene' (134), and, rather than Tess's subjective experience analysed, the novel's realism is to offer scenes that in every way *involve* her.

So Tess and Angel Clare in 'the diminishing daylight' take the Talbothays' milk churns in a waggon to the railway station: time, place and history yield a margin for tenuous contact between 'Modern life', which 'stretched out its steam feeler', and 'native existences', which it touched 'and quickly withdrew its feeler again' (251). Like, and unlike, the telegraph poles of *Nostromo* – 'a slender vibrating feeler of that progress waiting . . . to enter and twine itself about the weary heart of the land' (166) – it is one of the great visionary moments of the novel, sudden, slight, and swiftly past, not fully explicable:

> Then there was the hissing of a train, which drew up almost silently upon the wet rails, and the milk was rapidly swung can by can into the truck. The light of the engine flashed for a second upon Tess Durbeyfield's figure, motionless under the great holly tree. No object could have looked more foreign to the gleaming cranks and wheels than the unsophisticated girl, with the round bare arms, the rainy face and hair, the suspended attitude of a friendly leopard at pause, the print gown of no date or fashion, and the cotton bonnet drooping on her brow. (251)

The naturalisation of Tess's sensations as the reader's own is suddenly, for a unique instant, turned on its head. Tess's world has been steadily brought within our comprehension and affections until, just at the moment when she reflects how insignificant is her experience to those who live in other worlds, she is thrust beyond us to be a mere 'figure' caught for a second in the exposing glare of an engine (it is the 'cranks and wheels' that are doing the looking), so much harsher than the indigenous 'feeble light' of the station's 'smoky lamp' (251).

She is caught long enough to be glimpsed as an 'object', one already made 'foreign' in her own county, the definite article that marks off each of the items that fall under the quick glance of the reader, no closer now than a passenger in the train passing through, denoting the figure to be that of a typical 'unsophisticated girl' of the country. But this is no pre-vision of 'Adlestrop'; no dim hinterland is briefly manifest, and Tess does not, as we read phrase by phrase, stand for several thousand other country farm girls undoubtedly like her. We see her only, though without the partiality almost amounting to ownership that the previous two hundred pages have drawn us into. We see her as strange, and she *escapes* us. The slow monosyllables of 'the round bare arms' do not invite touch; and, of course, as the narrator attempts to account for a striking particularity in her whole bodily aspect, it is the phrase 'the suspended attitude of a friendly leopard at pause' that makes the reader pause at something foreign indeed. Full of a potential for movement and graceful power, this is not the domesticated plaything that Alec would have, nor the child that Angel twice over in the present chapter insists that she is. After this strangely confrontative phrase, the sentence moves on to give a picture of individual particularity being absorbed almost to erasure, the print gown 'of no date or fashion', the cotton bonnet, having lost its shape in the rain, 'drooping on her brow'. Momentarily irradiated as she is, we are losing Tess as we glimpse her. The darkening and rainy scene takes its place as a small pause in the wider movement of the brooding chapter 30 to display a vein of apprehension that runs deeply in the novel, of the margin between individuation and dissolving, between a unique experience of life and the common and disregarded existence produced and left behind by history.

The precariousness of *Tess* derives from the pervasive vision of Tess's existence as that of a particle in a medium, brilliantly described by Peter Conrad when he writes that 'Hardy's characters are all the time being unmade, rescued from the subtractions of selfhood and sent to wander, like genes or spores, at random through the world.'[23] Whether the novel endorses this apparent acquiescence in dissemination by natural forces, whether selfhood is merely a 'subtraction', are questions that surface in various guises as we look at how *Tess*, and later *Nostromo*, depict the margins within which expressions of identity and impressions of the world meet. The terms of the writing are empirical, not in the popular conception of an uncomplicated objective attention to a free-standing external reality, but

---

[23] Peter Conrad, *The Everyman History of English Literature* (1985), 513.

in the manner of Bain, Lewes and Spencer, which has been so well explained by Peter Garratt:

> If our knowledge claims must be made ultimately referable to sense experience, then self, knowledge, and reality soon threaten to shade into one another. Their boundaries become drastically difficult to draw, as reality becomes bound up inextricably with its perception ... Empiricism ... certainly did not automatically initiate or undergird a naïve representationalism. Instead, it troubled the neat ontologies of self and world implicit in such a view. As Bain put it, 'the object, or extended world, is inseparable from our cognitive faculties' [*Logic*, 2nd edn (1873), vol. 2, 277]. In effect, this position denied there were any simple external facts of reality. Instead, somewhat arbitrarily, outer and inner realms constructed one another mutually.[24]

Among Hardy's characters, it is Tess, constantly distinguished from the *intellectual* awareness of the author/narrator, whose 'cognitive faculties' in the more intuitive, visceral sense are brought closest to his. With little recourse to free indirect discourse, she thus infuses the novel's envisioning of the world in a manner different from the way in which Henchard dominates *The Mayor of Casterbridge*.[25]

The most critical of these moments of uncertain distinction between the objective and the subjective world is undoubtedly that which closes Phase the First, portraying the violation of Hardy's inviolable heroine. It arrives as the conclusion of a long sequence in which indistinctness itself is as much the subject as the events for which the hazy and dwindling light is the medium. The struggle between 'lights' and 'shades' which constitutes 'the atmosphere itself' (106) is continued at every level in the Chaseborough dance and the progress home of the Trantridge dancers, until, eventually, with Tess and Alec separated from the others, 'a faint luminous fog, which had hung in the hollows all the evening, became general and enveloped them' (114). The margin of separation between self and surrounding is diminished as rhythmic repetition extends this pervasiveness to penetrate Tess's state of mind: 'Whether on this account, or from absent-mindedness, or from sleepiness, she did not perceive that they had long ago passed the point at which the lane to Trantridge branched from the highway' (114). The mode of

---

[24] Peter Garratt, *Victorian Empiricism* (2010), 18.
[25] Mike Davis's fine essay, 'Hardy, *Tess*, and Late Victorian Theories of Consciousness', *Thomas Hardy Journal* 27 (Autumn 2012), 46–69, is pertinent to the whole of this chapter. He considers *Tess* in relation to Lewes, James and Bergson.

unanswered querying that this sentence initiates sustains the suspended quality of the episode, entertaining both possibilities and doubts in the chain of cause and effect, to the chapter's end. In different mode, Tess's individuality is eroded by four four-word sentences which carry the burden of the story in elemental form: 'Thus the thing began' (82); 'She was inexpressibly weary' (115); 'There was no answer' (118); 'It was to be' (119). Each bears the falling cadence of a gathering weight upon Tess of the forces of class, gender, work, history and tradition to which she loses the identity with which she tries to resist or negotiate these things. This is not passivity – she fights the 'moment of oblivion' in which she sinks on Alec and proceeds nearly to push him off the horse in her own defence – it is a subtle, long, slow overwhelming of the individually conscious self by the given self, the only self left to her in this situation.

Despite Tess's resistance, this is the whole tendency of Phase the First; and the point wherein the possibilities of her subjectivity are lost to the narrator is quite precise. Significantly it is a moment when the narrator lets go of the claim of Tess's own sense-world and allows her to become an object absorbed into the surrounding darkness. Alec has set her down in a nest of leaves and gone off into 'the webs of vapour' to discover where in the 'thick darkness' of The Chase they have wandered to:

> She could hear the rustling of the branches as he ascended the adjoining slope, till his movements were no louder than the hopping of a bird, and finally died away. With the setting of the moon the pale light lessened, and Tess became invisible as she fell into reverie upon the leaves where he had left her. (118)

Between the first and the second sentence the acute and characteristic sense of hearing is abandoned for an envisioning of Tess from quite a different point of view, made 'invisible' and abandoned indeed. The vital complex of nerves and sensations, feelings and thoughts, that Hardy has so managed that the reader conceives them as 'Tess', is disembodied to become merely Alec's dim sense of her as 'nothing but a pale nebulousness at his feet, which represented the white muslin figure he had left upon the dead leaves' (118). This culmination of so many previous images of indistinctness is explicit in offering Tess as a pictorial representation, robbed of the flesh and the blood so important to her being and agency elsewhere. As an artistic means of sanitising rape, with Tess unsullied because her active self is absent, the objection was long ago cogently expressed by Hardy's admirer, Havelock Ellis, in terms of the character losing ownership over her own story: 'to regard Tess as unimplicated is to deny her the right of participation in her own life. Robbed of responsibility, she is deprived of tragic status – reduced throughout to the victim she does indeed become.'[26] However, the event that Hardy proposes, included as it is with the 'primaeval yews and oaks', the 'gentle roosting birds' and the 'hopping rabbits and hares' (119) in the final unhurried vision of the episode, leads Philip Weinstein to speak of 'Tess's involuntary participation in a natural scheme'.[27] And yet that isn't quite right either. For if the violation of Tess is the 'natural scheme', then Hardy's world is that of a relentless Social Darwinism, a perversion of Darwin's observations of contingency into a doctrine of power similar to that which Auden expresses so succinctly in 'The Shield Of Achilles': 'That girls are raped, that two boys knife a third / Were axioms to him'. But this dispenses with so much in *Tess* that invests 'cruel Nature's law' with pleasurable and life-giving energies that include love. Although Hardy claimed that he agreed with Sophocles, that 'not to have been born is best', this is decidedly *not* the feeling given by *Tess of the d'Urbervilles*.[28] And Hardy so writes this scene (having jettisoned his earlier conception of a wickedly contriving Alec d'Urberville, replete with drugs) that neither Tess, nor Alec, nor the reader can distinguish where 'surrounding nature' and human agency or volition, where mental representation or material presence, have their beginnings and ends. For many readers this is simple evasion of the thoroughly human cruelty of an act by placing it at the margins of visibility; for others, Garrett's description of the uncertain borders that are inherent in empiricism goes right to the point of an 'interpenetrating' that had begun the Trantridge evening as comic extension of selfhood and now is tragic loss.

*

While Conrad writes about what is irremediable, an exhilarating feature of Hardy's fiction, in contrast, is the possibility it allows for organic recovery, and nowhere is this more directly and fully represented than in *Tess*. It is a process which is always under threat, from social regulation, from conscience, from contingent encounter,

---

[26] Havelock Ellis in *The Savoy* 6 (October 1896), 40.
[27] Philip Weinstein, *The Semantics of Desire* (1984), 112.
[28] See William Archer, *Real Conversations* (1904), 47.

and from the fact, despite Tess's resolution that 'The past was past; whatever it had been it was no more at hand' (141), that it has a continuing existence *as* the past. Yet the centre of the novel is filled with not only a restorative but also an exploratory energy that belongs to a profusion of spontaneous growth rather than meditated intention. What constitutes the self as autonomous – the boundary of an individual body, unique sensations, thoughts and determinations – and what constitutes the self as a participant in a greater flow of energy, is interrogated in this part of *Tess* with an intensity that is physiological more than psychological, that is drawn to organic movement and the impressions of environment rather than to the reconstitution of experience in the language of inner reflection. So, as she walks to Talbothays, Tess's 'hopes mingled with the sunshine in an ideal photosphere which surrounded her as she bounded along against the soft south wind' (157). Yet such a sentence is not as simple as it seems: it raises without answering the question – is it the mental, 'ideal', construction of this radiance, or the physical contact with the warm wind that produces hope? 'With', 'in', 'as', 'against' – all the little co-ordinators keep self and environment, the mental and physical aspects of experience, in a stream of changing involvement with each other, all the way through to 'I am ready' (487).

The recuperation which yields the climactic 'gravitation' of 'The Rally' has been preparing itself since the reaping scene of chapter 14. In a statement that binds together the sensations of ecstasy, acquiescence and disintegration which permeate the novel, the narrator asserts that 'A field-man is a personality afield; a field-woman is a portion of the field; she has somehow lost her own margin, imbibed the essence of her surrounding, and assimilated herself with it' (137–8). The gender-bias of this generalised loss of self has drawn much critical dissent, but 'imbibed' and 'assimilated' here are active verbs: a loss of 'margin' is not envisioned as a reduction of responsive action. While a man asserts but is bound by his own 'personality', a woman makes her sense of self co-existent with her surrounding, an *extension* which cannot be dissociated from the sense of connection to fruitful (as well as destructive) natural processes, which nearly all readers ascribe to *Tess* as its particular, enriching, quality.

Tess's own sense of an enlarged life must wait for the next phase, 'The Rally', where the generalised proposal about loss of margin is finely re-imagined in the depiction of an individual experience both rapturous and fraught with anxiety. Here *Tess* becomes Hardy's most extensive exploration of the borders and boundaries of the self, an issue inherent in an epistemology of sensations and relations, and one which all of the novels in this study differently investigate.[29] The sympathy in *Tess* for tendencies, currents and relations as forming our physical experience of the world, as opposed to free-standing facts and completely determinable entities, can be matched to the transformative vision in the physical sciences of the physicist Ernst Mach, Hardy's almost exact contemporary. Familiar in discussions of German literature of this period – his 'Das Ich ist unrettbar' (the self is unsalvageable) was the watchword of the Young Vienna writers of the 1890s, and his methodology as a scientist was the subject of Robert Musil's PhD – Mach's appearance here is consistent with the endeavour in this book to set the scenic realism practised in their different ways by Hardy and Conrad within contemporary thinking about the senses in the empirical sciences. 'My epistemological standpoint', as Mach puts it in his Author's Preface to an early pamphlet, 'is based on a study of the physiology of the senses . . . in so far as it concerns physics'.[30] It is exactly this engagement of the internal world of human sensations with the external world of impersonal processes, of physiology with physics, whose literary expression I have been seeking to explore. As with Hardy and Conrad, for Mach the world is event, successive events made coherent by human mental construction: 'Nature exists once only. Our schematic mental imitation alone produces like events.'[31] Although humanity constructs the world it knows, the external scene is not, in this view, subsumed as an appendage of consciousness. Rather, Mach says, our sensations 'exist, in other words, in a *spatial* field, in which our body fills but a part'.[32] Much has been written recently in both literary and scientific criticism about the embodiment of knowledge, but this claim by Mach seems to me an accurate description of what is constructed in a Hardy or Conrad novel – 'a *spatial* field, in which our body fills but a part'.

---

[29] Tom Lloyd's comment on the 'field-woman abroad' passage is pertinent here: 'The focus on disappearing margins suggests that Hardy has more in common with Conrad – especially with Marlow's trip down the Congo – than may at first seem to be the case' (*Crises of Realism: Representing Experience in the British Novel, 1816–1910*, 1997, 145).

[30] Ernst Mach, *History and Root of the Principle of the Conservation of Energy* (1911, originally 1872), 9.

[31] Address to the Imperial Academy of Sciences, Vienna, 25 May 1882, quoted in J. Kockelmans, *Philosophy of Science: The Historical Background* (1968), 179.

[32] Ernst Mach, *Contributions to the Analysis of the Sensations* (1998, originally 1886), 188.

On a longer view it is possible to see Mach as participating in a much wider late-century empiricist debate about the boundary of identity which would include, for instance, the feeling of Samuel Butler in *Life and Habit*, that 'Everything melts away into everything else; there are no hard edges; it is only from a little distance that we see the effect as of individual features and existences. When we go close up, there is nothing but a blur and confused mass of apparently meaningless touches, as in a picture by Turner.'[33] In the final chapter of *Contributions to an Analysis of the Sensations*, called 'Physics', far from hard edges Mach takes us towards the compound of passion, love, work, companionship, heat, photosynthesis, cattle-meads, times of day, hierarchy and history which make up the gravitational flow of the marvellous scenes at Talbothays. He says,

> There is no rift between the psychical and the physical, no *within* and *without*, no *sensation* to which an outward, different *thing* corresponds. There is but *one kind of elements*, out of which this suppositious within and without is formed – elements which are themselves within and without according to the light in which, for the time being, they are viewed.[34]

The light within which 'inner' and 'outer' experience is viewed is most delicately explored in 'the time being' of chapter 20, the high point of Tess's happiness, in which 'Tess and Clare unconsciously studied each other, ever balanced on the edge of a passion, yet apparently keeping out of it' (185). In their walks to gather the cows, when 'In the twilight of the morning light seems active',

> They could then see the faint summer fogs in layers, woolly, level, and apparently no thicker than counterpanes, spread about the meadows in detached remnants of small extent. On the gray moisture of the grass were marks where the cows had lain through the night – darkgreen islands of dry herbage the size of their carcasses, in the general sea of dew. From each island proceeded a serpentine trail, by which the cow had rambled away to feed after getting up, at the end of which trail they found her; the snoring puff from her nostrils, when she recognized them, making an intenser little fog of her own amid the prevailing one. Then they drove the animals back to the barton, or sat down to milk them on the spot, as the case might require. (187–8)

---

[33] Samuel Butler, *Life and Habit* (1878), 107.
[34] Mach, *Analysis of the Sensations*, 151.

Mach writes, 'The physiology of the senses demonstrates that spaces and times may just as appropriately be called sensations as colours and sounds.'[35] Hardy depicts the growing love between Tess and Angel Clare 'at this dim inceptive stage of day' (186) by having the reader look through the eyes of two people who are intensely alive to the world they move in because they are alive, unconsciously, to each other. Sight and touch are so bound together that we feel through the characters' pores the 'woolly' fogs and the 'intenser little fog' of the cow's breath. Tess's and Angel's senses are not divided but presented as one in their heightened receptiveness to this vivid dawn world in which they participate as explorers of moisture and depressions upon grass, and skeins of breath upon air. In their isolation from the other denizens of the dairy, this is as a world new made by their shared and enlarging senses, yet the only note of personal feeling belongs not to them but to the cow 'when she recognized them, making an intenser little fog of her own', the anapaestic rhythm of the last ten syllables conveying little peaks of pleasure without any vitiating sentimentality. Throughout, we look *with* Tess and Clare, not *at* them, but without being 'in their heads' because there is no interior mental world separable from this exterior physical one. Heightened sensation leads not to a disclosure of interiors but to an enlargement of that margin in which human consciousness does not select and reflect upon matter but partakes with it in a universe in which self and other are of one element.

What is appealing about Mach's sensationism is that, like Hardy's, it intuitively faces towards our participation *in* the world, rather than retreating to the necessary solipsistic exclusion *from* it envisaged by his disciple Karl Pearson and by Walter Pater's narrow chamber of the mind. Mach seeks likeness and integration more readily than difference and separation: '*Our* body, like every other, is part of the world of sense; the boundary line between the physical and the psychical is solely practical and conventional.'[36] The most concentrated form of this 'world of sense' is the few minutes in which Tess hears Angel playing his harp at the Talbothays dairy. These four paragraphs, 390 words, have occasioned more critical discussion than

---

[35] Ibid., 7.

[36] Ibid., 152. In modern psychology this is mirrored by Teresa Brennan: 'The notion that the sense of self is different from that which is outside it (because that which is outside is unconscious, passive, and material) is clearly untenable. It is untenable as a substantial distinction, because insofar as the self has substance and is embodied, it too is matter' (*The Transmission of Affect*, 2004, 92).

any other passage in Hardy (Knight on the cliff must be second by a margin) but, in a study of the literary representation of the senses, I make no apology for quoting them in their entirety, however familiar they may be. Tess has gone into the garden at Talbothays, regretting that her earnest tone to Angel Clare earlier had betrayed feelings whose nature she has not yet acknowledged to herself:

> It was a typical summer evening in June, the atmosphere being in such delicate equilibrium and so transmissive that inanimate objects seemed endowed with two or three senses, if not five. There was no distinction between the near and the far, and an auditor felt close to everything within the horizon. The soundlessness impressed her as a positive entity rather than as the mere negation of noise. It was broken by the strumming of strings.
>
> Tess had heard those notes in the attic above her head. Dim, flattened, constrained by their confinement, they had never appeared to her as now, when they wandered in the still air with a stark quality like that of nudity. To speak absolutely, both instrument and execution were poor; but the relative is all, and as she listened Tess, like a fascinated bird, could not leave the spot. Far from leaving she drew up towards the performer, keeping behind the hedge that he might not guess her presence.
>
> The outskirt of the garden in which Tess found herself had been left uncultivated for some years, and was now damp and rank with juicy grass which sent up mists of pollen at a touch; and with tall blooming weeds emitting offensive smells – weeds whose red and yellow and purple hues formed a polychrome as dazzling as that of cultivated flowers. She went stealthily as a cat through this profusion of growth, gathering cuckoo-spittle on her skirts, cracking snails that were underfoot, staining her hands with thistle-milk and slug-slime, and rubbing off upon her naked arms sticky blights which, though snow-white on the apple-tree trunks, made madder stains on her skin; thus she drew quite near to Clare, still unobserved of him.
>
> Tess was conscious of neither time nor space. The exaltation which she had described as being producible at will by gazing at a star, came now without any determination of hers; she undulated upon the thin notes of the second-hand harp, and their harmonies passed like breezes through her, bringing tears into her eyes. The floating pollen seemed to be his notes made visible, and the dampness of the garden the weeping of the garden's sensibility. Though near nightfall, the rank-smelling weed-flowers glowed as if they would not close for intentness, and the waves of colour mixed with the waves of sound. (178–9)

To question whether the passage portrays Tess's feelings as absorbed *by* or as diffused *into* a wider 'world of sense' asks us to register how acutely the writing conveys conflicting agencies here. The episode does not begin with Tess's felt sense of things but, on the contrary, with the endowment of 'inanimate objects' with sensory capacities in a profligacy of observation that does not close upon recorded items but keeps all open as subjects. The peculiarly Hardyan compound of sensory arousal and impersonal receptiveness lends the scene a general aerial condition of vivid alertness rather than the urgent response of an individual consciousness. Not only is it 'an auditor', rather than Tess herself, who feels 'close to everything within the horizon' (as it had been, all those years previously, 'a spectator', and not initially Cytherea, to whom the picture of events in Hocbridge Town Hall had been 'presented'); but also a notably Latinate vocabulary of 'equilibrium', 'transmissive', 'inanimate', 'entity', 'negation' extends a scientific objectivity that fends off representation of Tess's subjective interior world. Tess is not straining to listen, rather 'a positive entity' is 'impressed' upon her, and that this is the apparent nonentity of 'soundlessness' sites the reader even more in the surrounding atmosphere, which is then inhabited not by Tess's reflections but by the compelling presence of musical notes, once 'dim' and 'flattened', now released into remarkable 'nudity'. From the 'entity' of sound's absence to the 'nudity' of the movement of notes in air, the sense of something coming into being is given immediacy by the quality of touch, which will through all four paragraphs remain the connecting fabric that keeps Tess's experience from receding into private vision. Unselfconscious and caught, 'like a fascinated bird', Tess is led on not by interior volition (the garden is one 'in which Tess found herself'), but as a participant in an event with a valency that combines human desire and non-human natural process.

Despite the abolition of near and far, in the previous paragraphs there was space within the closeness for notes to wander; no free wandering is permitted by the 'profusion of growth' in the garden itself, where the previous suggestion of touch in the auditory world now closes in upon the slightest movement to become the defining quality of the event. Yet interpretations of sensation differ: for Gillian Beer and Rosemarie Morgan touch here is immersion and assimilation, while for James Krasner it is edges and distinction.[37] To look as objectively as we can, the first of the two sentences of the paragraph

---

[37] Gillian Beer, *Darwin's Plots* (1983), 239; Rosemarie Morgan, 'Passive Victim? *Tess of the D'Urbervilles*', *Thomas Hardy Journal* 5:1 (January 1989), 33; James Krasner, *The Entangled Eye* (1992), 84.

concerns the activity of the vegetation in the garden, the second that of Tess herself as she moves through it to get closer to Angel's playing. The condition of this untended 'outskirt' provokes in the writing such an active interplay of vowels and consonants that the reader's senses are assailed by too much for a single reading; textures, surfaces and audible displacements jostle for supremacy. Certainly the disturbed natural world is no longer soundless, though I doubt it would be possible to gain agreement as to which sense predominates in the rendering of the most active growth of all – 'tall blooming weeds emitting offensive smells'. The vigour of every one of these words strains together and against each other, with no article, preposition or conjunction to ease a space for the reader to pass through the sensory onslaught unassaulted.

Equally difficult to determine is who has greater agency in the account of Tess's progress through this profusion: Tess, her skirts and feet, or the thistles, slugs and apple-tree trunks against which she brushes. 'Stealthily as a cat' declares a more positive intent than any which has possessed Tess up to this point in the novel, the two triplets of its movement suggesting a precise lifting and placing of paws to preserve the boundary of self-containment. But its elegant intention turns out to contrast markedly with the accumulation of contact Tess's steps actually produce, represented in the percussive concatenation of an extraordinary series of phrases that push forward with quite a different rhythm: 'gathering cuckoo-spittle on her skirts, cracking snails that were underfoot, staining her hands with thistle-milk and slug-slime . . .'. Tess intends a silent and delicate approach to Clare but finds herself involved in an action in which latent mutual aggression is what is heard by the reader. That Hardy consciously develops this is confirmed by noting that the explosive 'cracking snails that were underfoot' had been the more tamely descriptive 'brushing off snails that were climbing the apple-tree stems' in the *Graphic* serial. An inherent violence in the movements prompted by desire is inescapable: after 'gathering', 'cracking' and 'staining', Tess is finally depicted 'rubbing off upon her naked arms sticky blights which, though snow-white on the apple-tree trunks, made madder stains on her skin'. The packed verbal compounds ('sticky blights', 'snow-white', 'apple-tree', 'madder stains') make reading this an experience of being held back and released upon a little series of tactile/auditory detonations. This prompts me, reluctantly, to question the reading of this episode as an *assimilation* to 'erotic consciousness' (Morgan), or 'voluptuous *acceptance*' (Beer, both emphases mine). There is a margin within which the actions upon each other of human and non-human organisms cannot be disentangled, and they are more discomfortingly frictional than these descriptions convey. As Tess passes among the apple-trees she rubs 'sticky blights' off their trunks and onto her bare arms, and in the transfer white growths become deep red stains; and yet, because of the awkward syntax, the clause 'and rubbing off upon her naked arms sticky blights' cannot be divested of the sense that the trees themselves are actively doing the 'rubbing off' (and 'naked' clearly plays its part in this), an agency which is intensified by ending the sequence with the blights as active subject, 'which . . . made madder stains on her skin'.[38] To repeat, everything in this description presents itself as subject.

If the evocation of this 'typical summer's evening' began with a relatively simple appeal to the auditory senses, there is by now nothing uninvolved for the reader who has made her way, as has Tess, through the dense undergrowth thrown up by this paragraph. Drawing closer to Clare's playing the reader re-emerges into an aerial world, but one now scarcely to be distinguished from a mental one, for the fourth paragraph, after the material and bodily density of the third, is about consciousness. For Tess to be 'conscious of neither time nor space' after the spatially crowded struggle through the garden is indicative in itself of the 'exaltation' produced by the notes of the harp under Clare's hands. The projected fulfilment as 'she drew quite near to Clare' is quite different from the progress itself, one that unifies what is traditionally thought of as inner and outer fields of experience. Now Tess's ecstatic awareness of what is transmitted auditorily, visually, tactilely, by the evening atmosphere ('the thin notes of the second-hand harp', 'the floating pollen', the dampness of the garden') is co-extensive with this transpiring external world: the synaesthesia which conflates the musical notes with the floating pollen to become visual items, and which permits the garden's dampness, seen through her own tears, to possess 'sensibility', has an unbounded mental dimension that is, as Mach says, of '*one kind of elements*' with material nature.[39] The wonderful closure upon the

---

[38] When Hardy changed 'blood-red' to 'madder' he alliteratively and rhythmically intensified the aggressive activity of the blights, while semantically remaining within the plant world.

[39] Tom Lloyd refuses to be taken in: 'Tess and Angel are close to unmediated experience; it is the narrator – and hence the reader – who realises that it is all a bit of a sham, that Tess's moment of timelessness seems a shoddy instance of Kant's belief that time and space are creations of the mind' (*Crises of Realism*, 150).

glowing 'weed-flowers' – which themselves stay open ('they would not close for intentness'), continuous, wave rather than particle – with their radiating energy, cannot, also, be other than a description of the enraptured Tess herself. All too briefly, self is of the air, as the transports of lightwave and soundwave become indeed the matter of not-yet realised desire. Yet the boundaries that mark out the self as distinct in body and in history, erased though they seem to be in the garden and beyond, will return upon Tess to influence her courses as strongly as these evening harmonies. But, for now, the tyranny of force is overcome and radiant energy rules in its stead.

*

Much of the tragic feeling in the second half of *Tess* derives from the reader's sense of how atomised becomes the world of the novel after the flush of suffusing energy of the Talbothays sections, and how its human figures are seen to be subjects of mechanical force rather than participants in a generative field. Machian notions of an unboundaried world of sensational qualities retreat before a thoroughly Newtonian physics of forces to create for Tess the constant feeling of an inner world to be defended against external circumstance. At her wedding she whispers to herself, 'for she you love is not my real self, but one in my image; the one I might have been!' (281). Sounds harden. In a remarkable acoustic moment, the crowing of the cock on the nearby palings 'thrilled their ears through, dwindling away like echoes down a valley of rocks' (282). This auditory threat is amplified to a more general oppressiveness as Tess and Angel make their poor attempt to settle into Wellbridge Manor:

> Out of doors there began noises as of silk smartly rubbed; the restful dead leaves of the preceding autumn were stirred to irritated resurrection, and whirled about unwillingly, and tapped against the shutters. It soon began to rain. (285)

This briefly heard exterior scene results for the reader in a sense of an interior that is tense in its uneasy alertness towards contingency. In the 'irritated resurrection' of the dead leaves outside is heard the common history of this uncommon young woman which, when told to the apparently generous-minded Clare, will find out his 'hard logical deposit' (311). The embracing ferment of Talbothays has been entirely, and with remarkable rapidity, replaced by a different landscape, and a language of pallor and obduracy pervades this part of the novel to thin the characters back to their self-enclosed, surviving, resisting selves. Tess narrates her history to Angel, and the result is an awful *withdrawal* of the world, leaving her, and Clare too, bare and exposed, not a part of anything:

> When she ceased the auricular impressions from their previous endearments seemed to hustle away into the corners of their brains, repeating themselves as echoes from a time of supremely purblind foolishness. (297)

They are deserted not only by their own former language but also by the language of the author, who could not have chosen words more at variance with his subjects and their new exposure to each other. Except, that is, for the fast-retreating 'hustle away into the corners of their brains', which tells us everything sensationally about their desperate situation. Clare had been able to feel that 'Upon her sensations the whole world depended for Tess' (214) – Hardy's fundamental empiricist tenet that structures the appeal made by his characters from Cytherea to Jude for their 'single opportunity of existence' (214) – but in the 'ashy and furtive' light of the dawn following their confessions 'it seemed as if nothing could kindle either of them to a fervour of sensation any more' (307), and correspondingly the vividness of the world recedes, most damagingly the reality of Tess's world for Angel.

Far from finding a correspondence in the anti-mechanical physics of Mach, the tragedy of the second half of *Tess* is illuminated by the more biologically-based observations about defended boundaries of the Geneva School literary critic, Jean Starobinski. His celebrated essay, 'The Inside and the Outside', would seem more immediately applicable to many works other than *Tess* (*Under Western Eyes* would be one of them); but his analysis reveals exactly the process of contraction that exerts its force at this point in Hardy's novel:

> A living organism exists only by virtue of the margin (dictated by the species, by the genetic code) through which it determines, defines and opposes itself, becoming individual: limit, finiteness, individuality, the struggle waged against the outside – all these are correlative. No inside is conceivable, therefore, without the complicity of an outside on which it relies.[40]

If such a view seems antipathetic to the inclusive circulating energies of *Tess of the d'Urbervilles*, its pertinence to 'The Woman Pays' and 'The Convert' penetrates to the nature of what *Tess* becomes

---

[40] Jean Starobinski, 'The Inside and the Outside', *The Hudson Review* 28:3 (Autumn 1975), 342.

and why it is so desolating. 'Becoming individual' is the defensive, wearying journey Tess undertakes in the second half of the novel, and Philip Weinstein writes of it, 'Tess is condemned – like all of Hardy's reflective people – to absorb the impress of nature's inhuman otherness. Not harmonious merging but sustained abrasion is her portion.'[41] This is a heartfelt summation, but one that silences the fact that a very human otherness – that of men – violates Tess in tissue and spirit. Indeed, Angel's refusal to hear in Tess's confession the true nature of the woman he has married is felt by many readers to be a more heinous disregard for her than Alec's treatment of the woman he seduces. Certainly it proceeds from Starobinski's defended 'inside' – the unreflecting imbibing of his culture's estimate of 'a pure woman' to which he sacrifices the living woman, defending it by silence about his own equivalent behaviour – just as surely as Jim deserts Jewel in order 'to celebrate his pitiless wedding with a shadowy ideal of conduct' (*Lord Jim* 313), while never disclosing to her that he wasn't 'good enough' on account of the *Patna* affair. So even the most moving avowal of love in the entire novel – Izz Huett's '"nobody could love 'ee more than Tess did! . . . She would have laid down her life for 'ee. I could do no more"' (343) – does not reconnect Angel to the outflowing current of his feelings; he would rather defend the entity of self deposited within by gender, class and culture. He is at the furthest remove, at this point, from an ameliorative, Comtean hope that Hardy entertained precisely at the time he was writing *Tess*: 'Mankind, in fact, may be, and probably will be, viewed as members of one corporeal frame' (*LW* 235). Angel holds to the unitary, the separate; he departs for Brazil because

> the facts had not changed. If he was right at first, he was right now. And the momentum of the course on which he had embarked tended to keep him going in it, unless diverted by a stronger, more sustained force than had played upon him this afternoon. (345)

The language of classical mechanics could not be more directly applied to a psychological condition. The radiant plenitude of *Tess* has fallen before a bleak vision of atoms and forces.[42]

---

[41] Weinstein, *The Semantics of Desire*, 122.
[42] Martha Turner's *Mechanism and the Novel: Science in the Narrative Process* (1993) offers a very good discussion of the persistence of mechanistic thought throughout the nineteenth century. See especially, 'Matter, motion, laws', 24–31.

The compulsion of Tess's movements is envisioned differently from the attractions and gravitations of much of the first half of the novel. Everywhere she is propelled by the stark necessity of economic forces, and she moves through the landscape disfigured or disguised in the attempt to preserve an inner self and faith in Angel untouched: 'Inside this exterior, over which the eye might have roved as over a thing scarcely percipient, almost inorganic, there was the record of a pulsing life' (355). On her desperate journey from Flintcomb-Ash to Emminster, 'She saw her purpose in such staring lines, and the landscape so faintly, that she was sometimes in danger of losing her way' (374). The direction prescribed by the forces brought to bear upon Tess almost obliterates the direction to be gleaned by one in tune with her surroundings; and when she receives no answer at the Vicarage, and rests briefly in the porch, she sees quite casually a mirror to her own desolate and fruitless compelled movement: 'A piece of blood-stained paper, caught up from some meat-buyer's dust-heap, beat up and down the road without the gate; too flimsy to rest, too heavy to fly away; and a few straws kept it company' (374). It is one of Hardy's greatest images, entirely without consequence, a small ekphrasis, suspending narrative action to focus on an aesthetic object, yet drawing into its fluctuating movements the deep narrative agitations, the taking up and discarding, the staining and marking, with which the whole novel is so concerned.

The unpicking of the integrity of life, and the wholeness felt in the Talbothays sections, into inner and outer worlds and selves is the tragedy of *Tess*. Life at Flintcomb-Ash is driven not only by Farmer Groby's severe exploitation, but more fundamentally by the engineer and his steam engine, a *'primum mobile'* tellingly designated his 'portable repository of *force*' (405, my emphasis). The fruitful margin wherein the body is not a defence system, as in Starobinski's biological account, but a participant in external process as in Mach's romantic physics, is lost to the rule of an unforgiving division. This loss reaches its most extreme manifestation at Sandbourne. Angel's tentative attempts at enquiry and restitution serve only to expose the compulsion of forces that play upon each of them when he and Tess finally encounter each other at The Herons:

> 'These clothes are what he's put upon me: I didn't care what he did wi' me! But – will you go away, Angel, please, and never come any more?'
>   They stood fixed, their baffled hearts looking out of their eyes with a joylessness pitiful to see. Both seemed to implore something to shelter them from reality.
>   'Ah – it is my fault!' said Clare.
>   But he could not get on. Speech was as inexpressive as silence. (467)

The mechanics of the second half of the novel has brought them both to this bare knowledge, which stares uncompromisingly in the face of Clare's faltering. 'But he could not get on': there is no shelter, connection or direction. If we are to look for atomised unitary existence in *Tess*, 'the little cell called your life' as *Jude* has it, we find it exposed and comfortless in the brief interchange across a room in The Herons.

There will be no recovery of Machian oneness offered in the closing pages of *Tess*. When the brief idyll at Bramshurst Court exactly reverses Angel's abandonment of her at Wellbridge Manor, the terms remain the same as those which have characterised the second half of the novel. Tess says,

> 'All is trouble outside there; inside here content.'
> He peeped out also. It was quite true; within was affection, union, error forgiven: outside was the inexorable. (481)

At Talbothays, the inexorable had been the tide of passion, both within and without. If inner content is now briefly possible, it is fatally out of harmony with the forces of the 'outside'. In the dawn in which the police net on Salisbury Plain closes in upon Stonehenge there is a separateness quite distinct from the dawns wherein Tess and Angel collected the cows:

> Presently the night wind died out, and the quivering little pools in the cup-like hollows of the stones lay still. At the same time something seemed to move on the verge of the dip eastward – a mere dot. (486)

In this marginal moment of night becoming day and temporary freedom becoming acknowledged captivity, there is a pause allowed in which Tess intimates that she knows all that there is to be known about her own condition of separateness and belonging, of an individual course and controlling forces: '"I am ready," she said quietly' (487). Tess certainly doesn't belong to *us*; her quiet declaration forbids intimacy, and in the final chapter, silent apart from the town clocks striking eight, she is lost to the successive vistas presented to the eye of the reader of the institutions that have condemned her, the landscapes that have nurtured and entrapped her, the sun which has generated all this, and she is present only as the extension upon the breeze of a black flag, and the obliterated reason why we are asked to look at this view of Wintoncester on a July morning. At the margin of the picture 'The two speechless gazers . . . joined hands again, and went on' (489). The effect is to leave Tess also out of the reach of the ever-desiring narrator, and quietly to resist the possessiveness of an author somewhat in love with his own fictional creation, and of readers who follow him.

*

That sort of possessiveness is never a danger when reading *Nostromo*, nor are the attractions of organicism. Nature in *Nostromo* is more august and removed than in *Tess*; it does not present itself in atmospheric conditions that can be imbibed or to which the novel's characters can assimilate themselves. Associated with stoppage, dissolution and expiry, it is grand, unprovocative and, above all, silent.[43] Not so clearly conceived as either energy or force as in *Tess*, its power lies in being distantly uninvolved with humanity; yet even in a novel of such human action,[44] of national politics and a predominantly urban scene, 'facing nature' will continue to be as unavoidable a demand in *Nostromo* as in Hardy's novel of rural retreat.[45] In a contrast to the focus upon the sounds of the thronged historical drama of the previous chapter, this second foray into *Nostromo* examines the widening margins within which the self is called upon to face nature's silence in a history as invasive, though not so immediately intimate, as that of *Tess*.[46]

Martin Decoud is a fictional figure as different from Tess Durbeyfield as it would be possible to conceive, though perhaps as close to Conrad intellectually as Tess is to Hardy emotionally. To take the urban dandy journalist as a prime means through which to explore a disintegration of self in the face of elemental forces indicates that the astringencies of *Nostromo* are remote from *Tess*'s visceral connect-

---

[43] Hardy's silences, in contrast, are closer at hand. See the 'gradients of silence' that Jean-Jacques Lecercle instances in his essay 'Thomas Hardy's Silences', *Cycnos* 26:2 (2010), 13–28.

[44] Letter to J. B. Pinker: 'I've never written anything with so much *action* in it' (*CL* 3:137).

[45] For an opposed view, see Geoffrey Galt Harpham's important essay, 'The Future of Conrad's Beginnings', in Kaplan, Mallios and White eds, *Conrad in the Twenty-First Century* (2005), 17–38.

[46] The nineteenth-century empirical tradition is virtually silent upon the nature of silence as a phenomenon. In Tyndall's eight lectures of 1867, published as *Sound*, it receives no mention. Max Picard's *The World of Silence* (1948), for all its extravagance, remains seminal for its opening assertion, 'Silence is an autonomous phenomenon' (15).

edness, but the expendability of the human spirit amid cosmic indifference, and the struggle to maintain it, are the tragic perception and urgent concern of both novels. Decoud's long night-time letter to his sister from the Albergo d'Italia Una keeps alive the human work of constructing a narrative amid the first intimations of the appalling vacancy which eventually will nullify that endeavour. After many pages of writing, he pauses:

> Decoud lifted his head to listen. But there were no sounds, neither in the room nor in the house, except the drip of the water from the filter into the vast earthenware jar under the wooden stand. And outside the house there was a great silence. (244)

The concentration of the ear upon the single sound of the drip close at hand extends the silence beyond to an infinitude exceeding audible range. In practice, Conrad is taking his talkative and aware character step by step towards a silence to which he will not be adequate, whose discomposing invasion he will not be able to resist.

At this stage, exhausted but engaged, Decoud is still able to look about him and describe in writing the pervasive silence of the scene, not yet lost nor overwhelmed, as Robert Penn Warren has it.[47] Between the press of events to which his unacknowledged idealism has committed him, and the impress of a non-human physics of which, as yet, he has no conception despite its encroaching presence, Decoud maintains the slender margin of the writer, able sufficiently to detach himself from his impressions to record them as a narrative. The end of the letter recalls Elizabeth-Jane's night vigil, but is altogether more assertive of the necessity for consciousness:

> 'But now it is a pause under the hovering wing of death in that silent house buried in the black night, with this dying woman, the two children crouching without a sound, and that old man whom I can hear through the thickness of the wall passing up and down with a light rubbing noise no louder than a mouse. And I, the only other with them, don't really know whether to count myself with the living or with the dead. "*Quién sabe?*" as the people here are prone to say in answer to every question. But no! feeling for you is certainly not dead, and the whole thing, the house, the dark night, the silent children in this dim room, my very presence here – all this is life, must be life, since it is so much like a dream.'
>
> With the writing of the last line there came upon Decoud a moment of sudden and complete oblivion. (249)

---

[47] 'Man is lost in this overwhelming scene.' Introduction, *Nostromo*, The Modern Library (1951), xxxv.

In so powerfully conveying 'the whole thing' – the night, the woman, the old man, the silent children – Decoud discovers something of the cadence that Conrad's younger friend Edward Thomas was to find in his poetry, in his own facing of a silent darkness. He has not yet approached the extremity that turns to face Thomas in late poems where 'Its silence I hear and obey / That I may lose my way / And myself' ('Lights Out'), or where the boundary is lost between self and other in the night, 'And I and star and wind and deer / Are in the dark together, – near, / Yet far' ('Out in the dark'), though this dissolution awaits.[48] Instead, throughout the letter we read a solitary but intensely active mind keeping a narrative going against the encroaching night, until a final, but only temporary, surrender and collapse. Decoud explicitly rejects the fatalistic *Quién sabe?* of the people to assert his individual feeling for his sister, and he recognises that dreams are a product of life, not death: he is as yet unassailed by the loss of will that overtakes him later. As Kenneth Graham acutely observes of his creator Conrad:

> the strong drift towards the dream, towards inanition and will-lessness, is in turn almost always challenged from within his narrative by the not-quite-paralysed forces of love, personal and communal, of fidelity, physical battle, yarn-spinning, justified scorn, and, at the very least, of rather grimly holding on.[49]

All of these forms of resistance act in some measure in Decoud's letter, against a deepening of the surrounding silence. But there is an anterior silence, one which requires a casting off from the visible and auditory contours of Costaguana to hear, that will discover more corrosive truths about will and holding on than the historical drama displays.

*

At this juncture Decoud is able to keep writing against the encroaching dark silence, for his life as it were; but later during the same night when they push off from land in the lighter, the speed with which he and Nostromo are engulfed in conditions which extinguish his talents

---

[48] Conrad was among the last people whom Thomas sought out while he was stationed at Lydd, before his posting to France in January 1917. On 7 December 1916 he wrote to Eleanor Farjeon, 'I shall just walk over and see Conrad, who is only 12 miles away.' And on the 11th he writes, 'I saw Conrad and in fact I stayed the night. Then he drove me back in the rain' (Eleanor Farjeon, *Edward Thomas: The Last Four Years*, 1979, 231.)

[49] Kenneth Graham, *Indirections in the Novel: James, Conrad and Forster* (1988), 4.

overtakes the reader as swiftly as it does the men themselves. It is effected in a single paragraph, in which Decoud's 'clear, ringing tones' of temporary farewell are lost to utterly new phenomena: 'it seemed to him that the wharf was floating away into the night . . . the effect was that of being launched into space. After a splash or two there was not a sound . . .', and by the end of the following paragraph 'the big, half-decked boat slipped along with no more noise than if she had been suspended in the air' (261). The strange suspensions enacted in the Gulf, a 'new experience' for Decoud, are a remove known to Conrad, as he tells the readers of his *Daily Chronicle* article, 'Well Done':

> In my early days, starting out on a voyage was like being launched into Eternity. I say advisedly Eternity instead of Space, because of the boundless silence which swallowed up one for eighty days – for one hundred days – for even yet more days of an existence without echoes and whispers . . . . An enormous silence, in which there was nothing to connect one with the Universe but the incessant wheeling about of the sun and other celestial bodies, the alternation of light and shadow, eternally chasing each other over the sky.[50]

For once, in the enormous imaginative effort of writing *Nostromo*, Conrad can draw upon his own remembered sensations of intelligence facing annihilating vacancy, a region beyond the range of all the deprivations in *Tess*, unless it lives in the eyes of the 'strange birds from behind the North Pole' (*Tess* 363) who visit Flintcomb-Ash on their migrations. The appeal of lapsing into 'this mysteriousness of the great waters spread out strangely smooth' (261) can be felt by the reader in the steady draw of a rhythm that contrasts with the purposeful alertness that keeps Decoud and Nostromo going in the smothering dark. So, after a sudden whisper from Nostromo, 'When his voice ceased, the enormous stillness, without light or sound, seemed to affect Decoud's senses like a powerful drug' (262). But far from any Machian extension or dissolution of the ego that discovers a larger self in its dispersal in the surrounding elements, Conradian physics here and elsewhere is one of resistant forces. Decoud's alertness is overcome as by a drug rather than partaking in any larger atmospheric event: 'Like a man lost in slumber, he heard nothing, he saw nothing' (262). Decoud is 'a man lost'; the excitements of listening which assure him of existence are extinguished, and 'The change

---

[50] Joseph Conrad, *Notes on Life and Letters* (1949), 182.

from the agitation, the passions and the dangers, from the sights and sounds of the shore, was so complete that it would have resembled death had it not been for the survival of his thoughts' (262). The man who professes belief in nothing but his own sensations, when the sources of sensation are withdrawn and 'nothing to connect one with the Universe' remains, not even 'the alternation of light and shadow', is left with almost nothing to persuade him of his own reality.

And yet it is exactly here that Conrad's imaginative art is finer than the formulations of his psychology, for the truth that emerges from his depiction, as opposed to his statements, is that Decoud's life does *not* depend on his sensations, but on his thoughts. With a Shelleyan idealism that might have enthused Hardy, but which is more ethereal than anything Hardy wrote about the inhabitants of consciousness, those thoughts are rendered as phenomena free from containment by the thinking mind:

> In this foretaste of eternal peace they floated vivid and light, like unearthly clear dreams of earthly things that may haunt the souls freed by death from the misty atmosphere of regrets and hopes. (262)

These life-confirming thoughts are embodiments refined beyond the wandering notes of Angel's harp in the garden which they resemble. Those visualised sounds depended upon sensation, while these dreams that look back upon the earth exist in a region without affect. These moments in the apparent vacuum of the Gulf are also a strange foretaste of Decoud's more violently synaesthesic experience on the Great Isabel, but one in which, for a period, an entirely mental sphere can sustain itself without external stimulus; thus the lost man, a man who has disappeared as far as the life confirmed by sensations goes, has not in fact lost possession of himself, and we discover a pure idealism at the heart of a novel so concerned with materialism.

Throughout the episode Decoud is portrayed as slipping away from a grasp of himself as present in the scene, and then again recovering attention. When feeling returns to overcome a 'languid but not unpleasant indifference' (267), it is from a region in which material forms have been dissolved, one that can be apprehended by the soul but not by the senses:

> He had the strangest sensation of his soul having just returned into his body from the circumambient darkness in which land, sea, sky, the mountains, and the rocks were as if they had not been. (262)

This is quite the opposite experience to Cytherea's reverie on the hill overlooking Lewborne Bay, or Tess's 'quiescent glide' in the woods near Marlott, in which the sense of self seems constituted from the external features it apprehends, not separate from them. Rather, Decoud's experience in the Gulf is of the necessity for a continual retrieval of a resistant self that has been on the point of surrendering its individual will. It is more analogous to the Tess of the second half of Hardy's novel, sustained in her resistance by *ideas* of Angel and her love for him, rather than by immediate sensations.

For Decoud, the night journey with Nostromo reveals that 'There was no bond of conviction, of common idea; they were merely two adventurers pursuing each his own adventure, involved in the same imminence of deadly peril' (295). For the reader, the effect of this prolonged immersion in the darkness of the Gulf is subtly to visit every succeeding episode with this knowledge of almost irresistible disintegration: all the major characters – Decoud, Nostromo, Monygham, Gould, Mrs Gould, Antonia, Father Corbelàn, Sotillo, Pedrito Montero, Giorgio Viola, Captain Mitchell – each in his or her own way is seen to become progressively and irretrievably a prey to solipsism, and it could be said of them all that they are adventurers pursuing each his own adventure (only Don Pépé would escape that censure). Despite the establishment of the Occidental Republic, the muted anaphoric rhythm of 'No bond of conviction, of common idea' is the murmur that sounds below Sulaco's success. And its architect, Decoud, must face nature alone.

*

Identity in *Nostromo*, apparently so certainly declared in intention, speech and action by all the Costaguanan politicos, is shown by the novel increasingly to be subject to invasion or erosion, to require defending, or rebuilding. It is unsurprising therefore that the second half of the novel brings to prominence Dr Monygham, the figure who has suffered most brutally the violation of corporeal and mental borders, who knows more intimately than the other characters how narrow is the margin for free and uncompelled choice in the self's interaction with the world. Monygham's awareness has been forced upon him by his experience of torture at the hands of Father Beron, acting in the service of the paranoia of the then Citizen-Saviour of the country, Guzman Bento. With broken body, it is an experience of being penetrated and possessed by another which overcomes 'all the force of his will striving its utmost to forget' (371). A dilapidated figure for much of the novel, Monygham, however, is not without force: the man who 'had made himself an ideal conception of his disgrace' (375) thereby finds a means to act, decisively and dangerously, in the narrow margin between his self-contempt and his disdain of others. Thinking only of the consequences to Mrs Gould of the fall of Sulaco to the Monteros, he exploits the damaged vanity of Nostromo to persuade him to undertake the difficult mission to retrieve Barrios and his forces from Cayta as the only expedient to save Sulaco. Monygham's need to generate an idealisation of Nostromo's courageous powers of endurance, as a counter to his own failure of nerve and body, yields a conception of man and nature that is central to the novel and to this whole study:

> Having had to encounter single-handed during his period of eclipse many physical dangers, he was well aware of the most dangerous element common to them all: of the crushing, paralyzing sense of human littleness, which is what really defeats a man struggling with natural forces, alone, far from the eyes of his fellows. He was eminently fit to appreciate the mental image he made for himself of the Capataz, after hours of tension and anxiety, precipitated suddenly into an abyss of waters and darkness, without earth or sky, and confronting it not only with an undismayed mind, but with sensible success. (433)

Focalised through the figure least susceptible to heroic claims for man, this is the novel's most heroic image of facing nature, 'a man struggling with natural forces, alone'. His vision of 'an undismayed mind' finds a uniquely apt word, containing the full knowledge of an utter want of adequacy while proclaiming a readiness to continue, which conveys the mind's capacity to counter the disintegrating formlessness of nature, fitting for this idealist.

The injunction laid upon its inhabitants by the Conradian universe is, in the words of the stoical Captain MacWhirr of 'Typhoon', to 'face it': 'Facing it – always facing it – that's the way to get through . . . . Face it. That's enough for any man' (217). A man has to bring his humanity to the test of being in a world of forces that require resistance, a world conceived as having a more rigid and unyielding physics than the energy-field of Hardy's equally exacting cosmology. The two figures who brave the Gulf, Nostromo and Decoud, bring very different psychological and physical equipment to that task of self-definition; for one it is 'the disenchanted vanity which is the reward of audacious action', while for the other it is 'the disillusioned weariness which is the retribution meted out to intellectual audacity' (501). Both are victims of their own gifts, and after the darkness of the Gulf both fail to confront in good faith the glittering silence of the natural world.

In Nostromo's case, newly awakened as he is to the meaning of his name, it is a matter of possession or, more accurately, re-possession. The re-enchantment of Nostromo as a jealous devotee of stolen treasure, and his re-birth as Captain Fidanza, is accomplished in a quietly dramatic moment when he is not 'in the thick of it', but has absented himself from the successful outcome of his greatest venture in the service of the Blancos of Sulaco. Having dived off Barrios's returning troop-ship at the sight of the lighter's empty dinghy drifting in the Gulf, Nostromo gazes out from the Great Isabel with an unseeing stare:

> Then slowly, without a limb having stirred, without a twitch of muscle or quiver of an eyelash, an expression, a living expression came upon the still features, deep thought crept into the empty stare – as if an outcast soul, a quiet, brooding soul, finding that untenanted body in its way, had come in stealthily to take possession. (493)

This reanimation of an empty husk by the legendary watchers over the treasure of the Azuera, enslaved by 'the fatal spell of their success' (5), creates in Captain Fidanza an inside and an outside, to revert to the terms of Jean Starobinski, more severely adhered to than that adopted by Tess. For the remainder of the novel, Fidanza's visible life is one of gravely maintained rectitude; the exterior world that had conferred upon Nostromo his identity is sundered by an unbreachable border from a newly-found sensible interior of appetite and obsession. But it is the sentence that follows which locates the barely noticeable moment of re-tenanting at the heart of Conrad's fictional enterprise: 'The Capataz frowned: and in the immense stillness of sea, islands, and coast, of cloud forms on the sky and trails of light upon the water, the knitting of that brow had the emphasis of a powerful gesture' (494). Human consciousness opposes itself to the infinite recession of silence and light. In a typically Conradian sudden juxtaposition of the near and the far, the mere frown of a new awareness is 'a powerful gesture', an imposition of definition upon the forms and immaterial formlessness within which human activity is cast. It is what human beings must do: 'In our activity alone do we find the sustaining illusion of an independent existence as against the whole scheme of things of which we form a helpless part' (497). And yet the magisterial statement is implacable, for we are no more than 'a helpless part' of 'the whole scheme of things', and all our activity creates only an 'illusion'. This summation of so much of what Conrad's fiction explores stands as his definition of identity and its margins. The senses, which confirm our singularity as organisms that harbour impressions by which the world is uniquely and separately known, also immerse us in a physics in which we are merely minute participants, caught up in the impersonal unfolding of a cosmic event. The world is all before us, but also around us, within us, and passing through us, and the best that we can do is to face this knowledge with a transparent self, and thereby find solidarity with others who are also caught up. Nostromo, despite the capacities that exact Dr Monygham's unwilling tribute, does so in the bad faith of being possessed by a secret hidden from others' eyes.

Yet while Captain Fidanza's assiduous attention to the borders of his identity procures a small margin for activity, much reduced from his days as Nostromo, Decoud fails entirely in this illusory yet necessary task of self-maintenance. Befitting this talker and child of noise and history, Decoud's encounter alone, unaided, with the forces of nature presents itself as an encounter with silence, and turns, too, on a matter of faith. Like Nostromo, he is another who has retreated to the margins of a history in which he had been central, and his fate on the Great Isabel remains suspended for 200 pages during which the reader is left to speculate upon his enforced solitude while Montero's counter-revolution, Sotillo's obsessive trawling for the silver, Monygham's coercion of Nostromo, the defeat of the Monterists and the creation of the Occidental Republic play themselves out in his absence. After the noise of history, when we return to Decoud it is to the silence which takes so few pages of direct description in the novel yet which has such a pervasive effect in our reading. For the intensely verbal Decoud, his first day on the Great Isabel 'had been a day of absolute silence – the first he had known in his life' (496). After five days the mental world which had preserved his self-possession in the Gulf proves inadequate:

> his intelligence and his passion were swallowed up easily in this great unbroken solitude of waiting without faith ... His sadness was the sadness of a sceptical mind. He beheld the universe as a succession of incomprehensible images. (498)

It is the sadness of Conrad's sceptical mind, too. To see the universe 'as a succession of incomprehensible images' is the disintegrating threat inherent in an impressionism of nervous shocks and phenomena minutely observed as kaleidoscopic fragments of sensational response; in this sense Decoud is the object lesson of a profound strain that Conrad recognises in his own art.

Decoud is unable to maintain that margin of distinction between self and other, however small, which is necessary to sustain the 'illusion of an independent existence' in the Conradian universe. His penetrative analyses of the political and linguistic game which constitutes the existence of all of the characters of the novel fall before the outright statement that 'The brilliant Costaguanero of the boulevards had died from solitude and want of faith in himself and others' (496). Faith in a continuous self is necessarily under attack from a temperament which resolves authenticity into the sensations of the moment, and Decoud has no principle of continuity with which to withstand evacuation and invasion.[51] When Conrad writes of his experience on the island that Decoud 'was not fit to grapple with himself single handed' (497), it is clear that he is pointing to a condition of silent solitude that has lain in wait for this social creature. He is found to be a fundamentally uninhabited figure, requiring the stimulus of some outward sensation to assure himself of his own existence:

> After three days of waiting for the sight of some human face, Decoud caught himself entertaining a doubt of his own individuality. It had merged into the world of cloud and water, of natural forces and forms of nature. (497)

This is not conceived as any sort of Machian extension of the indeterminate boundaries of the ego; this is the absorption and dissolution of an organism which can no longer raise a gesture to resist its own defeasibility. For this sentence of Decoud's merging contrasts explicitly with that of Nostromo's knitting of his brow, which had proved such a 'powerful gesture', three pages previously: Nostromo had been able to compel 'cloud forms on the sky and trails of light upon the water' (494) into a picture serving his understanding of things, while 'the world of cloud and water' is met with no such shaping power in Decoud and overwhelms him.

'Weighted by the bars of San Tomé silver', Decoud 'disappeared without a trace, swallowed up by the immense indifference of things'

---

[51] Torsten Pettersson says, 'The logic of Decoud's disintegration is thus: without social context, no 'belief'; without some kind of belief, no activity; and without activity, no sense of temporally continuous identity' (*Consciousness and Time*, 1982, 131).

(501), an absorption as complete as Tess's erasure from the final chapter of *Tess*. It comes as no surprise to conclude that Conrad's vision in *Nostromo* is more nihilistic than that of Hardy in *Tess*. Yet that feeling cannot arise from a contemplation of what happens to the characters: Tess is tracked and cut down by the forces arrayed against her in a manner more pitiless than that which contingently befalls the characters of *Nostromo*. But for all that the Natural Law in *Tess* is as indifferent to the plight of the individual as the Social Law is cruel, Nature in Hardy's novel allows a participation, a burgeoning and a fullness of embodied pleasure, which is absent from *Nostromo*, and which Conrad's pervasive sense of the nothingness at the back of everything ultimately denies.[52] Conrad writes more recognisably than Hardy in a tradition of European metaphysics that rejoices, almost, in acknowledging 'the void', such as can be found, for instance, in Sénancour's epistolary novel *Oberman* (1802):

> Nothing is possessed as it is conceived, nothing is conceived as it exists. We perceive relations, not essences; we never enjoy the things themselves, only their images. Thus Nature, which appears elusive without and impenetrable within us, is everywhere shadowy. 'I feel' is the only word for the man who wants nothing but truth.[53]

Condensed here is the psychic condition for a credo of truth to sensations, and also the solipsism that threatens to follow from such authenticity. Oberman's accent is that of Conrad in letter after letter to Cunninghame Graham. One such performance of despair in order to disillusion the idealist Graham (here translated from French) reads:

> And words fly away; and nothing remains, do you understand? Absolutely nothing, oh man of faith! Nothing. A moment, a twinkling of an eye and nothing remains – but a clot of mud, of cold mud, of dead mud cast into black space, rolling around an extinguished sun. Nothing. Neither thought, nor sound, nor soul. Nothing. (*CL* 2:70)

---

[52] The ways in which this affects Conrad's style has been brilliantly examined by Werner Senn in *Conrad's Narrative Voice* (1980/2017), chapter 3 in particular. Senn provides the finest and most extensive linguistic analysis in modern Conrad studies, equivalent in significance to what Dennis Taylor has done for Hardy's poetry (*Hardy's Literary Language and Victorian Philology*, 1993).

[53] Quoted in Robert Martin Adams, *Nil: Episodes in the Literary Conquest of Void in the Nineteenth Century* (1966), 25. Conrad used a passage from Sénancour as the original epigraph to *Chance*. The hand-written extract on the typescript is heavily scored over in blue pencil, making further identification difficult.

In place of this 'nothing', the different tenor of Hardy's pessimistic sensibility embraces an 'unknown': 'beyond the knowable, there must always be an unknown', he writes to C. W. Saleeby in 1915 (*LW* 400). Conrad's 'nothing' lays the fiercer injunction upon man to impose immediate meaning upon it; Hardy's 'unknown' more generously permits to man indeterminate dimensions into which to expand.

*

In *Nostromo*, the expansion to generosity of the human spirit, attenuated almost to extinction by the unanswering, unconsoling silence that surrounds all human activity, is most poignantly located in a silent garden and in the person of Mrs Gould. In chapter 11 of Part Third, about ten years after the successful establishment of the Occidental Republic, the First Lady of Sulaco hears by telephone message that '"The master remains to sleep at the mountain tonight"' (519). It has become the pattern of her married life, and in the profound silence which follows in the garden of the Casa Gould, Dr Monygham abruptly departs, ending the most sustained intimate conversation of the novel and taking with him his unuttered devotion to her. In the still silence that reigns through the three paragraphs that take the reader to the end of the chapter, the novel approaches with the utmost delicacy the 'distant regions' usually kept hidden by this most subtle and swiftly intelligent of women.[54]

> Had anybody asked her of what she was thinking, alone in the garden of the Casa, with her husband at the mine and the house closed to the street like an empty dwelling, her frankness would have had to evade the question. It had come into her mind that for life to be large and full, it must contain the care of the past and of the future in every passing moment of the present. Our daily work must be done to the glory of the dead, and for the good of those who come after. She thought that, and sighed without opening her eyes – without moving at all. Mrs Gould's face became set and rigid for a second, as if to receive, without flinching, a great wave of loneliness that swept over her head. And it came into her mind, too, that no one would ever ask her with solicitude what she was

---

[54] The phrase is from Conrad's essay on Alphonse Daudet of 1898: 'The road to these distant regions ... is a path of toilsome silence upon which travel men simple and unknown, with closed lips, or, may be, whispering their pain softly – only to themselves' (*Notes on Life and Letters*, 22).

thinking of. No one. No one, but perhaps the man who had just gone away. No; no one who could be answered with careless sincerity in the ideal perfection of confidence. (520–1)

'Had anybody asked', he would have found that Mrs Gould is granted two thoughts, one providing the novel's greatest statement of continuity and connection, the other voicing its most intense awareness of lonely separation. The careful, poised phrase 'It had come into her mind' is so moving because, despite sometimes seeing through her eyes and hearing her ironic rejoinders or expressive small cries of dismay, we have not been quite fully privy to that *mind* for a long time in our reading, not since Part First, chapter 6, the long chapter of the Goulds' courtship and early life in Sulaco. And now the sentence which conditionally and judiciously approaches the contents of that mind eventually arrives at 'her frankness', which it then has to suppose to be defeated by something unnamed (but which we know) to become the opposite of frankness. Not exactly indirect, this treats Mrs Gould with the intuitive tact and 'solicitude' that we know she will receive from no one in the novel, except 'perhaps the man who had just gone away', but it does not quite prepare us for the largeness which comes when the question is, in fact, taken up.

'It had come into her mind' – from where? Really, from the whole novel, as, typically, she looks beyond her own privations to contemplate the nature of attachment which creates of life more than a succession of images or a buzzing of phrases. If there is a 'moral centre' to be found in *Nostromo* it is in a mind into which can come a thought large enough to transcend individual experience but which is grounded in every individual's experience. 'She thought that' has an air of completion to it, but the 'akoumena' of this deep silence has not finished with her,[55] and for a second time a thought about the defining nature of a human condition is given words as 'it came into her mind'. It does not destroy the first thought, and she receives it 'without flinching', but it confirms that she will never experience what she, alone in the novel, has the power to conceive, a life that is 'large and full'. It does so through the extraordinary measure of five successive negations, and the thought completes itself with the perfect expression of just what is forever denied her, the ability to *answer* such a solicitous question ('What are you thinking of?') 'with

---

[55] 'that which is to be listened to' in any environmental ambience: Mark Muldoon, 'Silence Revisited', *The Review of Metaphysics* 50:2 (1996), *passim*.

careless sincerity in the ideal perfection of confidence'. That sort of absolute assurance in the intimacies of private intercourse is found nowhere in *Nostromo*; but in the silence of the garden of the Casa Gould it has found articulation as an ideal, an unspoken thought in the mind of the novel's most emotionally agile character, now wearied into a 'still and sad immobility' (521). The margins within which the self might find expression have contracted to a compass even smaller than that allowed to Elizabeth-Jane.

And it might come into our mind also that what is so often designated 'background' or 'setting' is, in these novels, the very matter of their scenic depictions: the margin within which vital exchange takes place between an organism and that which immediately or more distantly surrounds it – every passing moment of the present, including past and future, even if, in novels with no surviving children, these are not specifically the dead and those who come after. There is a losing of the self's enclosing boundary and outline which is enriching and expansive; and there is a losing of the sense of self which is annihilating, not productive of exchange, and which must be resisted as long as is possible. Hardy was more attuned to the former, Conrad more strenuously braced for the latter, but neither exclusively so, and their compatible field-apprehension of the constitution of identity enables a new relation between psychological and material space to enter late-realist fiction.

Chapter Six

Minding the Senses
Jude the Obscure and Under Western Eyes

It is unusual for a novelist's most autobiographical work to come late in his career, but this is the case with both Hardy and Conrad. *Jude the Obscure* and *Under Western Eyes* are their authors' most personal books, each a searching exploration of a psychic region of loneliness and exclusion transposed from the writers' own complex relations to mid- and late-century Victorian England and the autocratic Russia of the same and a slightly later period.[1] In order to write them, both authors required not exactly a new style, but a new epistemology in which truth to sensation is diminished in favour of analysis of mental contents and antagonisms of ideas. This final chapter thus offers an account of how and why reading *Jude the Obscure* and *Under Western Eyes* is a different experience from reading the novels previously considered, but also why they are essential novels upon which to conclude a study of the senses.

The narrowing down to interior life yields a new and different intensity. It is wrung from a paucity of the rich sensory surrounding world made available to the reader that had been so characteristic of earlier works. In both novels the presence of the natural world is attenuated and the senses confined – in *Jude* they exist largely to be repressed, and in *Under Western Eyes* a tight rein of consciousness diverts their action into hallucination. Conrad's novel certainly maintains a considerably larger role for the senses than Hardy's: in *Jude* they suffer from an ideological disdain conducted by both Jude and Sue, though they retaliate, while in *Under Western Eyes* they are everywhere ready to act disruptively, threatening the control exercised by thought and

---

[1] However, we should be aware of Hardy's direct repudiation of this view: 'There is not a word of autobiography in "Jude the Obscure"' (to Samuel Chew, 17 September 1922, CL vi. 154).

intention. For the direct claims of the physical world Hardy and Conrad have substituted a field of mental, one might even say *mentalised*, activity, which constantly obtrudes into the engagement of the characters with their immediate tasks and surroundings. These minds are very much inhabited by *words*, and commentary, rather than description, is their typical mode. Equally, both novels are written in dialogue with others that precede them. Hardy recasts into the starker form of *Jude* the detailed realism of Mrs Humphrey Ward's examination of engagement and detachment, of faith, good works and intellect, in *Robert Elsmere*, her popular success of 1888.[2] Hardy's contest with the Oxford that is celebrated, though not uncritically, in that novel is not unrelated in impulse to Conrad's rewriting, in still more oppositional terms, of Dostoyevsky's spiritualised nationalism in *Crime and Punishment* in order to confront an anti-rational messianic exaltation that he was forced to recognise as part of his own inheritance too.[3] For this final chapter, however, I will take only those aspects of *Jude* and *Under Western Eyes* that serve to show the transformations wrought to an art of scenic realism based on sensory experience as they find out a new medium in the mental theatre of tormented consciousness.

*

What is the experience of the senses in *Jude*? It is frequently one of rebuff, as when Jude, hearing the talk of his great-aunt Drusilla and other villagers, feels 'the impact of their glances like slaps upon his face' (51).[4] When Jude throws away the clacker with which he is meant to scare off the local rooks, its sharp sound 'announced to his surprised senses' (54) that Farmer Troutham is beating him with it, and the only resonance in the rural scene is punitive and harsh, the echoes of the offending clacker and the blows it administers. The feeding of the visual sense seems deliberately starved by 'the uniformity of the scene' (52) at

---

[2] Hardy extracts fifteen passages from *Robert Elsmere* in his *Literary Notebooks*. John Goode has an excellent page on the novel in his chapter on *Jude* in *The Offensive Truth* (1988, 157).
[3] See Keith Carabine's indispensable *The Life and the Art: A Study of Conrad's 'Under Western Eyes'* (1996) for the most detailed study of this issue and many others in the novel.
[4] All references to *Jude the Obscure* are to the 1978 Penguin English Library edition, edited by C. H. Sisson, which follows the text of the 1912 Wessex Edition. In 'Amy Foster', Conrad's 1901 story of a comparable tragic dourness to *Jude*, the first appearance of Amy's face is 'as if her flat cheeks had been vigorously slapped' (Joseph Conrad, *The Nigger of the 'Narcissus', Typhoon and Other Stories*, 1983, 229).

Marygreen, where the working of the vast field is seen to be 'depriving it of its history' (53), evacuating the world of the senses in a manner new in Hardy's fiction, leaving a featureless expanse more austere even than that at Flintcomb-Ash. Edmund Gosse's well-known plea, 'We want our novelist back among the rich orchards of the Hintocks, and where the water-lilies impede the lingering river at Shottsford Ash', expresses a feeling of sensory impoverishment in reading the novel, and a resistance to the flatter, more declarative style, that is not simply a sentimentalist's reading of Hardy.[5] In a village in which the church has been 'cracked up into heaps of road metal' (50), the only remnant of its history is the well into which Jude stares, and which appears to him 'a long circular perspective ending in a shining disk of quivering water at a distance of a hundred feet down' (49). But the well is not an invitation to 'set the darkness echoing', as for Heaney, nor does it discover 'For once, then, something', as for Frost; far from such inclusive resonances, this ocular glimmer is an occasion for a child's verbalised thought about his schoolmaster, who was 'too clever to bide here any longer' (49). In *Jude* sensory experience, limited and constrained as it is, does not make its own declarations but waits on a verbal commentary that proceeds from a debate with the conditions of life itself. It is a small step from 'the melodramatic tones of a whimsical boy' (49) to the narrator's 'But nobody did come, because nobody does' (72), so often felt to be the novelist putting 'his thumb in the scale' as Lawrence has it.[6] The narrator's tone, after all, is little more than an extension of Jude's. When Jude wanders away from Marygreen for the first time we hear the same cadence in the chastened brevity of comment on the 'ancient track': 'But it was now neglected and overgrown' (59). The novel's primary drive is consistently that of Jude himself, and later Sue, to come to consciousness *about* life, rather than representing the feeling of living *in* life of the earlier novels.

The supreme moment in the early pages of the novel in which a sensory awareness of life is urged towards a conscious awareness of predicament, lies in the extraordinary paragraph in which Jude, discouraged by Aunt Drusilla's placing of Christminster beyond his reach, goes out to lie on his back near the pig-sty. It is a debate with life that has a significant relationship to the author's own experience:

> The fog had by this time become more translucent, and the position of the sun could be seen through it. He pulled the straw hat over his face, and peered through the interstices of the plaiting at the white brightness,

---

[5] Edmund Gosse, 'Mr Hardy's New Novel', *Cosmopolis* 1 (January 1896), 62.
[6] D. H. Lawrence, 'Morality and the Novel', in *Phoenix* (1970), 528.

vaguely reflecting. Growing up brought responsibilities, he found. Events did not rhyme quite as he had thought. Nature's logic was too horrid for him to care for. That mercy towards one set of creatures was cruelty towards another sickened his sense of harmony. As you got older, and felt yourself to be at the centre of your time, and not at a point on its circumference, as you had felt when you were little, you were seized with a sort of shuddering, he perceived. All around you there seemed to be something glaring, garish, rattling, and the noises and glares hit upon the little cell called your life, and shook it, and warped it. (57)

The episode as recounted in *Life and Work* makes 'Tommy' – 'a boy of that sort', fragile, intense, drawn to dramatising – conclude 'that he did not wish to grow up' (*LW* 20). *Jude* takes that feeling and *thinks* about it, more impersonally: the three abrupt declarations that find out Jude's unfitness for this cruel world are followed by a style of free indirect thought whose more complex syntax ('That mercy . . .'), and multiplying loose clauses ('As you got . . .'), create a reflective present in the boy's head, but one that blends the seriousness of Jude's mental encounter with the narrator's sad humour at his earnestness. His literary cousin is Stevie in *The Secret Agent*, and the hard, shuddering, glaring percussion that produces Jude's conception of the solitary self as a 'cell', physically assaulted, prefigures the jolting cab-ride of Conrad's novel and Stevie's 'Bad world for poor people'.[7] For both protagonists at this point it is a general mental conception of things rather than a recalled event which is of overwhelming importance, the struggle into expression making memorable this momentous facing of the world. The particular poignancy of Jude's effort of realisation is that it even manages an intimation of the future – 'and warped it'. This constant and painful mental awareness of the human position arising out of every sensory experience, and the need to articulate it, makes *Jude* a different book from Hardy's previous novels.

Jude's ideal conception of Christminster is a major factor in directing the novel more persistently than Hardy's earlier novels towards the portrayal of mental as opposed to material worlds. As the boy gazes upon the 'halo or glow-fog over-arching the place', he becomes 'entirely lost to his bodily situation' while performing a 'mental leap' (63), and his dream of 'some place which he could call admirable' sanctifies 'the spot mentally to him as he pursued his dark way' (66). The four solemn declarations that Jude then formulates to represent his mental election of Christminster as a New Jerusalem – 'It is a

---

[7] John Goode's discussion of the passage allows, rather, a fleeting thought of *Lord Jim* as he concludes that Jude is 'one of us' (*The Offensive Truth*, 139).

city of light . . . manned by scholarship and religion' (66) – is characteristic of the move the book makes towards articulating ideals, and which secures the recurrent effect: comical, sad, not uplifting, excruciatingly painful.

The idealising 'mind-sight' (127) with which Jude is gifted – or afflicted – makes him a descendent of Clym and Angel, but also of Elizabeth-Jane, whose circumspection is always holding an inner dialogue with itself. Thus, as he finally sets off towards Christminster, he is markedly different from Tess in her analogous journey to Talbothays: 'Now and then as he went along he turned to face the peeps of country on either side of him. But he hardly saw them; . . . the one matter that really engaged him was the mental estimate of his progress thus far' (78). The smack of the pig's pizzle which interrupts this accountancy of his intellectual achievements is the least subtle of incursions of the material world upon the ideal, though certainly a welcome interruption for the reader. But it does not lead to a real inhabitation of the senses either by Jude or the narrator. After this first encounter with Arabella, 'Jude Fawley shouldered his tool-basket and resumed his lonely way, filled with an ardour at which he mentally stood at gaze' (83). The 'new atmosphere' of sexuality, which 'had somehow been divided from his actual breathing as by a sheet of glass' (84), does not pervade the novel and, unlike *Tess*, is nothing to do with those 'peeps of country' to which Jude is as blind as Phillotson. It is all high-minded from first to last, from Jude's reading of the 'Carmen Saeculare' causing him to sing a hymn to the moon as 'His mind had become so impregnated with the poem' (75), to his feeling that '"courting" was too coolly purposeful to be anything but repugnant to his ideas' (88), to 'His idea of her was the thing of most consequence, not Arabella herself, he sometimes said laconically' (102). Of course, the writing drily satirises this disembodied idealism, but it no longer has available to it as a counterpoise the sensuous trust in eyes and ears and touch, in ground and air, that so marked the earlier novels. *Jude* is set less outdoors than Hardy's other novels, and the chamber within which it works is decidedly a mental one. The occasional sensational note contains the anguish of consciousness, as when, on his first evening walk in Christminster, 'Jude began to be impressed with the isolation of his own personality, as with a self-spectre, the sensation being that of one who walked but could not make himself seen or heard' (126). One can see so much of the whole novel in those phrases, which are then not worked out upon the senses but in sometimes vibrant, sometimes exhausted, *debate* with Sue Bridehead.

Hardy's artistic stance in *Jude* falls outside the frame of the literary sensationism with which I have characterised the other novels, though it is not unconnected to that other late critique of idealism written from an idealist perspective, *The Well-Beloved*.[8] David DeLaura, in his deservedly well-known essay, '"The Ache of Modernism" in Hardy's Later Novels', quotes from a letter by Matthew Arnold to his friend Arthur Hugh Clough, lamenting 'the modern situation in its true *blankness* and *barrenness* and *unpoetrylessness*', and in *Jude* Hardy adopts a style in which the senses have all but expired in order both to face and to embody this 'unpoetrylessness'.[9] This can be exemplified in the final chapter of Part One as Jude and Arabella pull apart. Suddenly giving up his anger at her, Jude acknowledges simply, 'Their lives were ruined, he thought; ruined by the fundamental error of their matrimonial union' (115). He goes out and jumps on the ice of the frozen pond, 'but he did not go down. . . . Jude went back to the edge, and stepped upon the ground.' The new paragraph begins, 'It was curious, he thought. What was he reserved for?' (116), and in the same affectless manner 'He began to see now why some men boozed at inns' (117) and he goes to get drunk. Deliberately divested of 'poetry', the succession of contingent events gains in artistic coherence from the articulations of thought which accompany each action. One might think, then, that *Jude* is of all Hardy's novels the driest empirical record; yet, to the contrary, my claim is that its animation derives from the ideal realm, which mounts, at the very least, a competing epistemology. When Arabella departs, and Jude stands out in the road after work, 'He could not realize himself' (119): we are reading one of those terse sentences that mark *Jude* for the new century – it could be Lawrence – and it is driven, to use a phrase of Conrad's, by the 'ideal conception of the self'. Mounting to the summit of the road, Jude makes out 'a small dim nebulousness' which, but only to 'the eye of faith' (120), is Christminster. Jude is the object of a sad satire; but the mental edifice of his yearnings is the subject and the vantage-point of the writing too.

The 'grimy' everyday, the 'squalid real life' (Hardy's words to Edmund Gosse, 10 November 1895 (*CL* ii. 93)) are everywhere in *Jude*, but so are the higher aspirations of Jude, the finer nature of Sue, their lives seeking an accomplishment in accord with the ideal aspect of humankind rather than the embrace of the senses. The immediate exchange of *ideas*, rather than those other sorts of energy exchanges in the realm of physics so pervasive in the earlier novels, is the prevailing

---

[8] In *Satire in an Age of Realism* (2010), Aaron Matz usefully distinguishes *Jude* from the other novels. He writes, 'In Hardy's staging of circumstance, satire is what happens when a person becomes *aware* of his own tragedy' (53).

[9] David DeLaura, '"The Ache of Modernism" in Hardy's Later Novels', *ELH* 34:3 (September 1967), 87.

artistic mode for much of the book. 'Transmutation into human stuff or idealisation is the condition under which man works' is the proud concluding assertion of 'Realism and Idealism' (1890) by John Addington Symonds, the poet, essayist and classical and renaissance scholar with whom Hardy had been in correspondence in 1889, when he was much preoccupied with the real and the ideal.[10] The 'human stuff' of *Jude* is made articulate to an extent unprecedented in Hardy's previous work, novels which more strictly respected an empiricist doctrine of impenetrability, attending more copiously to the reflecting surfaces of the observable. In *Jude*, Jude's textual studies, Sue's irreverent talk, the debates between the two of them, and between Phillotson and Gillingham, Jude's bar-room addresses, the rituals of Christminster, Sue's final desperate reliance on doctrine, all mean that the 'transmutation' of which Symonds speaks has an intensely *verbal* nature, that idealisation cannot be separated from language in this novel. Jude and Sue speak their own self-conceptions; as Phillip Mallett comments, 'The language Sue and Jude speak to each other, then, values one set of terms over another: spirit, noble, fine, high etc. over flesh, gross, coarse, low etc.'[11] Marjorie Garson goes further in the direction of naming the artistic stance of the novel: 'What particularly marks this novel, indeed, is the tone of what might be called "logocentric wistfulness" . . . . And Jude's author shares his logocentric desire.'[12] Christminster is, of course, the perfect venue for the senses to fall chastened before the word of learning and the Word of scripture, but the logocracy of the novel is deeper than its subject, it is its method too. To have characters so invested in words as are Jude and Sue moving amid the spare reports from the exhausted unspeaking world offered them is the novel's peculiar power.

*

With Sue's entry into the novel the senses revive a little, an irony that the reader will come to feel as tragic by the novel's end. There is a brief conjunction before Sue knows who Jude is:

> She looked right into his face with liquid, untranslatable eyes, that combined, or seemed to him to combine, keenness with tenderness, and mystery with both, their expression, as well as that of her lips, taking

---

[10] John Addington Symonds, *Essays Speculative and Suggestive* (1890), vol. 2, 303.
[11] Phillip Mallett, '*Jude the Obscure*: A Farewell to Wessex', *Thomas Hardy Journal* 11:3 (October 1995), 56.
[12] Marjorie Garson, *Hardy's Fables of Integrity* (1991), 153.

its life from some words just spoken to a companion, and being carried on into his face quite unconsciously. She no more observed his presence than that of the dust-motes which his manipulations raised into the sunbeams. (136)

The movement described in that first sentence, and its own movement through so many clauses and phrases, contains refreshing intimations of Sue's light and eager vivacity. The medium, the sunbeams with their dust-motes, is physical, but in the lovely sequence from 'lips' to 'unconsciously' it conveys what is richly, elusively, human, the 'mystery' of Sue's spiritedness that stays with her even as it passes from her. If the novel is starved of such real beauty it is because so much of the narration is coloured by Jude's mood and tone. Thus, although he receives the 'revelation' that 'She was so vibrant that everything she did seemed to have its source in feeling' (151), before they meet he reproduces Sue as 'an ideal character' (136) and, with fitting abstraction, 'an ideality' (146), a mental construction from which she is only rarely liberated into full physical being, even when she is his comrade, lover and mother of his children. With her clothes drying in front of the fire, and dressed in his, having 'Walked through the largest river in the county' (197), Jude yet sees in her 'almost a divinity' (199).[13] And in the second half of the novel, the epithet 'little' everywhere applied to her, by the narrator as well as Jude, imprisons Sue in an *idea* of her, one that consistently makes her a victim of her thoughts rather than a self-possessed observer of life. At the Great Wessex Agricultural Show the narrator feels compelled to add in protection of her winsomeness that 'a moderately strong puff of wind would float her over the hedge into the next field' (360). How different is that opening glimpse of her vibrancy of feeling, when 'An exciting thought would make her walk ahead so fast that he could hardly keep up with her' (151). A '*thought*': intellect and senses are at one, impelling her in a marvellous integrity ahead of Jude's 'dogged, mouse-like subtlety of attempt' (73) to acquire erudition. The sharpest tragedy in *Jude*, a novel which Hardy came to think of as 'the Sue story', is that these two aspects of Sue become disengaged, and that

---

[13] Al Alvarez takes the situation in this scene to be 'exactly the same as that of the masterpiece of double identity, Conrad's "The Secret Sharer"' ('The Poetic Power of *Jude the Obscure*', New American Library edition, 1961, reprinted in *Jude the Obscure*, Norton, 1978, 417).

she herself uses the hard edge of ideas to punish the senses, bringing them to rule.[14]

The novel allows occasional glimpses of the adult Jude's sensory world. After Sue's marriage to Phillotson, 'He could no longer endure the light of the Melchester lamps; the sunshine was as drab paint; and the blue sky as zinc' (234). When he goes drinking, Jude's eyes and ears briefly acquire something of Joyce's 'scrupulous meanness' in *Dubliners*:

> On the inside of the counter two barmaids leant over the white-handled beer-engines, and the row of little silvered taps inside, dripping into a pewter trough . . . . The moment was enlivened by the entrance of some customers into the next compartment, and the starting of the mechanical tell-tale of monies received, which emitted a ting-ting every time a coin was put in. (236)[15]

The itemised separateness of these observations suggests why descriptive writing is so sparse in *Jude*: there is little rooted connection to external life to allow it to become abundant. An earlier paragraph from the first Christminster section, where the church appears the entirety of that external world, shows just what happens in *Jude* to the senses and atmospheres that have been the stuff of this study. Jude and Sue, separately, are listening to the same church service:

> The girl for whom he was beginning to nourish an extraordinary tenderness, was at this time ensphered by the same harmonies as those which floated into his ears; and the thought was a delight to him. . . . To an impressionable and lonely young man the consciousness of having at last found anchorage for his thoughts, which promised to supply both social and spiritual possibilities, was like the dew of Hemon, and he remained throughout the service in a sustaining atmosphere of ecstasy. (139)

The awkwardly lovely verb 'ensphered' conveys precisely the transport of surrounding sound to the ideal realm, and the impression

---

[14] Letter to Florence Henniker, 4 August 1895 (*CL* ii. 84). For Sue, see Kay Young's excellent chapter in *Imagining Minds* (2010): 'In Sue, Hardy has imagined a woman character unlike any other in the nineteenth-century English novel – a character who is more her "self" than she is a representation of "woman" . . . . she is not "one of us"' (131).

[15] Joyce wrote, 'It seems so improbable that Hardy, for example, will be spoken of in two hundred years' (Letter to Stanislas, 19 July 1905, Richard Ellmann ed., *Letters of James Joyce* (1966), vol. 2, 99).

upon this 'lonely young man' of the atmosphere is unsurprisingly emptied of all bodily charge to become an 'anchorage for his *thoughts*' indeed. The satirical rejoinder which follows, suggesting that the atmosphere 'blew as distinctly from Cyprus as from Galilee' (139), coolly points up the extent to which Jude's free indirect speech has invaded the narrative, but it does not seek to restore sensuous apprehension. Despite her claim, after she has practised the marriage ceremony in St Thomas's with Jude, that 'My curiosity to hunt up a new sensation always leads me into these scrapes' (229), of Sue's sensory world we get practically nothing at all. As opposed to Jude's evaporation of her initially sensuous presence into an ideality 'living largely in vivid imaginings' (245), the realisation of her independent reality is largely her *talk*.

The world of *Jude* is more entirely human and verbal than the other novels, and the superb series of scenes at Melchester and Shaston exemplify at a microcosmic, utterance by utterance, level Ian Gregor's sense of 'vexed movement' rather than 'imposed design' in the form of the novel.[16] Conversation becomes debate, mounting to challenges which incorporate declarations and pleas, in the fluctuations so marvellously observed by Hardy in the exchanges between Sue and Jude prior to and after her marriage to Phillotson. Sitting in his clothes after her escape from the Training School, it is Sue who initially takes the conversation to Jude:

> 'You called me a creature of civilization, or something, didn't you?' she said, breaking a silence. 'It was very odd you should have done that.'
> 'Why?'
> 'Well, because it is provokingly wrong. I am a sort of negation of it.'
> 'You are very philosophical. "A negation" is profound talking.'
> 'Is it? Do I strike you as being learned?' she asked, with a touch of raillery.
> 'No – not learned. Only you don't talk quite like a girl – well, a girl who has had no advantages.' (201)

Hardy catches the quizzing exchange of two people who are highly self-conscious, and conscious above all about words. They pick each other up on the form of what they say, and even though, as the relationship between them progresses, the narrator will say 'there was ever a second silent conversation passing between their emotions' (263), it is remarkable how far the novel eschews description of the silent, the more sensational, for the expressed and more intellectual.

---

[16] Ian Gregor, *The Great Web* (1974), 207.

There is always a finely observed drawing towards and shying away from this undercurrent; and in this opening conversation in Jude's room in Melchester the quickness and forcefulness is all with Sue as 'Jude felt much depressed; she seemed to get further and further away from him with her strange ways and curious unconsciousness of gender' (203). The Sue that Hardy gives us, refusing to conform to the ideal, is highly conscious of the oppression of *both* genders by institutions, as so many of her later words and actions – famously, 'licensed to be loved on the premises' – go to show. It is her consciousness of the distortions wrought by sanctioned language that here directs the debate:

> 'You are on the side of the people at the Training School – at least you seem almost to be! What I insist on is, that to explain such verses as this: "Whither is thy beloved gone, O thou fairest among women?" by the note: "*The Church professeth her faith*" is supremely ridiculous!'
> 'Well then, let it be! You make such a personal matter of everything!' (207)

And what an interesting moment this is – the supposedly sexless Sue diverting her passionate response to beauty into an argument for the sensuousness of language to be allowed to stand as itself. This is the complexly imagined Sue, freed from Jude's idealising mind, and from the critics who would conventionalise what Hardy knows about women, men and sexuality by calling her frigid.[17] She reverses her asperity in little notes the following day; she feels directness as an assault, yet from behind the small protection of a window-sill can express her affection for Jude and her knowledge of herself as 'a woman tossed about, all alone, with aberrant passions and unaccountable antipathies' (266), knowingly using the judgements of a society bewildered at her feelings and behaviour. To see Sue as 'a terrible study in pathology', as Gosse did, or as a sexless flirt, as Jude sometimes does, is to be like Gabriel Oak and seek to read off Bathsheba as Vanity.

What Hardy imagines through the central part of *Jude* are living situations in which Sue and Jude regard each other with 'a mutual distress' that things are as they are and that they are as they are. This,

---

[17] Gosse, though often lampooned, has many successors to his view that 'the splendid success' of Hardy's portrait of Sue is of 'a poor, maimed "degenerate", ignorant of herself and of the perversion of her instincts' ('Mr Hardy's New Novel', 67). For a fine antidote to this reading of Sue, see Jane Wood, *Passion and Pathology in Victorian Fiction* (2001), 163–85, 199–214.

in a phrase, is what the novel consistently dramatises. Sue has just confided that the 'parting piece of advice' from the Training School was 'vulgar and distressing', and winds up her account of their relations, 'It is all my fault. Everything is my fault always!' The paragraph that follows is poignant in its brevity and its concentration of the fundamental and persistent 'scene' of the novel:

> The speech seemed a little forced and unreal, and they regarded each other with a mutual distress. (212)

The awareness of a strained linguistic discourse as a medium from which there is no escape, and a 'regard' which knows that it cannot alter anything as it contemplates complex natures and social appearances, is a configuration to which the novel returns many times. There are, indeed, times when, in the oscillations that the novel traces, it seems that the pair will escape the constrictions of a language which in practice also binds them, simpletons and insurgents against its cultural definitions as they are.[18]

Jude's visit to Sue in the schoolhouse at Shaston, in the first chapter of that section, is the high point of the novel in this respect. Jude picks out an air on the piano in the empty schoolroom, which Sue more skilfully takes over from him, her presence announced by her fingers laid lightly upon his. It does not release the pair from the necessity of words, but the response of hand to hand, each with an intelligence and vitality of its own, with Sue's meeting Jude's half-way and allowing his grasp, precipitates in the short utterances which follow a direct, spare language which also allows the sensuous fluctuations between them:

> 'It is odd,' she said, in a voice quite changed, 'that I should care about that air; because – '
> 'Because what?'
> 'I am not that sort – quite.'
> 'Not easily moved?'
> 'I didn't quite mean that.'
> 'O, but you *are* one of that sort, for you are just like me at heart!'
> 'But not at head.'
> She played on, and suddenly turned round; and by an unpremeditated instinct each clasped the other's hand again.

---

[18] *Jude the Obscure* first appeared as a serial in *Harper's Monthly Magazine* in twelve parts from December 1894 to November 1895. The first part was entitled *The Simpletons*, the remaining eleven parts *Hearts Insurgent*.

> She uttered a forced little laugh as she relinquished his quickly. 'How funny!' she said.
> 'I wonder what we both did that for?' (262)

And Sue lets go the moment she had initiated when she rested her fingers on his playing bass hand. Al Alvarez maintains that the connection between Sue and Jude 'is of the sensibility, not of the senses'.[19] Here is the moment in the novel where the division between those terms might have been acknowledged and healed. The 'vexed movement' of the chapter does not end there, of course, and could be examined through to its conclusion, with Sue's statement that she is 'not really Mrs Richard Phillotson' (266), the agreement to meet again in a week, and Sue seen through the window, contemplating a photograph – of whom, each reader will differently elect. But mutual distress is not displaced as 'the overwhelming scene'[20] of the novel, within which this chapter is a local moment of partial relief. And neither does the encounter at Shaston dispel the claim that *Jude* is different from the previous novels in its location in the mind rather than the senses. As Jude and Sue together go to visit the dying Aunt Drusilla, Jude was 'convinced that she was unhappy, although she had not been a month married' (247). He 'knew the quality of every vibration in Sue's voice, could read every symptom of her mental condition' (247). It is this last phrase which is new; and the senses do little more than offer material for a diagnosis.

The word 'distress' is everywhere in *Jude*. Sue says to Jude it is wrong of her to 'tell my distress to you' (276), but does so with a powerful sense of where its origins lie: 'When people of a later age look back upon the barbarous customs and superstitions of the times we have the unhappiness to live in, what *will* they say!' (276).[21] Arabella also proclaims 'I really am in great distress' (329), and although hers is both more material and easy to resolve, the scene – with Arabella down in the street, Jude at the window, and Sue at the bedroom door, 'at gaze, in painful tension, hearing every word, but speaking none' (329) – is again one of those scenes of 'a mutual distress' in which the novel repeatedly finds its picture of the human situation, almost geometrically, as Hardy himself pointed out

---

[19] Alvarez, 'Poetic Power', 419.
[20] See Robert Penn Warren on *Nostromo* in the previous chapter.
[21] This is strikingly similar to the conclusion of Alfred Russel Wallace's *The Malay Archipelago* (1869), which declares to its British readers that in comparison to Malay 'savages', 'we are in a state of social barbarism' (546). Though the book was a favourite of Conrad's, Hardy was closer to its cultural relativism.

in letters to Gosse. More intense and imaginatively realised is the distress experienced in their marriage by Sue and Phillotson, far from mutual in feeling but one that encompasses them both. The aversion to physical contact, the contraction of sleeping space to the clothes closet under the stairs with spiders, and of open conversation to written notes read either side of a glazed partition, is painful to read in the unheightened domestic ordinariness of its scene. The string with which Sue has tied the door of the closet, and which is broken at one tug, is the most silently eloquent item in the novel. But there is a vocalised dimension too. Sue's breakfast plea for mutual freedom, which so distresses Phillotson in its 'importunity' as he strives to hold on to the outlines of normal and expected life, is Hardy's last great appeal in the sequence that originates with Cytherea and which holds all his fiction together, lending an immediately recognisable Hardyan note to the vision of distressed humanity in the sweep of sidereal time: 'O Richard, be my friend and have pity! We shall both be dead in a few years, and then what will it matter to anybody that you relieved me of constraint for a little while?' (285).

Jude the Obscure portrays a tragic divorce from the senses. Little Father Time, all mental consciousness, is the emblem of this condition, while Sue's denial of the senses and abject abasement before the Word makes her the true tragic hero of the novel; Jude was lost from the start. The final time that they see each other, in the church at Marygreen, Jude pleads with Sue, 'We've both re-married out of our senses' (470), meaning, of course, out of our *minds*; but the novel takes his exasperated colloquial utterance more literally, presenting both of them as characters whose sensory selves have nearly always suffered chastisement from their ideas. Sue's tragic acquiescence in this would be grotesque farce were it not for the few moments at the last which so painfully declare it *as* tragedy and not numbness, when love and desire demand utterance and expression together:

> 'Kiss me, O kiss me lots of times . . .' . . . She rushed up to him and, with her mouth on his, continued: 'I must tell you – O I must – my darling love! . . .' . . .
>
> 'But there, there, darling; I give you back your kisses; I do, I do!' (469–70).

When later she initially recoils from Phillotson's marital embrace, she excuses herself by saying 'I – was not *thinking* – ' (478, emphasis mine). She wasn't; and, even in defeat, the senses speak truth. But the appalling moment in which, in response to Phillotson's embrace and kiss, 'A quick look of aversion passed over [Sue's] face, but clenching her teeth she uttered no cry' (479), is observed by no one, and the novel portrays no enduring natural or sensory world in whose plenitude the reader, if not the characters, can shelter from the antagonisms of mental election. 'Sheathe- and shelterless', Hopkins writes, 'thoughts against thoughts in groans grind'.[22]

*

Until *Jude*, it would seem, Hardy was reluctant to find direct articulation for what lay in the mind because that made too precipitous a way to the personal. It is an avoidance of treating directly in fiction aspects of his own experience which, when broached, yields the distinctive tonality of *Jude*. In more wracked and hallucinatory form, this finds an exact match in *Under Western Eyes*, of which Conrad wrote to J. B. Pinker on 7 January 1908, 'The subject has long haunted me. Now it must come out' (*CL* 4:14). And thus two of the great studies of loneliness in modern fiction are born from a late circumvention of the desire *not* to represent a personal trauma, a loneliness compounded by their authors' holding at bay through many years a too-revealing subject.[23] Twice on the same day Hardy writes – to Florence Henniker and Edmund Gosse, 10 November 1895 – that *Jude* 'is really addressed to those into whose souls the iron of adversity has deeply entered at some time of their lives' (*CL* ii. 93), a phrase I would join to Marlow's 'it is as if loneliness were a hard and absolute condition of existence' in *Lord Jim* (137).

The language for this address, as we have already seen in *Jude*, is barer, the syntax more concise than in previous novels, just as the evocation of the exterior world is distinctly sparser. Conrad's own consciousness that he was doing something new in *Under Western Eyes* is suggested in a letter to his French translator, H.-D. Davray, concerning 'Razumov', which proclaims 'For the rest, analysis – but movement enough all the same – that's the *tone* of the novel' (*CL* 4:59). This indicates an artistic procedure quite contrary to that which served *The Rescue*, for instance, summed up in the letter to Garnett already quoted in Chapter 1: 'No analysis. No damned mouthing. Pictures – pictures – pictures' (*CL* 1:392). A 1911 letter to Pinker speaks of *Under Western Eyes* as 'so utterly unlike in subject *and treatment* from

---

[22] Gerard Manley Hopkins, 'Spelt From Sybil's Leaves'.
[23] This is an uncontroversial statement as far as Conrad goes. The claim can justifiably be applied to Hardy too when one remembers what we know of the subject and attitudes of *The Poor Man and the Lady*, which re-surface, in a form modulated towards comedy, in *The Hand of Ethelberta*.

anything I had done before' (*CL* 4:477, my emphasis); and when Conrad came to write the Author's Note in 1920, he claimed, 'I had never been called on before to a greater effort of detachment; detachment from all passions, prejudices, and even from personal memories' (6). More intimately known to his author than any other of his creations, yet held aloof in this way, Razumov is a figure 'as lonely in the world as a man swimming in the deep sea. The word Razumov was the mere label on his solitary individuality' (16). The spare denotations suggest in themselves the diminished scope for selfhood allowed by a 'word', a 'mere label'; yet in *Under Western Eyes* the senses do not make their abashed, already-defeated counter-claim against words and the Word as in *Jude*, but pursue a violently eruptive narrative tenaciously held under control until Natalia Haldin demands 'the story' (269), and they declare it.

Until that point – and Razumov can write to Natalia Haldin after his confession, 'there is air to breathe at last' (274) – the lack of air and space afflicting *Under Western Eyes* is because the processes of autocracy, the apparatus of a vast state, and the machinations of the revolutionaries who oppose it both in St Petersburg and in Geneva, are not rendered with the descriptive dystopian urban sublime of *The Secret Agent*: they are depicted, compressed and intensified, as processes of Razumov's brain. This loss of air is the condition in which the novel's particular intensity is incubated, as the visual faculty is turned inward towards mental re-presentation as sudden vision. The irruption of the revolutionary assassin Victor Haldin into Razumov's lonely existence is absolute and immediate: 'And so . . . here I am', he declares simply (22). Immediately contaminated by contact, Razumov 'saw himself shut up in a fortress . . . saw himself deported by an administrative order . . . saw himself creeping, broken down and shabby, about the streets' (24). These visions of a psychological state, and of relations into which, as he conceives them, he has already entered, are, like 'the words and events of that evening', according to the teacher of languages, 'graven as if with a steel tool on Mr Razumov's *brain*' (26, my emphasis). In this account of taking an impression wrung from Razumov's pen, both the impressible surface and the hard, sharp impressive agent belong to the same suffering self. It is an image further intensified when, having betrayed Haldin to the authorities, Razumov is interviewed by Councillor Mikulin, and holds an inner debate as to whether 'misunderstood' or 'mistrusted' rightly portrays his relation to the Secretariat:

> At that moment Razumov beheld his own brain suffering on the rack – a long pale figure drawn asunder horizontally with terrific force in the darkness of a vault and whose face he failed to see. . . . he records a remarkably dream-like experience of anguish at the circumstance that there was no one, no one whatsoever near the pale and extended figure. The solitude of the racked victim was particularly horrible to behold. (73)

The unconscious identification here with Haldin lying stretched in solitude in the snow in Razumov's mind, and already racked and dead in actuality, is a connection saved up in the words of his journal for the reader alone to make very much later. In pained intensity, the equivalent moment in *Jude* is when Jude sees Sue in the unlit church, 'a heap of black clothes . . . prostrate on the paving' under the life-size cross 'suspended in the air by invisible wires' (425). 'One person split in two' (293), as Phillotson perceives them, Sue has become that reactive part of Jude which abases himself before the ideal; for Razumov, the horror in this vision of self-division is not that of wilful abjection but of the naked stripping of the organ of private thought, exposed like a specimen, but not even attended to by his investigators.

We are, then, in *Under Western Eyes* much closer to a Paterian concept of experience as a private and self-enclosed event reserved in 'the narrow chamber of the individual mind' than in any previous novel in this study, including *Jude*. Through 'material contacts that make one day resemble another' (48), Razumov strives to reconnect himself to a shared exterior world as he makes his way, having 'given up' the revolutionist to Prince K and General T, back to the room in which Haldin lies waiting. But the substance that has materialised so disruptively within his walls refuses to belong simply to any single order of experience, real or ideal:

> Haldin appeared like a dark and elongated shape – rigid with the immobility of death. This body seemed to have less substance than its own phantom walked over by Razumov in the street white with snow. It was more alarming in its shadowy, persistent reality, than the distinct but vanishing illusion. (49)

As the security of material contacts recedes before the manifestations of vision, Razumov is faced by two phenomena, the product of his brain more 'distinct' and with more 'substance' than the Haldin who is on his bed, yet the latter, 'rigid', bearing an 'alarming', 'shadowy, persistent reality'. Not only Razumov, but also the reader, has entered a state of contest before competing phenomena which will engulf him until the end of the novel. What 'Haldin' *is* – shadowy, indistinct, already given up to the authorities, yet maintaining an undeniable, persistent reality, an ineradicable presence – is a bewilderment that plunges Razumov into unrelieved agitation and revolt. Driven to speaking with ever less control, Razumov 'almost shrieked', 'Why! I am responsible for you' (53), and unable to separate his own identity as an individual under autocracy from Haldin's presence in his room, he finally cries 'in a vibrating, subdued voice' that what Russia needs 'is not a lot of haunting phantoms that I could walk through – but a man!' (54).

These oblique statements wrenched from Razumov about the relations of individuals to each other and to the state remain suspended and incomplete, curtailed by Haldin's understanding of Razumov's revulsion and his almost silent farewell. The vanishing of this incubus from his room, so desired and yet anguishing, as it takes Haldin to certain torture and death at the hands of the security services, produces the most descriptively sensational passage in the novel:

> There was a faint rustling in the outer room, the feeble click of a bolt drawn back lightly. He was gone – almost as noiseless as a vision.
> Razumov ran forward unsteadily, with parted, voiceless lips. The outer door stood open. Staggering out on the landing he leaned far over the bannister. Gazing down into the deep black shaft with a tiny glimmering flame at the bottom he traced by ear the rapid spiral descent of somebody running down the stairs on tiptoe. It was a light swift pattering sound, that sank away from him into the depths: a fleeting shadow passed over the glimmer – a wink of the tiny flame. Then stillness.
> Razumov hung over, breathing the cold raw air tainted by the evil smells of the unclean staircase. All quiet. (55)

In this extraordinary evocation of something wished away, slipping away, longed for, expelled and lost, apparition and whisper lap at each other and lapse away to silence. The noiselessness of the visionary Haldin is transferred to the 'voiceless' Razumov, whose 'gazing' becomes a tracing 'by ear' as he is left suspended over a receding phenomenon compounded of 'a light swift pattering' and 'a fleeting shadow'. Haldin is attenuated to a 'wink', a momentary eclipse of a weak flame as his form passes in front of it, but he has indeed sunk away into the depths of Razumov's consciousness, waiting to be re-encountered under the reassuring 'All quiet'. These are the strangely heightened, vivid phenomena of dream. In practice, the complex interaction that runs the length of the novel between Razumov's desire for silence, and the unbound disconnection it promises, and his need to hear precisely the sounds that convey his release from the bonds that he loathes, starts here. Not seeing, but listening to the forced conversations in which Razumov does not wish to participate, is the mode of *Under Western Eyes*.

Even more than *Jude*, Conrad's great novel of lonely self-enclosure is conducted upon a series of verbal encounters, interviews almost – Razumov with Mikulin, the teacher of languages with Natalia, Natalia with Tekla, Razumov with Peter Ivanovitch and with Sophia Antonovna, finally, Razumov with Natalia. In the case of *Jude* there is a hopeful, expressive function in each engagement, however awry this is driven, while in *Under Western Eyes*, as Aaron Fogel has shown, the coerced nature of these debates makes of each of them a contest in which guarding against expressiveness is the norm.[24] *Lord Jim*, too, is made up of a series of interviews, but the atmospheric density surrounding the participants which we examined in Chapter 2 is here replaced by a wily tension between them. Now, the question has narrowed and concentrated itself down to 'What is each thinking?' rather than the 'What is the sensational quality of this moment as it passes?' of the earlier novel. 'What is in his *mind*?' is the constant question for characters in the novel, and also for the reader.

Conrad's concern for impressions upon the senses is thus put to a service far removed from any that comes under the rubric 'facing nature'. Nothing conveys more clearly the direction and the distance travelled in this study than the almost unbreakable attachment in *Under Western Eyes* of impressions to *words* rather than to the phenomena of the material world. In Part Second, equipped with Razumov's journal, the teacher of languages is able to exceed Natalia Haldin's account of finding herself alone with 'the new arrival from Russia' by saying, 'Every word uttered by Haldin lived in Razumov's memory. They were like haunting shapes; they could not be exorcised. The most vivid amongst them was the mention of the sister. The girl had existed for him ever since' (132). In the mental atmosphere of this novel, living existence depends upon the connections established by words, and Natalia's account to the teacher of languages of this first meeting with Razumov is a brilliant dramatisation by Conrad of the antagonistic yet compelled interrelation between words and impressions. Uncommunicative as she is about Razumov, the teacher of languages presses her:

> 'Well – but you can tell me at least your impression.'
> She turned her head to look at me and turned away again.
> 'Impression,' she repeated slowly, almost dreamily; then in a quicker tone:

[24] Aaron Fogel, *Coercion to Speak* (1985), 180–218.

> 'He seems to be a man who has suffered more from his thoughts than from evil fortune.'
>
> 'From his thoughts, you say?'
>
> 'And that is natural enough in a Russian,' she took me up. 'In a young Russian; so many of them are unfit for action and yet unable to rest.'
>
> 'And you think he is that sort of man?'
>
> 'No, I do not judge him. How could I, so suddenly. You asked for my impression – I explain my impression. I – I – don't know the world nor yet the people in it; I have been too solitary – I am too young to trust my own opinions.'
>
> 'Trust your instinct,' I advised her. 'Most women trust to that and make no worse mistakes than men. In this case you have your brother's letter to help you.'
>
> She drew a deep breath like a light sigh.
>
> '"Unstained, lofty and solitary existences,"' she quoted as if to herself. But I caught the wistful murmur distinctly.
>
> 'High praise,' I whispered to her.
>
> 'The highest possible.' (133)

To recognise the Miranda situation here ('O brave new world / That has such people in't') is only to increase, if possible, the intense sadness of Natalia's later 'It is impossible to be more unhappy' (270). In her solitary Russian existence, it has been the capacity of words to turn a mirror – 'Unstained, lofty and solitary existences' – into mystical exaltation, which has sustained her. The demand for a transparent unity of thought, action and words (the 'highest possible' praise) is peculiarly intense for this young woman, a need for integrity that is quite at odds with Razumov's strategies for immediate survival.

The teacher of languages continues:

> She ceased on that note and for a space I reflected on the character of the words which I perceived very well must tip the scale of the girl's feelings in that young man's favour. They had not the sound of a casual utterance. . . .
>
> 'Very well . . . . you must have made for yourself a representation of that exceptional friend, a mental image of him, and – please tell me – you were not disappointed?'
>
> 'What do you mean? His personal appearance.'
>
> 'I don't mean precisely his good looks or otherwise.'
>
> We turned at the end of the alley and made a few steps without looking at each other.
>
> 'His appearance is not ordinary,' said Miss Haldin at last.
>
> 'No, I should have thought not – from the little you've said of your first impression. After all one has to fall back on that word. Impression!' (134)

In that first meeting with him, eventually Natalia had come out with 'You are Mr Razumov'; evidently her difficulty with both words and impressions has not dissipated between the event and the account of it. Asked for an 'impression', both Natalia and the teacher of languages find themselves driven back upon the priority of Haldin's *words*: the 'representation', the 'mental image', coheres around them more readily than around Razumov's immediate 'appearance' (indeed, his appearance in Geneva at all). And 'impression' itself ends by being no more than a word – and yet, in the guise of 'instinct', it is all we have to fall back on, finally. The result of Natalia's examination of her own impressions is, eventually, 'His appearance is not ordinary', but whether this is, indeed, the first impression of her senses, an expectation created by her brother's words, or an evasive verbal formula produced under the duress of questioning, is not clear. We cannot say that the word operates *against* the senses, as in the logocracy of *Jude*, but the need for the senses to demonstrate the truth they are witness to, innocent of words, will become the imperative of Conrad's novel.

*

The isolated and suffering mind, wanting, and yet not wanting, to be understood is the subject of Razumov's journal, the self-examination of a rawly exposed brain. It finds itself impelled towards the question implicit in *Lord Jim* – in what medium can truth be found? – and the more that Razumov in Geneva veils himself behind inscrutability, the more he is aware of the mental and linguistic medium within which his name and Haldin's circulate. Literally, Razumov watches words. Thus in the prolonged, thrilling, verbal contest with Sophia Antonovna in Part Third, one of the highlights of the novel, the name of Haldin at last falls 'from the rapid and energetic lips of the woman revolutionist', bringing the reader in sudden close-up to the narrowed scope of Razumov's intense concentration. Razumov has prepared for this, has 'made for himself a mental atmosphere of gloomy and sardonic reverie, a sort of murky medium', in which 'Haldin' retains only an 'air of discreet waiting in the dusk' (190). Conrad's management of this inner medium and its disconnected sensational surface, and the part played by words in and upon both, achieves a rare dialogic subtlety. When Sophia Antonovna suddenly tries to pull the discreetly waiting figure of Haldin into the daylight, by asking 'What was *he* like?' (190), Razumov responds, 'How like a woman. What is the good of concerning yourself with his appearance. Whatever it was, he is removed beyond all feminine influences now' (191). It will prove to be, precisely, 'feminine influences' that will recover Haldin's full moral force in Razumov's eyes. Meanwhile, the immediate surface of the exchange is sensory as well as verbal, as Sophia Antonovna's 'black eyes never left Razumov's face' (191) and 'At any instant ... some momentous words might fall on his ear' (192). The compensation for this unremitting effort of attention is the disconnected inner chamber in which 'Silently he indulged his wounded spirit in a feeling of immense moral and mental remoteness' (192), and in which he can speak his conviction, 'I am a match for them all' (196). But this protected and purely mental sphere, in which so much of the novel takes place, will not, finally, provide an adequate medium to convey the truth of Razumov's situation.

Sophia Antonovna is a worthy antagonist, one who knows more deeply than Razumov the nature and cost of commitment and the involvement with life that it exacts: 'You have either to rot or burn. And there is not one of us [women], painted or unpainted, that would not rather burn than rot' (193). In her capacity sympathetically to detect Razumov's bitterness she comes close to the truth and provokes in him the sense of being touched, against which, above all, he is defending himself:

> 'What are you flinging your very heart against? Or perhaps you are only playing a part?'
> Razumov had felt that woman's observation of him like a physical contact, like a hand resting lightly on his shoulder. At that moment he received the mysterious impression of her having made up her mind for a closer grip. He stiffened himself inwardly to bear it without betraying himself. (194)

Feeling the friendly hand become a detaining hand, he counter-attacks by citing Cabanis: 'Man is a digestive tube' (194). In other words, he claims a purely physical basis for his bitterness. But the irony which escapes Razumov is that the reference to a materialist physiologist implicitly empowers the body, over which he is constantly seeking to exert mental control; and the masterstroke of deception that he opportunistically but with perfectly controlled execution now practises on Sophia Antonovna leads him to a psychic region quite beyond his intention.

Her admiration at his apparent coolness in walking away from the assassination and attending his university lectures immediately afterwards emboldens him to re-imagine the scene in telling the story: 'The snow was coming down very thick, you know' (197). The readiness of this detail, which so engages Sophia Antonovna, in fact comes from the first time in the novel that Razumov's perceptions are touched by sensation in Conrad's typical early manner, when he goes himself to seek Ziemianitch: 'Along the roadway sledges glided phantom-like and jingling through a fluttering whiteness on the black face of the night' (28). Razumov finds himself taking over Haldin's narrative of his own actions after the assassination. He 'remembered something he had heard. "I turned into a narrow side street, you understand . . . I felt inclined to lie down and go to sleep there"' (198). The cynical re-use of Haldin's 'turned left into a narrow street' and his 'almost irresistible longing to lie down on the pavement and sleep' (21), projects Razumov into his marvellous creative invention to explain to Sophia Antonovna how he was seen with a notebook at the lecture. He had simply been home to get it. But far from simply declaring this, Razumov rediscovers the great sensory scene recently quoted which has, as it were, like Haldin, been lying in wait for him:

> 'I went up like a shadow. It was a murky morning. The stairs were dark. I glided up like a phantom. Fate? Luck? What do you think?'
> 'I just see it!' The eyes of the woman revolutionist snapped darkly. 'Well – and then you considered . . .'
> Razumov had it all ready in his head.
> 'No. I looked at my watch, since you want to know. There was just time. I took that notebook, and ran down the stairs on tip toe. Have you ever listened to the pit-pat of a man running down round and round the shaft of a deep staircase? They have a gaslight at the bottom burning night and day. I suppose it's gleaming down there now. . . . The sound dies out – the flame winks. . . .'
> He noticed the vacillation of surprise passing over the steady curiosity of the black eyes fastened on his face as if the woman revolutionist received the sound of his voice into her pupils instead of her ears. He checked himself, passed his hand over his forehead, confused like a man who had been dreaming aloud. (198)

If Razumov has his account 'all ready in his head', in the telling it excites a sensory evocation that escapes from his mental preparations. The vision of Haldin as a 'fleeting shadow' has passed down into the depths of Razumov's subconscious, now to revive itself as the consciously employed picture of himself as a 'phantom' gliding up those same stairs. And it is here that the earlier reference to Cabanis finds its force, because Razumov has, indeed, at a more somatic level than that planned by mental selection, *incorporated* Haldin into himself, running down the stairs 'on tip toe'. As extraordinarily, he invites Sophia Antonovna to become his own listening self, and the whole earlier scene reassumes him into its sights and sounds, with its sensory presence alive again: 'They have . . . down there now . . . The sound . . . the flame . . .'.

The striking physiology of Sophia Antonovna's heightened attention to Razumov's strange performance, receiving 'the sound of his voice into her pupils', reflects the complex synaesthetic transfer between Razumov, Haldin and Sophia Antonovna, in which the haunted Razumov's 'dreaming aloud' visibly speaks his unconscious identification with the expelled intruder Haldin. Later, ejected himself, Razumov will even more literally embody this figure in the Rue de la Cité, the steep street in which Julius Laspara's house stands. Here, it is significant that it is Sophia Antonovna who is both the observer and auditor of this first intimation of Razumov's dramatic confession. It is impossible, I would judge, for a reader not to collude with Razumov in his deception of the Geneva revolutionary cell; yet Sophia Antonovna's view of Russia, of revolutionary activity, and of Razumov himself, has an integrity shared with Natalia and Tekla, and strikingly lacking in Razumov and the male figures gathered in Geneva. Demanding that Razumov 'Listen to [her] story', the 'short, vibrating sentences' (202) in which she delivers it convey an authenticity in her experiences and her reactions that commands respect, and which allows to the reader a different perspective from Razumov's sardonic inner reflection, 'Good that', as he outwits her 'black and impenetrable' eyes, that he conceives of as 'the mental caverns where revolutionary thought' sits plotting (201).

Part Third concludes with Razumov sitting under the statue of Rousseau on its little island in the river, writing his report to Councillor Mikulin. After an excited 'mental soliloquy' about 'the idea of writing' (222), he sits down to write in a strangely public secluded safety, where 'His fine ear could detect the faintly accentuated murmurs' (223) of the river's current. '"Extraordinary occupation *I am giving myself up to*," he murmured' (224, my emphasis):

> And it occurred to him that this was about the only sound he could listen to innocently and for his own pleasure as it were. 'Yes, the sound of water, the voice of the wind – completely foreign to human passions. All the other sounds of this earth brought contamination to the solitude of a soul.' (224)

What we have read of the discourses generated by the passions for autocracy and revolution bears out Razumov's desire for a natural world without human voices. But the novel does not take place in the sort of Wordsworthian imaginary in which contact with the non-human is cleansing. Razumov *will* be 'washed clean' (271), but by forces which impel him towards articulation of human connection, contamination even; and he will be maintained in his state of redemption from the blight of solitude not by any mystical connection with nature, but by the integrity of three women who are all implicated in the discredited revolutionary babble, the talk of the era of Peace and Concord, which Razumov, the teacher of languages, and, generally, Conrad himself, dismiss alike.

*

Part Fourth is suffused in an atmosphere of tempestuous gloomy suppression in which the senses are accorded glimpses and overhearings, as when the teacher of languages comes upon the Genevan revolutionary cell in Peter Ivanovitch's apartment. Light is dim, or casts only a small circle of illumination; Conrad extends generally a sense of airless confinement, so that the reader is overtaken by a forced inclusion in Razumov's own mental condition, even while the plot conducts us from location to location under the guidance of the teacher of languages. The climax arrives in the bleak glare of an anteroom, typically robbed of any grandeur and removed from the redemptive sound of wind and water: 'The light of an electric bulb high up under the ceiling searched that clear square box into its four bare corners, crudely, without shadows, a strange stage for an obscure drama' (260). This scoured cell shares the pitiless exposure of Wellbridge Manor after Tess's murmured confession; but in the teacher of languages' observation of Razumov and Natalia there is an extension of sensory sympathy that recalls the organic attentiveness of earlier Hardy:

> I perceived that with his downcast eyes he had the air of a man who is listening to a strain of music rather than to articulated speech. And in the same way, after she had ceased, he seemed to listen yet, motionless as if under the spell of suggestive sound. (264)

What the sound suggests of the invisible and seemingly unattainable world of love compels Razumov into an honesty that he knows will be his perdition. To tell Natalia that he loves her also requires him to avow his other true relationship to her as her brother's betrayer.

Throughout the ten pages of this climactic confrontation between guile and innocence, 'the truth struggling on his lips' (268) is indeed obscure (and for the first-time reader too), as Razumov's words disclose 'the precarious hold he had over himself' (265) more readily than 'the story' that Natalia finally demands from him. Physical and bodily references multiply as Razumov seeks to exert mental and verbal control over senses in revolt at the continuation of deception; and thus in a bizarre simile which the teacher of languages vividly flashes upon us, 'It was as though he had stabbed himself outside and had come in there to show it. That was the impression rendered in physical terms' (266). Ultimately, it requires absolutely literal physical terms to replace the verbal fabrication of deceit structurally woven into the novel by its procedures of interview, conversation and debate:

> 'The story, Kirylo Sidorovitch, the story!'
> 'There is no more to tell!' He made a movement forward and she actually put her hand on his shoulder to push him away but her strength failed her and he kept his ground though trembling in every limb. 'It ends here – on this very spot.' He pressed a denunciatory finger to his breast with force and became perfectly still. (269)

In this sensory counterpart to Sue clenching her teeth as Phillotson lifts her in his arms, bodily gesture announces a self in the act of freeing itself from the evasions and ambiguities of language. It thus acts in precisely the reverse direction from Sue's self-suppression which preserves an abject continuation of an ideal world of rectitude; in *Under Western Eyes* the mental narrative we have been forced to follow so intimately 'ends here', comes to a dead stop in the authentic declaration of touch. As the teacher of languages says of Razumov's 'atrocious confession', 'A wonder came over me that the mysterious force which had torn it out of him had failed to destroy his life, to shatter his body' (270). It is a gesture already answered by another gesture: Natalia has not spoken, but 'pointed mournfully at the tragic immobility of her mother, who seemed to watch a beloved head lying in her lap' (269). In his immediately following comment, the teacher of languages cannot be merely dismissed as the uncomprehending Western observer of a peculiarly Russian scene: 'That gesture had an unequalled force of expression, so far-reaching in its human distress, that one could not believe that it pointed out merely the ruthless working of political institutions' (269). A silent 'distress' equal to *Jude*'s wrings from language an expression not altogether a foe to reality.

If the end of *Under Western Eyes* is primarily characterised by cessation and rupture – upon which the seal is set by the actions of Nikita – Conrad also pays regard to the diminished yet cleansed possibilities for continuing emotional life. In *The Transmission of Affect*, Teresa Brennan defines feelings as 'sensations that have found a match in words'.²⁵ Such an integration might serve as an indicator of a healthy human life, with a capacity to construct continuity and to repair the atomising action of the 'succession of incomprehensible images' that finally afflicts Decoud in *Nostromo*. The explosion of words in Razumov's journal that immediately follows his forcefully expressive gesture is, in fact, the beginning of some sort of reintegration into a shared world, recording how he 'came to *feel* this so deeply' (my emphasis), how 'In giving Victor Haldin up, it was myself after all whom I have betrayed most basely' (274). The cost of such integration of scattered sensation into coherent feeling is its demand that Razumov give up his safety among the Genevan revolutionists just as it has been securely established by 'the story' of Ziemianitch. Razumov finds that 'Life is a public thing' (48), after all, in quite a different way from his more comforting earlier formulation. Yet he cannot simply write himself back into a shared and social normality. He is, in this, like Jude and Sue, who have no one to turn to with any hope of understanding except each other, but who can only destroy each other in doing so, as no social arrangement exists in which they can live and fulfil themselves. Conrad casts Razumov into an even greater extremity of moral loneliness, but likewise it is to Natalia Haldin alone that he must turn, as he declares, 'Do you understand what I say? No one to go to. Do you conceive the desolation of the thought: no one to go to . . .' (268).

Neither novel grants to its protagonists reconstitution or fulfilment as part of society, family or couple. Fractured between idealism and convention these figures are all but wrecked from without and within: Councillor Mikulin's quietly resonant 'Where to?' applies as much to Jude and Sue as to Razumov.²⁶ Both novels portray figures who have in various ways come adrift from their moorings, but to Ian Watt's unsettling question, 'Alienation, of course; but how do we get out of it?', it is *Under Western Eyes* that surprisingly returns the more positive answer.²⁷ Eschewing, like *Jude*, any hint of a transcendent resolution, and facing the extremes of human distress without metaphysical props, the more romantic *Under Western Eyes* allows Razumov – at the cost of almost everything – to regain the 'sanity of

---

[25] Teresa Brennan, *The Transmission of Affect* (2004), 19.

[26] Paul Kirschner's 'Revolution, Feminism, and Conrad's Western "I"' discusses the place of ideas and idealism in *Under Western Eyes*, and their 'catastrophic effect' (*The Conradian* 10:1, May 1985, 4–25). See also his illuminating 'Making You See Geneva: The Sense of Place in *Under Western Eyes*', *L'Epoque Conradienne* (1988), 101–28, and 'Topodialogic Narrative in *Under Western Eyes*', in Moore ed., *Conrad's Cities* (1992).

[27] Ian Watt, *Conrad in the Nineteenth Century* (1979), 33.

the senses', as Tony Tanner puts it, and thereby an integrity Hardy does not accord the self- and sense-punishing Jude.[28]

Postscript

In his incomparable memoir-essay about canoeing the Kentucky River in flood, 'The Rise' (1969), Wendell Berry writes:

> To sense fully the power and the mystery of it, the eye must be close to it, near to level with the surface. I think that is the revelation of George Caleb Bingham's painting of trappers on the Missouri.... And there they are, isolated in the midst of it ... all so strangely and poignantly coherent on the wild plain of the water, a sort of island.
>
> But impressive as the sights may be, the river's wildness is most awesomely announced to the ear. Along the channel, the area of the most concentrated and the freest energy, there is silence. It is at the shore line, where obstructions are, that the currents find their voice.[29]

I need not labour the ways in which this evocation takes up the preoccupations with the senses, 'all the mighty world of eye and ear' as Wordsworth puts it, with nature, and with the art that offers a mediation between humankind and the non-human world, that have been the subject of this book. For despite their resolutely human, moral and ethical concerns, the novels examined in this study show us that we live our lives amidst other processes of life, systems and worlds both smaller and larger than that to which we are habituated, and other than those we regard as 'ours'. Gillian Beer has written that 'a besetting preoccupation of Hardy's work' is to find 'a scale ... which will accept evanescence and the autonomy of systems not serving the human'.[30] We can see that while 'acceptance' recommends itself rather less to Conrad, the issue of human endeavour facing a material universe other than human in its constitution remains the same in outline.[31] Both Hardy and Conrad give us depictions of human life made

---

[28] Tony Tanner, 'Nightmare and Complacency', *Critical Quarterly* 4:3 (Autumn 1962), 213.
[29] Wendell Berry, *The World-Ending Fire* (2017), 346.
[30] Gillian Beer, *Darwin's Plots* (2009), 233.
[31] See Laurence Davies, '"With all that multitude of celestial bodies": Conrad's Sense of Scale', *The Conradian* 43:1 (Spring 2018), 99–120. See also, somewhat in contest with Beer, Benjamin Morgan, 'Scale as Form: Thomas Hardy's Rocks and Stars' (in Menely and Oak Taylor eds, *Anthropocene Reading*, 2017), which faces 'the fundamental problem of bringing nonhuman scales into the domain of the senses' (133).

passive, or overwhelmed, by sensations of belittlement in the face of nature's cosmic indifference; but equally these novels afford instances of their characters finding a scale for effective human action, the senses alert to their environment and the touch of the external world vivifying and sustaining. The reader of Hardy will think of Gabriel Oak, Giles Winterborne and Elizabeth-Jane as fulfilling Berry's prescription: 'we must not work or think on a heroic scale. . . . We must work on a scale proper to our limited abilities.'[32] Conrad is certainly far more attracted to heroism, and to the appeal of the infinite conveyed by the sense of unrestricted space. But from *Lord Jim* we take the French Lieutenant's 'One has done one's possible' (109), and the small voice of MacWhirr's 'All right' from 'Typhoon'. 'Most of the working truths on this earth are humble, not heroic', says Conrad directly in 'A Familiar Preface' to *A Personal Record* (xii): the ideal world must always meet the exactions of material circumstance.

It does so differently in these novels. Conrad, the disappointed absolutist, writes, 'The only indisputable truth of life is our ignorance. Beside this there is nothing absolute, nothing uncontradicted', revealing the desire for truth, the absolute, the uncontradictable.[33] For Hardy, on the other hand, 'Nothing is permanent but change' (*LW* 380), revealing a tolerance of the relative and a greater capacity, cautiously, to look forward.[34] Hardy's comparative optimism arises from an imagination inhabited by a gradualist vision of nature; he says to William Archer in an interview at Max Gate in 1901, 'When we have got rid of a thousand remediable ills, it will be time enough to determine whether the ill that is irremediable outweighs the good.'[35] For Conrad, irremediability is a central fact of human experience and it shapes his natural world more catastrophically. Whether from personal temperament or a more riven inheritance, it is Conrad who would restore the 'static nature' that he imputes to Hardy, despite the 'dynamic, active nature' that agitates his fictions. Yet the important fundamental empiricist affinity deserves to be re-asserted. In *A Personal Record*, Conrad memorably writes that 'the unwearied, self-forgetful attention to every phase of the living universe reflected in our consciousness may be our appointed task on this earth' (92), which takes us directly back to Hardy's 'humbly

---

[32] Berry, 'The Future of Agriculture', in *The World-Ending Fire*, 338.
[33] Letter to the *New York Times*, Saturday Review, 2 August 1901 (*CL* 2:348).
[34] Thomas Huxley, *Evolution and Ethics*: 'the most obvious attribute of the cosmos is its impermanence. It assumes the aspect not so much of a permanent entity as of a changeful process' (*Collected Essays*, vol. 9, 2001, 49).
[35] William Archer, *Real Conversations* (1904), 47.

recording diverse readings of its phenomena' with which this book began. There is, in this, something barer and more confronting than the subtle appreciation of life we expect of the nineteenth-century novel, a physical awareness of the human species clinging to the planet which makes the word 'existence' the single most important term in the vocabulary of both writers. The 'ingenuous transparent life' disclosed by the fleeting changes on Thomasin Yeobright's face gives way to the more elemental, 'it was as if the flow of her existence could be seen passing within' (*Native* 41). Tom Lingard finds 'the tense feeling of existence far superior to the mere consciousness of life', something which 'could not be faced and yet was not to be evaded' (*The Rescue* 432). Both writers look on this existence with Victorian courage and modern irony, with the astringent attitude expressed by Conrad when he contemplates the characters in Daudet's novels:

> Inevitably they *marchent à la mort* – and they are very near the truth of our common destiny: their fate is poignant, it is intensely interesting, and of not the slightest consequence.[36]

---

[36] Joseph Conrad, 'Alphonse Daudet' (1898), in *Notes on Life and Letters* (1949), 24.

Bibliography

Abercrombie, Lascelles. *Thomas Hardy: A Critical Study*. London: Martin Secker, 1912.

Adams, Henry. *The Education of Henry Adams* (1907). Oxford: Oxford University Press, 1999.

Adams, Robert Martin. *Nil: Episodes in the Literary Conquest of Void During the Nineteenth Century*. New York: Oxford University Press, 1966.

Allen, Grant. *Physiological Aesthetics*. New York: Garland Publishing Inc., 1997. Facsimile of 1877 edition, London: H. S. King.

Alvarez, Al. 'The Poetic Power of *Jude the* Obscure', Afterword, New American Library edition, 1961, reprinted in *Jude the Obscure*. New York: Norton, 1978, 414–22.

Arata, Stephen. 'The Impersonal Intimacy of *Marius the Epicurean*', in Rachel Ablow ed., *The Feeling of Reading: Affective Experience and Victorian Literature*. Ann Arbor: University of Michigan Press, 2010.

Archer, William. *Real Conversations*. London: William Heinemann, 1904.

Armstrong, Tim. *Modernism: A Cultural History*. Cambridge: Polity Press, 2005.

Arnheim, Rudolph. *Visual Thinking*. London: Faber & Faber Ltd., 1970.

Asquith, Mark. *Thomas Hardy: Metaphysics and Music*. Basingstoke: Palgrave Macmillan, 2005.

Babbage, Charles. *The Ninth Bridgewater Treatise: A Fragment*. London: Frank Cass & Co. Ltd, 1967. Facsimile of 2nd edition, London: John Murray, 1838.

Bain, Alexander. *The Senses and the Intellect*. London: John Parker & Son, 1855.

Bain, Alexander. *The Emotions and the Will* (1859). London: Longmans, Green & Co., 2nd edition, 1865.

Bain, Alexander. 'On the Correlation of Forces and its Bearing on Mind', *Macmillan's Magazine* no. 95, September 1867, in Vol. 16, May–Oct 1867, 373–83.

Bain, Alexander. *Mind and Body: The Theories of Their Relation*. London: Henry S. King & Co., 1873.

Barker, Simon and Gill, Jo eds. *Literature as History: Essays in Honour of Peter Widdowson*. London: Continuum, 2010.

Barrow, John D. and Tipler, Frank J. *The Anthropic Cosmological Principle*. Oxford: Oxford University Press, 1986.

Baxter, Katherine Isobel. 'The Strange Spaces of *The Rescue*', *The Conradian* 29:1 (Spring 2004), 68–83.

Baxter, Katherine Isobel. '*The Rescuer* Synopsis: A Transcription and Commentary', *The Conradian* 31:1 (Spring 2006), 117–27.

Baxter, Katherine Isobel. *Joseph Conrad and the Swan Song of Romance*. Farnham: Ashgate, 2010.

Baxter, Katherine and Robert Hampson eds. *Conrad and Language*. Edinburgh: Edinburgh University Press, 2016.

Bayley, John. *An Essay on Hardy*. Cambridge: Cambridge University Press, 1978.

Beach, Joseph Warren. *The Technique of Thomas Hardy* (1922). New York: Russell & Russell, 1961.

Beach, Joseph Warren. *The Twentieth Century Novel: Studies in Technique*. New York: The Century Co., 1932.

Beer, Gillian. *Darwin's Plots: Evolutionary Narrative in Darwin, George Eliot and Nineteenth-Century Fiction*. London: Routledge & Kegan Paul, 1983.

Beer, Gillian. *Open Fields: Science in Cultural Encounter*. Oxford: Clarendon, 1996.

Beer, Gillian. '"Authentic Tidings of Invisible Things": Vision and the Invisible in the Later Nineteenth Century', in Martin Jay and Teresa Brennan eds, *Vision in Context: Historical and Contemporary Perspectives on Sight*. London: Routledge, 1996.

Békésy, Georg von. *Experiments in Hearing*, trans. E. V. Wever. New York: McGraw-Hill Book Company Inc., 1960.

Bennett, Arnold. *The Journals*. Selected and ed. Frank Swinnerton. Harmondsworth: Penguin Books, 1971.

Bennett, Jane. *Vibrant Matter: A Political Ecology of Things*. Durham, NC: Duke University Press, 2010.

Benson, Donald R. '"Catching Light": Physics and Art in Walter Pater's Cultural Context', in George Levine ed., *One Culture: Essays in Science and Literature*. Madison: Wisconsin University Press, 1987.

Benson, Donald R. 'Impressionist Painting and the Problem of Conrad's Atmosphere', *Mosaic* 22:1 (1989), 29–41.

Benson, Donald R. 'The Crisis of Space: Ether, Atmosphere and the Solidarity of Men and Nature in "Heart of Darkness"', in Joseph Slade and Judith Yaross Lee eds, *Beyond the Two Cultures: Essays on Science, Technology and Literature*. Ames: Iowa State University Press, 1990.

Benson, Donald R. 'Constructing an Ethereal Cosmos: Late Classical Physics and *Lord Jim*', *Conradiana* 23:2 (Summer 1991), 133–49.

Berger, Sheila. *Thomas Hardy and Visual Structures: Framing, Disruption, Process*. New York: New York University Press, 1990.

Berkson, William. *Fields of Force: The Development of a World View from Faraday to Einstein*. London: Routledge & Kegan Paul, 1974.

Berry, Wendell. *The World-Ending Fire: The Essential Wendell Berry*. Selected by Paul Kingsnorth. London: Allen Lane, 2017.
Bivona, Daniel. *Desire and Contradiction: Imperial Visions and Domestic Debates in Victorian Literature*. Manchester: Manchester University Press, 1990.
Bjork, Lennart. *The Literary Notebooks of Thomas Hardy*. 2 vols. Basingstoke: Macmillan, 1985.
Blake, Kathleen. 'Pure Tess: Hardy on Knowing a Woman', *Studies in English Literature 1500–1900* 22:4 (1982), 689–705.
Blumenberg, Hans. 'Light as a Metaphor for Truth' (1957), in David Levin ed., *Modernity and the Hegemony of Vision*. Berkeley: University of California Press, 1993.
Bock, Martin. 'The Sensationist Epistemology in Conrad's Early Fiction', *Conradiana* 26:1 (1984), 3–18.
Bodanis, David. *Electric Universe: How Electricity Switched on the Modern World*. London: Abacus, 2006.
Bohlmann, Otto. *Conrad's Existentialism*. Basingstoke: Macmillan, 1991.
Boring, Edwin G. *Sensation and Perception in the History of Experimental Psychology*. New York: D. Appleton-Century Company, 1942.
Bregman, Albert S. *Auditory Scene Analysis: The Perceptual Organisation of Sound*. Cambridge, MA: MIT Press, 1990.
Brennan, Teresa. *The Transmission of Affect*. Ithaca: Cornell University Press, 2004.
Brooks, Jean R. *Thomas Hardy: The Poetic Structure*. London: Elek Books, 1971.
Brooks, Jean R. '*Tess of the d'Urbervilles*: The Move towards Existentialism', in F. B. Pinion ed., *Thomas Hardy and the Modern World*. Dorchester: Thomas Hardy Society, 1974.
Brooks, Peter. *Reading for the Plot: Design and Intention in Narrative*. Oxford: Clarendon Press, 1984.
Bullen, J. B. *The Expressive Eye: Fiction and Perception in the Work of Thomas Hardy*. Oxford: Clarendon, 1986.
Butler, Samuel. *Life and Habit*. London: Trübner & Co., 1878.
Cantor, G. N. *Optics After Newton: Theories of Light in Britain and Ireland 1704–1840*. Manchester: Manchester University Press, 1983.
Cantor G. N. and Hodge M. J. S. eds, *Conceptions of Ether: Studies in the History of Ether Theories 1740-1900*. Cambridge: Cambridge University Press, 1981.
Carabine, Keith. *The Life and the Art: A Study of Conrad's 'Under Western Eyes'*. Amsterdam: Rodopi, 1996.
Carpenter, Edward. *The Art of Creation: Essays on the Self and Its Powers*. London: George Allen, 1904.
Carpenter, William. *Principles of Mental Physiology*. London: Henry S. King & Co., 1874.
Cassirer, Ernst. *Substance and Function* and *Einstein's Theory of Relativity* (1910). Chicago: Open Court Publishing, 1923.

Chapple J. A. V. 'Conrad's Brooding over Scientific Opinion', *The Conradian* 10:1 (May 1985), 59–67.
Chew, Samuel. *Thomas Hardy, Poet and Novelist*. New York: A. A. Knopf, 1928.
Choi, Tina Young. 'Forms of Closure: The First Law of Thermodynamics and Victorian Narrative', *ELH* 74:2 (Summer 2007), 301–22.
Clarke, Bruce. *Energy Forms: Allegory and Science in the Era of Classical Thermodynamics*. Ann Arbor: Michigan University Press, 2001.
Classen, Constance. *Worlds of Sense: Exploring the Senses in History and Across Different Cultures*. London: Routledge, 1993.
Classen, Constance ed. *A Cultural History of the Senses* (6 vols). Vol. 5, *In the Age of Empire*. London: Bloomsbury, 2014.
Clifford, W. K. *Seeing and Thinking*. London: Macmillan & Co., 1879.
Clifford, W. K. *Lectures and Essays*. 2 vols. Ed. Leslie Stephen and Frederick Pollock. London: Macmillan, 1901.
Cohen, William A. *Embodied: Victorian Literature and the Senses*. Minneapolis: University of Minnesota Press, 2009.
Connor, Steven. *Dumbstruck: A Cultural History of Ventriloquism*. Oxford: Oxford University Press, 2000.
Conrad, Joseph. *Almayer's Folly*. Ed. Jacques Berthoud. Oxford: Oxford University Press, 1992.
Conrad, Joseph. *Last Essays*. Ed. Harold Ray Stevens and J. H. Stape. Cambridge: Cambridge University Press, 2010.
Conrad, Joseph. *Lord Jim*. Ed. J. H. Stape and Ernest W. Sullivan II. Cambridge: Cambridge University Press, 2012.
Conrad, Joseph. *The Mirror of the Sea & A Personal Record*. Ed. Zdzisław Najder. Oxford: Oxford University Press, 1988.
Conrad, Joseph. *The Nigger of the 'Narcissus'*. Ed. Allan Simmons. London: Everyman, 1997.
Conrad, Joseph. *The Nigger of the 'Narcissus'*. Ed. Allan H. Simmons. Cambridge: Cambridge University Press, 2017.
Conrad, Joseph. *The Nigger of the 'Narcissus', Typhoon and Other Stories*. Harmondsworth: Penguin Books Ltd., 1983.
Conrad, Joseph. *Nostromo*. London: J. M. Dent and Sons Ltd., 1947.
Conrad, Joseph *Notes on Life and Letters*. London: J. M. Dent and Sons Ltd., 1949.
Conrad, Joseph. *The Rescue*. London: J.M. Dent and Sons Ltd., 1949.
Conrad, Joseph. 'The Rescuer' manuscript, 1896-1898, Ashley 4787. London: The British Library.
Conrad, Joseph. *The Rover*. Ed. Alexandre Fachard and J. H. Stape. Cambridge: Cambridge University Press, 2018.
Conrad, Joseph. *Sea Stories*. Ed. Keith Carabine. Ware: Wordsworth Editions Ltd., 1998.
Conrad, Joseph. *The Secret Agent*. Ed. Bruce Harkness and S. W. Reid. Cambridge: Cambridge University Press, 1990.

Conrad, Joseph. *The Shadow-Line*. Ed. J. H. Stape, Allan Simmons and Owen Knowles. Cambridge: Cambridge University Press, 2013.
Conrad, Joseph. *The Sisters*, with an Introduction by Ford Madox Ford. New York: Crosby Gaige, 1928.
Conrad, Joseph. *Tales of Unrest*. Ed. Allan H. Simmons and J. H. Stape. Cambridge: Cambridge University Press, 2012.
Conrad, Joseph. *Under Western Eyes*. Ed. Roger Osborne and Paul Eggert. Cambridge: Cambridge University Press, 2013.
Conrad, Joseph. *Victory*. Ed. J. H. Stape, Alexandre Fachard and Richard Niland. Cambridge: Cambridge University Press, 2016.
Conrad, Joseph. *Within the Tides*. Harmondsworth: Penguin Books, 1978.
Conrad, Joseph. *Youth, Heart of Darkness, The End of the Tether*. Ed. Owen Knowles. Cambridge: Cambridge University Press, 2010.
Conrad, Joseph and Hueffer, Ford Madox. *Romance*. London: Thomas Nelson and Sons, 1909.
Conrad, Peter. *The Everyman History of English Literature*. London: Dent, 1985.
Cook, Susan E. '*Nostromo*'s Uncanny Light', *Conradiana* 44:2/3 (Fall/Winter 2012), 126–44.
Coombs, David Sweeney. 'Reading in the Dark: Sensory Perception and Agency in *The Return of the Native*', *ELH* 78:4 (Winter 2011), 943–66.
Cooper, James Fenimore. *The Deerslayer* (1841). New York: Signet Classics, 1963.
Corbin, Alain. *Village Bells: Sound and Meaning in the Nineteenth-Century French Countryside*. Basingstoke: Macmillan, 1999.
Cosslett, Tess. *The 'Scientific Movement' and Victorian Literature*. Brighton: Harvester Press, 1982.
Cox, R. G. ed. *Thomas Hardy: The Critical Heritage*. London: Routledge, 1979.
Crossland, Rachel. *Modernist Physics: Waves, Particles, and Relativities in the Writings of Virginia Woolf and D. H. Lawrence*. Oxford: Oxford University Press, 2018.
Curle, Richard. *Joseph Conrad: A Study*. London: Kegan Paul, Trench, Trübner & Co. Ltd, 1914.
Daleski, H. M. *Joseph Conrad: The Way of Dispossession*. London: Faber & Faber, 1977.
Daleski, H. M. *Thomas Hardy: The Paradoxes of Love*. Columbia: University of Missouri Press, 1997.
Dalziel, Pamela and Michael Millgate eds. *Thomas Hardy's 'Poetical Matter' Notebook*. Oxford: Oxford University Press, 2009.
Danius, Sara. *The Prose of the World: Flaubert and the Art of Making Things Visible*. Uppsala: Uppsala University Press, 2006.
Danziger, Kurt. *Naming the Mind: How Psychology Found its Language*. London: Sage Publications, 1997.

Darwin, Charles; Thomas Henry Huxley. *Autobiographies*. Ed. Gavin de Beer. Oxford: Oxford University Press, 1983.

Davie, Donald. 'Hardy's Virgilian Purples', *Agenda* 10:2–3 (Spring and Summer 1972), 138–56.

Davies, Laurence. '"With all that multitude of celestial bodies": Conrad's Sense of Scale', *The Conradian* 43:1 (Spring 2018), 99–120.

Davis, Mike. 'Hardy, *Tess*, and Late Victorian Theories of Consciousness', *Thomas Hardy Journal* 27 (Autumn 2012), 46–69.

Dawson, Gowan. 'Walter Pater's *Marius the Epicurean* and the Discourse of Science in Macmillan's Magazine: "A Creature of the Nineteenth Century"', *English Literature in Transition 1880–1920* 48:1 (2005), 38–54.

Dean, Dennis. '"Through Science to Despair": Geology and the Victorians', in James Paradis and Thomas Postlewait eds, *Victorian Science and Victorian Values: Literary Perspectives*. New Brunswick, NJ: Rutgers University Press, 1981.

DeLaura, David. '"The Ache of Modernism" in Hardy's Late Novels', *ELH* 34:3 (September 1967).

Deleuze, Gilles and Parnet, Claire. *Dialogues* (1971), trans. Hugh Tomlinson & Barbara Habbejam, London: Athlone Press, 1987.

DeMille, Barbara. 'Cruel Illusions: Nietzsche, Conrad and Hardy and the Shadowy Ideal', *Studies in English Literature 1500–1900* 30:4 (Autumn 1990), 697–714.

Dewey, John. *Art as Experience*. New York: G. P. Putnam's Sons, 1958.

Dixon, Thomas. *From Passions to Emotions: The Creation of a Secular Psychological Category*. Cambridge: Cambridge University Press, 2003.

Dolar, Mladen. *A Voice and Nothing More*. Cambridge, MA: MIT Press, 2006.

Dryden, Linda, Stephen Arata and Eric Massey eds. *Robert Louis Stevenson and Joseph Conrad: Writers of Transition*. Lubbock: Texas Tech University Press, 2009.

Einstein, Albert. *Ideas and Opinions* (1954), trans. Sonja Bergmann. New York: The Modern Library, 1994.

Einstein, Albert and Infeld, Leopold. *The Evolution of Physics: Growth of Ideas from Early Concepts to Relativity and Quanta*. Cambridge: Cambridge University Press, 1938.

Eliot, George. *Adam Bede*. Edinburgh: William Blackwood and Sons, 1912.

Eliot, George. *Middlemarch*. Edinburgh: William Blackwood and Sons, 1912.

Elkins, James. *The Object Stares Back: On the Nature of Seeing*. New York: Simon and Shuster, 1996.

Elliott, Dorice Williams. 'Hearing the Darkness: The Narrative Chain in Conrad's "Heart of Darkness"', *English Literature in Transition 1880–1920* 28:2 (1985), 162–81.

Ellis, Havelock. 'Thomas Hardy's Novels', *Westminster Review* (April 1883), 163–77.

Ellis, Havelock. *The Philosophy of Conflict, And Other Essays in War-time*. London: Constable and Company Ltd, 1919.

Ellmann, Richard ed. *Letters of James Joyce*. 3 vols. London: Faber and Faber, 1966.

Epstein, Hugh, '*Bleak House* and Conrad', in Gene Moore, Owen Knowles and J. H. Stape eds, *Conrad: Intertexts and Appropriations*. Amsterdam: Rodopi, 1997.

Erchinger, Philipp. *Artful Experiments: Ways of Knowing in Victorian Literature and Science*. Edinburgh: Edinburgh University Press, 2018.

Farjeon, Eleanor. *Edward Thomas: The Last Four Years*. Oxford: Oxford University Press, 1979.

Fechner, Gustav. *Elements of Psychophysics* (1860). Ed. Davis H. Howes and Edwin G. Boring, trans. Helmut Adler. New York: Holt, Reinhard, Winston Inc., 1966.

Fernandez, Ramon. 'The Art of Conrad', in *Messages*, trans. Montgomery Belgion. London: J. Cape, 1927. (Translation of 'L'art de Conrad', *La Nouvelle Revue française*, 1924, 730–7.)

Fogel, Aaron. *Coercion to Speak: Conrad's Poetics of Dialogue*. Cambridge, MA: Harvard University Press, 1985.

Follett, Wilson. *Joseph Conrad: A Short Study*. New York: Russell and Russell, 1966. A facsimile re-issue of the 1915 edition, New York: Doubleday Page & Co.

Ford, Ford Madox. *A History of Our Own Times*. Ed. Solon Beinfeld and Sondra J. Stang. Manchester: Carcanet Press Limited, 1989.

Ford, Ford Madox. *Joseph Conrad, A Personal Remembrance*. London: Duckworth & Co., 1924.

Ford, Mark. *Thomas Hardy: Half a Londoner*. Cambridge, MA: The Belknap Press of Harvard University Press, 2016.

Freedman, William. *Joseph Conrad and the Anxiety of Knowledge*. Columbia: University of South Carolina Press, 2014.

Garnett, Edward. *Letters from John Galsworthy 1900–1932*. London: Jonathan Cape, 1934.

Garratt, Peter. *Victorian Empiricism: Self, Knowledge, and Reality in Ruskin, Bain, Lewes, Spencer, and George Eliot*. Madison: Fairleigh Dickinson University Press, 2010.

Garson, Marjorie. *Hardy's Fables of Integrity: Woman, Body, Text*. Oxford: Clarendon Press, 1991.

Gerber, Helmut E. and Davis, W. Eugene eds. *Thomas Hardy, An Annotated Bibliography of Writings About Him*. DeKalb: Northern Illinois University Press, 1973.

Gibson, James J. *The Senses Considered as Perceptual Systems*. London: George Allen & Unwin Ltd, 1968.

Gibson, James J. *The Ecological Approach to Visual Perception*. Boston: Houghton Mifflin Company, 1979.

Gissing, George. *In the Year of Jubilee*. Brighton: The Harvester Press, 1976.

Glendening, John. *The Evolutionary Imagination in Late Victorian Novels: 'The Entangled Bank'*. Aldershot: Ashgate, 2007.
Goode, John. *Thomas Hardy: The Offensive Truth*. Oxford: Basil Blackwell, 1988.
Gosse, Edmund. 'Mr Hardy's New Novel', *Cosmopolis* 1 (January 1896).
Graham, Kenneth. *Indirections in the Novel: James, Conrad and Forster*. Cambridge: Cambridge University Press, 1988.
Greenberg, Steven. 'Auditory Function', in *Encyclopaedia of Acoustics*. Ed. Malcolm J. Cocker. 4 vols. New York: John Wiley & Sons, 1997, Vol. 3, 123–30.
Gregor, Ian. *The Great Web: The Form of Hardy's Major Fiction*. London: Faber & Faber, 1974.
Gregory, R. L. *Eye and Brain: The Psychology of Seeing*. London: Weidenfeld & Nicolson, 1966.
Grove, W. R. *The Correlation of Physical Forces*. London: S. Highley, 1850.
Guerard, Albert J. *Thomas Hardy*. Cambridge, MA: Harvard University Press, 1949.
Guerard, Albert J. *Conrad the Novelist*. Cambridge, MA: Harvard University Press, 1958.
Gurney, Edmund. *The Power of Sound*. London: Smith, Elder & Co., 1880.
Gwynn, Frederick L. and Joseph L. Blotner eds. *Faulkner in the University* (1959). Charlottesville: University of Virginia Press, 1995.
Haley, Bruce. *The Healthy Body and Victorian Culture*. Cambridge, MA: Harvard University Press, 1978.
Halliday, Sam. *Sonic Modernity: Representing Sound in Literature, Culture and the Arts*. Edinburgh: Edinburgh University Press, 2013.
Hamlyn, D. W. *Sensation and Perception: A History of the Philosophy of Perception*. London: Routledge & Kegan Paul, 1961.
Hands, Timothy. *A Hardy Chronology*. Basingstoke: Macmillan, 1992.
Hardy, Barbara. *Tellers and Listeners: The Narrative Imagination*. London: The Athlone Press, 1975.
Hardy, Thomas. *Desperate Remedies*. Ed. Patricia Ingham. Oxford: Oxford University Press, 2003.
Hardy, Thomas. *The Dynasts*. London: Macmillan and Co., 1924.
Hardy, Thomas. *Far From the Madding Crowd*. London: Smith, Elder & Co., 1874.
Hardy, Thomas. *Far From the Madding Crowd*. Ed. Ronald Blythe. Harmondsworth: Penguin Books, 1978.
Hardy, Thomas. *Jude the Obscure*. Ed. C. H. Sisson. Harmondsworth: Penguin Books, 1978.
Hardy Thomas. *Jude the Obscure*. Ed. Norman Page. New York: W.W. Norton & Company, 1978.
Hardy, Thomas. *A Laodicean*. Ed. Jane Gatewood. Oxford: Oxford University Press, 1991.
Hardy, Thomas. *The Mayor of Casterbridge*. Ed. Martin Seymour-Smith. Harmondsworth: Penguin Books, 1978.

Hardy, Thomas. *A Pair of Blue Eyes*. Ed. Pamela Dalziel. London: Penguin Books, 2005.
Hardy, Thomas. *The Pursuit of the Well-Beloved* and *The Well-Beloved*. Ed. Patricia Ingham. Harmondsworth: Penguin Books, 1997.
Hardy, Thomas. *The Return of the Native*. Ed. Simon Gatrell. Oxford: Oxford University Press, 2008.
Hardy, Thomas. *The Return of the Native: a facsimile of the manuscript with related materials*. Ed. Simon Gatrell. New York: Garland, 1986.
Hardy, Thomas. *Tess of the d'Urbervilles*. Ed. A. Alvarez. Harmondsworth: Penguin Books, 1978.
Hardy, Thomas. *The Trumpet-Major*. Ed. Charles Pettit. Ware: Wordsworth Editions Ltd., 2002.
Hardy, Thomas. *Two on a Tower*. Ed. Sally Shuttleworth. Harmondsworth: Penguin Books, 1999.
Hardy, Thomas. *Under the Greenwood Tree*. Ed. Tim Dolin. Harmondsworth: Penguin Books, 1998.
Hardy, Thomas. *The Woodlanders*. Ed. Patricia Ingham. Harmondsworth: Penguin Books, 1999.
Hardy, Thomas. *The Complete Poems*. Ed. James Gibson. London: Macmillan London Ltd., 1988.
Hardy Thomas. *The Life and Work of Thomas Hardy*. Ed. Michael Millgate. Basingstoke: Macmillan, 1989.
Harpham, Geoffrey Galt. 'The Future of Conrad's Beginnings', in Carola Kaplan, Peter Mallios and Andrea White eds, *Conrad in the Twenty-First Century*. New York: Routledge, 2005.
Hayles, N. Katherine. *The Cosmic Web: Scientific Field Models and Literary Strategy in the Twentieth Century*. Ithaca: Cornell University Press, 1984.
Helmholtz, Hermann von. *On the Sensations of Tone as a Physiological Basis for the Theory of Music* (1862). Bristol: Thoemmes Press, 1998. Facsimile of the first English edition, London: Longman, Green & Co., 1875.
Helmholtz, Hermann von. *Popular Lectures on Scientific Subjects*, trans. E. Atkinson. 2 vols. London: Longman, Green & Co., 1893.
Henchman, Anna. *The Starry Sky Within: Astronomy and the Reach of the Mind in Victorian Literature*. New York: Oxford University Press, 2014.
Henshaw, John. *A Tour of the Senses*. Baltimore: Johns Hopkins University Press, 2012.
Herbert, Christopher. *Victorian Relativity: Radical Thought and Scientific Discovery*. Chicago: University of Chicago Press, 2001.
Hervouet, Yves. *The French Face of Joseph Conrad*. Cambridge: Cambridge University Press, 1990.
Hillis Miller, J. *Poets of Reality: Six Twentieth-Century Writers*. Cambridge, MA: Harvard University Press, 1966.
Hillis Miller, J. *Thomas Hardy: Distance and Desire*. Cambridge, MA: Harvard University Press, 1970.
Hoenselaars, Ton and Moore, Gene. 'Joseph Conrad and T. E. Lawrence', *Conradiana* 27:1 (Spring 1995), 3–20.

Horowitz, Seth. *The Universal Sense: How Hearing Shapes the Mind*. New York: Bloomsbury, 2012.

Howe, Irving. *Thomas Hardy*. London: Weidenfeld and Nicolson, 1966.

Hughes, John. *'Ecstatic Sound': Music and Individuality in the Works of Thomas Hardy*. Aldershot: Ashgate, 2001.

Hughes, John. *'Affective Worlds': Writing, Feeling and Nineteenth-Century Literature*. Brighton: Sussex Academic Press, 2011.

Hughes, Linda K. and Michael Lund. 'Linear Stories and Circular Visions: The Decline of the Victorian Serial', in N. Katherine Hayles ed., *Chaos and Order: Complex Dynamics in Literature and Science*. Chicago: University of Chicago Press, 1991.

Humphrey, Nicholas. *A History of the Mind*. London: Chatto & Windus, 1992.

Hunt, Bruce J. *Pursuing Power and Light: Technology and Physics from James Watt to Albert Einstein*. Baltimore: The Johns Hopkins University Press, 2010.

Huxley, Aldous ed. *The Letters of D. H. Lawrence*. London: William Heinemann Ltd, 1937.

Huxley. T. H. *Collected Essays*. Vols 6 and 9. Bristol: Thoemmes Press, 2001.

Huysmans J. K. *Against the Grain (À Rebours* 1884). New York: Dover Publications Ltd, 1969.

Ihde, Don. *Listening and Voice: Phenomenologies of Sound* (1974). Albany: SUNY Press, 2007.

Ingold, Tim. *Being Alive: Essays on Movement, Knowledge and Description*. Abingdon: Routledge, 2011.

Ireland, Ken. *Thomas Hardy, Time and Narrative: A Narratological Approach to his Novels*. Basingstoke: Palgrave Macmillan, 2014.

Irwin, Michael. *Reading Hardy's Landscapes*. Basingstoke: Macmillan, 2000.

Irwin, Michael. 'Seen in a New Light: Illumination and Irradiation in Hardy', in Phillip Mallett ed., *Thomas Hardy: Texts and Contexts*. Basingstoke: Palgrave, 2002.

James, David. 'Hearing Hardy: Soundscapes and the Profitable Reader'. *Journal of Narrative Theory* 40:2 (2010), 131–55.

James, Henry. *The Golden Bowl* (1905). Harmondsworth: Penguin Books, 1966.

James, William. *Principles of Psychology*. 2 vols. New York: Dover Publications Inc. 1950. Unaltered re-publication of New York: Henry Holt & Co., 1890.

Jameson, Fredric. *The Antinomies of Realism*. London: Verso, 2013.

Jay, Martin. 'In the Realm of the Senses: An Introduction', *The American Historical Review* 116:2 (2011), 307–15.

Jeans, James. *The New Background of Science*. Cambridge: Cambridge University Press, 1933.

Jenkins, Alice. *Space and the 'March of Mind': Literature and the Physical Sciences in Britain, 1815–1850*. New York: Oxford University Press, 2007.
Jevons, William Stanley. *The Principles of Science: A Treatise on Logic and Scientific Method*. 2 vols. London: Macmillan & Co., 1874.
Johnson, Bruce. *Conrad's Models of Mind*. Minneapolis: University of Minnesota Press, 1971.
Johnson, Bruce. *True Correspondence: A Phenomenology of Thomas Hardy's Novels*. Tallahassee: University Presses of Florida, 1983.
Johnson, Lionel. *The Art of Thomas Hardy*. London: Elkin Mathews & John Lane, 1894.
Jütte, Robert. *A History of the Senses, From Antiquity to Cyberspace*, trans. James Lynn. Cambridge: Polity Press, 2005.
Kaplan, Carola, Mallios, Peter and White, Andrea eds. *Conrad in the Twenty-First Century: Contemporary Approaches and Perspectives*. New York: Routledge, 2005.
Karl, Frederick R. and Davies, Laurence et al. eds. *The Collected Letters of Joseph Conrad*. 9 vols. Cambridge: Cambridge University Press, 1983–2007.
Kearns, Michael S. *Metaphors of Mind in Fiction and Psychology*. Lexington: University of Kentucky Press, 1987.
Kirschner, Paul. *Joseph Conrad: The Psychologist as Artist*. Edinburgh: Oliver and Boyd, 1968.
Kirschner Paul. 'Revolution, Feminism, and Conrad's Western "I"', *The Conradian* 10:1 (May 1985), 4–25.
Kirschner, Paul. 'Making You *See* Geneva: The Sense of Place in *Under Western Eyes*', *L'Epoque Conradienne* (1988), 101–28.
Knowles, Owen ed. *'My Dear Friend', Further Letters to and About Joseph Conrad*. Amsterdam: Rodopi, 2008.
Kockelmans, Joseph J. *Philosophy of Science: The Historical Background*. New York: The Free Press, 1968.
Korg, Jacob. 'Hardy, Conrad and the Agnostic Novel', in Francesco Marroni and Norman Page eds, *Thomas Hardy*. Pescara: Edizione Tracce, 1995.
Kramer, Dale ed. *Critical Approaches to the Fiction of Thomas Hardy*. London: Macmillan, 1979.
Kramnick, Jonathan. *Paper Minds: Literature and the Ecology of Consciousness*. Chicago: University of Chicago Press, 2018.
Krasner, James. *The Entangled Eye: Visual Perception and the Representation of Nature in Post-Darwinian Narrative*. New York: Oxford University Press, 1992.
Kreilkamp, Ivan. 'A Voice Without a Body: The Phonographic Logic of "Heart of Darkness"', *Victorian Studies* 40:2 (Winter 1997), 211–44.
Ladd, George Trumbull. *Elements of Physiological Psychology*. Bristol: Thoemmes Press, 1998. Facsimile of New York: Scribner & Son, 1887.

Lawrence, D. H. *Phoenix: The Posthumous Papers of D. H. Lawrence* (1936). Ed. Edward D. McDonald. London: Heinemann, 1970.

Lecercle, Jean-Jacques. 'Thomas Hardy's Silences', in *Thomas Hardy: Far From the Madding Crowd*, Cycnos 26:2 (2010).

Ledger, Sally and Scott McCracken eds. *Cultural Politics at the Fin de Siècle*. Cambridge: Cambridge University Press, 1995.

Lee, Vernon and C. Anstruther-Thomson. *Beauty and Ugliness and Other Studies in Psychological Aesthetics*. London: John Lane, 1912.

Lester, John A. *Journey Through Despair 1880–1914: Transformations in British Literary Culture*. Princeton: Princeton University Press, 1968.

Levine, George. *The Realistic Imagination*. Chicago: Chicago University Press, 1981.

Levine, George. *Darwin and the Novelists*. Cambridge, MA: Harvard University Press, 1988.

Levine, George. *Dying to Know: Scientific Epistemology and Narrative in Victorian England*. Chicago: Chicago University Press, 2002.

Levine, George. *Realism, Ethics and Secularism: Essays on Victorian Literature and Science*. Cambridge: Cambridge University Press, 2008.

Lewes, G. H. *The Physiology of Common Life*. 2 vols. Leipzig: Bernhard Tauchnitz, 1860.

Lewes, G. H. *The Physical Basis of Mind*. Bristol: Thoemmes, 1998. Facsimile of Second Series, Trübner & Co., 1877.

Lewes, G. H. *Problems of Life and Mind*. First and Third Series. London: Trübner & Co., 1879.

Lewis, Geraint and Luke Barnes. *A Fortunate Universe: Life in a Finely Tuned Cosmos*. Cambridge: Cambridge University Press, 2016.

Lloyd, Tom. *Crises of Realism: Representing Experience in the British Novel 1816–1910*. Lewisburg: Bucknall University Press, 1997.

Lodge, Oliver. *The Ether of Space*. London: Harper and Brothers, 1909.

Lommel, Eugene. *The Nature of Light with a General Account of Physical Optics*. London: Henry S. King & Co., 1875.

Lord, Ursula. *Solitude versus Solidarity in the Novels of Joseph Conrad: Political and Epistemological Implications of Narrative Innovation*. Montreal: McGill-Queen's University Press, 1998.

Lorentz, H. A. *Clerk Maxwell's Electromagnetic Theory* (The Rede Lecture for 1923). Cambridge: The University Press, 1923.

Losey, Jay B. 'Conrad's Moments of Awakening', *Conradiana* 20:2 (Summer 1988), 89–108.

Lukács, Georg. *Writer and Critic and Other Essays*. London: Merlin Press, 1978.

Macfarlane, Robert. *The Old Ways: A Journey on Foot*. London: Hamish Hamilton, 2012.

Mach, Ernst. *Contributions to the Analysis of the Sensations*. Bristol: Thoemmes Press, 1998. Facsimile of Chicago: Open Court Publishing Company, 1897.

Mach, Ernst. *History and Root of the Principle of the Conservation of Energy* (1872). Chicago: Open Court Publishing, 1911.
Macpherson, Fiona ed. *The Senses: Classic and Contemporary Philosophical Perspectives*. New York: Oxford University Press, 2011.
Mallett, Phillip. '*Jude the Obscure*: A Farewell to Wessex', *Thomas Hardy Journal* 11:3 (October 1995), 48–59.
Mallett, Phillip ed. *The Achievement of Thomas Hardy*. Basingstoke: Macmillan, 2000.
Mallett, Phillip ed. *Thomas Hardy: Texts and Contexts*. Basingstoke: Palgrave, 2002.
Mallett, Phillip ed. *Palgrave Advances in Thomas Hardy Studies*. Basingstoke: Palgrave, 2004.
Mallios, Peter. *Our Conrad: Constituting American Modernity*. Stanford: Stanford University Press, 2010.
Marle, Hans van. 'A Novelist's Dukedom: From Joseph Conrad's Library', *The Conradian* 16:1 (September 1991).
Matz, Aaron. *Satire in an Age of Realism*. New York: Cambridge University Press, 2010.
Matz, Jesse. *Literary Impressionism and Modernist Aesthetics*. Cambridge: Cambridge University Press, 2001.
Maxwell, James Clerk. 'The Telephone' (The Rede Lecture at Cambridge, 1878), *Nature* 18: 449 (6 June 1878), 159–63.
Maxwell, James Clerk. *The Scientific Papers of James Clerk Maxwell*. Ed. W. D. Niven. Vol. 1. Cambridge: Cambridge University Press, 1890.
Meisel, Perry. *The Myth of the Modern: A Study in British Literature and Criticism after 1850*. New Haven: Yale University Press, 1987.
Meredith, George. *Diana of the Crossways*. London: Virago Limited, 1980.
Merleau-Ponty, Maurice. *Sense and Non-Sense*, trans. Hubert L. and Patricia Allen Dreyfus. Chicago: Northwestern University Press, 1964.
Meyering, Theo C. *Historical Roots of Cognitive Science: The Rise of a Cognitive Theory of Perception from Antiquity to the Nineteenth Century*. Dordrecht: Kluwer Academic Publishers, 1989.
Mill, James. *Analysis of the Phenomena of the Human Mind*. Ed. J. S. Mill, with notes by Alexander Bain et al. London: Longmans Green Reader and Dyer, 1869.
Mill, J. S. *On Liberty and Other Essays*. London: Macmillan, 1926.
Millgate, Michael ed. *The Life and Work of Thomas Hardy*. Basingstoke: Macmillan, 1989.
Millgate, Michael. *Thomas Hardy: His Career as a Novelist*. Basingstoke: Macmillan, 1994.
Millgate, Michael ed. *Thomas Hardy's Public Voice: The Essays, Speeches and Miscellaneous Prose*. Oxford: Clarendon, 2001.
Moore, Gene M. ed. *Conrad's Cities: Essays for Hans van Marle*. Amsterdam: Rodopi, 1992.

Morell, J. D. *An Historical and Critical View of the Speculative Philosophy of Europe in the Nineteenth Century*. 2 vols. London: William Pickering, 1846.
Morgan, Benjamin. *The Outward Mind: Materialist Aesthetics in Victorian Science and Literature*. Chicago: University of Chicago Press, 2017.
Morgan, Benjamin. 'Scale as Form: Thomas Hardy's Rocks and Stars', in Tobias Menely and Jesse Oak Taylor eds, *Anthropocene Reading: Literary History in Geologic Times*. University Park: Pennsylvania State University Press, 2017.
Morgan, Rosemarie. 'Passive Victim? *Tess of the D'Urbervilles*', *Thomas Hardy Journal* 5:1 (January 1989), 31–54.
Morrell, Roy. *Thomas Hardy: The Will and the Way*. Kuala Lumpur: University of Malaya Press, 1965.
Morrison, Toni. *Beloved*. London: Pan Books Ltd., 1988.
Morus, Iwan Rhys. *When Physics Became King*. Chicago: University of Chicago Press, 2005.
Moses, Michael Valdez. *The Novel and the Globalisation of Culture*. Oxford: Oxford University Press, 1995.
Muir, Edwin. *Latitudes (Essays)*. New York: W. B. Huebsch Inc., 1924.
Muldoon, Mark S. 'Silence Revisited: Taking the Sight Out of Auditory Qualities', *The Review of Metaphysics* 50:2 (December 1996), 275–98.
Murfin, Ross C. ed. *Conrad Revisited: Essays for the Eighties*. Birmingham: University of Alabama Press, 1985.
Murfin, Ross C. 'Prestidigitations of Discourse: The Problem(s) with *Tess of the D'Urbervilles*', *The Hardy Review* 10:2 (Autumn 2008), 120–8.
Musselwhite, David. *Social Transformations in Hardy's Tragic Novels: Megamachines and Phantasms*. Basingstoke: Palgrave Macmillan, 2003.
Neilson, Brett. 'Hardy, Barbarism, and the Transformations of Modernity', in Tim Dolin and Peter Widdowson eds, *Thomas Hardy and Contemporary Literary Studies*. Basingstoke: Palgrave Macmillan, 2004.
Neuhoffer, John G. ed. *Ecological Psychoacoustics*. San Diego: Elsevier Academic Press, 2004.
Noë, Alva. *Action in Perception*. Cambridge, MA: MIT Press, 2004.
Noë, Alva. *Varieties of Presence*. Cambridge, MA: Harvard University Press, 2012.
Nudds, Matthew and O'Callaghan, Casey eds. *Sounds and Perception: New Philosophical Essays*. Oxford: Oxford University Press, 2009.
Nuttall, A. D. *A Common Sky: Philosophy and the Literary Imagination*. London: Chatto & Windus, 1974.
O'Callaghan, Casey. *Sounds: A Philosophical Theory*. Oxford: Oxford University Press, 2007.
O'Hanlon, Redmond. *Changing Scientific Concepts of Nature in the English Novel from 1850 to 1920, with Special Reference to Joseph Conrad*. Oxford: unpublished PhD thesis, 1977.

O'Hanlon, Redmond. *Joseph Conrad and Charles Darwin: The Influence of Scientific Thought on Conrad's Fiction*. Edinburgh: The Salamander Press, 1984.

Okuda, Yoko. 'East Meets West', *The Conradian* 23:2 (Autumn 1998), 73–87.

Ong, Walter J. *The Presence of the Word: Some Prolegomena for Cultural and Religious History*. New Haven: Yale University Press, 1967.

Paccaud, Josiane. 'Speech and the Nature of Communication in Conrad's "Heart of Darkness"', *The Conradian* 8:1 (Winter 1983), 41–8.

Paradis, James and Postlewait, Thomas eds. *Victorian Science and Victorian Values: Literary Perspectives*. New Brunswick, NJ: Rutgers University Press, 1985.

Park, David. *The Fire Within the Eye: A Historical Essay on the Nature and Meaning of Light*. Princeton: Princeton University Press, 1997.

Parkes, Adam. *A Sense of Shock: The Impact of Impressionism on Modern British and Irish Writing*. Oxford: Oxford University Press, 2011.

Pasnau, Robert. 'What is Sound?', *The Philosophical Quarterly* 49:156 (July 1999), 309–24.

Pater, Walter. *Appreciations, With an Essay on Style*. London: Macmillan, 1907.

Pater, Walter. *Marius the Epicurean*. London: J. M. Dent & Sons Ltd, 1960.

Pater, Walter. *The Renaissance: Studies in Art and Poetry* (1873). Oxford: Oxford World's Classics, 1986.

Pearson, Karl. *The Grammar of Science*. London: Walter Scott, 1892.

Pecora, Vincent. '"Heart of Darkness" and the Phenomenology of Voice', *ELH* 52:4 (1985), 993–1015.

Peters, John G. ed. *Conrad in the Public Eye: Biography / Criticism / Publicity*. Amsterdam: Rodopi, 2008.

Pettersson, Torsten. *Consciousness and Time: A Study in the Philosophy and Narrative Technique of Joseph Conrad*. Åbo (Finland): Åbo Akademi, 1982.

Picard, Max. *The World of Silence* (1948). London: The Harvill Press, 1952.

Pippin, Robert B. *Modernism as a Philosophical Problem: On the Dissatisfactions of European High Culture*. Oxford: Basil Blackwell, 1991.

Poincaré, Henri. *Science and Hypothesis*. New York: Walter Scott Publishing, 1905.

Potter, Richard. *Physical Optics or the Nature and Properties of Light. Part II: The Corpuscular Theory of Light, Discussed Mathematically*. Cambridge: Deighton, Bell & Co., 1859.

Purdy, Richard Little and Michael Millgate eds. *The Collected Letters of Thomas Hardy*. 7 vols. Oxford: The Clarendon Press, 1978–1988.

Purssell, A. M. '"The End of the Tether": Conrad, Geography and the Place of Vision', *The Conradian* 33:2 (Autumn 2008), 30–43.

Pye, Patricia. 'A City that "disliked to be disturbed": London's Soundscape in *The Secret Agent*', *The Conradian* 32:1 (Spring 2007), 21–35.

Radford, Andrew. *Thomas Hardy and the Survivals of Time*. Aldershot: Ashgate, 2003.

Ray, Martin. 'The Gift of Tongues: The Languages of Joseph Conrad', *Conradiana* 15:2 (Summer 1983), 83–109.

Ray, Martin. 'Language and Silence in the Novels of Joseph Conrad', *Conradiana* 16:1 (Spring 1984), 19–41.

Ray, Martin. 'Interviews and Recollections', *The Conradian* 13:1 (1988).

Ray, Martin. 'Hardy and Conrad', *Thomas Hardy Journal* 12:2 (May 1996), 82–4.

Ray, Martin. *Thomas Hardy Remembered*. Aldershot: Ashgate, 2007.

Rée, Jonathan. *I See a Voice: A Philosophical History of Language, Deafness and the Senses*. London: Harper Collins Publishers, 1999.

Reed, Edward S. *From Soul to Mind: The Emergence of Psychology from Erasmus Darwin to William James*. New Haven: Yale University Press, 1997.

Reilly, Jim. *Shadowtime: History and Representation in Hardy, Conrad and George Eliot*. London: Routledge, 1993.

Rezelman, Betsy Cogger. 'Discovering the Scientific Frame of Mind in the Late-Victorian Artistic Experiments of James McNeill Whistler and Stanhope Forbes'. *Australasian Victorian Studies Journal* 2 (November 1996), 139–52.

Russolo, Luigi. *The Art of Noises*, trans. Barclay Brown (1916). New York: Pendragon Press, 1986.

Ryan, Vanessa L. *Thinking Without Thinking in the Victorian Novel*. Baltimore: The Johns Hopkins University Press, 2012.

Rylance, Rick. *Victorian Psychology and British Culture 1850–1880*. Oxford: Oxford University Press, 2000.

Scarry, Elaine. *Resisting Representation*. New York: Oxford University Press, 1994.

Schafer, R. Murray. *The Soundscape: Our Sonic Environment and the Tuning of the World*. Rochester, VT: Destiny Books, 1994.

Schnauder, Ludwig. *Free Will and Determinism in Joseph Conrad's Major Novels*. Amsterdam: Rodopi BV, 2009.

Schneider, Eric D. and Sagan, Dorian. *Into the Cool: Energy Flow, Thermodynamics and Life*. Chicago: Chicago University Press, 2005.

Schwartz, Hillel. *Making Noise: From Babel to the Big Bang and Beyond*. New York: Zone Books, 2011.

Schwarz, Daniel. *The Transformation of the English Novel 1890–1930*. Basingstoke: Macmillan, 1989.

Sears, Sally and Lord, Georgianna eds. *The Discontinuous Universe: Selected Writings in Contemporary Consciousness*. New York: Basic Books Inc., 1972.

Senn, Werner. *Conrad's Narrative Voice: Stylistic Aspects of his Fiction* (1980). Leiden: Brill Rodopi, 2017.

Seremetakis, C. Nadia. *The Senses Still: Perception and Memory as Material Culture in Modernity*. Boulder: Westview Press, 1994.
Sherry, Norman ed. *Joseph Conrad: The Critical Heritage*. London: Routledge, 1997.
Shires, Linda M. *Perspectives: Modes of Viewing and Knowing in Nineteenth-Century England*. Columbus: Ohio State University Press, 2009.
Simmons, Allan H. '"He was misleading": Frustrated Gestures in *Lord Jim*', *The Conradian* 25:1 (Spring 2000), 31–47.
Simmons, Allan H. *Conrad's 'Heart of Darkness'*. London: Bloomsbury, 2007.
Simmons, Allan H. ed. *Joseph Conrad in Context*. Cambridge: Cambridge University Press, 2009.
Simons, Mark. 'Hardy's Stereographic Technique', *Thomas Hardy Journal* 13:3 (October 1997), 86–93.
Smith, Mark M. *Sensory History*. Oxford: Berg, 2007.
Sokołowska, Katarzyna. *Conrad and Turgenev: Towards the Real*. New York: Columbia University Press, 2011.
Somerville, Mary. *On the Connexion of the Physical Sciences*. London: John Murray, 1834.
Soper, Kate. *What is Nature? Culture, Politics and the non-Human*. Oxford: Blackwell, 1995.
Spencer, Herbert. *First Principles* (2nd edition 1867), in *Collected Writings*, Vol. V. London: Routledge/Thoemmes Press, 1996.
Spencer, Herbert. *The Principles of Psychology*. 2 vols. 2nd edition. London: Williams and Norgate, 1870.
Spiegel, Alan. *Fiction and the Camera Eye: Visual Consciousness in Film and the Modern Novel*. Charlottesville: University Press of Virginia, 1976.
Starobinski, Jean. 'The Inside and the Outside', *The Hudson Review* 28:3 (Autumn 1975), 333–51.
Stauffer, Ruth M. *Joseph Conrad, His Romantic Realism*. Boston: The Four Seas Company, 1922.
Steege, Benjamin. *Helmholtz and the Modern Listener*. New York: Cambridge University Press, 2012.
Stewart, Balfour and Tait, Peter Guthrie. *The Unseen Universe, or Physical Speculations on a Future State*. London: Macmillan & Co., 1886.
Stiles, Anne ed. *Neurology and Literature 1860–1920*. Basingstoke: Palgrave Macmillan, 2007.
Straus, Nina Pelikan. 'The Exclusion of The Intended from Secret Sharing in Conrad's "Heart of Darkness"', *Novel* 20:2 (Winter 1987), 123–37.
Strauss, D. F. *The Old Faith and the New: A Confession*. London: Asher & Co., 1873.
Sully, James. *Sensation and Intuition: Studies in Psychology and Aesthetics*. London: Henry S. King & Co., 1874.

Sumner, Rosemary. *Thomas Hardy: Psychological Novelist*. Basingstoke: Macmillan, 1981.
Symonds, John Addington. *Essays Speculative and Suggestive*. London: Chapman and Hall Limited, 1890.
Symons, Arthur. *Notes on Joseph Conrad*. London: Myers & Co., 1925.
Tanner, Tony. 'Nightmare and Complacency: Razumov and the Western Eye', *Critical Quarterly* 4:3 (Autumn 1962), 197–215.
Tanner, Tony. 'Butterflies and Beetles: Conrad's Two Truths', *Chicago Review* 16 (Winter–Spring 1963), 123–40.
Tanner, Tony. 'Colour and Movement in *Tess of the d'Urbervilles*', *Critical Quarterly* 10 (1968), 219–39.
Tanner, Tony. '"Gnawed Bones" and "Artless Tales": Eating and Narrative in Conrad', in Norman Sherry ed., *Joseph Conrad: A Commemoration*. London: Macmillan, 1979.
Taylor, Dennis. *Hardy's Literary Language and Victorian Philology*. Oxford: Clarendon Press, 1993.
Taylor, Richard H. *The Neglected Hardy: Thomas Hardy's Lesser Novels*. London: Macmillan, 1982.
Thomas, Edward. *Walter Pater: A Critical Study*. London: Martin Secker, 1913.
Thomas, Edward. *Collected Poems*. Ed. R. George Thomas. Oxford: Clarendon Press, 1978.
Thompson, Emily. *The Soundscape of Modernity: Architectural Acoustics and the Culture of Listening in America, 1900–1933*. Cambridge, MA: MIT Press, 2002.
Thompson, Sylvanus P. *Light Visible and Invisible. A Series of Lectures Delivered at the Royal Institution of Great Britain, at Christmas 1896*. London: Macmillan & Co. Ltd, 1897.
Turner, Martha. *Mechanism and the Novel: Science in the Narrative Process*. Cambridge: Cambridge University Press, 1993.
Tutein, David. *Joseph Conrad's Reading: An Annotated Bibliography*. West Cornwall, CT: Locust Hill Press, 1990.
Tyndall, John. *Six Lectures on Light, delivered in America in 1872–1873*. New York: D. Appleton & Co., 1873.
Tyndall, John. *Fragments of Science: A Series of Detached Essays, Addresses, and Reviews*. 6th edition. London: Longmans, Green, and Co., 1879.
Tyndall, John. *Sound*. 5th edn. London: Longmans, Green, and Co., 1893.
Verschoyle, Derek ed. *The English Novelists: A Survey of the Novel by Twenty Contemporary Novelists*. London: Chatto & Windus, 1936.
Vigar, Penelope. *The Novels of Thomas Hardy: Illusion and Reality*. London: The Athlone Press, 1974.
Wade, Nicholas ed. *The Emergence of Neuroscience in the Nineteenth Century*, Vol. 4. London: Routledge/Thoemmes Press, 2000.
Wallace, Alfred Russel. *The Malay Archipelago* (1869). Oxford: John Beaufoy Publishing, 2009.

Walpole, Hugh. *Joseph Conrad*. London: Nisbet & Co. Ltd, 1916.
Ward, Mrs Humphrey. *Robert Elsmere*. New York: Wm. L. Allison, 1889.
Warodell, Johan. '"Arrows by Jove!": Delayed Miscoding in "Heart of Darkness"', *The Conradian* 40:1 (Spring 2015), 7–22.
Warren, Robert Penn ed. Introduction, *Nostromo*. New York: The Modern Library, Random House, 1951.
Watt, Ian. *Conrad in the Nineteenth Century*. Berkeley: University of California Press, 1979.
Watts, Cedric. *Conrad's 'Heart of Darkness': A Critical and Contextual Discussion*. Milan: Mursia International, 1977.
Weinstein, Philip. *The Semantics of Desire: Changing Models of Identity from Dickens to Joyce*. Princeton: Princeton University Press, 1984.
White, Andrea. *Joseph Conrad and the Adventure Tradition*. Cambridge: Cambridge University Press, 1993.
Whitworth, Michael H. *Einstein's Wake: Relativity, Metaphor and Modernist Literature*. Oxford: Oxford University Press, 2001.
Wickens, Glen G. 'Romantic Myth and Victorian Nature in *Desperate Remedies*', *English Studies in Canada* 8:2 (June 1982), 154–73.
Widdowson, Peter. *Hardy in History: A Study in Literary Sociology*. London: Routledge, 1989.
Wilczek, Frank. *A Beautiful Question: Finding Nature's Deep Design*. New York: Penguin Press, 2015.
Wiley, Paul L. *Conrad's Measure of Man*. Madison: University of Wisconsin Press, 1954.
Williams, Linda ed. *'Viewing Positions': Ways of Seeing Film*. New Brunswick, NJ: Rutgers University Press, 1995.
Williams, Raymond. *The English Novel from Dickens to Lawrence*. London: Chatto & Windus, 1970.
Wilson, Keith ed. *A Companion to Thomas Hardy*. Chichester: Wiley-Blackwell, 2009.
Wise, M. Norton. 'Electromagnetic Theory in the Nineteenth Century', in R. C. Olby, G. N. Cantor, J. R. R. Christie and M. J. S. Hodge eds, *Companion to the History of Modern Science*. London: Routledge, 1996.
Wittenberg, Judith Bryant. 'Early Hardy Novels and the Fictional Eye', *Novel* 16:2 (Winter 1983), 151–64.
Wittenberg, Judith Bryant. 'Angles of Vision and Questions of Gender in *Far From the Madding Crowd*', *The Centennial Review* 30:1 (1986), 25–40.
Wood, Jane. *Passion and Pathology in Victorian Fiction*. New York: Oxford University Press, 2001.
Woolf, Virginia. *A Writer's Diary*. Ed. Leonard Woolf. London: The Hogarth Press, 1953.
Woolf Virginia. *Collected Essays*. 4 vols. Ed. Leonard Woolf. London: Chatto & Windus, 1966.

Woolf, Virginia. *Moments of Being*. Ed. Jeanne Schulkind. London: Pimlico, 2002.
Wordsworth, William. *Poetical Works*. Oxford: Oxford University Press, 1965.
Worringer, Wilhelm. *Abstraction and Empathy*. Chicago: Ivan R. Dee, 1997.
Wotton, George. *Thomas Hardy: Towards a Materialist Criticism*. Totowa NJ: Gill & Macmillan, Barnes and Noble Books, 1985.
Yeazell, Ruth Bernard. 'The Lighting Design of Hardy's Novels', *Nineteenth-Century Literature* 64:1 (Spring 2009), 48–75.
Youmans, Edward ed. *The Correlation and Conservation of Forces*. New York: D. Appleton and Company, 1865.
Young, Kay. *Imagining Minds: The Neuro-Aesthetics of Austen, Eliot and Hardy*. Columbus: Ohio State University Press, 2010.
Zabel, Morton Dauwen. 'Hardy in Defense of his Art: The Aesthetic of Incongruity', *The Southern Review* 6 (July 1940).
Zabel, Morton Dauwen. 'Joseph Conrad: Chance and Recognition', *Sewanee Review* 53:1 (Winter 1945), 1–22.
Zabel, Morton Dauwen ed. *The Portable Conrad*. New York: Viking Press, 1947.
Zemka, Sue. *Time and the Moment in Victorian Literature and Society*. New York: Cambridge University Press, 2012.

Index

Abercrombie, Lascelles, 3, 79n
Achebe, Chinua, 169n
Adams, Henry, 49–50
aerial experience, 141, 147, 192
  in Conrad, 56, 168, 171, 177, 189
  in Hardy, 140–1, 155, 159, 161–2, 221, 223
air, 12n, 27, 44, 99, 139, 141, 145, 147, 154, 158–9, 193
  in Conrad, 30, 54, 55–6, 57, 105–6, 114, 115, 135, 147n, 163, 165, 166–7, 168, 171, 175–6, 177, 179, 183, 190, 232, 258, 260
  in Hardy, 3, 23–4, 26, 46, 95, 124, 125, 140, 151, 153, 154, 158, 162, 219, 220–1, 224, 259
'akoumena', 241
Allen, Grant, 186
Alvarez, Al, 250n, 255
Anstruther-Thomson, Clementina, 41n
Arata, Stephen, 72n
Archer, William, 215, 271
Aristotle, 162
Arnold, Matthew, 248
Arscott, Caroline, 82
Asquith, Mark, 49n, 145n, 147n, 150n
Athenaeum, The, 13, 175
atmosphere, 70, 82, 99, 133, 154, 158–9, 165
  in Conrad, 31, 53n, 76, 111, 165, 173–4, 229, 232, 233, 261, 263
  as an effect of description, 3, 7, 12n, 23, 35, 46, 49, 53, 56, 74–5, 133, 173–4, 247, 267
  in Hardy, 25, 46, 87–9, 94, 94n, 98, 125, 151, 158–9, 160, 161, 213, 220–1, 223, 251–2

Auden, W. H., 175, 215
Authorised Version of the Bible, 12

Babbage, Charles, 158–9, 160
Bain, Alexander, 22n, 38–9, 40, 43, 50n, 65, 80, 85, 126, 184, 185n, 198–9, 199–200, 202, 213
Balfour, Arthur, 50
Barrie, J. M., 8, 8n
Bates, H. E., 10–11
Baxter, Katherine Isobel, 28n, 57n, 105n
Bayley, John, 4, 22n, 28n, 150n
Beach, Joseph Warren, 16
Beer, Gillian, 17, 17n, 63n, 140n, 221, 222, 270
Békésy, Georg von, 146, 146n
Bellini, Giovanni, 92
Bell-Magendie law, 35–6
Bennett, Arnold, 1, 1n, 8, 8n, 14, 73, 73n
Bennett, Jane, 66, 67
Benson, Donald, 53n, 80n, 110–11, 111n, 114, 133
Berkson, William, 96n, 111n
Berry, Wendell, 270–1
Blackmore, R. D., 12
Blackwood, William, 22, 29, 52
Blake, Kathleen, 210n
Blind, Mathilde, 61
Blumenberg, Hans, 111n, 137
Bock, Martin, 21n
Bohlman, Otto, 19n
Bonington, Richard, 64
Boring, Edwin, 36
Boumelha, Penny, 89n
Bowen, Elizabeth, 80

brain, 38, 38n, 39, 64, 71, 84, 96, 100, 128, 141, 158, 225, 258–9, 263
Bregman, Albert S., 147, 147n
Brennan, Teresa, 219n, 268–9
Brewster, David, 107n
Brontës, the, 12
Brooks, Jean R., 19n, 210n
Brooks, Peter, 173, 173n, 175
Brown, Thomas, 57, 85
Bullen, J. B., 25n, 80n
Butler, Samuel, 38n, 218

Cabanis, Pierre Jean Georges, 264, 265
camera, 69n, 71n, 129, 132, 196
Carabine, Keith, 244n
Carpenter, Edward, 109–10
Casseres, Benjamin de, 70
Cassirer, Ernst, 85
Cézanne, Paul, 6, 6n
Chapple, J. A. V., 18
Chew, Samuel, 12, 13n, 243n
Clifford, W. K., 2, 83, 83n, 119
Clodd, Edward, 60, 62
Clough, Arthur Hugh, 248
Cohen, William A., 16n, 153, 156
Colvin, Sidney, 8, 65, 81n
Common Prayer, Book of, 12
Comte, Auguste, 37, 226
Connor, Steven, 152, 172, 206
Conrad, Joseph
    ESSAYS
    'Alphonse Daudet', 240n, 272
    'Autocracy and War', 126
    'Guy de Maupassant', 61
    'Henry James', 42
    The Mirror of the Sea, 142
    Notes on Life and Letters, 42, 61, 126, 232, 240n, 272
    A Personal Record, 143, 171, 271
    'Well Done', 232
    NOVELS AND STORIES
    Almayer's Folly, 81
    'Amy Foster', 244n
    The Arrow of Gold, 9
    Chance, 239n
    'The End of the Tether', 119, 127–38
    'Heart of Darkness', 14n, 34, 51, 119, 122n, 128, 135, 148, 162–76
    'The Idiots', 5–6
    The Inheritors, 113
    'Karain', 131
    'The Lagoon', 135
    Lord Jim, 10n, 84, 86, 95, 103–19, 159, 174, 226, 246n, 257, 261, 263, 271
    The Nigger of the 'Narcissus', 7, 64, 68, 72, 73, 73n, 86, 150, 176
    Nostromo, 12n, 33, 72, 76, 77, 116n, 142, 148, 171, 175, 177–92, 194, 209, 210, 211, 212, 229–42, 269
    The Rescue, 21–3, 28–35, 51–8, 141, 257, 272
    'The Return', 117n
    Romance, 144
    The Rover, 3, 30, 81, 142n
    The Secret Agent, 10, 51, 130, 183n, 246, 258
    'The Secret Sharer', 250n
    The Shadow-Line, 59
    The Sisters (Introduction by Ford), 6, 178
    Tales of Unrest, 6n, 117n, 135
    'Typhoon', 235, 271
    Under Western Eyes, 20, 225, 243–4, 244n, 257–70
    Victory, 72, 76, 147n, 177
    Within the Tides, 74–5
    'Youth', 13, 14, 128, 175
Conrad Peter, 212
consciousness
    in Conrad, 30, 31, 56–7, 72, 106, 113, 115–16, 233, 236, 243, 260, 265, 271–2
    in Hardy, 25–6, 27, 30, 33, 46–7, 48–9, 51, 89, 90–1, 92, 94, 97, 101, 159, 194–6, 196n, 197, 198, 202–3, 205, 208, 219, 220–3, 245, 247, 251, 252–3, 256
    literary presentation of, 2, 14, 25, 27, 39, 56, 70, 141, 244
    and philosophy, 63, 198
    scientific exploration of, 32, 35, 38n, 40, 50, 62n, 69, 83n, 111, 184, 184n, 217

Cooper, James Fenimore, 12, 12n
Corbin, Alain, 141–2, 142n
The Cornhill, 126
Corti, Alfonso, 146
Cosslett, Tess, 18n
Crabbe, George, 37, 37n
Crane, Stephen, 59
Crary, Jonathan, 71n
Crivelli, Carlo, 92, 121
Curle, Richard, 7, 74n, 81n, 111
Cussen, Eoin, 107n

Daily Chronicle, 232
Daily Telegraph, 180
Daleski, H. M., 17
Danius, Sara, 5
Danziger, Kurt, 37
darkness
  in Conrad, 31, 33, 34, 42, 52, 53–4, 55–6, 105, 106, 111, 116, 128, 131, 134, 136, 165, 166–7, 175, 176, 191, 230, 231, 233–4, 235, 259
  in Hardy, 103, 123, 152, 163, 210, 214, 246
  in Heaney, 245
  in Meredith, 68
  in Thomas, 231
Darwin, Charles, 61, 63n, 207, 215
Davie, Donald, 125n
Davis, Mike, 213n
Davray, H.-D., 257
Dean, Dennis, 12
DeLaura, David, 248
'delayed decoding', 34, 34n
Deleuze, Gilles, 76–7
dematerialising, 34, 56, 71, 115
description, 5, 8, 25, 32, 40n, 50, 58, 68, 69n, 70, 82, 112, 151, 154n, 244
determined, determinism, 2, 11, 15–16, 44n, 50, 57, 62n, 153, 198
Dewey, John, 19, 19n
Dickens, Charles, 13, 107, 157
'disproportioning', 6, 48, 72, 101, 201
dissolve, dissolving, 52, 67, 76, 116, 125, 127, 129, 145, 160, 186, 212, 233
Dolar, Mladen, 170

Dolin, Tim, 74n, 86
Don Quixote (Cervantes), 12
Dostoyevsky, Fyodor, 244
Doubleday, F. N., 58, 176

Eagleton, Terry, 102
Einstein, Albert, 82, 110
Eliot, George, 1, 12, 18, 62n, 69n, 72, 76, 91, 92n, 99n, 137
Elkins, James, 83n, 124–5
Ellis, Havelock, 28, 214–15
Empfindung, 201
empirical, empiricist, 3, 8, 11n, 38, 39, 72, 83, 110n, 140, 141, 212–13, 215, 217, 218, 229n
  in Conrad, 55, 65, 132, 271
  in Hardy, 64, 64n, 77, 86, 161, 208, 225, 248, 249, 271
energy (physics), 41n, 43–4, 43n, 47, 81, 82n, 96n, 128, 145, 157, 163, 200, 270
  in Conrad, 56, 112, 113, 114, 141, 186, 235
  in Hardy, 44, 45, 47, 56, 95, 96, 99, 141, 224, 229, 235, 248
entropy, 44, 54, 112, 157
epiphany, 105, 117, 131, 187
epistemology, 2, 21n, 40n, 48, 104, 114, 132, 217, 243, 248
Erchinger, Philipp, 18n, 66n
ether, 25, 70, 82, 88, 109–14, 139, 140, 159, 166, 174, 233
'event', 67, 70, 80, 165–6, 204, 217, 237
  in Conrad, 56, 112, 168, 182, 237
  in Hardy, 19, 26, 47, 77, 89, 96, 204, 215, 221
Everett, John, cover image, 29n
'existence'
  in Conrad, 20, 56, 64, 74, 75, 104, 144, 206, 232, 236, 238, 262, 272
  in Hardy, 45–8, 49, 50, 51, 73, 96, 151, 160, 205, 206, 211, 225, 272

Faraday, Michael, 8, 43, 82, 96n, 110n
Faulkner, William, 2, 80
Fauvism, 6, 6n

Fechner, Gustav, 22n, 36
Fernandez, Ramon, 16–17, 17n, 34, 56
field, electromagnetic, 8, 43, 43n, 81–2, 133, 147
field theory, 18, 43n, 82, 96n, 114, 193, 200
Fielding, Henry, 12
Flaubert, Gustave, 13, 68, 69, 69n, 75, 130n
Fogel, Aaron, 147n, 180, 261
Follett, Wilson, 15
force (physics), 7n, 8, 43–4, 43n, 50, 51–2, 96n, 110n, 111, 145, 193, 226n
   in Conrad, 31, 56, 186, 227, 232, 235
   in Hardy, 28n, 101, 224, 226
Ford, Ford Madox, 6, 11, 13, 144, 178
Ford, Mark, 9n
Freedman, William, 109n
Frost, Robert, 245

Galsworthy, John, 8, 9, 10, 14
Garland, Hamlin, 8
Garneray, Ambroise Louis, 12
Garnett, Edward, 3, 9, 28, 35, 40, 52, 56, 76, 131, 136, 257
Garratt, Peter, 11n, 64n, 213
Garson, Marjorie, 199, 249
Geneva, 258, 263, 266, 267, 269, 269n
Gibson, James J., 7, 36n, 80
Gissing, George, 1, 8, 17, 84
gleams
   in Conrad, 53, 55, 106, 117, 118, 265
   in Hardy, 94–5, 94n, 97, 211
glimpses, 80
   in Conrad, 104, 105n, 106, 118, 170, 172, 267
   in Hardy, 81, 162, 212, 250, 251
Goode, John, 196n, 244n, 246n
Gosse, Edmund, 8, 181n, 245, 248, 253, 253n, 256, 257
Graham, Cunninghame, 9, 32, 54, 60, 61, 62, 116, 239
Graham, Kenneth, 231

Graphic, 222
Greenberg, Steven, 188
Gregor, Ian, 97, 252
Gregory, R. L., 91, 93n
Grove, W. R., 7n, 44
Guerard, Albert, 17
Gurney, Edmund, 139, 154–5, 177

Hamlet, 205
Hamlyn, D. W., 22
Hardy, Barbara, 160
Hardy, Thomas
   ESSAYS ETC.
   '*Poetical Matter*' *Notebook*, 61, 77
   'The Profitable Reading of Fiction', 73, 86–7
   'The Science of Fiction', 73
   NOVELS
   Desperate Remedies, 21–8, 29, 37, 43–51, 54, 81, 92, 118, 120, 143–4, 156, 199, 221, 225, 234, 256
   Far From the Madding Crowd, 19, 68, 86–103, 104, 119, 140–1
   The Hand of Ethelberta, 257n
   'An Indiscretion in the Life of an Heiress', 49
   Jude the Obscure, 9, 11, 14n, 17–18, 142, 225, 228, 243–57, 258, 259, 261, 263, 268, 269, 270
   A Laodicean, 119–27, 129, 135
   The Mayor of Casterbridge, 14, 148, 194–209, 213
   A Pair of Blue Eyes, 92, 92n, 220
   The Poor Man and the Lady, 49n, 257n
   The Return of the Native, 9, 148–62, 163, 164, 173, 197, 272
   Tess of the d'Urbervilles, 2, 51, 61–2, 126, 142, 194, 197, 209–29, 232, 234, 236, 239, 247, 267
   Two on a Tower, 5–6, 84
   The Trumpet-Major, 66
   Under the Greenwood Tree, 86, 151
   The Well-Beloved, 80, 248
   The Woodlanders, 10n, 64, 210n
   POEMS
   The Dynasts, 10n, 62
   'Her Dilemma', 175n

'A Kiss', 159
'I Look Into My Glass', 205
'Neutral Tones', 27
'Self-Unconscious', 25
'She to Him II', 50n
'The Voice', 159–60, 160n
Harper's, 110
Harper's Monthly Magazine, 254n
Harpham, Geoffrey, Galt, 229n
Harrison, Frederic, 60
Hayles, N. Katherine, 107n
Heaney, Seamus, 245
hearing, 19, 139–92, 270
  in Conrad, 28, 30–1, 33, 52, 55, 144, 164, 165, 167, 168–9, 171, 173–5, 177, 178–9, 181–2, 189, 191, 230, 231, 241, 260, 265, 266, 267
  in Fenimore Cooper, 12n
  in Hardy, 16n, 97, 144, 148, 150–2, 158, 159, 160, 160n, 161, 203, 206, 214, 219–24, 244, 247
  and philosophy, 19, 143, 145, 157, 179, 191, 203, 206
  and physiology, 139, 140, 141, 146, 147, 152–3, 153–4, 158, 161, 167, 168, 183, 186, 188, 203
Hegel, G. W. F., 60
Heinemann, William, 58
Heisenberg, Werner, 65, 66, 70
Helmholtz, Hermann von, 21, 35, 36, 40n, 42, 50, 83–4, 96n, 127, 128, 144n, 145, 146–7, 152, 154, 154n, 167, 183, 184, 193
Henchman, Anna, 62n, 151n
Henniker, Florence, 251n, 257
Herbert, Christopher, 11n
Herschel, John, 88
Hertz, Heinrich, 35, 37, 145
Hidaka, Tadaichi, 1, 13n, 59
history
  in Conrad, 180, 181, 181n, 183, 185, 187, 188, 189, 192, 229, 237
  in Hardy, 204, 207, 211, 212, 214, 218, 224, 225, 245, 255
Hopkins, Gerard, Manley, 79, 257
horizontal(s), 48, 56, 92, 121, 186, 259
Horowitz, Seth, 139
Hughes, Linda K., 10n
Hugo, Victor, 12
Hunt, Bruce J., 43n
Huxley, T. H., 22n, 60, 63, 65, 271
Huysmans, J. K., 146

ideal, idealism
  in Conrad, 36, 42, 54, 58, 65, 72, 86, 107, 116, 116n, 119, 179, 183, 226, 230, 233, 235, 239, 242, 269, 269n, 271
  in Hardy, 36, 37, 45, 64, 64n, 72, 73, 86, 216, 234, 246, 247, 248, 249, 250, 251, 252, 253, 259, 268, 269
  and philosophy, 19, 41n, 43, 63, 70, 138, 184, 201, 249
  and physics, 42, 140n, 216
  and physiology, 19, 36, 40, 42, 65, 73, 184, 200
Ihde, Don, 140, 152, 158, 162
illumination, 83, 168
  in Conrad, 34, 35, 64, 104, 115, 132, 134, 136–7, 183, 267
  in Hardy, 5, 16n, 24, 48, 49, 87, 101, 103
image
  in audition, 140, 167, 179, 188, 191
  in Conrad, 32, 41–2, 56, 76, 118n, 128, 133–4, 167, 171–2, 179, 188, 191–2, 235, 237, 241, 258, 262–3, 268
  in Eliot, 92n
  in Hardy, 27, 28, 34, 48, 62, 93, 125, 151, 196, 202, 224, 227
  in physiological psychology, 38, 40n, 84, 133, 134, 200–1
  in Woolf, 14, 14n
impressionism, 3n, 16n, 17, 32, 34, 34n, 42, 79n, 237
impressions
  in Conrad, 2, 34, 95, 114, 212, 230, 237, 261, 263
  in Hardy, 2, 3, 19, 48–9, 95–6, 212, 216, 225
  in other literary presentation, 16, 39n, 40–1
  in physical science, 3, 38, 39–40, 83n, 98n, 139

Infeld, Leopold, 82
Ingold, Tim, 139n
inner life, 50, 123, 180, 198, 208, 209
Ireland, Ken, 5n
Irwin, Michael, 16n, 80n, 143n, 147n

James, David, 16n, 160n
James, Henry, 1, 17, 25, 26–7, 39n, 40n, 42, 56, 69n, 74n, 76, 80, 137
James, William, 22n, 65, 70, 184, 184n, 213n
Jameson, Frederic, 90n
Jeans, James, 80
Jenkins, Alice, 18, 193
Jevons, William Stanley, 154n
Johnson, Bruce, 17, 34n, 116n
Johnson, Lionel, 3
Joule, James, 43, 44
Joyce, James, 14, 251, 251n
Jütte, Robert, 15n, 19

kaleidoscope, 107, 107n, 237
Kearns, Michael, 69n
Keats, John, 36n, 62, 84n
Kipling, Rudyard, 1, 1n
Kirschner, Paul, 89n, 269n
Korg, Jacob, 17
Kramnick, Jonathan, 71n
Krasner, James, 17n, 221
Kubovy, Michael, 168

landscape, 5, 41, 68, 71, 99, 149, 163, 178
  in Conrad, 58, 134, 163, 178
  in Hardy, 6, 33, 46–7, 64, 99, 143n, 150n, 151, 154, 195, 203, 224, 227, 228
Lawrence, D. H., 3, 13, 47, 101, 186, 245, 248
Lawrence, T. E. 176, 176n
Lecercle, Jean-Jacques, 229n
Lee, Vernon (Violet Paget), 4n, 41n
Lester, John A., 11–12
Levine, George, 17, 17n, 40n, 63n, 72
Lewes, G. H., 22n, 38, 40n, 64n, 69, 88n, 184n, 200–1, 202, 203, 204, 209, 213

light, 79–138, 80, 88
  in Conrad, 52–3, 55–6, 64, 80n, 81, 86, 103, 105n, 106–7, 108–9, 111–12, 115–18, 119, 127–8, 129–30, 131, 133–4, 136, 163, 182, 232, 236, 265, 267
  and contemporary physics, 47, 56, 63, 80, 81–2, 83, 83n, 88, 109–11, 110n, 133, 139, 145
  corpuscular or particle theory of, 81, 88, 88n, 224
  in Hardy, 3, 27, 28n, 45, 46–7, 74, 80n, 81, 86–8, 89, 92, 93–5, 97, 99, 100–3, 122–3, 124, 125–6, 125n, 160–1, 211, 213, 224, 225, 247, 251
  and other writers, 12n, 70–1, 80, 80n, 99, 175
  and philosophy, 85, 103, 109, 137–8
  and physiology, 87, 93n, 136
  and Turner, 46
  wave theory of, 46, 47, 56, 81–2, 88, 110n, 154n, 224
Lloyd, Tom, 217n, 223n
Lodge, Oliver, 110, 113
Lommel, Eugene, 88
London in Hardy and Conrad, 10
Lorentz, H. A., 82n, 113
Losey, Jay B., 131
Lukács, Georg, 69n
Lund, Michael, 10n
'Lycidas' (Milton), 72

Macfarlane, Robert, 99, 153n
Mach, Ernst, 22n, 39n, 50, 104, 193, 217–18, 219, 223, 224, 225, 227, 228, 232, 238
McIntyre, John, 56
Macpherson, Fiona, 15n, 19n
magnesium, 131
Mallett, Phillip, 2n, 60n, 63n, 249
Marryat, Captain Frederick, 12
Marx, Karl, 11, 19
materialism, materialist, 11, 17, 21, 41n, 42, 57, 59–60, 63, 67, 70, 166, 183, 198, 233, 264
Matz, Aaron, 248
Matz, Jesse, 3n, 32, 33
Maugham, Somerset, 53

Maupassant, Guy de, 1, 13, 61
Max Gate, 9, 9n, 271
Maxwell, James Clerk, 8, 43, 44, 81–2, 82n, 110, 113, 154n, 200
mechanical, mechanics, 56, 111n, 113–14, 128, 186, 224, 225, 226, 226n
medium
   in Conrad, 6, 31, 52, 57–8, 86, 103, 104, 113, 114, 115, 116, 117, 133, 135, 139, 167, 171, 181, 263–4
   in Hardy, 6, 45, 48, 58, 74, 86, 87, 94, 120, 125, 139, 151, 162, 210, 212, 213, 250, 254
   mental, 114, 125, 128, 141, 179, 244, 263–4
   in physics, 23, 45, 58, 80, 81–2, 82n, 88, 109–11, 110n, 133, 140–1, 145, 166, 167
   in physiology, 83, 120, 128, 140, 147
mental experience, 7, 15, 43, 62n, 69, 71, 75–6, 103, 166, 243–4
   in Conrad, 32, 33, 41–2, 75, 112, 117, 130–2, 133–4, 163, 171, 179, 183, 233, 235, 237, 258, 261–6, 268
   in Hardy, 27–8, 33, 44, 48, 71, 73–4, 88, 92, 100, 194, 195–6, 196n, 198, 211, 215, 216, 219, 223, 223n, 246–7, 248, 250, 255, 256–7
   in Pater, 41, 71–2, 196n, 198
   in physiology, 43, 69, 71, 83, 183–5, 184n, 198–9, 217
   see also mind
Meredith, George, 1, 1n, 68, 73, 99n
Merleau-Ponty, Maurice, 6
Meyering, Theo C., 42, 96n, 128
Michelson–Morley experiment, 25, 110
Mickiewicz, Adam, 12
Mill, James, 19, 22n, 43
Mill, John Stuart, 59–60, 60n
Miller, J. Hillis, 17, 75–6, 150, 196n
Millet, Jean-François, 86
Millgate, Michael, 120n, 199
mind, 19, 27, 37, 39n, 42, 62n, 66, 67, 69n, 81, 84, 140, 243–4
   in Conrad, 20, 32, 34, 42, 54, 56, 104, 106, 108, 116n, 132, 136, 179, 182, 231, 233, 235, 237, 240–2, 259, 261, 263
   in Hardy, 23, 25–6, 27, 28, 49, 62, 70, 73–4, 95, 100, 101, 122, 126, 127, 196, 196n, 197, 199, 213, 223n, 247, 253, 255, 256, 257
   in Pater, 41, 41n, 219, 259
   in philosophy, 19, 109, 166, 223n
   in physiology, 4n, 37, 38–9, 63, 81, 84, 87, 184n, 198–9, 200
   see also mental experience
Mitchell, Judith, 89
Modernism, Modernist, 2, 5, 11, 11n, 15, 16, 37, 39, 42, 79n, 85, 96, 154, 165, 248
Monet, Claude, 6n
mood, 3, 37, 49, 203
   in Conrad, 3, 6, 73, 75, 122n, 176
   in Hardy's novels, 3, 6, 48–9, 88, 92, 92n, 102, 144, 203, 211, 250
   in Hardy's thought, 73, 77
Moore, George, 17
Morell, J. D., 21
Morgan, Benjamin, 41n, 62n, 79n, 270n
Morgan, Rosemarie, 221, 222
Morrison, Toni, 163n
Morus, Iwan Rhys, 112n
Mudie's, 10
Muir, Edwin, 15, 52
Muldoon, Mark S., 143, 191, 241
Müller, Johannes, 22n, 35, 36, 36n, 71n, 83n
Munch, Edvard, 'The Scream', 169n
Murfin, Ross C., 17
music, 140n, 144, 145n, 154–5, 154n, 177–8, 183
   in Conrad, 142, 177–8, 181, 185, 267
   in Hardy, 149–50, 150n, 154–6, 178, 221, 223, 267
Musil, Robert, 217
Musselwhite, David, 199, 199n

Naturalism, 69n
nature, 1, 59–78, 62, 70, 71, 209, 243, 270, 271
  in Conrad, 1, 13, 59, 60, 61, 62, 63n, 76, 112, 115–16, 122n, 163, 180, 229, 234, 235–8, 239, 261, 266, 267, 271
  in contemporary science, 21, 59, 63, 63n, 65, 83n, 84, 112n, 217
  in contemporary thought, 2, 17, 21, 59–60, 61, 70, 146, 155, 198, 239
  in Hardy, 3, 13, 28n, 51, 59, 60, 61, 62, 62n, 64, 66, 77, 93, 97, 151, 210, 212, 215, 216, 221–2, 223, 226, 239, 246, 257, 271
  in literary presentation, 1, 37, 68–9, 70–1, 99n, 146, 239, 270
  in modern thought, 11n, 65–7, 157, 166, 167, 178
nerves
  in Conrad, 65, 81, 81n, 129, 185, 237
  in Hardy, 65, 70–1, 81, 95, 214
  and physics, 47
  and physiology, 35–6, 38, 39, 40n, 71n, 84, 141, 184, 185n, 186
New York Times, 113, 271
Newton, Isaac, 4n, 66, 81, 103, 113, 114, 143, 145, 154n, 224
Noble, Edward, 108
Nobel Prize, 58
Noë, Alva, 71, 71n
Noel, Roden, 51
noise, 178, 183, 184
  in Conrad, 84, 148, 165, 177–8, 180, 183, 230, 232, 237
nothing
  in Conrad, 55, 62, 114, 232–3, 239–40, 271
  in Hardy, 62, 84, 96, 205, 214, 225, 271
  in other nineteenth-century writing, 39–40, 61, 70, 75, 239
Nouvelle Revue française, La, 9, 17n
Nudds, Matthew, 145
Nuttall, A. D., 69, 69n

O'Callaghan, Casey, 165–6, 167
O'Hanlon, Redmond, 4n, 62n

Ong, Walter, 169, 203
onset, 188
O'Shaughnessy, Brian, 145
Oswalds, 1, 9

Paccaud, Josiane, 168n
Parnet, Claire, 76–7
Pasnau, Robert, 145
Pater, Walter, 39, 40–2, 51, 61, 71–2, 79, 79n, 96, 128, 174, 196n, 198, 219, 259
Pawling, S. S., 58
Pearson, Karl, 22n, 39–40, 40n, 41, 50, 51, 174, 219
Pecora, Vincent, 172, 172n
perception, 4n, 7, 30, 33, 35–6, 37, 39–40, 51, 68, 70, 71n, 85–6, 91, 113, 197, 198, 213, 239, 246
  auditory, 128, 146, 166, 179, 182, 188
  visual, 26–7, 32, 36n, 46, 62n, 74, 84, 86, 95, 106, 126–7, 128, 135–7, 196–7, 201–2, 265
pessimistic, pessimism, 2, 15, 51n, 63, 65, 118n, 173, 240
Pettersson, Torsten, 61, 61n, 238n
Phelps, William Lyon, 8n
phenomena, 3, 7, 30, 45, 63, 67, 70, 99, 140, 157, 162, 170, 198
  in Conrad, 28, 34, 35, 41, 57n, 59, 104, 113, 167, 169, 182, 185–6, 232, 233, 237, 259, 260, 261
  in contemporary science, 3–4, 18, 42, 70, 72, 81, 82, 113, 128, 229n
  in Hardy, 3, 28, 44, 45, 91, 100, 121, 125, 144, 149, 160–1, 195, 272
photography, 73, 126, 131, 255
physics, 18, 63, 65–6, 66n, 79–119, 96, 139n, 165, 209, 217–18, 237
  in Conrad, 4n, 28, 31, 42, 62–3n, 106, 133–4, 165, 179, 186, 230, 232, 235, 237
  in contemporary science, 3–4, 7n, 8, 43–4, 47, 50, 81, 82, 85, 103, 109–11, 112n, 114, 193, 217–18
  of energy, 43–4, 45, 47, 81, 145, 186, 224, 235

in Hardy, 44, 46–7, 50, 89, 94, 95, 143–4, 159, 218, 221, 224, 226, 227, 235
of light, 46, 80, 81, 82, 88, 94, 106, 109–11, 139
of sound, 139, 143–4, 145–7, 157, 179, 186
physiology, 21–58
　in Conrad, 4, 7, 28, 32, 57, 134, 182, 186, 264, 266
　and description, 68, 146
　in Hardy, 7, 28, 48–9, 50, 64, 73, 92, 97, 119, 120, 127, 143–4, 194, 195, 201, 216
　and hearing, 139, 141, 146, 188
　and philosophy, 57, 64, 198
　and physics, 7, 18, 43, 62n, 81, 85, 134, 193, 217, 219
　and psychology, 22, 22n, 28, 32, 35–6, 37, 38, 57, 58, 62n, 65, 198, 201
　and sight, 83, 83n, 86, 120, 127
Picard, Max, 229n
Pinker, J. B., 79, 229n, 257–8
Pippin, Robert B., 11n
Platonic, 118, 118n
Poincaré, Henri, 104, 134
Popular Educator, The, 12
Potter, Richard, 88

Quiller Couch, Arthur, 86

Radford, Andrew, 149n
Ray, Martin, 1, 8n, 17, 17n
realism, 8, 12n, 17, 37, 37n, 41n, 42, 70, 71, 72–4, 74n, 75, 76, 89, 133, 211, 217, 244
Rée, Jonathan, 157, 167
Reed, Edward S., 3–4
relativity, 4, 4n, 16, 66, 255n
Relativity, Theory of, 110
Rezelman, Betsy Cogger, 82n
Röntgen machine, 56
Russell, Bertrand, 2
Russia, 243, 258, 260, 261, 262, 266, 268
Russolo, Luigi, 177–8, 181
Ryan, Vanessa, 69n
Rylance, Rick, 11n, 200, 202

Sadler, T. H., 6n
Savoy, The, 5, 6n, 215n
Scarry, Elaine, 16
'scenic realism', 8, 12n, 42, 70, 74, 74n, 76, 89, 133, 217, 244
scepticism, 4, 11n, 15, 41, 63, 66, 108, 116n, 193, 237
Schafer, Murray, 139, 142n, 149n
Schnauder, Ludwig, 2n, 15–16
Schneider, Eric, 96
Schwartz, Hillel, 183, 187
Schwarz, Daniel, 17n, 60n
Scott, Sir Walter, 12
Secker, Martin, 79
seeing, 19, 71, 79, 80, 83–4, 83n, 85, 119–38, 136n, 140, 141, 146, 158, 161, 162, 163, 218, 270
　in Conrad, 29, 32, 33, 35, 52, 55, 103, 105–6, 107, 117, 118, 130–2, 133–4, 135–8, 164, 170, 175, 237, 259, 265–6
　in Hardy, 16n, 23–5, 27–8, 46, 64, 73n, 88–92, 93–4, 97, 99–100, 101–2, 103, 120–2, 124, 126–7, 161–2, 196–7, 201–2, 203, 204–5, 212, 218–19, 227
　and movement, 41n, 80, 122n
　see also sight
Sénancour, Étienne Pivert de, 239, 239n
Senn, Werner, 239n
sensation(s), 7, 21–58, 32, 43, 61, 128, 183, 243, 268–9, 271
　in Conrad, 4, 6, 28, 31, 32, 33, 34, 35, 51, 54, 56–7, 58, 65, 75, 95, 114, 116, 118, 144, 164, 165, 167, 169, 174, 182, 186, 188, 189, 232, 233–4, 237–9, 260, 261, 263, 265, 269
　in contemporary science, 4, 21, 22, 22n, 23, 35, 37, 38, 40, 56–7, 62n, 80, 83, 83n, 84, 154, 184, 184n, 193, 201, 217–19
　in Hardy, 4, 6, 19, 23, 26, 37, 45, 46, 47, 49, 50–1, 76–7, 94, 95, 99n, 125, 151, 159, 195, 198, 199, 201, 202, 208, 209, 210, 211, 214, 216–17, 219, 221, 224–5, 247, 252
　in literary presentation, 16, 32, 36, 41, 42, 49, 146

sensationism, sensationist, 21, 21n, 32, 36, 40, 40n, 42, 48–9, 67, 85, 118, 127, 146, 184, 219, 247
sensation novel, 22, 22n, 58
sensorium, 24, 38, 200, 209
sentience, 69–70, 92, 201
Shaw, G. B. 8, 8n
Shelley, Percy Bysshe, 36, 47n, 233
Shires, Linda, 11n, 89n
shock, 183–5, 186, 188, 189, 237
sigh
  in Conrad, 165, 174, 240, 262
  in Hardy, 50, 158–9, 164, 205
sight
  in Conrad, 6, 29, 52, 76, 81, 106, 119, 129, 133, 135, 136, 137, 180, 236, 238, 265–6
  in Hardy, 14n, 24, 27, 73, 89–90, 100, 119, 120, 123, 125, 151, 161, 202, 208, 219, 247
  in literary sensationism, 36
  in philosophy, 19, 140n, 162
  in physiology, 83, 83n, 84, 139, 144, 144n, 147, 152, 161, 183
silence, 143n, 229n, 241, 241n
  in Conrad, 35, 58, 142n, 144, 166, 168, 177, 178, 180, 181, 192, 210, 229, 230, 231, 232, 236, 237, 240, 240n, 241, 260
  in Hardy, 24, 121, 148–9, 194–5, 206–7, 229n
Simmons, Allan, 14n, 86n, 105n
Simons, Mark, 122n
Singapore, 129, 135
Słowacki, Juliusz, 12
Smith, W. H., 10
Sokołowska, Katarzyna, 118n
solipsism, 36, 37, 40n, 41, 42, 51, 61, 69n, 219, 234, 239
Somervell, Arthur, 140n
Soper, Kate, 66–7
Sorenson, Roy, 145
sound, 139–92
  in Conrad, 30–1, 33, 52, 55, 76, 136, 141, 142–3, 144, 147n, 148, 163–76, 177–92, 230, 260–1, 265–6, 267
  in contemporary thought, 140, 140n
  event view of, 165–6, 168
  in Hardy, 45, 47, 48, 94n, 140, 142, 143–4, 143n, 148–62, 194–5, 204, 208, 220–1, 224, 244, 251
  and modernity, 177–8
  and philosophy, 143, 144, 151, 157, 166, 167, 169, 179, 191, 203
  and physics, 31, 56, 139, 140, 141, 144, 145, 147, 152, 154, 157, 158–9, 161, 163, 165, 167, 168, 174, 179, 180–1, 183–4, 186–7, 189
  and physiology, 36, 139, 141, 146, 147, 158, 167, 174, 183–4, 188
  property view of, 145, 165
  wave view of, 145, 146, 165, 176, 179, 190, 220, 224
  see also music; noise; voice; waves
soundscape, 139, 139n, 160n, 169, 173, 177, 178, 190
space, 119–38
  in Conrad, 28, 30, 34–5, 53–4, 55–6, 58, 81, 105–6, 115, 134, 136, 141, 165, 174, 188, 232, 239, 258, 271
  in contemporary physics, 47, 81, 82, 110–11, 180, 193, 219
  in Hardy, 24, 27–8, 30, 45, 81, 103, 122n, 123–4, 127, 140–2, 152, 194–5, 220–3, 256
  sensory apprehension of, 152, 157, 242
  in visual art, 82
Speaker, The, 76
Spectator, 23, 24
Spencer, Herbert, 22n, 51, 184, 198, 199, 200, 209, 213
Spiegel, Alan, 5, 69, 69n
Stagg, Hunter S., 3
Stallo, J. B., epigraph, 104
Starobinski, Jean, 225, 226, 227, 236
Stauffer, Ruth, 74n
Steege, Benjamin, 146n, 193
Stephen, Leslie, 126
Stevenson, Robert Louis, 80, 81n
Stewart, Balfour, 109
Straus, Nina Pelikan, 173n
Strauss, D. F., 61
Sully, James, 22n, 36, 83, 145
Sumner, Rosemary, 89n, 101

Symonds, John Addington, 59, 249
Symons, Arthur, 4, 41

Tait, Peter Guthrie, 109
Tanner, Tony, 17, 91, 118n, 122, 269–70
Tate and Brady, 12
Taylor, Dennis, 105n, 239n
Taylor, Richard, 22n
teleology, 5, 138, 157, 162
The Tempest, 124, 127, 262
thermodynamics, first law of, 43, 44, 157, 163
thermodynamics, second law of, 44, 68, 157
Thomas, Edward, 79, 99, 231, 231n
Thompson, Emily, 178
Thompson, Sylvanus, 110n
Thomson, William (Lord Kelvin), 43, 44, 113
time
  in Conrad, 33, 53–4, 62, 106, 136, 180–1, 189, 230, 241, 265, 271
  in Hardy, 27, 46–7, 48–9, 89, 121, 122n, 150, 160, 162, 194–5, 206, 210, 211, 218–19, 220, 223n, 228, 245, 246, 256, 271
  and identity, 61, 230, 238, 246
  literary treatment of, 4–5, 150
  and sound, 139, 140, 143, 145, 157, 180–1, 187
  and transmission, 54, 145, 162
Times Literary Supplement, 13, 14
Tinsley Brothers, 23
touch, 6, 7, 36, 218, 271
  in Conrad, 28, 106, 132, 137, 264, 268, 271
  in Hardy, 24–5, 46, 73–4, 153, 153n, 155–6, 195, 211, 212, 219, 220–1, 247, 271
transmission
  in Conrad, 52, 54, 107, 168, 180, 189, 190, 192
  in Eliot, 18
  in Hardy, 25, 28n, 45, 45n, 100, 126, 192, 220–1
  and physics, 139, 145, 146, 154
  and physiology, 21, 23, 40, 141
Trollope, Anthony, 12
Turner, J. M. W., 46, 218

Turner, Martha, 226n
Tylor, E. B., 149n
Tyndall, John, 63, 65, 83, 83n, 140, 140n, 141, 145, 147, 154, 229n

Ulysses (Joyce), 14
unconscious experience, 2, 71, 128, 219n
  in Conrad, 143, 259, 266
  in Hardy, 24–6, 28n, 47, 78, 87, 89, 101–2, 218–19, 250, 253
Unwin, T. Fisher, 78

Van Valkenburg, David, 168
Victorian
  literature, 2, 4–5, 18n, 40, 127
  outlook, 9, 10, 11, 18, 85, 173, 243, 272
  science, 4, 8, 15, 18n, 62n, 103, 113, 163
  thought, 11n, 43, 62n, 63, 64n, 113, 145, 165, 166
visual cortex, 84, 136n
voice
  in Conrad, 30–1, 32, 54, 141, 143, 164, 168, 169–70, 171, 172, 173, 175, 181, 189, 192, 260, 265–6, 271
  in Hardy, 47, 141, 144, 151, 152, 154, 155, 156, 158–9, 206, 207, 208, 255
Vorstellung, 201, 202

Wagner, Richard, 139
Wallace, Alfred Russel, 255n
Walpole, Hugh, 74n, 176n
Ward, Mrs Humphrey, 244
Warodell, Johan, 34n
Warren, Robert Penn, 116n, 230, 230n, 255
Watt, Ian, 34, 104, 269
wave theory, 44, 56, 81–2, 88, 110n, 140, 141, 145, 146, 154, 154n, 165–6, 179
waves
  of light, 46, 47, 81–2, 88, 110n, 220, 224
  of sound, 31, 45, 140, 141, 145, 154, 165–6, 167, 176, 179, 187, 189, 190, 191, 220, 224

Weber, Ernst, 36
Weinstein, Philip, 17, 215, 226
Wells, H. G., 8, 8n, 14, 73n, 185
Wessex, 5n, 86, 162, 250
whisper
   in Conrad, 58, 143, 164, 165, 170, 171, 172, 173, 174, 189, 191, 232, 240n, 260, 262
   in Hardy, 25–6, 50, 155–6, 159, 224
Whistler, James McNeill, 82, 82n
Wickens, Glen, 28n, 47n
Widdowson, Peter, 74n
Wilczek, Frank, 139n
Wiley, Paul, 53
Williams, Raymond, 11
Wise, M. Norton, 43n
Wittenberg, Judith Bryant, 45n, 89n, 91n, 92
Wood, Jane, 253n

Woolf, Virginia, 8, 8n, 11, 13–15, 25, 56, 78, 80, 80n
Wordsworth, William, 16n, 50, 68, 71, 84, 94, 140, 140n, 160, 266, 270
Worringer, Wilhelm, 86
Wotton, George, 64n
Wuthering Heights, 193

X rays, 56

Yeats, W. B., 114, 172
Youmans, Edward, 44, 47, 51
Young, Kay, 33, 251n
Young, Thomas, 81
'Young Vienna', 217

Zabel, Morton Dauwen, 17
Zelie, John Sheridan, 9
Zola, Émile, 1, 37n, 69n, 90n